(In)Formalizing Jobs in Latin America and the Caribbean

This book, along with any associated content or subsequent updates, can be accessed at https://hdl.handle.net/10986/43535.

Reproducible Research Repository

https://reproducibility.worldbank.org

A reproducibility package is available for this book in the Reproducible Research Repository at https://reproducibility.worldbank.org/catalog/330/.

Scan to see all titles in this collection.

INTERNATIONAL DEVELOPMENT IN FOCUS

(In)Formalizing Jobs in Latin America and the Caribbean

Taxes, Benefits, and Labor Market Incentives

KATHARINA FIETZ, CLEMENT JOUBERT, HUGO ÑOPO, ALBERTO J. OCAMPO, TRUMAN PACKARD, JOSEFINA POSADAS, LOURDES RODRIGUEZ CHAMUSSY

WORLD BANK GROUP

Contents

Boxes

Figures

Tables

Acknowledgments

This report is the culmination of a two-year analytical project conducted by the World Bank's Poverty and Equity and Social Protection and Labor teams for Latin America and the Caribbean under the leadership of Willam Maloney, Jaime Saavedra, Oscar Calvo-Gonzalez, Carlos Rodriguez Castelan, and William Wiseman. The authors are grateful for their support, guidance, and patience throughout the production of this report.

From the beginning, the authors sought to ensure the relevance of the project by keeping World Bank staff who work at the front lines of policy dialogue in the lead of the seven country case studies on which this report is based. The authors recognize and thank the following colleagues for their professionalism, painstaking work, and excellent contributions: Gonzalo Aguilar, Ignacio Apella, Clemente Avila, Gaston Blanco, Ana Lucia Cardenas, Luis Castellanos, Teodoro Crisologo, Maria Davalos, Elisa Failache, Samuel Freije, Alexandra Gordina, Sofia Hidalgo Berrios, Roy Katayama, Gabriel Lara, Mattia Makovec, Fernando Marin, Juan Manuel Monroy, Claudio Montenegro, Gonzalo Rivera, Eliana Rubiano, Kajetan Wladyslaw Trzcinski, Diego Tuzman, and Gonzalo Zunino. The contributions of these colleagues increase the likelihood that the recommendations made in this report will be closely considered.

The authors are additionally grateful for the excellent data management and research assistance provided by Sofia Hidalgo Berrios throughout the analysis and report writing. Her sense of urgency, tireless attention to detail, and persistence was vital in preparing the reproducible research package for this report.

Finally, the authors are indebted to Santiago Levy Algazi for hours of dialogue and advice throughout the course of the project, as well as to World Bank colleagues who read early drafts and provided excellent suggestions that have greatly strengthened this report. We thank Melis Guven, Gabriela Inchauste Comboni, Marcela Melendez Arjona, Matteo Morgandi, Ana Maria Oviedo Silva, Gonzalo Reyes Hartley, Iamele Rigolini, Ernesto Schargrodsky, Liliana Do

Couto Sousa, and Ekatarina Vostroknutova. Special thanks goes to Sebastian Nieto Parra for serving as external peer reviewer of the report.

We are grateful for the support of a highly professional editing and production team. Cindy Fisher was the acquisitions editor, Christina Davis was the production editor, Sandra Gain was the copy editor, and Greg Edmondson was the proofreader for this book. Lily Franchini provided excellent administrative support throughout.

About the Contributors

Katharina Fietz is an economist consultant at the World Bank, specializing in social protection and labor market policies in Latin America. She also is a research fellow at the German Institute for Global and Area Studies, focusing on informality, tax-benefit systems, and the design and evaluation of employment and social assistance programs. She holds a PhD in economics from the University of Göttingen in Germany.

Clement Joubert is a research economist in the World Bank's Development Research Group. An applied microeconomist, he is interested in how households work and save in high-informality settings, the economic risks they face, and how to optimally design social protection programs for them. His research also covers gender inequality, underemployment, and radicalization. Before joining the World Bank, he was an assistant professor at the University of North Carolina at Chapel Hill. His research has been published in the *Journal of Econometrics,* the *Review of Economics and Statistics,* and the *International Economics Review*. He holds a PhD in economics from the University of Pennsylvania.

Hugo Ñopo is a senior economist in the Poverty and Equity Practice of the World Bank. He previously served as regional economist at the International Labor Organization and as lead education economist at the Inter-American Development Bank. He also has been a senior researcher at the Group for the Analysis of Development in his native Peru and an assistant professor at Middlebury College in Vermont. He has published extensively on a variety of topics in academic journals and books and, more recently, has participated in outreach and dissemination through opinion columns and TED talks. Currently, he is a research affiliate at the Institute for the Study of Labor in Bonn, Germany. He holds a PhD in economics from Northwestern University in Evanston, Illinois.

Alberto J. Ocampo is an economist consultant at the World Bank, working on labor markets, social protection, and gender inequality in Latin America. He has conducted research with academic and policy institutions on labor economics, health economics, social welfare, migration, and economic development. As a lecturer, he has taught microeconomics and game theory at Universidad del Rosario and Universidad Jorge Tadeo Lozano, both in Colombia. He holds an MSc in economics from Universidad del Rosario.

Truman Packard is a lead economist in the Social Protection and Labor Practice of the World Bank. His last operational assignment was as human development practice leader for Colombia, Mexico, and the República Bolivariana de Venezuela. He was lead author of the Social Protection and Labor white paper "Protecting All: Risk Sharing for a Diverse and Diversifying World of Work" and led the team for the report "East Asia Pacific at Work: Employment, Enterprise, and Well-being." He also led the Human Development program in the Pacific Islands, Papua New Guinea, and Timor Leste and has been part of teams delivering financial and knowledge transfer services to governments in the East Asia and Pacific, Europe and Central Asia, and Latin America and the Caribbean regions. Trained as a labor economist, his work has focused primarily on the impact of social insurance, including pensions, unemployment insurance, and health coverage, on household labor supply decisions, saving behavior, and risk preferences. He holds a PhD in economics from the University of Oxford in the United Kingdom.

Josefina Posadas is a lead economist in the Social Protection and Labor Practice of the World Bank, where she works with client countries to develop and implement policies and programs to improve labor market access and success, particularly for vulnerable populations. Her most recent World Bank publications focus on developing advanced labor market information systems. Additional areas of expertise include entrepreneurship, gender equality, social assistance, delivery systems, aging, and poverty. She has provided policy advice to governments in East Asia, Eastern and Central Europe, and Latin America. Before joining the World Bank, she worked at the Inter-American Development Bank and the Universidad Nacional de La Plata in Argentina, as well as for national and local government offices on employment and fiscal federalism matters. She holds a PhD in economics from Boston University in Massachusetts.

Lourdes Rodriguez Chamussy is a senior economist in the Poverty and Equity Practice of the World Bank, where she has worked in the Europe and Central Asia and Latin America and the Caribbean (LAC) regional units. Her work focuses on applied microeconomics, labor markets, political economy of development, and gender. She led the Gender Innovation Lab for the LAC region between 2019 and 2021. Before joining the World Bank, she worked at the Inter-American Development Bank, George Washington University, and the

Government of Mexico. She has published articles and reports on poverty measurement, gender gaps in the labor market, the poverty impacts of climate shocks, and the distributive effects of government investments. She co-authored the book *Cashing in on Education: Women, Childcare and Prosperity in Latin America and the Caribbean*. She holds a PhD in agricultural and resource economics from the University of California, Berkeley.

Abbreviations

AFAM–PE	Asignaciones Familiares–Plan de Equidad (Family Allowance and Equity Plan) (Uruguay)
AI	artificial intelligence
ARG$	Argentine peso
BPC	Beneficio de Prestação Continuada (Continuous Cash Benefit) (Brazil)
CCF	Cajas de Compensación Familiar (Family Compensation Funds) (Colombia)
CIT	corporate income tax
CLT	Consolidation of Labor Laws (Brazil)
Col$	Colombian peso
CREE	Contribución Empresarial para la Equidad (Business Contribution to Equity) (Colombia)
ECLAC	United Nations Economic Commission for Latin America and the Caribbean
FTR	formalization tax rate
GDP	gross domestic product
HEART	Human Employment and Resource Training (Jamaica)
HICs	high-income countries
ILO	International Labour Organization
IMSS	Mexican Social Security Institute
INCRA	Instituto Nacional de Colonização e Reforma Agrária (National Institute for Colonization and Agrarian Reform) (Brazil)
ISSSTE	Institute for Social Security and Services for State Workers in Mexico
LAC	Latin America and the Caribbean
LM	labor market

MEI	Individual Micro-Entrepreneur System (Brazil)
Mex$	Mexican peso
MIS	management information system
MW	minimum wage
OECD	Organisation for Economic Co-operation and Development
OLS	ordinary least squares
OOP	out of pocket
p.p.	percentage point
PAP	Second Pillar Pension Benefit
PBU	Universal Basic Pension
PCA	principal component analysis
PIT	personal income tax
PMG	Guaranteed Minimum Pension
PNC	noncontributory pension
PPP	purchasing power parity
QoG	Quality of Government Institute
R$	Brazilian real
S/.	Peruvian sole
SEDLAC	Socio-Economic Database for Latin America and the Caribbean
SENATI	National Training Service of Industrial Work (Peru)
SI	social insurance
SIMPLES	Simplified Tax Regime (Brazil)
SISBEN	System of Identification of Social Program Beneficiaries (Colombia)
SR	reference salary
SS	social security
SSW	social security wealth
SUS	Sistema Único de Saúde (Unified Health System) (Brazil)
TA	acquisition rate
UMA	Unidad de Medida y Actualizacion (Measurement and Updating Unit) (Mexico)
UNESCO	United Nations Educational, Scientific and Cultural Organization
Ur$	Uruguayan peso
WDI	World Development Indicators
WGI	Worldwide Governance Indicators
WHO	World Health Organization
WVS	World Values Survey

1 Introduction

WHY THIS REPORT NOW?

Designing and administering effective national social protection systems has long been a challenge for policy makers worldwide. For decades, the principal objection to social protection policies was that they encouraged sloth. Today, voters and the governments they put in place are less worried that taxes and social protections unintentionally create poverty traps than that they encourage workers to be static rather than dynamic, or to be averse to risk with new technologies scaling their economic activity (World Bank 2024).

The task of policy makers is to balance the objectives of greater inclusion, equity, and effective risk sharing at a sustainable cost (Guven and Wiseman 2022; Packard et al. 2019). On one side of the scale, governments seek to ensure that all people are protected from impoverishment regardless of their circumstances; can maintain an adequate standard of living; and have opportunities to build, preserve, and renew their human capital. On the other side, it is important to encourage people's labor market participation, enterprise, and risk taking so that work is as productive as possible and fuels economic growth.

Governments in the Latin America and the Caribbean (LAC) region are particularly challenged to achieve and sustain the right balance. The region has the longest institutional history of social protection outside Europe, featuring deeply rooted institutions that provide opportunities as well as impose constraints on policy makers. As an example, on the one hand, in many countries the network of social insurance offices has grown to reach farther into remote areas than has other public service providers. On the other hand, the administrative procedures and operating systems have been in place so long that they have become politicized and difficult to modernize. Despite the region's long history of social protection, in many LAC countries, the percentage of working people who are effectively protected from

A reproducibility package is available for this book in the Reproducible Research Repository at https://reproducibility.worldbank.org/catalog/330/.

impoverishment and other risks to their well-being via coverage by social insurance plans—typically still the largest segments of social protection systems—has remained stubbornly low. The low share of working people who regularly contribute to social insurance has been a decades-long challenge.

In reaction to this widespread vulnerability, almost all governments in LAC have established so-called *noncontributory* programs alongside their *contributory* social insurance plans. *Noncontributory* programs provide a semblance of risk-pooling entitlements based on residence, citizenship, and need rather than the sector, manner, or place of employment. They are financed from sources of government revenue other than earmarked levies on firms' payrolls and profits. In contrast, the eligibility conditions and financing structure of the so-called *contributory* plans grant benefits conditional on a personalized record of contributions and have been left relatively unchanged since their inception in several LAC countries during the interwar period. This has kept the relationship between what people are mandated to contribute and their eventual benefits difficult to understand and value relative to alternative insurance and savings options (Bozio et al. 2024).

All social insurance plans receive some subsidy financed from the government's general revenues, to which almost all people *contribute* in one form or another. Therefore, the words *contributory* and *noncontributory* are italicized to emphasize that these labels are more cosmetic than categorical. In the era of human rights and given the codification in many of the region's national constitutions of the rights of all people to health, education, and economic opportunity, the distinction created by social insurance laws between those "with rights" ("derechohabientes") and others is a relic, albeit one with clear welfare, fiscal, and distributional implications. Yet, even if these distinctions may be arcane and mainly semantic from the perspective of those who design and finance these programs, they matter greatly to working people's day-to-day choices.

In most countries in the LAC region, many of the shocks covered by *contributory* benefits are mirrored by coverage from seemingly "free" *noncontributory* benefits. In some cases, the latter are almost equal in generosity and quality to the former. Although the push to expand protection is well motivated and urgently needed, many scholars believe that it has created strong incentives for people to remain in relatively unproductive, "informal" work where government mandates can be minimally adhered to or avoided altogether but that impose a heavy burden on the productivity gains that sustain growth (Eslava et al. 2023; Levy and Cruces 2021; Perry et al. 2007). Hence, the best efforts of governments in LAC to kick-start growth are hindered by widespread, deeply rooted, and normalized avoidance and evasion of laws, regulations, and taxation (OECD 2024). Although full or even partial compliance can be an economic nonstarter for many workers and firms, in the aggregate, a self-reinforcing culture of noncompliance can trap countries at low- and middle-income levels of development and sustain social exclusion (World Bank 2024).

Whether cash transfer programs disincentivize or boost formal jobs can vary across contexts. Not all research shows that the advent of assistance through cash transfers in LAC has disincentivized formal work. It is important to distinguish between social protection policies and to scrutinize incentives and outcomes that are likely to differ both in character and in their significance across labor markets.

In some settings, the increased cash injections from social assistance transfers stimulate aggregate demand, even leading to a boost in formal employment (Gerard, Naritomi, and Silva 2021). Moreover, recent broad and rigorous reviews of the literature conclude that the published empirical evidence on whether social protection encourages or discourages informal work is mixed (Ghorpade, Franco Restrepo, and Castellanos Rodriguez 2024; Orozco Corona and Vélez-Grajales 2024; Torm and Oehme 2024). Results vary across countries, with changes in focus across different programs, profiles of people, and even minor changes in data. These reviews also make the important point that the absence of integrated analyses of social assistance, social security, and taxation weakens the conclusions that can be drawn. It also reduces the set of reform recommendations to guide the design of comprehensive, coherent national social protection systems. This report is a response to the lack of integrated, systemwide analyses of incentives for formal employment.

Without an integrated, systemwide view of the problem, policy makers fail to account for the second-hand effects and individual responses to policies. That the impact on labor market incentives was not given greater consideration by policy makers when *noncontributory* programs were launched may reflect two aspects of policy making. First, governments felt that the need to extend protection was urgent. Second, governments lacked political strength in the face of powerful stakeholders and seemingly intractable challenges to reforming social insurance and labor institutions, which had proven over the years to be resilient, even during the region's many episodes of economic and political instability.

Yet, the importance of incentives should not be underplayed. "Hecha la ley, hecha la trampa" ("once the law is made, so is the 'work-around'") is a common saying in the region, usually delivered with a wry smile and even some pride in the viveza criolla (cleverness) and ubiquitous jeitinhos (work-arounds of questionable legality). The latter are small, daily instances of strategic gaming to which market participants resort when the proverbial "rules of the game" allow and where gaming is socially acceptable because people perceive that government mandates are unreasonable and entitlements are of little value. Indeed, in societies where government corruption is long standing and even endemic, this gaming may be justified and even considered admirable.

That the share of social protection financed from general revenues has grown so quickly is not the problem. On the contrary, *noncontributory* programs are a welcome evolution of policy making, which is quickly making up for the decades-long limitations and exclusions of purely "Bismarckian," employment-based models through the nominal contributions of the working head of household (Esping-Andersen 1990).[1] Equitable, effective, and sustainable social protection systems should include a variety of financing and eligibility requirements, determined principally according to the nature of the specific shocks that they intend to cover, labor market conditions, and governments' administrative capacities (Packard et al. 2019). The crux of the matter is the harmony in which all *contributory* and *noncontributory* programs coexist without generating unintended perverse effects.

Most reforms to date have been episodic, opportunistic, incremental, and implemented with little regard for the labor market and the broader existing system of benefits and taxation. This policy-making challenge is the subject of this report. In most LAC countries, further reforms to all branches of the social protection and personal taxation systems are needed so that *noncontributory* and *contributory* programs will work coherently and cohesively to achieve more-effective inclusion, redistribution, and risk sharing, while creating stronger incentives for people to take more risks and work more productively. Politically powerful interests stand as an obstacle. However, as pointed out in the 2024 *World Development Report*, "the handful of countries that have made speedy transitions from middle- to high-income status have done so by disciplining vested interests, building their talent pool, and modernizing policies and institutions" (World Bank 2024). Even if the nature of policy making in pluralistic representative democracies is necessarily episodic, opportunistic, and incremental, policy makers can still benefit greatly from a set of principles and a "roadmap" to keep their efforts moving in the right direction.

STRUCTURE OF THE REPORT

This report examines the incentives that people face as they encounter the opportunities and constraints that social protection policies and institutions create in the labor market. These institutions are cogs in a country's broader public revenue and expenditure machine, and from the perspective of most market participants, they are inseparable from personal income taxation. Indeed, in many high-income countries, the objectives of social protection are increasingly pursued directly and explicitly through income taxation channels, as the growing preference for earned income tax credits and other so-called "negative income taxes" in many high-income countries attests. Although social insurance specialists are fastidious in distinguishing statutory "social contributions" from other mandated payments, these programs all entail a ration on the consumption of services—either more or less than people would consume if left to their own devices—provided by a single or tightly limited set of providers. This ration gives any mandated participation in a benefit plan—even one that is actuarially fair—an element of taxation, creating incentives for people to avoid and evade.

What makes a mandated payment a "tax" rather than a "contribution" from a working person's perspective? This report responds to this key question. With the answers provided, the report identifies a course for policy making as well as specific reforms that could have substantial positive effects on people's incentives to formalize their work.

The report is structured as follows:

- Chapter 2 sets the scope of the report by identifying the aspect of informal work that is of primary interest: the choices that working people make—whether they are working for themselves or for someone else—when government-mandated protections are partially or not fully enforced, leaving room for choice. This dimension is illustrated empirically, with a more-granular and -specific categorization of working people than the usual, simplistic, and increasingly ambiguous "formal" versus "informal" dichotomy. Using representative survey microdata, chapter 2 strives for greater precision, measuring among those who are subject to national mandates the shares that are "compliant" and "noncompliant." Among those who are legally free to choose whether to contribute to social protection schemes, the chapter distinguishes the "participating" from the "nonparticipating" shares. The chapter analyzes informality in 2019, just prior to the COVID-19 pandemic, and in 2022, showing how little the shares of workers falling into the previously mentioned categories changed, even in the wake of such systemic and deep social and economic upheaval as the pandemic.

- Chapter 3 presents a conceptual framework grounded in microeconomic theory and evidence, which is used to analyze incentives along three dimensions. The three dimensions are (1) the economic context—specifically, the labor market—which is determined in part by government regulations and product market outcomes; (2) the perceived value that working people assign to the protections and entitlements they are awarded for their compliance with and participation in the social protection system; and (3) the likelihood that the government can detect noncompliance and, when it does, the penalties that it exacts. Each dimension of this conceptual framework is discussed and underpinned with detailed references to an already large and growing theoretical and empirical literature, much of which is not coincidentally focused on countries in LAC.

- Chapter 4 presents the results of de jure tax and benefit models drawn from seven country case studies (described in box 1.1). The de jure models detail the composition of income taxes, benefits, social insurance contributions, and other payroll levies at each point of the distribution of labor earnings as mandated by the government. The modeling allows easy visual identification of incentive "pressure points." For example, the models show where in the earnings distribution a worker may lose eligibility for a social assistance transfer, the level of earnings at which workers are required to contribute to social insurance, the point at which this obligation changes abruptly with a higher contribution rate, or where exemptions to personal income taxation end or the marginal rate of taxation starts to steepen. The de jure modeling is presented so that readers can consider the perspectives of an employee and an employer, as well as that of a self-employed person. In countries where alternative legal ways of contracting employees or different forms of self-employment recognized by regulations are available, the de jure modeling captures these differences, showing clear cost and benefit advantages of one form of contracting over others. The modeling is also presented from a household perspective, as many of the taxes and benefits involve the family and not just the individual.

Selection and design of the Latin American and Caribbean country case studies

Seven country case studies were chosen to reflect the diversity of the Latin America and the Caribbean (LAC) region. The seven countries—Brazil, Colombia, El Salvador, Jamaica, Mexico, Peru, and Uruguay—make up slightly more than two-thirds of LAC's population. All the subregions in LAC are represented in this study.

Although the informal economy in most LAC countries is large, the prevalence of informal work and the form that it takes vary substantially across countries. Such variation is clearly mediated by legislation. Current social protection and tax policies—and their historical evolution—also differ substantially. For example, Brazil and Uruguay represent one extreme with almost no exemptions to the mandates for workers to contribute to social insurance and around one-third of workers not contributing. Colombia, El Salvador, and Mexico show similar distributions: one-third of workers mandated and complying, one-third mandated and noncomplying, and one-third exempt and noncomplying. Peru is an extreme case in which three-fourths of the working population are exempt from contributing and, indeed, noncomplying.

Similarities and differences exist along the income divide. Across all countries, formality is almost inexistent among working people in the lowest deciles of the income distribution, and informality is also present among the richest. The starkest contrasts are between the rates of formal work among those with higher household incomes.

At one extreme, in Brazil, Colombia, and Uruguay, the share of formality among those with the highest incomes is around four-fifths. At the other extreme, in Peru, 1 in 5 workers is obliged to contribute. El Salvador and Mexico are in the middle. Other clear commonalities across countries are that informal jobs are concentrated in the service sectors and small firms. Workers who are not complying with mandates are predominantly men, and those who can choose and are not participating are predominantly women.

With one exception, the analysis of the country case studies focuses on 2019—or the closest prior year—for three important reasons. First, this focus avoids the systemic impact of the COVID-19 pandemic confounding attempts to identify individual and household incentives created by social protection programs. Second, it helps to steer clear of temporary policy responses to the pandemic crisis. Third, it provides a solid baseline and a substantial subsequent period of analysis for future efforts to measure the impacts of reforms on those incentives.

Each country case discusses changes to social protection and labor market policies and programs since 2019. Several of these changes form part of the analysis, along with ideas for future reform measures. For Uruguay, due to significant changes to the household survey of core relevance, the year of the analysis is 2021.

Note: Further details are available in the annexes to chapter 4.

- Chapter 5 expands on the traditional analysis of labor market incentives, centered on the tax wedge, by using a renewed definition of the formalization tax rate (FTR). The FTR is a composite measure of the incentives created by social protection and personal income taxation policies, originally conceived by Koettl and Weber (2012) for analysis of incentives to formalize work in Central and Southern European countries (Packard, Koettl, and Montenegro 2012). The advantage of using the FTR is that it consolidates assistance transfers, social insurance contributions, mandated in-work benefits, and personal income taxation into a single indicator, calculated for all individuals according to their observed work and personal and household characteristics. The FTR is shown to be a statistically significant and important factor when used in econometric analysis of workers' observed formal or informal employment. More importantly, it serves as the incentive "benchmark" for comparing the impact of competing or complementary policy reforms.

- Chapter 6 presents an analysis of specific reforms to the personal income tax and benefit policies and how these reforms alter labor market incentives. The reform measures analyzed here are drawn from World Bank policy dialogues since 2019 or have been identified in earlier analysis as important to encourage greater participation in social insurance plans. The chapter discusses the arguments for each reform measure, the share of workers who are likely to be impacted by the measure where they are in the household income distribution, and the extent to which incentives are altered with reductions (and, in some cases, increases) in the FTR.

- Chapter 7 presents a deeper assessment of the factors determining perceived value, specifically how "tax morale" is related to the prevalence of informal work. Given the importance of how mandates are valued by working people to the FTR and their likely impact on labor supply and employment decisions, looking beyond the explicit costs of regulations and mandates is vital. Most social insurance plans in LAC present a net subsidy for most participants, although this varies across countries. The level of income at which current plans "subsidize" or "tax" participants also varies across workers according to their accumulated history of contributions ("contribution density"). This chapter compares estimates of the "social security wealth" measure given different levels of observed contribution history, as well as measures of net subsidies and net taxes in four countries. Furthermore, although it may indeed be necessary to minimize structural distortions caused by taxation and social protection policies, that alone is not a sufficient condition to shift economic activity to regulated and taxed markets. The nature of governance, institutional credibility, and social norms of compliance must be factored into the discussion to arrive at truly effective policy solutions that will bring more workers into formal work (Tommasi and Saavedra-Chanduvi 2007). Exploiting data on perceptions of government credibility and analysis of cross-country measures of governance, the chapter examines tax morale and its importance, controlling for labor regulations and other relevant contextual factors.

- Chapter 8 concludes the report with a summary of findings and guidance for policy makers in the region. The report's most-important message to this audience is as follows. In countries in LAC where national social protection policies have been in place since the early 20th century, the option to start from a proverbial "clean slate" is not available. Nonetheless, population aging, the structural evolution of markets, and the imperative to raise productivity and grow make reforms urgent. Many of the incentive problems created by current policies are well known, and more are being identified as talented analysts in the region make increasingly sophisticated use of more and better data. Over the years, as governments have attempted reforms, many features of social protection—especially social insurance—have been fiercely defended by powerful interest groups.[2] Few governments have the political space to enact comprehensive reforms all at once, even if they have a well-crafted blueprint for structural changes in hand. As such, politically feasible reforms are likely to be only incremental, partial measures. Pessimists would point out that it was this aspect of tax and social protection policy making that brought about the current incoherence across programs and resulting incentive problems. More optimistically, in a policy-making environment where only incremental, partial reforms are possible, these can have meaningful, positive impact if they are guided by a clear vision of the eventual social protection systems the countries need, and based on sound policy principles and a roadmap to keep the reform efforts on the right course.

KEY STYLIZED FACTS

The existing literature and inference from the country case studies presented in this report led to the identification of several common features of social protection and personal income taxation in the region that are likely to shape incentives against compliance and participation.

Social protection policies still reflect outdated norms around work.

Most social protection systems in the region reflect views of the labor market and the nature of work that were adopted from Continental Europe in the 1920s and 1930s. Yet, even at that time, those norms were far from the work experiences of most of the people in LAC countries, which is still the case today (Frolich et al. 2014; Kaplan and Levy 2014; Ribe, Robalino, and Walker 2012). This institutional inertia contrasts with a dynamic, diverse, and still diversifying world of work, leaving entire groups and large numbers of people explicitly or implicitly (statutorily) excluded.

Dependent workers on so-called "nonstandard" contracts, self-employed workers, and many women struggle to fit into the "mold" of the early-20th-century industrial worker. In the first third of the 20th century, the expectation held by policy makers in Latin America was that most economically active people would work in subordinated, dependent employment in factories and firms for the long employment spells necessary to meet stringent vesting requirements. The labor market was assumed to be a man's world; women would dedicate most of their time to home and family responsibilities. Little thought was given to how mandates and incentives would change with more women choosing market work over remaining in their homes.

Only recently have Brazil's social protection and labor systems been altered to allow less than full-time work. In Mexico, affiliation with social insurance requires the place of work to be a business with a fixed location. The Bismarckian, employment-based model of the welfare state in Continental Europe was yet to be tested by shocks to full employment, rising labor turnover, deindustrialization, and demographic change. The model also offered a convenient solution to national governments with limited administrative capacity or power to assess and collect taxes: "delegation" of policy implementation to firms, requiring them to collect contributions on behalf of the state. This further bound effective protection to whether, where, and how people work (Frolich et al. 2014; Kaplan and Levy 2014; Palier 2010). Systemic shocks, sectoral and occupational mobility, production automation, and a large and growing share of people combining market and nonmarket activities, even maintaining a portfolio of concurrent jobs, are all characteristics of today's world of work that challenge the foundational assumptions on which social protection systems still rest (Packard et al. 2019).

Policies segment the labor market, creating barriers to mobility and challenging the continuity of coverage.

Policies can create barriers to mobility and challenge the continuity of coverage, even for people in mainly formal standard employment. Reflecting the origins of national social insurance plans in the region, segmentation by sector or occupation—taking the form of separate plans or special treatment of certain forms of work—is still common.

For example, in Mexico, the mandate to participate in social insurance is constitutionally limited to people in subordinated, dependent employment, but it takes different forms for work in the public and private sectors and even across subnational governments. Brazil is similarly plagued by disparities based on sector, geography, and even occupation. This segmentation can exacerbate the gaps in participation among workers who choose to relocate or find themselves in changed circumstances—whether moving in and out of public employment, switching sectors and geographies, or altering the nature of their economic activity.

Recent efforts to remedy and bridge this segmentation have created additional segments, with special treatment of certain groups, most notably various forms of self-employment and online gig platform workers. Inequities, inconsistencies, and incoherence in how policies and programs are designed to create ample opportunities for arbitrage, gaming, and outright evasion. Many people simply fall out of coverage as life events move them across the cleavages that lie between these segments.

Levies on payroll are intensively used, and indeed abused, for purposes beyond financing social insurance.

Nominally Bismarckian systems, which are designed to tie benefit levels and eligibility tightly to contributions, have been redirected to achieve ambitious redistribution, inclusion, and other social policy objectives for which the original model is poorly suited. The employment relationship—specifically, the earmarked taxation of firms' payrolls—has become a primary source of finance for interventions designed to redistribute resources to the wider population, including those not or not yet working, and to help resolve social problems unrelated to the workplace or even to the labor market. However, in many instances, this repurposing has led to fiscally regressive outcomes.

As presented painstakingly in this report, nonwage labor costs vary widely, defying simple cross-country comparisons based only on averages. However, the intensity with which governments in the region use payroll taxes for broader social policy conflates the original *contributory* and "insurance" principles, resulting in levies that bear little relationship to benefits. The de jure mapping from the seven country cases in chapter 4 shows that Jamaica is an extreme case in this regard, with between 5 and 10 percentage points of payroll taxes financing "indirect" programs (although it admittedly has a different social policy tradition than the Continental European model on which other countries' programs are based).

For example, in Brazil, about 5.8 percent of the levies on payroll finance programs to which workers—in whose name these payments are made—may or may not have a claim. In Colombia, between 4 and 17 percentage points of payroll taxes have a similar character. The explicit and implicit redistribution and cross-subsidization that result make it difficult for contributing workers to accept mandated contributions as deferred remuneration. Population aging and unrevised or even rising expectations of what social insurance should provide make greater fiscal effort an imperative for most LAC governments and raise the costs of poor taxation practices.

Administrative rules, although operationally convenient, create exclusion.

First and foremost among these is the minimum "base" of earned income on which social insurance contributions can be applied, which is typically set equal to the statutory monthly minimum wage for full-time work. A statutory floor on wages can be an effective policy tool to encourage labor supply and improve employment outcomes when it is deployed carefully in monopsonistic and oligopsonistic labor markets. However, when the minimum wage is used as the minimum basis for participation in social insurance, the parameter becomes a de facto barrier to participation for any person whose capacity to earn falls below the floor. This exclusion is most salient in Colombia.

Few statutory minimum wages in LAC countries are set with strict regard to the level of and changes in median worker productivity. As statutory wage floors are raised relative to the earnings capacity of the median worker, a greater share of working people will be "priced out" of government risk-sharing instruments. Other effectively exclusionary parameters include minimum contribution history requirements to become "vested" for benefits, which are often set with little regard to workers' likely total spells in formal work, and discrete benefit levels that bear little relation to what most workers can contribute. Many such parameters were chosen to make administration, assessment of eligibility, and benefit delivery possible when governments' capacity was constrained by analog technologies—a constraint that is loosening and could be loosened faster or eliminated altogether with the right investments to augment governments' administrative capacity.

MAIN MESSAGES FOR POLICY MAKERS

Few policy areas are as notoriously controversial, polarizing, and provocative of popular protest as social protection, labor, and personal income taxation. Interest groups with strong stakes in the status quo are among the best organized, and some are as economically as they are politically powerful. Opposition to well-thought-through and thoroughly appraised reform proposals presented in the past creates curious confederacies that might not otherwise catalyze and that quickly disband when the threat of change subsides.

Many changes and additions to social protection and personal income taxation in recent years, although well motivated, introduced or aggravated the inconsistencies in and incoherence of existing policies and programs. This critique may be too easy to make from a technocratic distance. Although specific countries' contexts and considerations are provided with the presentation of the reform analysis in chapter 6, the report (humbly) suggests that policy makers should keep the following messages in mind. A fuller discussion of these points is provided in chapter 8, which concludes the report.

Job creation and greater productivity are the priority policy means to achieve sustained reductions of poverty and inequality.

This priority entails reforms that move social protection systems in a direction that matches the evolution of the labor market. Income earned through the labor market is consistently found to be the strongest, most-effective instrument for helping people overcome and stay out of poverty. Governments interested in eradicating poverty should release the labor market mechanism so that it is as unconstrained as possible to create jobs and growth. Yet, as is the case with most markets, the market for labor is rife with failures.

Those issues most germane to this report include the uneven distribution of bargaining power, inadequate information between sellers and buyers of labor, and missing or unaffordable insurance. These market failures are among the foundational motivations for social protection and labor policies, but it is important for policy makers to remember that these are intended as remedial to improve job quality and help people to manage risks rather than as ends in themselves. As such, they would ideally be dynamic and evolve as the communities, societies, economies, and nature of risks in the world of work evolve.

A neutral, agnostic policy stance with respect to how people earn their living is paramount.

Borrowed from the taxation principle of avoiding favorable treatment of income from one source over another, "neutrality" should also apply to how mandates on market work are designed and deployed. Although it remains a matter of debate, the rationale for having a mandate to guide people's savings and insurance choices is widely accepted. It is not easy to defend the notion that this rationale no longer applies if a person moves from one form of work to another. It is difficult to argue that individuals somehow overcome myopia and other cognitive limitations when they move from a subordinated, dependent form of employment to working for themselves.

If a mandate to save and insure is legitimate, it should be so for all people. Similarly, the arguments for fetishizing certain sectors or ways of working over others, with special tax treatment and exemptions, are growing stale, as work in service sectors grows to be as productive as or more productive than manufacturing jobs (Nayyar and Cruz 2018; Nayyar and Davies 2023). Overnight elimination of the special regimes that have opened the doors of social security to many self-employed workers—like the special social insurance system for self-employed persons registered as small contributors (Monotributo) in Uruguay or the Simplified Tax Regime (SIMPLES) and Individual Micro-Entrepreneur (MEI) registration option in Brazil—would be rash.

However, ensuring that the application of mandates and taxes is consistent across the ways people work would eliminate incentives to avoid and evade. A careful analysis of special regimes and reforms that would ensure proportionality—steps toward consistency and eventual convergence—could eliminate incentives for strategic gaming, which today often takes the form of firms and workers disguising their employment as self-employment, outsourcing, and subcontracting.

Program financing should be steered toward best taxation practices.

Although the debate over earmarking taxes is ongoing, sufficient consensus exists for aspects that are core to social protection financing. Namely, the use of statutory, individualized payroll taxes should be reserved for programs that cover risks and losses influenced by the parties to employment contracts and the nature of the workplace, such as the risk of work injury and termination of employment. These losses typically have few or no externalities, for which coverage entitlements and benefits are fully owned by the contributing individuals and their dependents. Inclusion and redistribution—poverty alleviation and prevention, the welfare of historically disenfranchised groups, and income redistribution—are laudable policy objectives but also are better pursued with financing from general revenues. This is the rationale for the restructuring of social insurance financing proposed by Palacios and Robalino (2020), albeit for a far-lower target pension benefit than those promised by social insurance plans in LAC.

If a program is important for social welfare—vis-à-vis the social consequences for society of someone going without it are dire—why make its financing reliant on the good behavior of employers and workers? Reserving the use of payroll taxes strictly for individual coverage and entitlements would dramatically lower the perceived tax element of mandates to save and insure (Palacios and Robalino 2020). In doing so, it would increase the value that working people place on participating and the benefits that flow from contributions.

With a few exceptions, the policies and programs for which a new financing model would be required if governments followed this advice can serve important ends. As a regional study, it is not within the scope of this report to present specific proposals for how they should be financed in lieu of payroll taxes, although some World Bank reports have presented the broad principles that can guide structural reforms (Packard et al. 2019; Ribe, Robalino, and Walker 2012). Rather, the analysis discussed here adds to the growing number of arguments for governments in LAC to broaden their tax bases and pursue a more-balanced deployment of revenue instruments (for example, refer to Vuletin 2024).

Administrative and enforcement capacity needs to be modernized, strengthened, and sustained.

The dangers of moral hazard and the temptations for people to "free ride" can be minimized with better-designed policies and programs, leveraging opportunities offered by digital technologies. However, moral hazard and free riding are human reactions to the availability of risk-pooling and other collective actions and, as such, cannot be eliminated entirely. Mitigating behavioral risks requires substantial investment in governments' monitoring and enforcement capacities, making full use of digital technologies and the growing predictive power of machine learning (Zaber, Casu, and Brodersohn 2024).

These investments can also bring the transaction costs of compliance to more-reasonable levels. The increasing focus on improvements in service delivery is a step in the right direction. Some of the region's innovations in the delivery of social assistance provide the best examples of the path to follow—such as registration and delivery procedures designed around the way people live and work, replacement of proxy measures with systems that observe actual income, and interoperability of administrative datasets to lighten the burden of identification and validation on households. By modernizing administrative capacity, outdated design features that create disincentives to registration and participation can be eliminated—for example, the assumed earned income base set equal to multiples of the minimum wage and long minimum contribution requirements to become vested for pensions.

Trust in policy promises and the credibility of government to follow through is the most-important factor and can be rebuilt.

Governments in LAC have been providing social protection directly or through para-governmental institutions for a sufficiently long period to have well-known track records. Somewhat paradoxically, although these institutions have stood the test of time and are among the strongest in LAC countries, whether due to inflation, administrative incompetence, or outright corruption, many are viewed with distrust and cynicism. This view has led to erosion of the perceived value of registering work and participating fully in social protection and other taxation systems (Perry et al. 2007; Tommasi and Saavedra-Chanduvi 2007).

When a sufficiently large proportion of the population shares these perceptions, it is more difficult for a single worker or firm to choose full or even partial compliance. This issue is a key insight into the nature of compliance: The importance of perceived fairness in tax systems—the psychological and social aspects of taxation—suggests that people are more willing to pay taxes when they believe others are also paying their fair share. The positive message for policy makers is that governments in countries with similar track records—most notably among countries in Southern and Central Europe—have been able to shift these perceptions in a positive direction, raising trust in institutions, tax morale, and compliance with mandates (for example, refer to Packard et al. 2012).

These key messages form the principles that underlie and orient recommendations for reform.

The key messages in this chapter form the principles that underlie and orient the specific reform recommendations made in chapter 8. As those charged with formulating policies are rarely afforded the choice of when and in what circumstances to propose or pass reforms, the chapter proposes a metaphorical "roadmap" and "milestones" to keep governments on track. Thus, if the reform process is inevitably incremental and opportunistic, hopefully this report—and the instruments for policy reform analysis that it develops—can serve as a tool for navigating the region's economies toward a system of taxation and social protection that delivers inclusion, equity, and risk sharing more effectively and in a way that attracts and facilitates compliance and participation.

NOTES

1. Bismarckian social insurance is a reference to the original mandated model of risk sharing first introduced in the late 19th century by German Chancellor Otto von Bismarck.
2. There have been efforts to create *contributory* social protection programs that are appealing to individuals working outside registered, dependent employment, with low, irregular incomes, who typically face financial exclusion and pressing liquidity constraints. However, there have been few success stories so far (Banerjee, Duflo, and Sharma 2021; Guven, Jain, and Joubert 2021; Hu and Stewart 2009).

REFERENCES

Banerjee, A., E. Duflo, and G. Sharma. 2021. "Long-Term Effects of the Targeting the Ultra Poor Program." *American Economic Review: Insights* 3 (4): 471–86.

Bozio, A., T. Breda, J. Grenet, and A. Guillouzouic. 2024. "Does Tax-Benefit Linkage Matter for the Incidence of Payroll Taxes?" PSE Working Papers halshs-02191315, HAL, Paris School of Economics, Paris.

Eslava, M., M. Meléndez, L. Tenjo, and N. Urdaneta. 2023. "Business Size, Development, and Inequality in Latin America: A Tale of One Tail." Policy Research Working Paper 10584, World Bank, Washington, DC.

Esping-Andersen, G. 1990. *The Three Worlds of Welfare Capitalism*. Princeton, NJ: Princeton University Press.

Frolich, M., D. Kaplan, C. Pages, J. Rigolini, and D. Robalino, eds. 2014. *Social Insurance, Informality and Labor Markets: How to Protect Workers While Creating Good Jobs*. Oxford, UK: Oxford University Press.

Gerard, F., J. Naritomi, and J. Silva. 2021. "Cash Transfers and Formal Labor Markets: Evidence from Brazil." Policy Research Working Paper 9778, World Bank, Washington, DC.

Ghorpade, Y., C. Franco Restrepo, and L. Castellanos Rodriguez. 2024. "Social Protection and Labor Market Policies for the Informally Employed: A Review of Evidence from Low- and Middle-Income Countries." Social Protection and Jobs Discussion Paper 2403, World Bank, Washington, DC.

Guven, M., H. Jain, and C. Joubert. 2021. *Social Protection for the Informal Economy: Operational Lessons for Developing Countries in Africa and Beyond*. Washington, DC: World Bank.

Guven, M., and W. Wiseman. 2022. *Charting a Course Towards Universal Social Protection: Resilience, Equity, and Opportunity for All*. Washington, DC: World Bank.

Hu, Y., and F. Stewart. 2009. "Pension Coverage and Informal Sector Workers: International Experiences." OECD Working Papers on Insurance and Private Pensions No. 31, Organisation for Economic Co-operation and Development, Paris.

Kaplan, D., and S. Levy. 2014. "The Evolution of Social Security Systems in Latin America." In *Social Insurance, Informality and Labor Markets*, edited by M. Frolich, D. Kaplan, C. Pages, J. Rigolini, and D. Robalino. Oxford, UK: Oxford University Press.

Koettl, J., and M. Weber. 2012. "Does Formal Work Pay? The Role of Labor Taxation and Social Benefit Design in the New EU Member States." IZA Discussion Paper No. 6313, Institute of Labor Economics, Bonn, Germany.

Levy, S., and G. Cruces. 2021. "Time for a New Course: An Essay on Social Protection and Growth in Latin America." UNDP LAC Working Paper No. 24, Background Paper for the UNDP LAC 2021 Regional Human Development Report, United Nations Development Programme, New York.

Nayyar, G., and M. Cruz. 2018. "Developing Countries and Services in the New Industrial Paradigm." Policy Research Working Paper 8659, World Bank, Washington, DC.

Nayyar, G., and E. Davies. 2023. "Services-Led Growth: Better Prospects after the Pandemic?" Policy Research Working Paper 10382, World Bank, Washington, DC.

OECD (Organisation for Economic Co-operation and Development). 2024. *Taxing Wages 2024: Tax and Gender through the Lens of the Second Earner*. Paris: OECD. https://doi.org/10.1787/dbcbac85-en.

Orozco Corona, M., and R. Vélez-Grajales. 2024. "Does Social Protection Cause Informality? A Critical Review of the Literature on the Relationship between Social Protection, Formal and Informal Employment." Women in Informal Employment: Globalizing and Organizing (WIEGO) Working Paper No. 48, WIEGO, Manchester, UK.

Packard, T., U. Gentilini, M. Grosh, P. O'Keefe, R. Palacios, D. Robalino, and I. Santos. 2019. *Protecting All: Risk Sharing for a Diverse and Diversifying World of Work*. Human Development Perspectives. Washington, DC: World Bank. https://openknowledge.worldbank.org/handle/10986/32353.

Packard, T., J. Koettl, and C. E. Montenegro. 2012. *In From the Shadow: Integrating Europe's Informal Labor*. Directions in Development: Human Development. Washington, DC: World Bank. http://hdl.handle.net/10986/9377.

Palacios, R., and D. Robalino. 2020. "Integrating Social Insurance and Social Assistance Programs for the Future World of Labor." IZA Working Paper No. 13258, Institute of Labor Economics, Bonn, Germany.

Palier, B., ed. 2010. *A Long Goodbye to Bismarck? The Politics of Welfare Reforms in Continental Europe*. Amsterdam: Amsterdam University Press.

Perry, G. E., W. F. Maloney, O. S. Arias, P. Fajnzylber, A. D. Mason, and J. Saavedra-Chanduvi. 2007. *Informality: Exit and Exclusion*. Latin American and Caribbean Studies. Washington, DC: World Bank. https://openknowledge .worldbank.org/handle/10986/6730.

Ribe, H., D. Robalino, and I. Walker. 2012. *From Right to Reality: Incentives, Labor Markets, and the Challenge of Universal Social Protection in Latin America and the Caribbean*. Washington, DC: World Bank. https://openknowledge.worldbank.org /handle/10986/6008.

Tommasi, M., and J. Saavedra-Chanduvi. 2007. "Informality, the State and the Social Contract in Latin America: A Preliminary Exploration." *International Labour Review* 146 (3–4): 279–309.

Torm, N., and M. Oehme. 2024. "Social Protection and Formalization in Low- and Middle-Income Countries: A Scoping Review of the Literature." *World Development* 181: 106662.

Vuletin, G. 2024. "Progressive Taxation for Growth in LAC." Draft Regional Study for the Chief Economist's Office, Latin America and Caribbean Regional Office, World Bank, Washington, DC.

World Bank. 2024. *World Development Report 2024: The Middle-Income Trap.* Washington, DC: World Bank.

Zaber, M., O. Casu, and E. Brodersohn. 2024. "Artificial Intelligence in Social Security Organizations." International Social Security Association and United Nations University, Geneva.

2 Focus and Scope of the Report

"INFORMALITY": WHAT IS IT, AND WHY SHOULD WE CARE?

Few public policy phenomena are as ambiguously defined and difficult to measure as the "informal sector." A form of economic activity that first captured the interest of anthropologists and development economists in the early 1970s (Harris and Todaro 1970; Hart 1973), the informal sector became a central focus of policy in the late 1980s and early 1990s, when sufficient data were first available to show that the informal economy was far more than cottage industries, taxi drivers, and children selling candy on street corners (de Soto 1989).

What is the informal economy? It is inherently difficult to observe something that, by its nature, people are trying to hide (Schneider and Enste 2000). Definitions change according to who is asking and what motivates their question. A minister of finance might ask to know where and how many untapped sources of additional tax revenue can be found. A minister of labor or the leader of a trade union might ask to have a better idea of where to concentrate their efforts to ensure that the rights and protections of labor market regulation are upheld. A minister of trade and industry or the head of the local chamber of commerce might ask to know where opportunities to expand sales, ensure fairer competition, and improve productivity might lie. From each perspective, a different definition of the informal economy can be drawn.

Why should policy makers be concerned about the extent and determinants of the informal economy and informal work? The most-reliable predictor of the size of the informal economy and the share of people working informally is a country's gross domestic product per capita (refer to figure 2.1). However, just as consistently, the data show that, even at similar levels of per capita income, substantial differences exist in the extent of

A reproducibility package is available for this book in the Reproducible Research Repository at https://reproducibility.worldbank.org/catalog/330/.

informal work across countries. What is going on? People work and do business outside the confines of social, labor, and business regulations for many reasons. Some choose to work in the informal economy to escape regulatory costs or enjoy greater flexibility. Others are excluded from the formal economy due to a lack of opportunities for advancement and actual barriers to better-protected, higher-productivity jobs.

Whether people are working informally because they exited or are excluded from formal work, widespread informal employment can be treated as evidence of inadequate and unsustainable social institutions. Thus, the extent of informality reveals the insufficiency of the institutions the state has put in place to help households build, sustain, and protect their investment in human capital as they enter the labor market to seek a return on this investment. Indeed, a large and growing informal economy can be seen as the consequence of a mass opting out of institutions by firms and individuals and "a blunt societal indictment of the quality of the State's services provision" (Perry et al. 2007, 2).

FIGURE 2.1

Share of people working informally and income per capita, 1955–2023

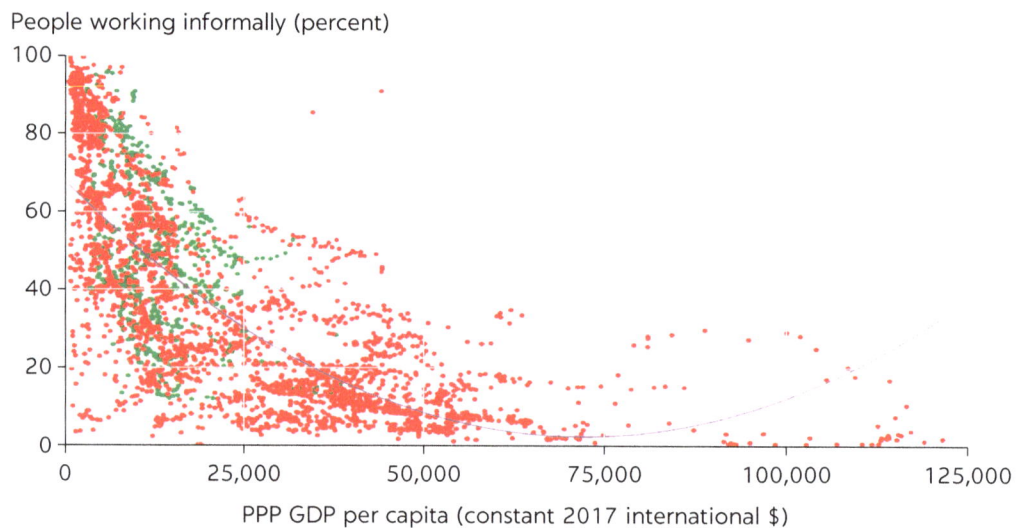

People working informally (percent)

PPP GDP per capita (constant 2017 international $)

Sources: Original figure for this publication, using calculations based on data from Ohnsorge and Yu 2022; International Labour Organization (ILO.org); the Income Inequality Distribution Database (I2D2), World Bank; the Luxembourg Income Study; and the Organisation for Economic Co-operation and Development.
Note: Observations for countries in Latin America and the Caribbean are in green, covering 21 countries, each with 60–78 observations over 1955–2023. "People working informally as a share of working people" is a composite indicator of people working in firms of 5 or fewer workers, self-employed workers, and nonremunerated family workers. Indicators of informal work from each source are positively correlated, with coefficients of 0.725 to 1.000. GDP = gross domestic product; PPP = purchasing power parity.

The extent of informal work has long concerned policy makers for several reasons:

- First, it is a problem for individuals and their families. People working informally and their dependents face explicit and implicit barriers to public and privately provided insurance instruments to manage potentially impoverishing shocks. Even if people can manage many risks to their well-being without help from the state, they may find it difficult to assess accurately the costs of certain needs. These needs may include health care, help during a period of job search, or sufficient provision for losses in the future, such as adequate income arrangements for when they can no longer work in old age. Nor do people who work informally have easy access to credit or recourse to rights and the legal protections these afford when things go wrong. Furthermore, few purely private risk management instruments can withstand a systemic shock. Households that depend solely on the informal economy are far more difficult to reach in the wake of a crisis, such as the recent COVID-19 pandemic.

- Second, it is a problem for firms. In countries with large informal economies, bigger, usually more-productive firms are often overtaxed to make up for the government's loss of revenue due to widespread evasion. This issue can discourage investment and hinder growth. Firms that operate within the rules face unfair competition from those operating outside the rules. Yet, firms that operate informally can be constrained to a small size to escape detection by the tax authorities. Those firms forgo a more-efficient scale of production, with aggregate consequences for the productivity of the economy (Eslava, García-Marín, and Messina 2023).

- Third, it is a problem for society. The larger the informal economy is, the more opportunities exist for households and firms to engage in transactions that bypass the formal rules. This issue occurs not only in the product and labor markets but also in the financial and other markets. A large informal economy imposes heavy costs that lead to deterioration of services and public goods. In extreme cases, it can corrode civic structures to such an extent as to contribute to state failure. This corrosive process can cause a country's social "risk pools"—such as public old age, unemployment, and health insurance, as well as the tax and transfer system—to become fragmented, inefficient, and too expensive to remain viable.

The productivity imperative has cast a spotlight on the informal economy. As governments attempt to keep up in the race to become more economically productive, what to do about the extent of informal employment is a dilemma that is gaining urgency. The forces that accompany technological change put a premium on mobility and skill renewal. Rapid population aging will require that people work longer and be far more productive. To achieve this, social institutions must be more "pro-work," encouraging greater participation and optimal matches in the labor market. As the rate of growth moderates, public financial resources will be increasingly scarce, making it imperative to implement measures that can significantly and sustainably increase tax revenue.

FOCUS AND SCOPE OF THIS REPORT

The size of the informal economy is correlated with but distinct from the extent of informal work (refer to figure 2.2). This report focuses on the "informality" that results from the negotiation of employment relationships and decisions of sole traders and self-employed workers with respect to social protection programs and policies, personal income taxation, and prevailing labor regulations (refer to figure 2.3).

Across countries in Latin America and the Caribbean (LAC), these policies, regulations, and taxes vary substantially. This variation includes the extent of mandates to participate in social insurance, which has been historically and continues to be the largest segment of social protection systems. The advent of social assistance transfers with broad coverage and entitlements to protection based on citizenship, residence, need, or a combination of these personal and household characteristics is relatively recent in LAC countries.

FIGURE 2.2

Average share of people working informally, by size of the informal economy in LAC countries, 1993–2019

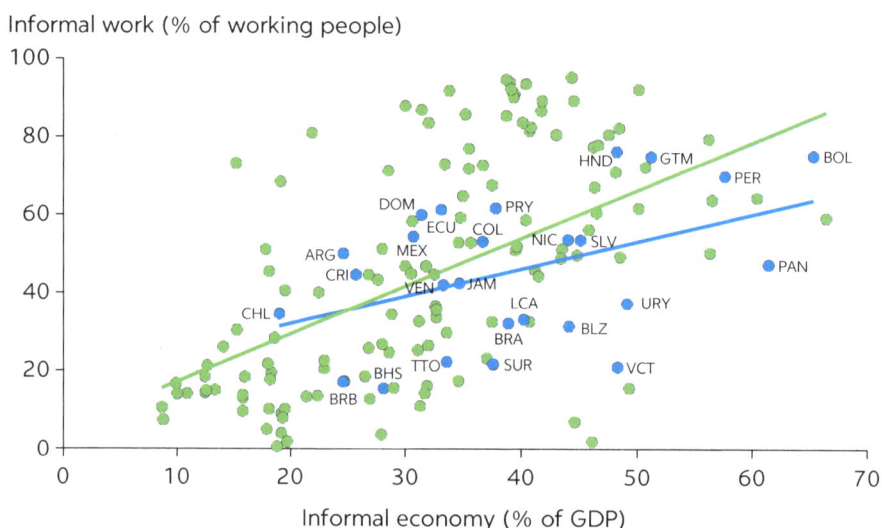

Informal work (% of working people)

Informal economy (% of GDP)

Sources: Original figure for this publication based on data from Ohnsorge and Yu 2022; International Labour Organization (ILO.org); the Income Inequality Distribution Database (I2D2), World Bank; the Luxembourg Income Study; and Organisation for Economic Co-operation and Development. The size of the informal economy is from Ohnsorge and Yu 2022.

Note: LAC countries are blue. For a list of country codes, refer to https://www.iso.org /obp/ui/#search. GDP = gross domestic product; LAC = Latin America and the Caribbean.

FIGURE 2.3

Informal work: Focus and scope of this report

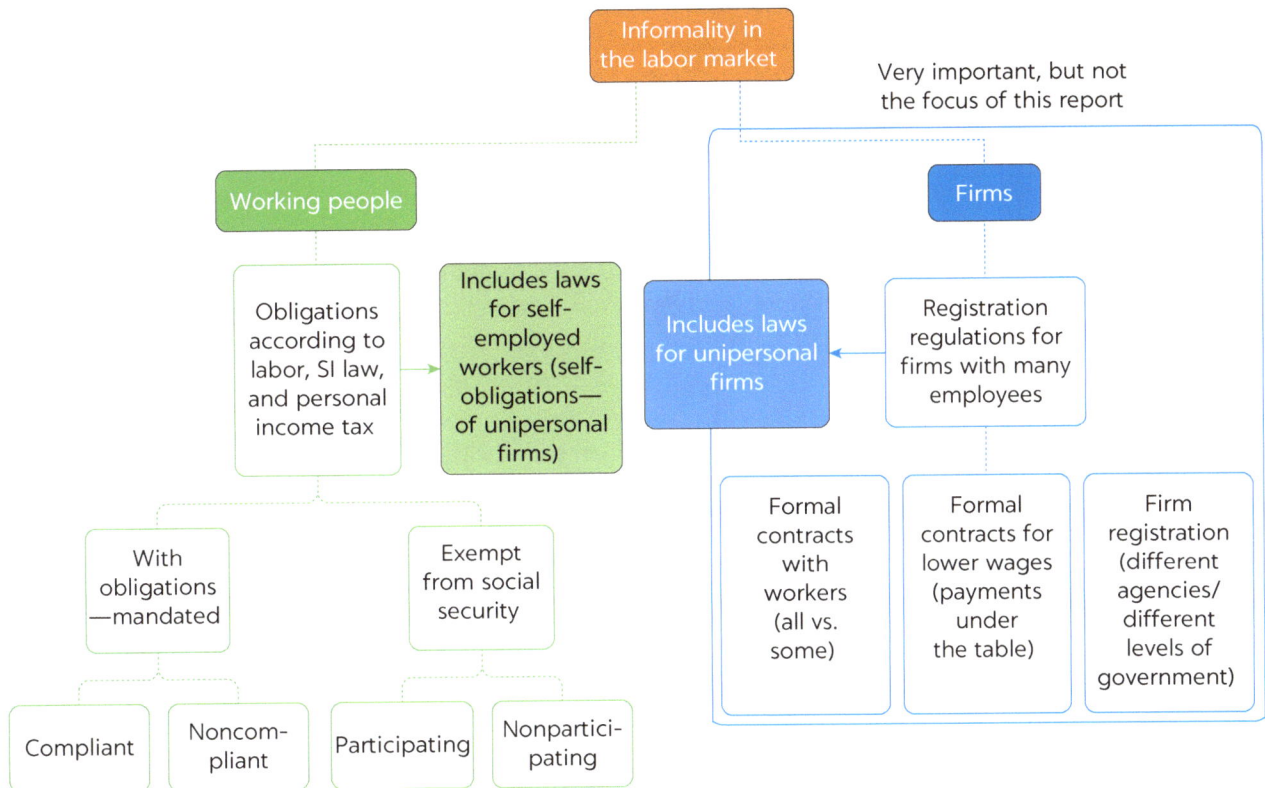

Source: Original figure for this publication.
Note: SI = social insurance.

Previously, entitlements that were de-linked from the workplace were scant and paltry. Thus, whether people are effectively protected from shocks is still highly correlated with their status as contributors to national social insurance programs. Hence, the narrow focus of the report's analysis of informality is those entitled to or gaining entitlement to protection by contributing to social insurance.

This report focuses on "informality" in a sense that is not synonymous with "illegality." Various ways exist in which people can work entirely legally while also completely or partially side-stepping social insurance. In countries such as Mexico and Peru, self-employed workers (and employers) are completely exempt from the mandate to participate in social insurance, which applies to dependent workers. In contrast, in Brazil and Uruguay, self-employed workers have long been mandated to participate, along with all other working people, although partial or total legal exemptions have emerged.

This chapter uses labor and household survey microdata to derive more-specific "dimensions" of informality. Although social insurance is mainly composed of pension and health services, the chapter focuses only on the pension dimension and its legislation. Therefore, it considers as informal workers all those who are employed in the labor market but do not contribute to or are not affiliated with the pension system. Among workers subject to legislative mandates, the chapter identifies those who are "complying" and "noncomplying," and among those who are legally exempt, it identifies those who are "participating" and "nonparticipating."[1]

Countries differ substantially in their shares of workers under these categories (refer to figure 2.4). "Mandated and complying" workers—those legally obligated to contribute to social insurance—represent most of the workers in countries such as Brazil and Uruguay at 67 and 78 percent, respectively; less than 50 percent in Colombia; about 33 percent in El Salvador and Mexico; and only 12 percent in Peru. Meanwhile, "mandated and noncomplying" workers—those who are in breach of the law—represent between one-fifth and one-third in Brazil, Colombia, and Uruguay. In Mexico, this category accounts for almost 50 percent of the workers, and in Peru, only 3 percent.

In contrast, the "exempt and participating" represent less than 1 percent in Brazil, Colombia, El Salvador, and Uruguay, showing that a limited percentage of workers freely choose to pay social insurance contributions. In Peru, this category accounts for 8 percent of the workers. Those who are "exempt and nonparticipating" represent almost 8 in 10 workers in Peru, where a high percentage of the workers are legally without social insurance. The share in this category is around a third in Colombia, El Salvador, and Mexico. Almost no workers are in this category in Brazil and Uruguay.

The differences in the shares of workers in the (in)formality categories across countries are linked to differences in legislation. Brazil and Uruguay have similar legislation, in which all workers are obliged to pay social insurance contributions. In Colombia, El Salvador, Mexico, and Peru, the legislation has some exceptions for certain types of workers. A commonality among these countries is that salaried workers in the public sector are obliged to pay social insurance contributions. In both Colombia and Mexico, all private salaried workers are required to contribute. In Peru, those in special regimes are excluded depending on the size of the firm, and in El Salvador, domestic and agricultural workers are excluded. In Colombia, self-employed workers and employers are obliged to contribute if their salary is greater than the minimum wage. However, in El Salvador, Mexico, and Peru, these workers are excluded.

Nonsalaried workers are not mandated to contribute in all six countries. Peru has the highest proportion of informal workers, mainly made up of those who do not contribute because of legislation (exempt and nonparticipating). Next are Colombia and El Salvador, where the percentages are similar for informal workers who violate the law (mandated and noncomplying) and those in line with the legislation (exempt and nonparticipating). In Brazil, Mexico, and Uruguay, informality is composed mainly of mandated and noncomplying workers.

FIGURE 2.4

Distribution of workers in select LAC countries, by informality category, 2022

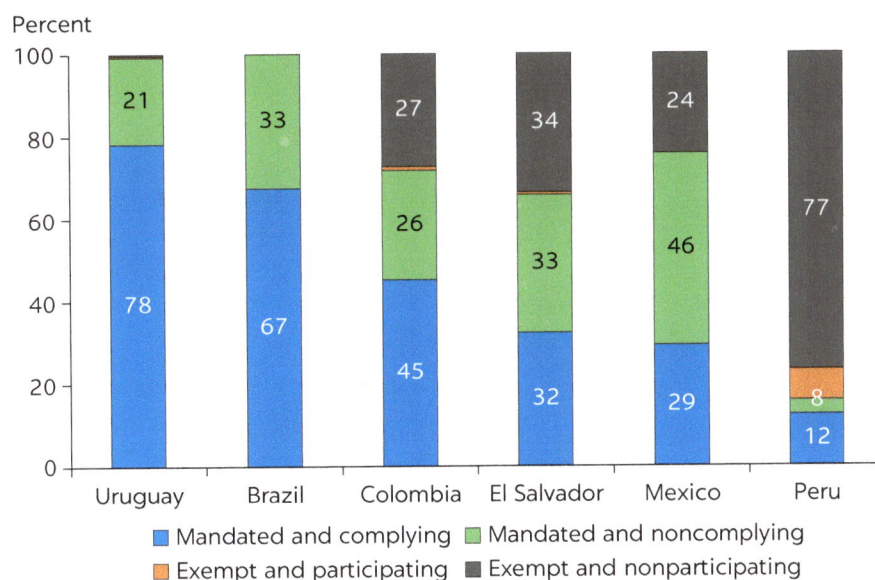

Source: Original figure for this publication, using data from SEDLAC 2022.
Note: LAC = Latin America and the Caribbean.

Worker type also plays a role in the links between the (in)formality categories and legislation. The incentives shaped by the legislation in the formality–informality margin (mainly exemptions from contributing to social insurance for certain types of workers) also operate through the decisions that individuals and firms make about the type of employment. Mandated and noncomplying workers are mainly self-employed in Brazil and Uruguay; are private salaried workers in Colombia, El Salvador, and Mexico; and are public salaried workers in Peru (refer to figure 2.5). Those who are "exempt and nonparticipating" are nonsalaried workers in Brazil and Uruguay and are mainly self-employed in the other countries.

Although workers across the (in)formality categories are present in all sectors, a substantial share is found in the service sector (refer to table 2A.1 in annex 2A). Service sector workers are the majority in most of the economies in this study. Both complying and noncomplying workers are predominantly employed in this sector. About 60 percent of noncomplying workers are in the service sector, and only 20 percent are in the industrial sector. The agriculture sector has a lower share of mandated workers, but the proportion increases for nonparticipating workers. Nonetheless, this type of worker is primarily found in the service sector across all the countries.

Small firms are characterized by a higher percentage of noncomplying and nonparticipating workers, compared to large firms (refer to table 2A.1 in annex 2A). Complying workers are mainly employed in large firms, and a significant share of noncomplying workers is found in small firms.

The proportion of exempt workers in large firms is relatively low, except in Peru, where more than 70 percent of participating workers are in large firms. The share of nonparticipating workers in small firms is considerable across nearly all the countries. In general, informal workers in public firms are few, except in Peru, where nearly 60 percent of noncomplying workers are in public firms.

FIGURE 2.5

Profile of workers in select LAC countries, by (in)formality category and job characteristics, 2022

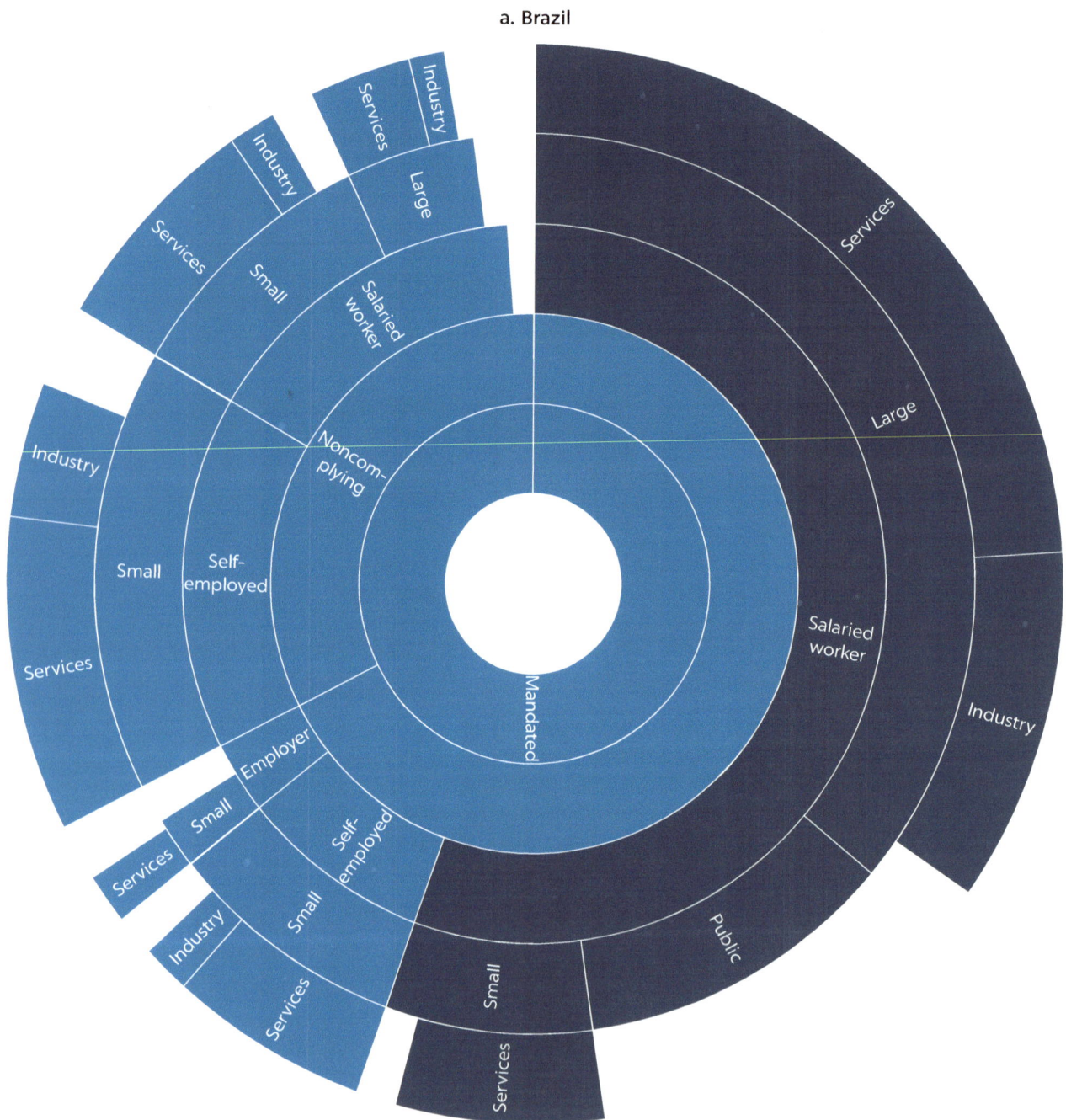

a. Brazil

continued

FIGURE 2.5 Profile of workers in select LAC countries, by (in)formality category and job characteristics, 2022, *(continued)*

b. Colombia

continued

FIGURE 2.5 Profile of workers in select LAC countries, by (in)formality category and job characteristics, 2022, *(continued)*

c. El Salvador

continued

FIGURE 2.5 Profile of workers in select LAC countries, by (in)formality category and job characteristics, 2022, *(continued)*

d. Mexico

continued

FIGURE 2.5 Profile of workers in select LAC countries, by (in)formality category and job characteristics, 2022, *(continued)*

e. Peru

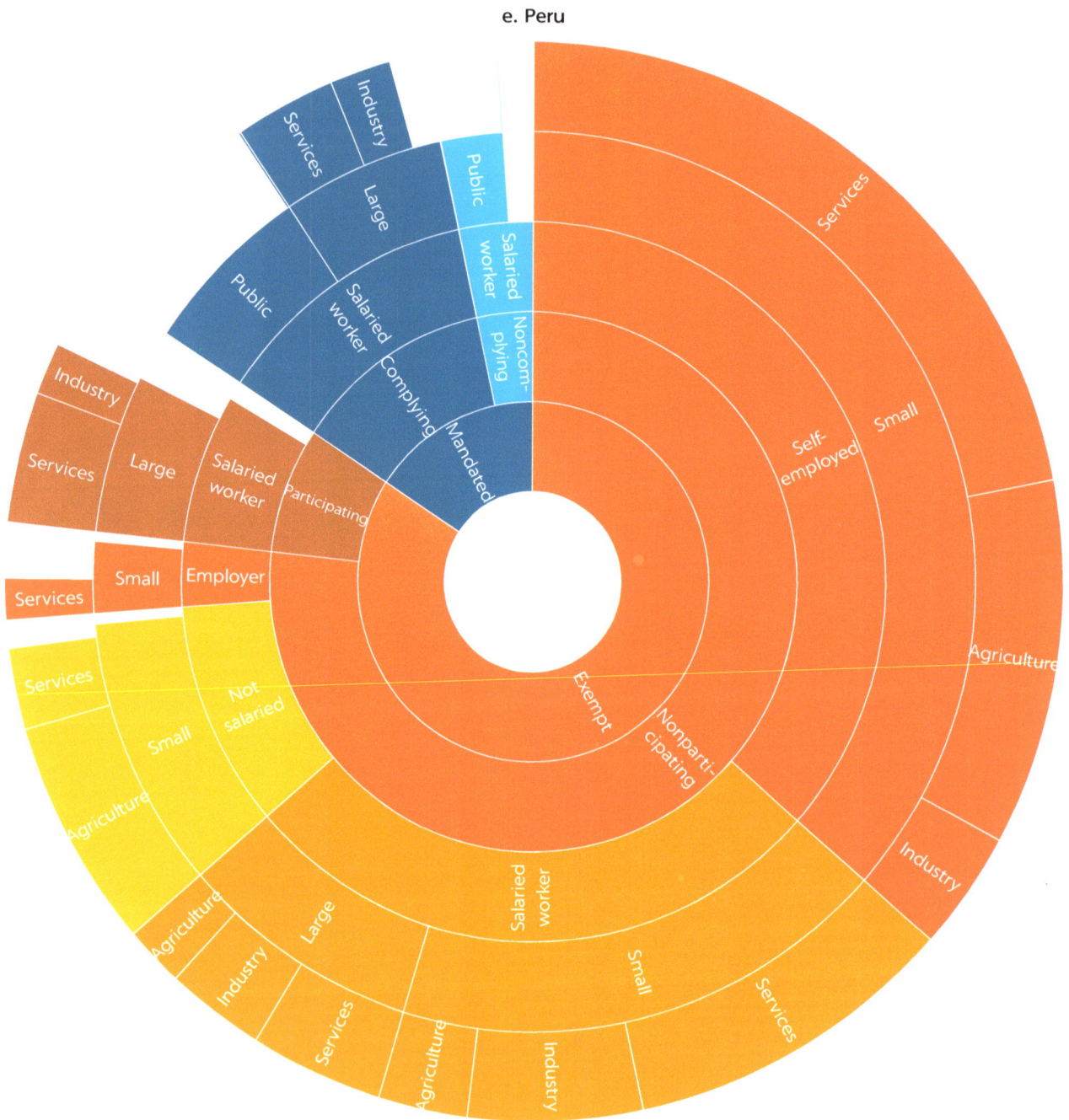

continued

FIGURE 2.5 Profile of workers in select LAC countries, by (in)formality category and job characteristics, 2022, *(continued)*

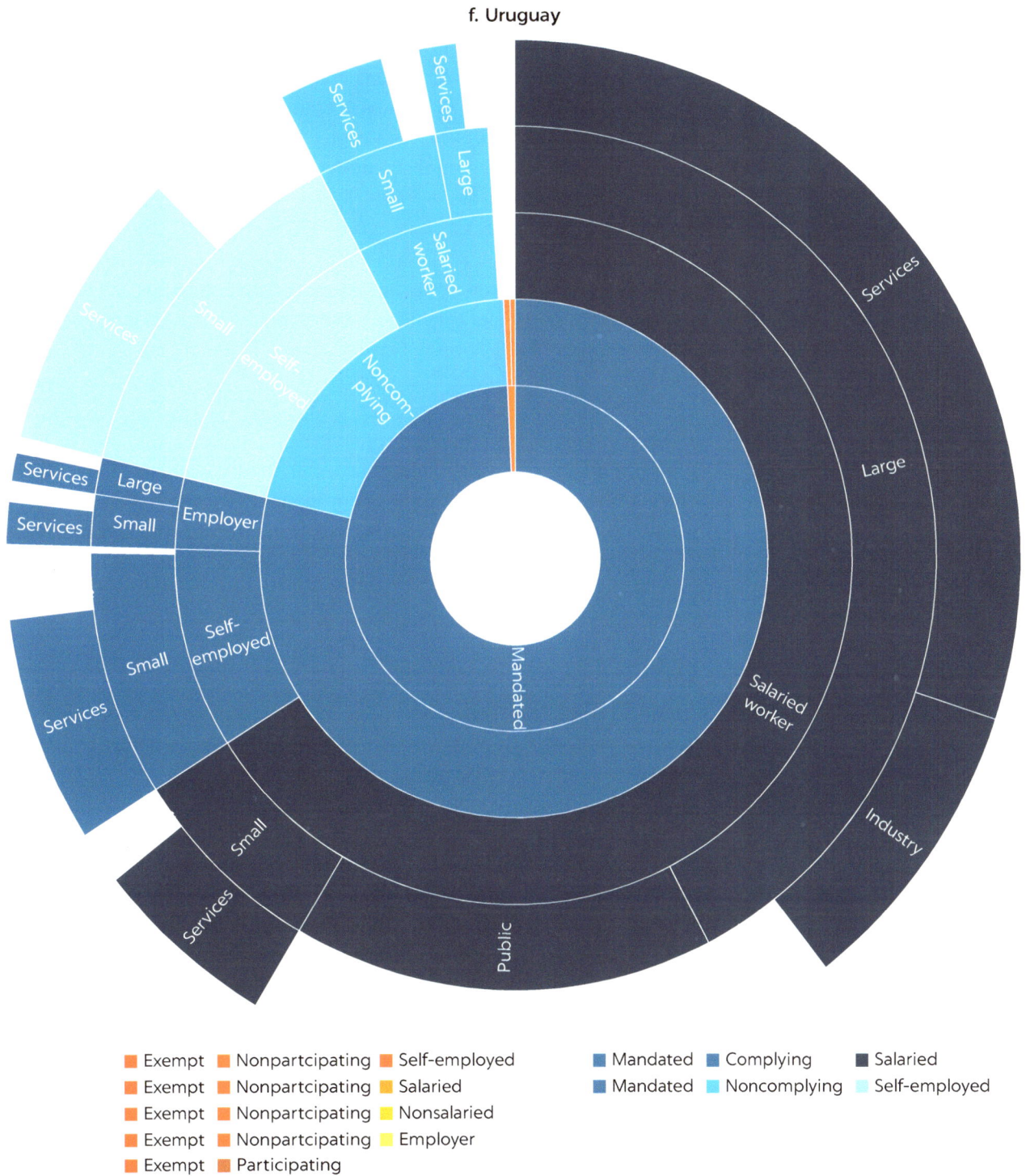

f. Uruguay

Legend:
- Exempt — Nonpartcipating — Self-employed
- Exempt — Nonpartcipating — Salaried
- Exempt — Nonpartcipating — Nonsalaried
- Exempt — Nonpartcipating — Employer
- Exempt — Participating

- Mandated — Complying — Salaried
- Mandated — Noncomplying — Self-employed

Source: Original figures for this publication, using data from SEDLAC 2022.
Note: LAC = Latin America and the Caribbean.

Noncomplying workers are predominantly men, and nonparticipating workers are mainly women (refer to table 2.1). Although the gender distributions of workers in the mandated and exempt categories are similar, noncomplying workers tend to be mostly men across all the countries, as are complying workers. In contrast, among nonparticipating workers, a higher proportion is women in Brazil, El Salvador, and Mexico. Participating workers are more likely to be men, except in Uruguay. These trends may reflect gender differences in employment rates and preferences, with women more often found in categories excluded from legislation, such as domestic work and part-time work.

Informal workers are generally in the most-productive age range and tend to reside in urban areas (refer to table 2.1). Most workers across all the categories are between ages 25 and 49 years. However, more frequently, noncomplying workers are ages 15 to 24 years, compared to complying workers. In contrast, a larger share of nonparticipating workers are between ages 50 and 65 years. In addition, noncomplying workers are often located in urban areas or in the capital city of their respective country, except in Brazil, where the presence of noncomplying or nonparticipating workers in the capital city is considerably low. Rural areas, by comparison, have a lower proportion of both noncomplying and nonparticipating workers.

Education levels also vary among informal workers. Noncomplying and nonparticipating workers generally have lower levels of education, with most having only primary or secondary education (refer to table 2.1). Few informal workers attain higher levels of education. Among mandated and complying workers, as well as exempt and participating workers, there is a higher proportion with tertiary education.

Complying and participating workers are scant at the bottom of the income distribution. Across countries, the share of working people complying or participating tends to increase as workers' per capita household income increases (refer to figure 2.6). In the lower deciles of per capita household income, the share of complying workers is near zero. In the highest income deciles, the share is higher than 80 percent of the employed population in Brazil, Colombia, and Uruguay; around 50 percent in El Salvador and Mexico; and above 20 percent in Peru. In contrast, the share of noncomplying and nonparticipating workers decreases slightly in the highest income deciles. For exempt and participating workers, the relationship is not as clear, as the share of workers in this category remains near zero. These results suggest that compliance and participation are more likely to be conditions for those with more-favorable economic circumstances. In this way, the poor population is restricted from accessing better jobs.

TABLE 2.1 **Profile of workers in select LAC countries, by informality category and individuals' characteristics, 2022**

		BRAZIL		COLOMBIA		EL SALVADOR		MEXICO		PERU		URUGUAY	
MANDATED, %		**M AND C**	**M AND NC**	**M AND C**	**M AND NC**	**M AND C**	**M AND NC**	**M AND C**	**M AND NC**	**M AND C**	**M AND NC**	**M AND C**	**M AND NC**
Gender	Female	44	40	44	34	39	36	41	40	43	47	47	44
	Male	56	60	56	66	61	64	59	60	57	53	53	56
Age (years)	15–24	13	19	10	17	15	27	12	24	8	17	9	16
	25–49	67	59	72	61	69	59	68	56	63	65	65	56
	50–65	20	22	18	22	16	14	21	20	29	18	26	28
Area	Urban	91	83	65	62	40	36	79	63	56	56	49	68
	Rural	7	16	7	24	18	43	9	22	5	15	6	5
	Capital city	2	1	28	13	42	21	13	15	39	29	45	27
Level of education	Less than primary	14	32	2	13	13	50	2	9	2	4	1	5
	Primary	11	19	10	32	25	30	33	53	6	13	50	78
	Secondary	48	40	35	40	43	18	32	25	34	40	27	14
	Tertiary	27	9	53	15	19	2	33	13	58	42	21	3

		BRAZIL		COLOMBIA		EL SALVADOR		MEXICO		PERU		URUGUAY	
EXEMPT, %		**E AND P**	**E AND NP**	**E AND P**	**E AND NP**	**E AND P**	**E AND NP**	**E AND P**	**E AND NP**	**E AND P**	**E AND NP**	**E AND P**	**E AND NP**
Gender	Female	40	57	41	34	27	52	—	52	36	49	90	47
	Male	60	43	59	66	73	48	—	48	64	51	10	53
Age (years)	15–24	3	33	5	15	0	11	—	11	11	18	6	38
	25–49	78	64	55	56	39	57	—	53	68	53	54	36
	50–65	20	4	40	29	61	32	—	36	21	28	40	26
Area	Urban	78	38	65	56	60	39	—	54	40	48	34	45
	Rural	22	62	18	37	7	36	—	34	4	26	58	18
	Capital city	0	0	17	7	33	25	—	11	56	27	8	37
Level of education	Less than primary	31	49	6	22	18	52	—	16	2	16	3	3
	Primary	7	10	16	37	16	25	—	51	7	29	72	70
	Secondary	37	40	36	33	22	19	—	22	47	44	22	22
	Tertiary	25	0	42	8	43	4	—	11	44	11	2	5

Source: Original table for this publication, using data from SEDLAC 2022.
Note: E and NP = exempt and nonparticipating; E and P = exempt and participating; LAC = Latin America and the Caribbean; M and C = mandated and complying; M and NC = mandated and noncomplying; — = not available.

FIGURE 2.6

Distribution of workers in select LAC countries, by informality category and per capita household income decile, 2022

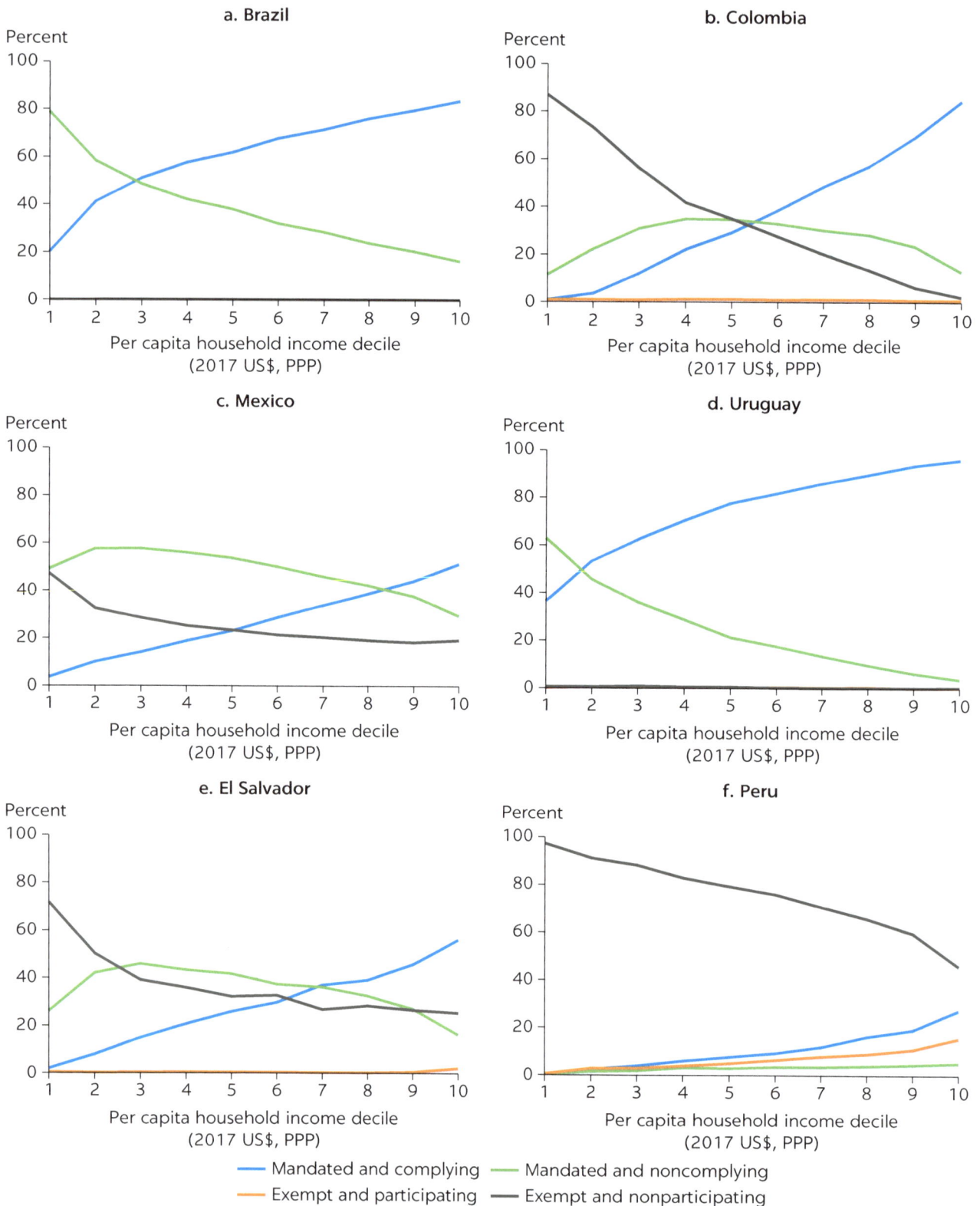

Source: Original figures for this publication, using data from SEDLAC 2022.
Note: LAC = Latin America and the Caribbean; PPP = purchasing power parity.

In the lower deciles, most of the labor income comes from noncomplying or nonparticipating jobs, while in the upper deciles, most of the labor income comes from complying jobs (refer to figure 2.7). Considering the share that the income of each category of workers represents within the deciles shows that the proportion from complying and participating jobs increases as the household income grows. In countries such as Brazil, Colombia, and Uruguay, in the highest deciles, labor income is almost entirely made up of income from complying and participating work. Indeed, this is consistent with the fact that these jobs among those in the lowest deciles are almost nonexistent. Notably, in Peru, the income of nonparticipating workers constitutes a substantial proportion across all the income deciles; however, this share also exhibits a decreasing trend as household income rises.

Those in the lowest income deciles not only are more likely to be in noncomplying employment or choose not to participate but also have lower incomes, perpetuating poverty. Complying and participating workers have higher incomes than noncomplying and nonparticipating workers. According to the distribution of labor income, the incomes of workers who do not comply or participate are concentrated at lower values. In all the countries, the distributions of complying and participating workers are to the right of their counterparts, indicating a higher amount of labor income, compared to that for noncomplying or nonparticipating workers (refer to figure 2.8). However, the labor income distributions also show that the categories overlap at higher levels of earnings, indicating that workers of all types appear across the earnings distribution, including noncomplying and nonparticipating workers who have high labor earnings.

People in uncovered work earn lower incomes, and most workers have incomes below the legal minimum wage. A large share of noncomplying and nonparticipating workers have incomes below the legal minimum wage threshold, worsening the precariousness associated with informality in the lowest income deciles. Figure 2.8 shows that the distributions for noncomplying and nonparticipating workers are clustered near the minimum wage (the red dashed line) and below the median labor income (the blue dashed line). Complying workers tend to be concentrated to the right of both lines. This pattern may arise partly from the definition of the legislation (for example, in Colombia, the exempt workers are those with wages below the legal minimum wage).

However, this situation reflects the vulnerability for workers in poverty. They not only lack the benefits and stability of formality but also earn incomes that are insufficient to meet what is socially assumed to be the minimum legally established level to ensure a decent standard of living. Dependence on low-income, informal jobs perpetuates their poverty and restricts their potential to improve their living conditions.

FIGURE 2.7

Share of total labor income in select LAC countries, by informality category and per capita household income decile, 2022

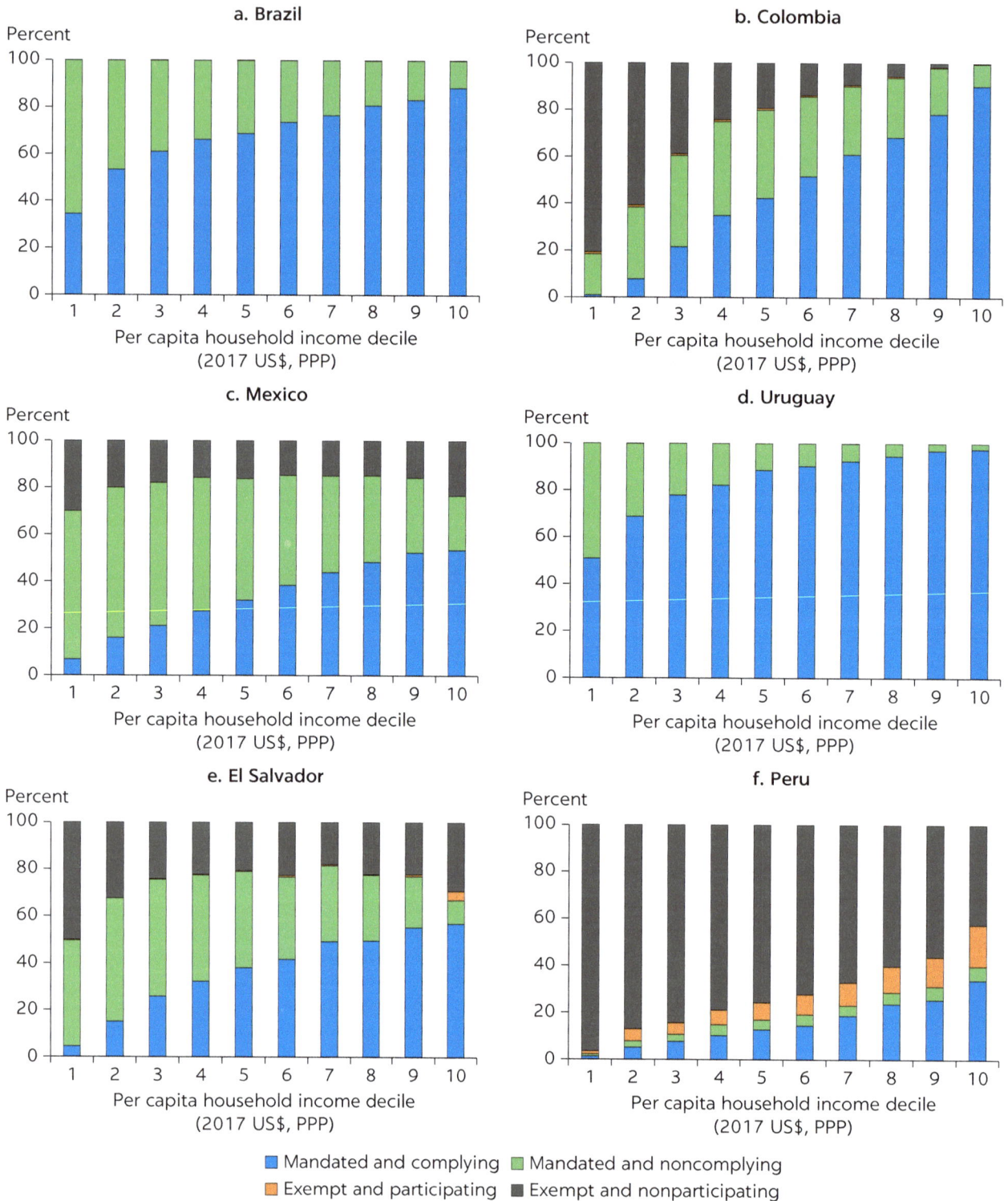

a. Brazil

b. Colombia

c. Mexico

d. Uruguay

e. El Salvador

f. Peru

■ Mandated and complying ■ Mandated and noncomplying
■ Exempt and participating ■ Exempt and nonparticipating

Source: Original figures for this publication, using data from SEDLAC 2022.
Note: LAC = Latin America and the Caribbean; PPP = purchasing power parity.

FIGURE 2.8

Income distribution in select LAC countries, by informality category, 2022

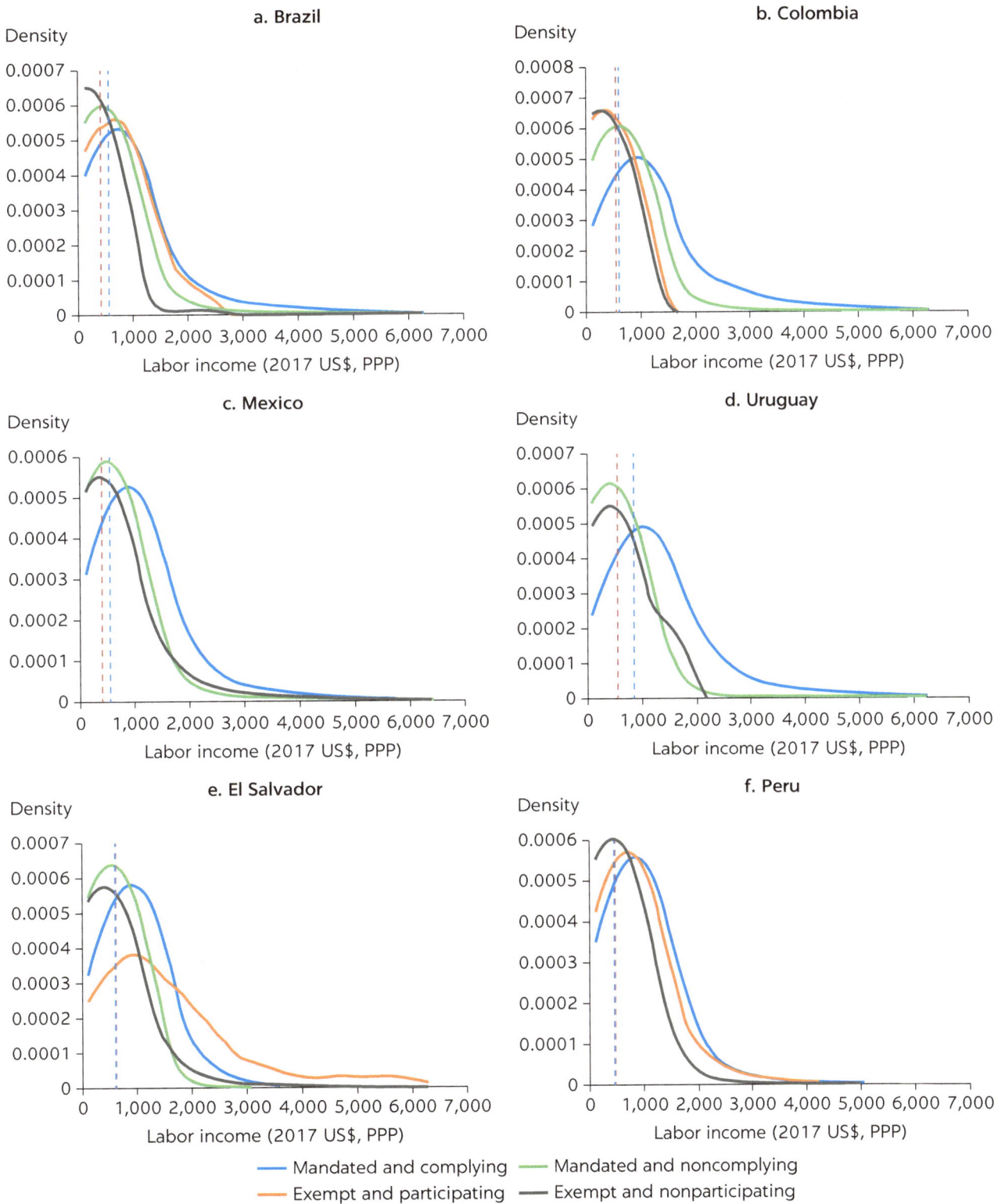

a. Brazil

b. Colombia

c. Mexico

d. Uruguay

e. El Salvador

f. Peru

— Mandated and complying — Mandated and noncomplying
— Exempt and participating — Exempt and nonparticipating

Source: Original figures for this publication, using data from SEDLAC 2022.
Note: The red dashed line represents the legal minimum wage, and the blue dashed line represents the median labor
income. LAC = Latin America and the Caribbean; PPP = purchasing power parity.

The average labor income of complying or participating workers is about twice as high as the average income of uncovered workers (refer to figure 2.9). This is the case for workers in all the per capita household income deciles. Within the group of mandated workers, the income of those complying is double the income of those who are noncomplying. Something similar occurs among those who are exempt, but the differences are smaller. Noncomplying and nonparticipating work is prevalent among those with lower incomes, although formality offers the incentive of higher wages. This issue may be linked to other barriers to formality.

TAXES, BENEFITS, AND OTHER INCENTIVES TO (IN)FORMALIZE: A WHISTLE-STOP TOUR OF THE EVIDENCE

Generally, the literature on the roles of taxation and social protection in the decision to comply or participate scrutinizes three channels through which the current policies and programs can shape incentives:

- *Taxes on individuals' labor supply and firms' hiring decisions.* Statutory contributions to social insurance programs (such as contributory pensions, unemployment insurance, and health insurance) increase firms' and workers' costs of entering formal employment relationships (that is, relationships that are observed contractually, regulated, and taxed). Meanwhile, social assistance transfer programs (such as cash or in-kind transfers) that cover some risks reduce the costs and risks of working informally.

- *Additional regulatory mandates on firms and individuals.* Costs are associated with overly restrictive labor regulation, such as restrictions on hiring, place of work, working hours and dismissal procedures, and mandated severance pay. These costs substantially increase the firms' costs of making formal employment offers, dissuading such offers, particularly to job-seekers with lower skill levels.

- *Firm behavior in the face of incentives and constraints.* The costs of compliance with taxation, social protection, and labor regulations can be burdensome. Combining these costs with special taxation regimes or exemptions can create strong incentives to "stay small" to avoid crossing the scale threshold into formality.

The following subsections discuss a brief literature review to assess the current state of knowledge on whether, and to what extent, the channels identified above operate to impact growth and productivity in the region.

FIGURE 2.9

Average labor income in select LAC countries, by informality category and per capita household income decile, 2022

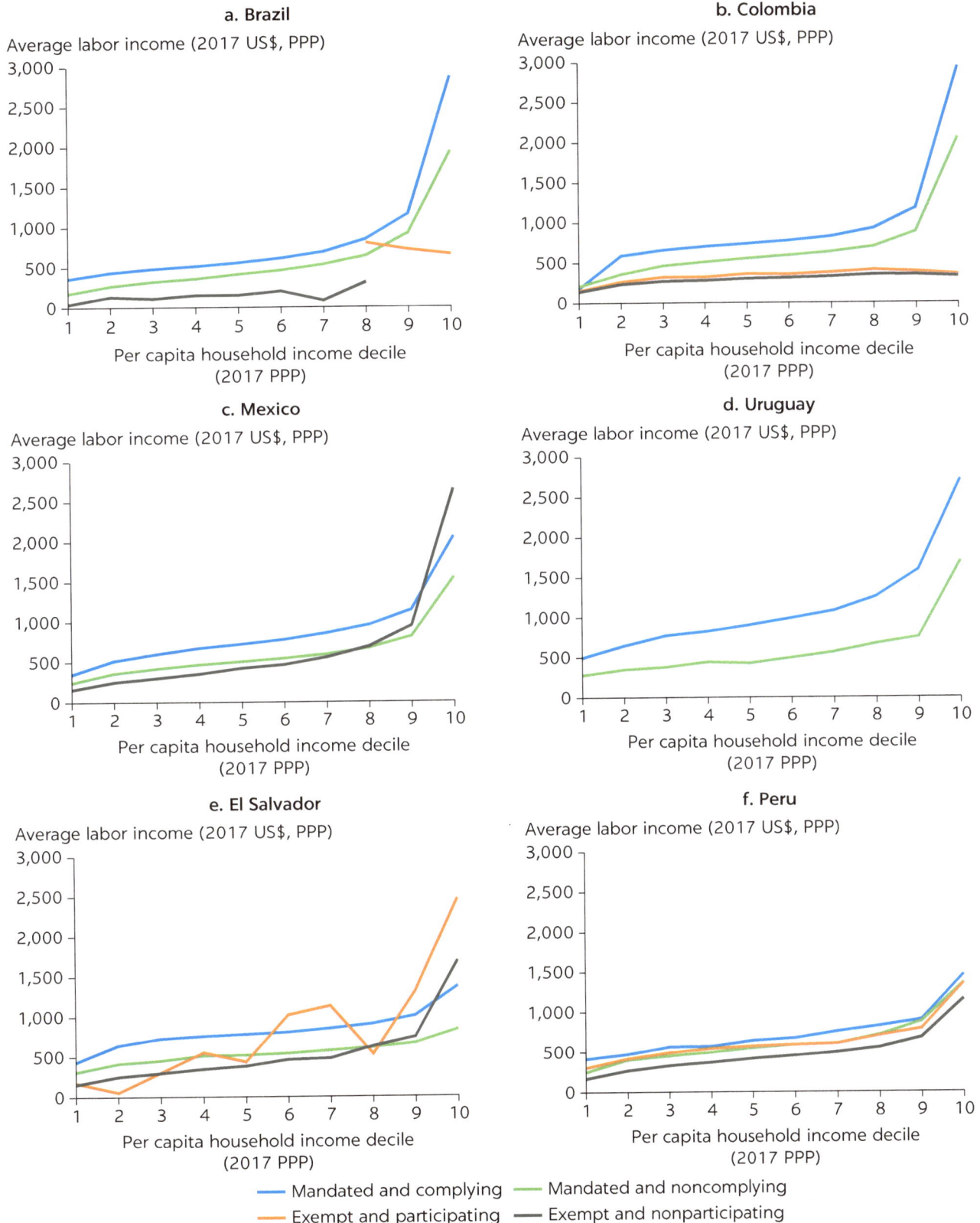

a. Brazil

Average labor income (2017 US$, PPP)

b. Colombia

Average labor income (2017 US$, PPP)

c. Mexico

Average labor income (2017 US$, PPP)

d. Uruguay

Average labor income (2017 US$, PPP)

e. El Salvador

Average labor income (2017 US$, PPP)

f. Peru

Average labor income (2017 US$, PPP)

Per capita household income decile (2017 PPP)

— Mandated and complying — Mandated and noncomplying
— Exempt and participating — Exempt and nonparticipating

Source: Original figures for this publication, using data from SEDLAC 2022.
Note: LAC = Latin America and the Caribbean; PPP = purchasing power parity.

Effects of taxes on individuals' labor supply and firms' hiring decisions

Researchers have investigated how health insurance, cash transfers, social insurance, and other payroll deductions, as well as how additional regulatory mandates on firms, can affect the extent of informality.

Health insurance

The incentives of parallel contributory and noncontributory health plans most consistently significantly impact the level of informal work. For example, in 2002, the Mexican government began an effort to improve access to health care for the 50 million uninsured individuals in the country through the Seguro Popular (Popular Insurance) program. This program offered nearly free health coverage to workers who were not affiliated with or contributing to a social health insurance plan.

The impact of expanding protection without increasing the cost of health care for households has been the focus of many studies. For example, Aterido, Hallward-Driemeier, and Pagés (2011) and Bosch and Campos-Vasquez (2014) found that the introduction of the Seguro Popular program to the uninsured population significantly reallocated labor toward the informal sector. However, Azuara and Marinescu (2013) and Hernandez and Ramirez (2011) found little or no overall effect.

In Colombia, the empirical evidence provides similarly ambiguous results. Camacho, Conover, and Hoyos (2013) found strong evidence of an increase in informal employment of approximately 4 percentage points, due to the expansion of a publicly subsidized health insurance program to those outside the formal sector. Although Calderon-Mejia and Marinescu (2012) found an increase in informal work in Colombia, they also indicated that the regulations that unified the system of payments for health insurance and pensions, which were part of the program, simultaneously increased formality.

That the strongest evidence of an impact on incentives arises from health care interventions is not surprising. Among state risk-sharing mechanisms, health coverage is a protection that people value and take time to learn a lot about (Baeza and Packard 2006). The literature also indicates that many noncontributory risk-pooling designs reduce the cost of being informal— particularly when a traditional contributory plan offering similar, if slightly better, benefits is still operating in parallel. This issue could generate perverse incentives.

Cash transfers

The empirical evidence on the impact of cash transfer programs to alleviate poverty also demonstrates a clear trend. Amarante et al. (2011) found a large disincentive effect on the level of formality (reduced formal employment, primarily among men) from the Uruguayan Plan de Atención Nacional a la Emergencia Social (National Social Emergency Response Plan). Gonzalez-Rozada and Pinto (2011) found that Ecuador's Bono de Desarrollo Humano (Human Development Grant) increased the probability that workers would leave formal employment. De Brauw et al. (2015) found that beneficiaries of Bolsa Familia (Family Allowance) in Brazil significantly shifted their working hours to the informal sector. Garganta and Gasparini (2015) found a statistically significant and economically large disincentive to formalize (namely, the probability of formalization reduced between 28 and 43 percent) for beneficiaries of the Asignacion Universal por Hijo (Universal Child Allowance) in Argentina, which is accessible to workers who have children and are not employed in the formal sector.

For households eligible for Uruguay's program, Bergolo and Cruces (2018) found a reduction of formal employment of around 8 percentage points, equally distributed between informal employment and nonemployment. In Türkiye, Alcan et al. (2016) found that a social assistance program disincentivized formal employment. Gasparini, Cruces, and Tornarolli (2009) analyzed another Argentinean transfer program, Jefes de Hogar (Household Heads), which was implemented after the crisis in 2002. They found that, although the initial impact of the program was to increase informal work, this effect disappeared as the value of the transfer, fixed in nominal terms, lost purchasing power relative to formal sector wages.

Not surprisingly, these results suggest that the value of benefits is likely to be an important factor in determining the scale of any potential impact on formality. Only Azuara and Marinescu (2013) found no effect of Mexico's erstwhile Oportunidades (Opportunities) program on informal employment. These findings on the incentives to work informally give nuances to the general finding in the literature that the receipt of cash transfers does not decrease labor force participation.

Social insurance and other payroll tax deductions

Both social insurance and payroll tax deductions offer natural experiments that researchers have exploited. For example, the 2014 payroll tax reduction in Colombia that aimed to reduce nonwage labor costs led to a significant shift of the workforce from informal to formal employment. Kugler, Kugler, and Herrera Prada (2017) found that this reduction increased the probability of workers having formal employment contracts and contributing to social insurance. The reform lowered the barriers for employers to hire formally, resulting in higher formalization rates and improved compliance with social insurance contribution mandates. In addition, Fernández and Villar (2016) observed that the reform stimulated formal job creation, which particularly benefited low-wage workers, who are typically more likely to work informally.

Consistent with the evidence from Latin American countries, the introduction of a social insurance contribution subsidy program in Türkiye was followed by an increase in registered workers, attributed to the formalization of existing employees (Aşık et al. 2022). The authors noted that the effect's magnitude does not justify the costs associated with subsidizing employment. However, if a worker remains with the same firm for the subsidy's entire duration (4 years), the subsidy costs are offset through the net present value of the worker's contributions and tax payments in less than 1 year.

Additional regulatory mandates on firms

Overly restrictive labor market regulations (including severance payments, statutory minimum wages, and overall employment protection legislation) are a feature of the social protection and labor policy landscape in all middle-income countries, especially those in LAC. These instruments are important and can be beneficial components of social protection policy. However, when set at stringent levels and unevenly enforced, these regulations can add substantially to the incentives for informal employment (Almeida and Carneiro 2012; David, Lambert, and Razafindrakoto 2020).

The labor market and employment protection regulations currently in place were established during a "high-inflation" era in most LAC countries, when labor markets adjusted through changes in real wages and governments pursued full employment policies through import-substituting industrialization (Silva et al. 2021). When the prevailing models of labor market regulation were put in place, it was assumed that the employer and firm were the superior providers of protection, primarily through continuity of stable employment relationships, seniority-based advancement, and "internal" labor markets. Partly due to the inexistence and inadequacy of government-provided risk-sharing arrangements like social protection programs, firms were reasonably expected to be the platform for protection and skills renewal. Statutory mandates on firms were the tools available to governments attempting to prevent in-work poverty and help to smooth consumption in the wake of shocks.

Yet, limited administrative and monitoring capacity resulted in only partial enforcement and created market segmentation. Even where mandates were fully enforced, these institutions had not evolved with other structural adjustments in the 1980s and 1990s and changes in the world of work, creating incentives for avoidance and evasion (Packard et al. 2019).

The Employment Protection Legislation indexes from the Organisation for Economic Co-operation and Development (OECD) and the International Labour Organization show that some Latin American countries mandate higher levels of de jure employment protection, compared to middle-income countries in other regions. In addition, for some countries, statutory protections are far more stringent than the OECD average (Argentina, Colombia, Honduras, Mexico, and the República Bolivariana de Venezuela). This issue keeps the de jure cost of formal employment and the cost of dismissing formal workers relatively higher for firms in LAC countries compared to other regions (Kugler 2019).

For example, Heckman and Pagés (2004) found that severance payments in LAC are among the highest in the world in relative terms and may substantially reduce formal job creation. Saavedra and Torero (2004) and Paes de Barros and Corseuil (2004) examined the likelihood of separations after reductions in the strictness of employment protection legislation in Peru and Brazil, respectively, finding evidence of increased turnover. Furthermore, using the World Bank's Enterprise Survey Database, Perry et al. (2007) identified that severance cost is the labor regulation described by firms in Argentina, Bolivia, Colombia, Panama, Paraguay, Peru, and Uruguay as the greatest obstacle to hiring workers formally. Additional disincentives for firms include the provision of social protection for employees, such as in Chile, where firms with more than 20 female employees are required to provide child care, which has negatively impacted starting wages for women (Prada, Rucci, and Urzúa 2015).

Firm incentives and behavior in the face of tax and regulatory constraints

Not all the incentives and constraints on firms' choices arise from social protection and labor policies and programs. Broader taxation policies and market regulations impact firms' behavior, including whether to invest and achieve a scale that is vital to raising productivity ((Eslava, García-Marín, and Messina 2023). Indeed, Perry et al. (2007) argued that overall productivity gains could be realized if a greater fraction of firms formalized and increased the scale of their operations, because most micro and small enterprises are informal. This finding is consistent with Levy and Cruces (2021) and others (for example, refer to Pagés 2010 and Bosch, Goni, and Maloney 2013; Bosch, Melguizo, and Pagés 2013), who argued that prevailing social protection and labor policies—principally contributions and eligibility requirements for social insurance, as well as statutory employment protection—combined with special tax regimes and market regulations strongly influence small firms' decision-making on whether formality is beneficial or not.

Firms operating at the margins between formal and informal economic activity must maneuver through thickets of taxation rules and market regulations, in addition to social protection and labor policies. Well-intentioned, although poorly designed and administered, special tax regimes directed at small firms make it beneficial to remain small (Levy 2008, 2018). Firm growth can translate into loss of tax benefits and exemptions, in addition to increased visibility and becoming the subject of enforcement (Levy 2008, 2018). Firms' decisions on whether to formalize or informalize their operations are further shaped by the quality of public services and governments' administrative capacity to enforce tax requirements and regulations (Ulyssea 2020).

In almost all of LAC's major economies, policy makers have introduced simplified tax systems in various ways to make formal work more attractive. These systems aim to streamline the business registration process and reduce compliance costs (Engelschalk 2007). Although in general registrations are increasing within these systems (Azuara et al. 2019), their causal effect on formalization remains debated. For example, studies on Brazil's SIMPLES tax system show mixed results. Fajnzylber, Maloney, and Montes-Rojas (2011) and Monteiro and Assunção (2012) reported significant effects on formalization, and Piza (2018) found no substantial impact. In Peru, tax incentives have led to the formalization of many micro and small enterprises (Jaramillo 2013).

The taxation policies and regulation of product and factor (other than labor) markets contain an array of incentives to "stay small." According to Levy and Cruces (2021), in Ecuador, firms with up to 10 workers may qualify for the special tax regime, but not if they hire an 11th worker. Furthermore, in Mexico, firms with sales of up to 1,999,999 pesos pay a tax of 2 percent on sales; however, if sales are greater than 2 million pesos, the tax on profits is 35 percent (Levy and Cruces 2021). In addition, Azuara et al. (2019) found that, in Peru, firms are bunched around the size eligibility thresholds of various tax regimes. They also found that, in Brazil, the introduction of a special tax regime benefiting self-employed workers generated incentives for the employees in many firms to register as sole traders. These examples clearly show the impacts on firms' decision-making, which at times disincentivize formality, expansion, and adherence to regulations.

NOTE

1. A recent joint study by the OECD and OISS (2024) derived the share of households in LAC countries that is completely without social insurance coverage, that is, no household member is complying or participating.

REFERENCES

Alcan, D., R. Can, T. Taskin, and W. Wiseman. 2016. "Impact of Social Assistance on Labor Market Mobility: The Case of Turkey." Policy Research Working Paper 7801, World Bank, Washington, DC. https://openknowledge.worldbank.org /handle/10986/25046.

Almeida, R., and P. Carneiro. 2012. "Enforcement of Labor Regulation and Informality." *American Economic Journal: Applied Economics* 4 (3): 64–89.

Amarante, V., M. Manacord, A. Vigorito, and M. Zerpa. 2011. "Social Assistance and Labor Market Outcomes: Evidence from the Uruguayan PANES." Technical Note IDB-TN-453, Inter-American Development Bank, Washington, DC.

Aşık, G., L. L. Y. Bossavie, J. Kluve, S. E. Nas Ozen, M. Nebiler, and A. M. Oviedo Silva. 2022. "The Effects of Subsidizing Social Security Contributions: Job Creation or Informality Reduction?" Policy Research Working Paper 9904, World Bank, Washington, DC.

Aterido, R., M. Hallward-Driemeier, and C. Pagés. 2011. "Does Expanding Health Insurance beyond Formal-Sector Workers Encourage Informality? Measuring the Impact of Mexico's Seguro Popular." IZA Discussion Paper No. 5996, Institute of Labor Economics, Bonn, Germany.

Azuara, O., R. Azuero, M. Bosch, and J. Torres. 2019. "Special Tax Regimes in Latin America and the Caribbean: Compliance, Social Protection, and Resource Misallocation." IDB Working Paper 9511, Inter-American Development Bank, Washington, DC.

Azuara, O., and I. Marinescu. 2013. "Informality and the Expansion of Social Protection Programs: Evidence from Mexico." *Journal of Health Economics* 32 (5): 938–50.

Baeza, C., and T. Packard. 2006. *Beyond Survival: Protecting Households from Health Shocks in Latin America.* Redwood City, CA: Stanford University Press.

Bergolo, M., and G. Cruces. 2018. "The Anatomy of Behavioral Responses to Social Assistance When Informal Employment Is High." Universidad de la República, Montevideo, Uruguay.

Bosch, M., and R. Campos-Vasquez. 2014. "The Trade-Offs of Welfare Policies in Labor Markets with Informal Jobs: The Case of the 'Seguro Popular' Program in Mexico." *American Economic Journal: Economic Policy* 6 (4): 71–99. doi:10.1257/pol.6.4.71.

Bosch, M., E. Goni, and W. F. Maloney. 2013. "The Determinants of Rising Informality in Brazil: Evidence from Gross Worker Flows." *Journal of Development Economics* 101: 232–43.

Bosch, M., A. Melguizo, and C. Pagés. 2013. *Better Pensions, Better Jobs: Towards Universal Coverage in Latin America and the Caribbean.* Washington, DC: Inter-American Development Bank.

Calderon-Mejia, V., and I. Marinescu. 2012. "Health Insurance and Informality in Colombia." *Labour Economics* 19 (4): 453–67.

Camacho, A., E. Conover, and A. Hoyos. 2013. "Effects of Colombia's Social Protection System on Informality." *Journal of Economic Behavior and Organization* 94: 215–33.

David, A., S. Lambert, and M. Razafindrakoto. 2020. "Employment Protection Legislation and Informal Employment in Developing Countries." *Labour Economics* 66: 101898.

De Brauw, A., D. O. Gilligan, J. Hoddinott, and S. Roy. 2015. "Bolsa Familia and Household Labor Supply in Brazil." *World Development* 70: 69–81.

de Soto, H. 1989. *The Other Path.* New York: Harper and Row Publishers Inc.

Engelschalk, M. 2007. "Designing a Tax System for Micro and Small Enterprises." Working Paper 42435, World Bank, Washington, DC.

Eslava, M., A. García-Marín, and J. Messina. 2023. "Inequality and Market Power in Latin America and the Caribbean." *Oxford Open Economics* 4 (S1): i416–25. https://doi.org/10.1093/ooec/odae037.

Fajnzylber, P., W. F. Maloney, and G. V. Montes-Rojas. 2011. "Does Formality Improve Micro-Firm Performance?" *World Development* 39 (9): 1580–93.

Fernández, C., and L. Villar. 2016. "Labor Formalization Policies and Their Effects on Employment, Wages, and Job Quality: The Case of Colombia's Payroll Tax Cut." *Economia* 17 (1): 95–129.

Garganta, S., and L. Gasparini. 2015. "The Impact of Social Protection Programs on Labor Informality: Evidence from Argentina's Asignacion Universal por Hijo." *Journal of Development Economics* 115: 99–110.

Gasparini, L., G. Cruces, and L. Tornarolli. 2009. "Recent Trends in Income Inequality in Latin America." ECINEQ WP 2009–132, Society for the Study of Inequality, CEDLAS–Universidad Nacional de La Plata, Argentina.

Gonzalez-Rozada, M., and F. Pinto. 2011. *The Effect of Ecuador's Bono de Desarrollo Humano on Employment and Poverty*. Washington, DC: World Bank.

Harris, J. R., and M. P. Todaro. 1970. "Migration, Unemployment and Development: A Two-Sector Analysis." *American Economic Review* 60 (1): 126–42.

Hart, K. 1973. "Informal Income Opportunities and Urban Employment in Ghana." *Journal of Modern African Studies* 11 (1): 61–89.

Heckman, J. J., and C. Pagés. 2004. *Law and Employment: Lessons from Latin America and the Caribbean*. Chicago, IL: University of Chicago Press.

Hernandez, R. D., and R. S. Ramirez. 2011. "Informality and Seguro Popular under Segmented Labor Markets." Preliminary Draft, Center for Research and Teaching in Economics, Mexico City, Mexico. https://hubs.worldbank.org/docs/imagebank /pages/docprofile.aspx?nodeid=437129.

Jaramillo, M. 2013. "Is There Demand for Formality among Informal Firms? Evidence from Microfirms in Downtown Lima." Avances de Investigación, 0013, Grupo de Análisis para el Desarrollo (GRADE), Lima, Peru.

Kugler, A. 2019. "Impacts of Labor Market Institutions and Demographic Factors on Labor Markets in Latin America." Working Paper No. 2019/155, International Monetary Fund, Washington, DC.

Kugler, A., M. Kugler, and L. O. Herrera Prada. 2017. "Do Payroll Tax Breaks Stimulate Formality? Evidence from Colombia's Reform." Working Paper 23308, National Bureau of Economic Research, Cambridge, MA.

Levy, S. 2008. *Good Intentions, Bad Outcomes: Social Policy, Informality, and Economic Growth in Mexico*. Washington, DC: Brookings Institution Press.

Levy, S. 2018. *Under-Rewarded Efforts: The Elusive Quest for Prosperity in Mexico*. Washington, DC: Inter-American Development Bank. http://dx.doi.org /10.18235/0001189.

Levy, S., and G. Cruces. 2021. "Time for a New Course: An Essay on Social Protection and Growth in Latin America." UNDP LAC Working Paper No. 24. Background Paper for the UNDP LAC 2021 Regional Human Development Report. Bureau for Latin America and the Caribbean, United Nations Development Programme, New York.

Monteiro, J. C. M., and J. J. Assunção. 2012. "Coming out of the Shadows? Estimating the Impact of Bureaucracy Simplification and Tax Cut on Formality in Brazilian Microenterprises." *Journal of Development Economics* 99 (1): 105–15.

OECD (Organisation for Economic Co-operation and Development) and OISS (Organizacion Iberoamericana de Seguridad Social). 2024. *Informality and Households' Vulnerabilities in Latin America: Data, Insights and Implications for Labour Formalization Policies*. Paris: OECD and OISS.

Ohnsorge, F., and S. Yu, eds. 2022. *The Long Shadow of Informality: Challenges and Policies*. Washington, DC: World Bank.

Packard, T., U. Gentilini, M. Grosh, P. O'Keefe, R. Palacios, D. Robalino, and I. Santos. 2019. *Protecting All: Risk Sharing for a Diverse and Diversifying World of Work*. Human Development Perspectives. Washington, DC: World Bank. https://openknowledge.worldbank.org/handle/10986/32353.

Paes de Barros, R., and C. H. Corseuil. 2004. "The Impact of Regulations on Brazilian Labor Market Performance." In *Law and Employment: Lessons from Latin America and the Caribbean*, edited by J. J. Heckman and C. Pagés. Cambridge, MA: National Bureau of Economic Research.

Pagés, C., ed. 2010. *The Age of Productivity: Transforming Economies from the Bottom Up.* Washington, DC: Inter-American Development Bank.

Perry, G. E., W. F. Maloney, O. S. Arias, P. Fajnzylber, A. D. Mason, and J. Saavedra-Chanduvi. 2007. *Informality: Exit and Exclusion.* World Bank Latin American and Caribbean Studies. Washington, DC: World Bank. https://openknowledge.worldbank .org/handle/10986/6730.

Piza, C. 2018. "Out of the Shadows? Revisiting the Impact of the Brazilian SIMPLES Program on Firms' Formalization Rates." *Journal of Development Economics* 134: 125–32.

Prada, F. M., G. Rucci, and S. S. Urzúa. 2015. "The Effect of Mandated Child Care on Female Wages in Chile." NBER Working Paper 21080, National Bureau of Economic Research, Cambridge, MA. https://ideas.repec.org/p/nbr/nberwo/21080 .html.

Saavedra, J., and M. Torero. 2004. "Labor Market Reforms and Their Impacts over Formal Labor Demand and Job Market Turnover: The Case of Peru." In *Law and Employment: Lessons from Latin America and the Caribbean*, edited by J. J. Heckman and C. Pagés. Chicago, IL: University of Chicago Press.

Schneider, F., and D. Enste. 2000. "Shadow Economies around the World: Size, Causes and Consequences." IMF Working Paper WP 00/26, International Monetary Fund, Washington, DC.

SEDLAC (Socio-Economic Database for Latin America and the Caribbean). 2018. "Base de Datos Socioeconómicos para América Latina y el Caribe." National University of La Plata, Argentina, and World Bank, Washington, DC. https://www.cedlas.econo .unlp.edu.ar/wp/estadisticas/sedlac/.

SEDLAC (Socio-Economic Database for Latin America and the Caribbean). 2019. "Base de Datos Socioeconómicos para América Latina y el Caribe." National University of La Plata, Argentina, and World Bank, Washington, DC. https://www.cedlas.econo .unlp.edu.ar/wp/estadisticas/sedlac/.

SEDLAC (Socio-Economic Database for Latin America and the Caribbean). 2022. "Base de Datos Socioeconómicos para América Latina y el Caribe." National University of La Plata, Argentina, and World Bank, Washington, DC. https://www.cedlas.econo .unlp.edu.ar/wp/estadisticas/sedlac/.

Silva, J., L. D. Sousa, T. G. Packard, and R. Robertson. 2021. *Employment in Crisis: The Path to Better Jobs in a Post-COVID-19 Latin America.* World Bank Latin America and Caribbean Studies. Washington, DC: World Bank.

Ulyssea, G. 2020. "Informality: Causes and Consequences for Development." *Annual Review of Economics* 12 (1): 525–46.

3 Incentives to (In)Formalize: A Conceptual Framework

CONCEPTUAL FRAMEWORK OF EMPLOYER AND WORKER DECISIONS

This chapter introduces the report's conceptual framework, built on well-established microeconomic foundations of the incentives to (in)formalize employment. First, the chapter constructs a comprehensive framework, as the underlying causes of informal employment vary substantially (Maloney 1999). This framework focuses on the decisions of workers and their employers (refer to figure 3.1). Second, building on the definitions and concepts introduced in chapter 2, the framework allows for distinguishing cases in which individuals are mandated to be covered and do not comply from cases in which insurance is voluntary and individuals choose not to participate.

This chapter focuses tightly on the status of working individuals with respect to government mandates and the parameters of the tax and benefit system. Hence, the chapter aims to avoid utilizing the broad (and generally ambiguous) terms "formal" and "informal," although they are used occasionally for simplicity.[1]

The conceptual framework is centered around employer and worker decisions, while acknowledging that the government plays an important role in setting the legal and regulatory framework, carrying out enforcement, and providing public goods and services. It is widely accepted in the academic literature that formality—or compliance with regulations—is an outcome that results from a negotiation between the employer and worker (Bobba, Flabbi, and Levy 2022; Flabbi and Tejada 2023). This negotiation, which may involve asymmetric power, determines the type of employment the worker is constrained to accept or incentivized to choose (self-employed versus dependent worker), as well as the degree of compliance with or participation in social insurance and the wage level. In other words, the observed outcomes of the negotiation are the type of employment taken up by the worker, the extent of compliance with regulations, and the wage.

A reproducibility package is available for this book in the Reproducible Research Repository at https://reproducibility.worldbank.org/catalog/330/.

FIGURE 3.1

Three factors that influence negotiations for formalization

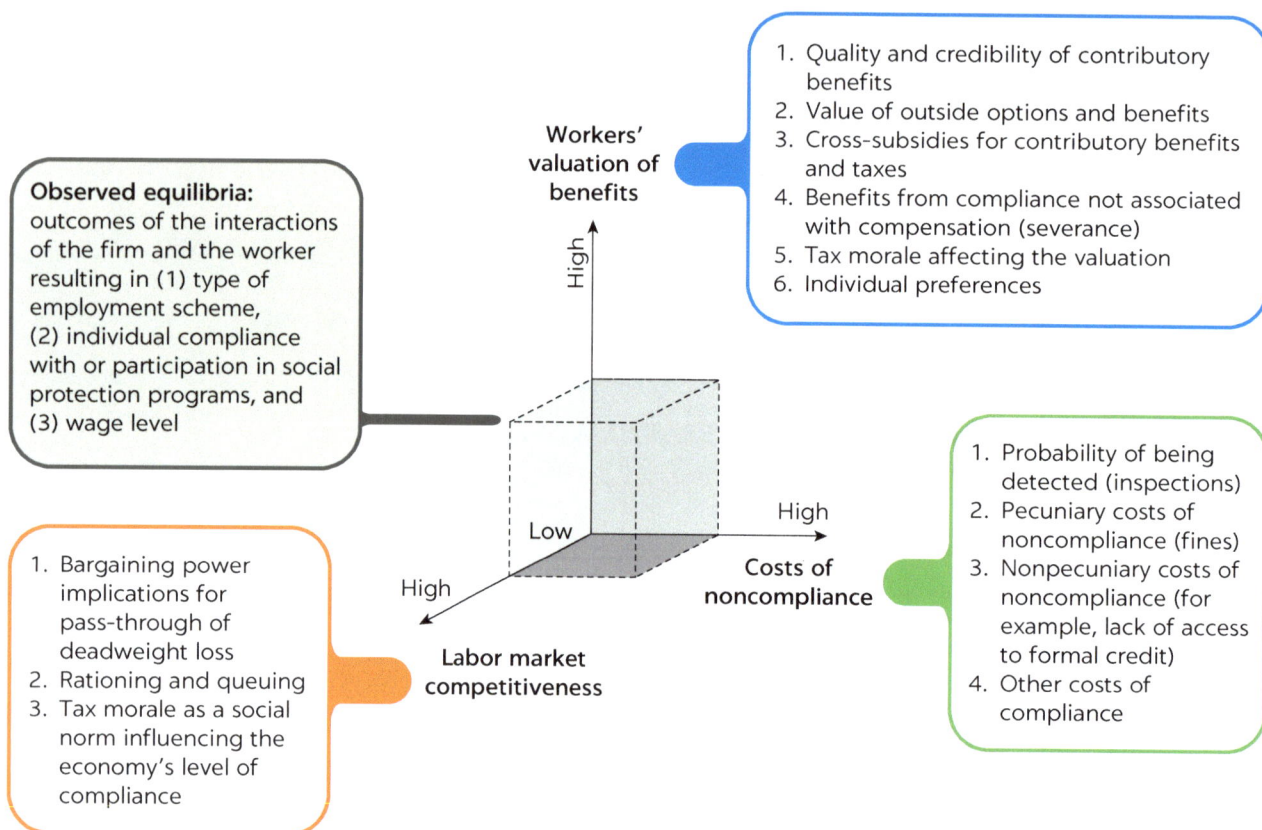

Observed equilibria: outcomes of the interactions of the firm and the worker resulting in (1) type of employment scheme, (2) individual compliance with or participation in social protection programs, and (3) wage level

Workers' valuation of benefits

1. Quality and credibility of contributory benefits
2. Value of outside options and benefits
3. Cross-subsidies for contributory benefits and taxes
4. Benefits from compliance not associated with compensation (severance)
5. Tax morale affecting the valuation
6. Individual preferences

Low

High

High

Labor market competitiveness

High

Costs of noncompliance

1. Bargaining power implications for pass-through of deadweight loss
2. Rationing and queuing
3. Tax morale as a social norm influencing the economy's level of compliance

1. Probability of being detected (inspections)
2. Pecuniary costs of noncompliance (fines)
3. Nonpecuniary costs of noncompliance (for example, lack of access to formal credit)
4. Other costs of compliance

Source: Adapted from Fietz (forthcoming).

The factors that influence the negotiation process and outcomes can be organized into three dimensions:

- Extent of market competitiveness,

- Workers' valuation of the benefits and services, and

- Perceived and actual costs of noncompliance.

Each dimension can be seen as a range because markets can be competitive to a lesser or greater extent; workers may value some benefits and not others to differing degrees; and the costs of compliance may be perceived as high or low, particularly as market participants assess governments' actual enforcement abilities. All the factors in these dimensions have been studied previously and indicated as potential reasons for noncompliance.

The three dimensions are represented along the three axes in figure 3.1. Although some factors may not apply for self-employed workers, others remain relevant and operate similarly to those explained for dependent workers (refer to figure 3A.1 in annex 3A), demonstrating the flexibility of the framework to describe different work contexts. Moreover, examining all these factors jointly allows stressing that the problem of noncompliance or nonparticipation cannot be addressed by just moving one of the parameters. Instead, it must be viewed as a complex, multidimensional challenge, in which policy makers may need to engage in a wide range of reforms to generate changes in the outcome of interest.

The complexity and interdependence of the factors also shows why many policy makers are involved. For example, a country's labor ministry may set the minimum wage, and the social ministry may be in charge of the noncontributory social protection programs.

DIMENSION 1. MARKET COMPETITIVENESS (LACK OF MARKET DISTORTIONS)

The labor market structure is an important determinant of the outcome of the negotiations between firms and workers. Various factors determine whether it is beneficial for workers and employers to comply. Although the parameters introduced in this chapter—minimum wage rationing, extent of labor market segmentation, bargaining power, and social norms influencing tax morale—are discussed one by one, they are all interconnected and should be considered together. These factors matter more for dependent workers who actually negotiate with employers, and they matter indirectly for self-employed workers. First, one outcome of the negotiation is the sorting of people between dependent work and self-employment. Second, the market equilibrium observed for compliant dependent workers also influences other labor markets through lighthouse-type effects.

A binding minimum wage can prevent employers from reducing wages too much so that they comply with the regulations. Standard economic theory predicts that, in competitive labor markets, the introduction of or increase in a minimum wage that lies above the (single) market-clearing wage will lower the demand for labor. Because the supply of labor surpasses the demand for labor, unemployment and labor market segmentation may appear (Stigler 1946). Where noncompliance with the rules is possible, employers may have an incentive to avoid paying the minimum wage (and the associated social security contributions) when it exceeds marginal labor productivity. Situations like this result in labor market segmentation, with low-productivity workers stuck in wage contracts that are noncompliant with labor regulations (Gramlich, Flanagan, and Wachter 1976; Mincer 1976).

Empirical evidence backs up this hypothesis in several contexts. For example, increases in minimum wages have led to decreases in covered employment in Colombia and Honduras (Bell 1997; Gindling and Terrell 2009) but had no effects in Brazil (Lemos 2009).[2]

High minimum wages also impact the types of employment and may lead to larger shares of self-employment. The negotiation between workers and firms also affects the contract type. Although a large overlap exists between self-employment and complying with or participating in social security systems and other labor market regulations, the overlap may result from common underlying factors, because high minimum wages may lead to higher noncompliance with regulations and higher shares of self-employment.

Using a sample of 59 developing countries, Lotti, Messina, and Nunziata (2016) found that a 1 percentage point increase in the minimum wage ratio is associated with a 0.204 percentage point increase in the self-employment rate. At the same time, evidence shows that higher minimum wages in the complying salaried worker segment of the market may result in higher wages in the noncompliant segment (Foguel et al. 2000; Messina and Silva 2017; Neri, Gonzaga, and Camargo 2001).[3] In addition, in several countries, the minimum wage serves as an administrative unit or "base" for calculating the contributions of self-employed workers. If self-employed workers comply or participate, the amount of contributions they pay varies with the minimum wage, leading to higher contributions when the minimum wage is higher.

Other labor market regulations that create barriers to jobs can also generate noncompliance with regulations. For example, the costs of hiring and dismissing workers may be high due to overly restrictive levels of labor market regulations and asymmetric information about workers' productivity, which may lead to noncompliance with regulations and labor market segmentation. In many cases, labor market regulations are relevant for some groups in the workforce, such as migrants, youth, and unemployed individuals (Fields 1975; Harris and Todaro 1970; Perry et al. 2007).

Asymmetric information arises when workers know more about their productivity than their employers know. This issue may increase the perceived cost of hiring, causing employers to hesitate to hire individuals who have not completed their studies or have no other way to signal information about their productivity. This can become a formidable barrier when the costs of hiring and dismissal are high.[4] For example, younger workers are potentially unable to signal their productivity because they lack work experience (Almeida, Orr, and Robalino 2014; Altonji and Pierret 2001; Farber and Gibbons 1996).

With respect to difficulty of dismissal, Peru and Mexico stand out for having the most-restrictive labor market regulations among the countries analyzed for this report. In figure 3.2, four indices measure the restrictiveness of labor market regulations: difficulty of hiring, rigidity of working hours, difficulty of dismissal, and dismissal costs. Each index is plotted against an index of overall labor regulation restrictiveness. Therefore, countries that are plotted in the top right quadrant of each panel in the figure are regional outliers with respect to each dimension of labor regulation.

FIGURE 3.2

Normalized indexes of labor market regulations in select LAC countries, 2019

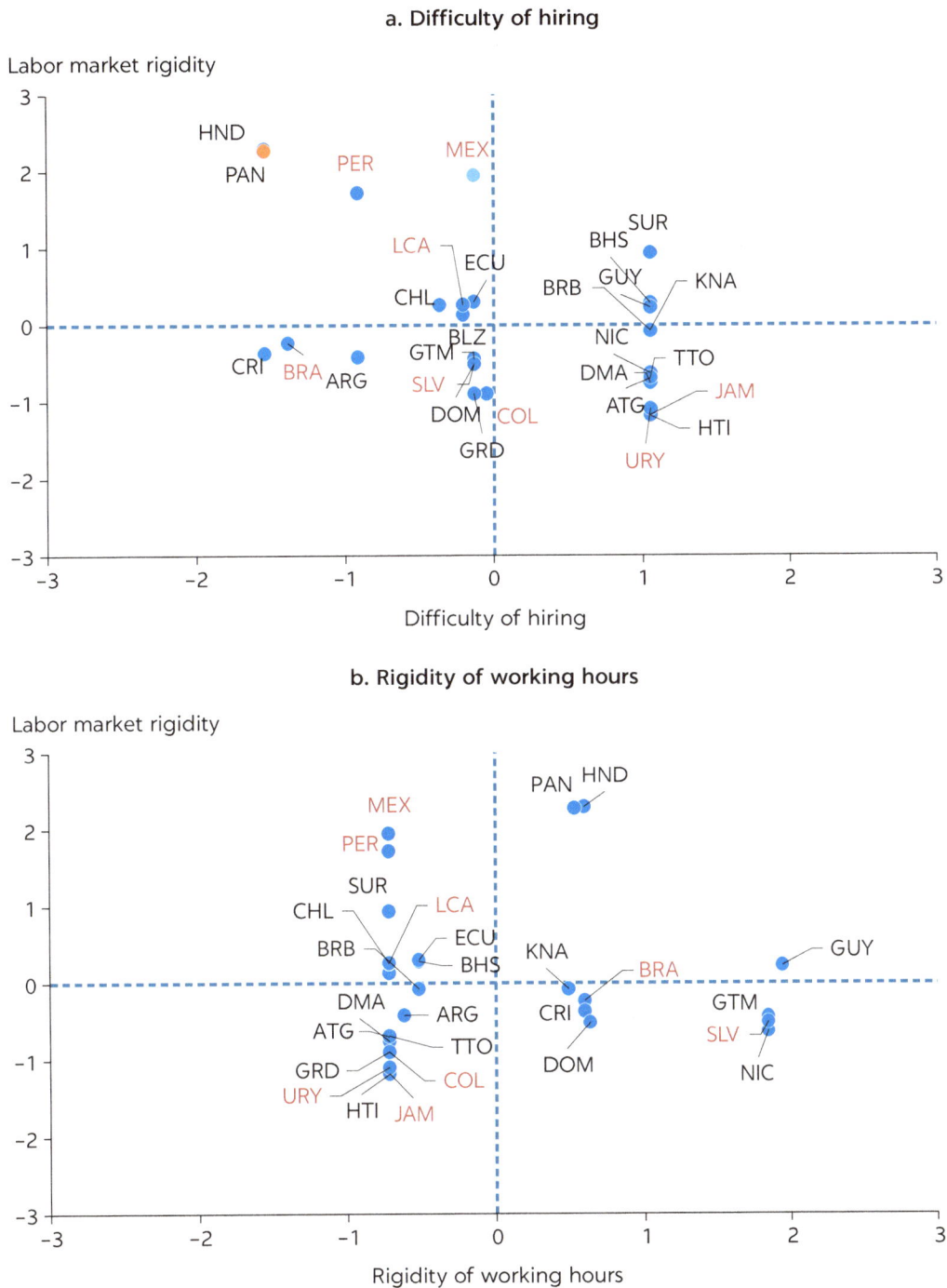

a. Difficulty of hiring

b. Rigidity of working hours

continued

FIGURE 3.2, **Normalized indexes of labor market regulations in select LAC countries, 2019, (continued)**

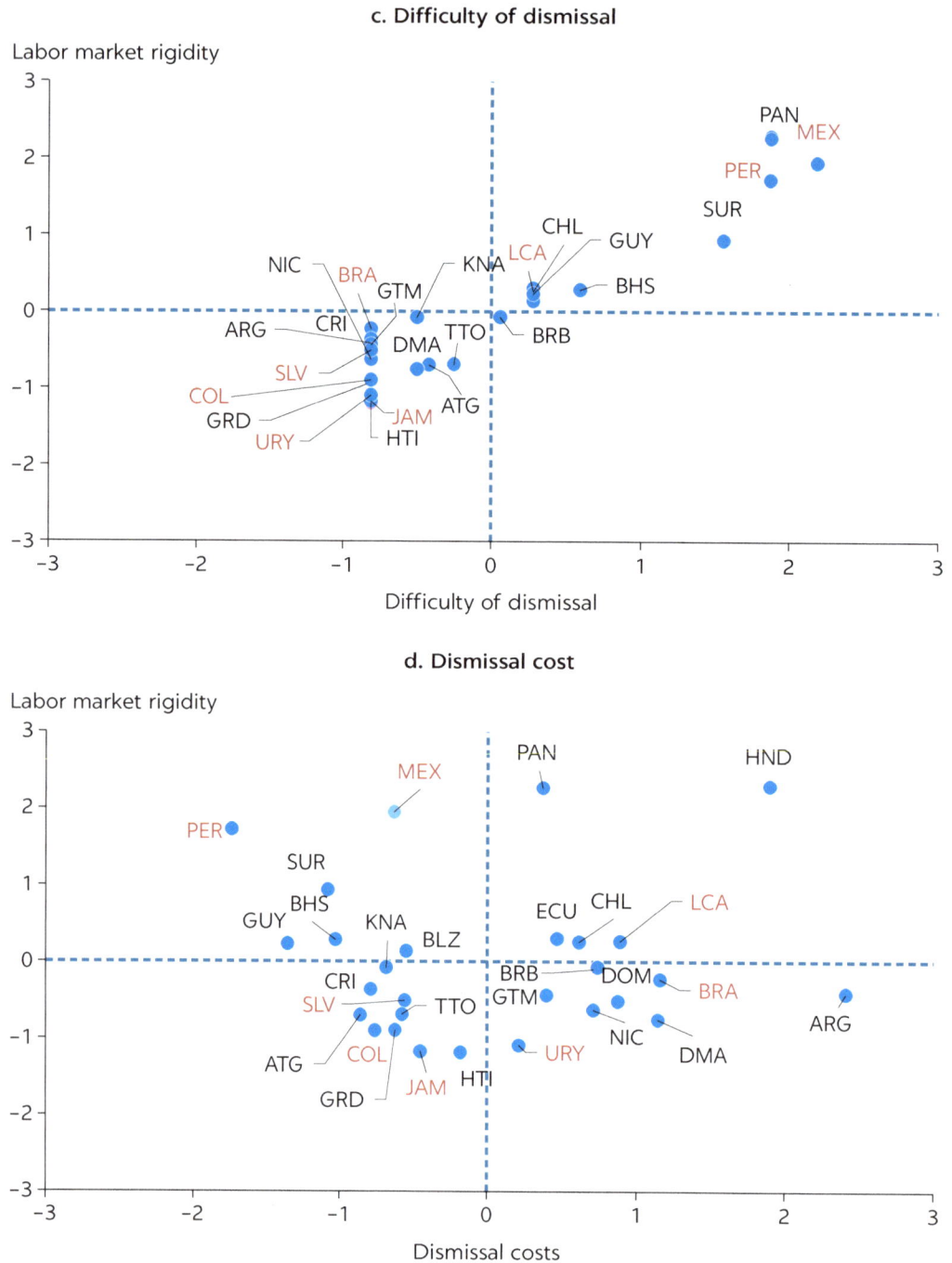

c. Difficulty of dismissal

Labor market rigidity

Difficulty of dismissal

d. Dismissal cost

Labor market rigidity

Dismissal costs

Sources: Silva et al. 2021; indices constructed by Maratou-Kolias et al. 2020 using Employing Workers data from the Doing Business project, World Bank.

Note: Following Packard and Montenegro 2017, five indices of de jure regulations were constructed using PCA: a composite "overall labor market regulation rigidity" index of all the Doing Business project's Employing Workers labor market regulation indicators (plotted on the vertical axis in each panel) and four indices for different subsets of regulation measures. PCA values have been normalized to the LAC regional mean values (indicated by blue horizontal and vertical dashed lines, respectively) to create a scale ranging from −3 (most flexible) to 3 (most rigid). For a list of country codes, refer to https://www.iso.org/obp/ui/#search. LAC = Latin America and the Caribbean; PCA = principal component analysis.

Both Mexico and Peru show high overall labor market rigidity, primarily driven by stringent de jure restrictions on dismissing workers. In contrast, Colombia, Jamaica, and Uruguay have more-flexible labor market regulations. Among these countries, only Jamaica and Uruguay show above-average restrictions in their hiring processes compared to other countries in Latin America and the Caribbean. However, as Kanbur and Ronconi (2018) pointed out, a comprehensive understanding of labor market flexibility requires looking at both de jure regulations and their enforcement through noncompliance costs, which are discussed in the last part of this chapter.

The bargaining power of each party underlies the negotiation between firms and workers, and labor market conditions influence bargaining power. During negotiations, workers and firms agree on the total compensation, which reflects how much the cost of labor departs from the workers' average or marginal productivity—the so-called "pass-through of the deadweight loss"—and how much of the cost is split between direct (wages) and indirect (benefits) compensation. Although standard economic theory assumes competitive labor markets, empirical evidence suggests that firms often possess a degree of monopsony power over employees (Manning 2021). Asymmetric market power on either side, emerging from monopsony or monopoly, influences the negotiation outcomes. Firms with greater monopsony power tend to achieve a higher pass-through of the deadweight loss through lower wages (Cazzuffi et al. 2023), in the form of lower direct or indirect compensation for workers.

Bargaining power is influenced by other factors, including labor market tightness. In a low-unemployment scenario, employees have greater bargaining power as firms are competing for fewer workers who are ready to start working. Conversely, in a high-unemployment case, the power shifts to employers. Moreover, the degree of tightness can be relevant within smaller markets defined by geographic areas or certain skills. In markets with a scarcity of a particular skill set, workers who possess it have a stronger bargaining position, as has been found for high-skilled individuals (Blanchard and Diamond 1994; Cahuc, Postel-Vinay, and Robin 2006).

Social norms influence people's sense of civic duty and fairness and the economywide level of compliance. The economic literature on tax morale examines *social norms*—defined as behaviors that society deems acceptable—and how they represent the degree to which individuals and firms perceive that it is "socially acceptable" to comply or not to comply with the tax and benefit system (Hashimzade, Myles, and Tran-Nam 2013). Whether it is socially acceptable to comply or not depends, in turn, on the initial level of compliance within the firm, industry, and labor market (Koettl-Brodmann, Montenegro, and Packard 2012). If a large share of the workforce within the firm is already complying, the firm will feel a stronger sense of civic duty, and the workers' bargaining position for compliance with a minimum degree of pass-through will be stronger.

The shares of other firms that are compliant and noncompliant will also influence the relative bargaining positions of employers and workers.

Koettl-Brodmann, Montenegro, and Packard (2012) built on previous work by Ades and Di Tella (1997) and Bardhan (1997), highlighting that the initial level of compliance is important for future levels of compliance.

In labor markets with few noncompliant jobs, having a compliant job is more beneficial for workers. However, as the number of noncompliant jobs increases, the benefits of compliance decrease, leading to a negative marginal benefit of compliance if most other workers are noncompliant. According to this framework, the marginal benefit of being noncompliant is always positive. Workers gain the most from noncompliance when a large portion of the workforce is noncompliant. This situation minimizes the risk of detection for noncompliant workers while keeping wages from being driven down due to the large share of noncompliant workers.

At high levels of noncompliance, shifting to a state in which all workers and firms comply is challenging. Conversely, if the initial level of noncompliance is low, society is more likely to move toward an equilibrium where everyone complies (Koettl-Brodmann, Montenegro, and Packard 2012). The next section discusses other social factors, such as trust in government and perceptions of fairness, which are determinants of individuals' valuation.

DIMENSION 2. WORKERS' VALUATION

The extent to which workers value a "formal job" determines whether social security contributions are perceived as a pure tax or a package of concurrent and deferred benefits. If benefits to be received in the future and other nonpecuniary perks of a formal job are of low value to a worker, then disincentives to comply with the legal framework emerge. However, if future benefits and accompanying perks are highly valued, workers and firms will be more likely to comply with social protection and other mandated benefit plans (Summers 1989).

When the perceived quality of future contributory benefits is higher, the value to the worker of making contributions is also higher. Contributory benefits, paid by the employer or the worker, are part of the worker's indirect compensation and typically include retirement pensions, financial protection from the costs of health care, unemployment insurance, and occupational injury insurance. Workers' valuation of these benefits depends on the size and quality of the benefits when compared with the forgone present consumption due to the contributions (Galiani and Weinschelbaum 2012; Gruber 1994; Levy 2008; Summers 1989). If the perceived quality of coverage is low, workers will potentially place a low value on making contributions to secure a certain benefit; that is, the workers will have low incentives to comply or participate.

The value of contributing to secure coverage is mainly determined by the probability of receiving the promised benefit when it is needed. First, this probability depends on the likelihood of meeting all the eligibility requirements. For example, the rules of contributory social insurance plans usually establish a minimum number of required years of contributions to receive a pension (a "vesting" period). If the number of years is high—or the worker perceives that it is high given the opportunities in the market and employment patterns—then that individual's perceived likelihood of eventually benefiting from the plan is low. Thus, the worker would not value the contributions and would consider them to be a pure tax.

Second, the perceived valuation is also heavily influenced by trust in government institutions and their resilience to systemic shocks, both economic and political. If workers and firms expect economic instability and inflation, or if they believe that the "rules of the game" will change by the time the contingency materializes, the incentives to comply with or participate in the system will be reduced.

Moreover, dependent workers may value benefits stemming from being registered that are not part of the compensation package, such as severance pay and protection from dismissal. As with the other benefits, this value will depend on the perceived probability of receiving them and the size of the benefits (for example, the amount of severance pay). If workers value severance pay, which is de jure included in the "package" of a formal work contract, but in practice, workers rarely receive severance pay, even having a de jure mandated severance pay will not increase compliance (Holzmann et al. 2011).

At the same time, workers could value other nonmonetary benefits that are not associated with a payment but rather with the dynamics of formal jobs. For example, workers usually perceive that wage jobs that comply with regulations are more stable. These jobs are usually valued because job turnover may be costly for the worker—even when there are no gaps between jobs. Switching jobs may require learning and adaptation that may be costly to the worker, and it may entail additional uncertainties about the characteristics of the new job.

The value of outside options and benefits, usually noncontributory benefits, potentially influences the valuation of contributory benefits to a large extent. In the example of pensions, it may be assumed that workers perceive that the pension system is a high-quality system and expect to reach the minimum contribution requirements to receive such pensions. In this case, generous noncontributory outside options might cause some workers to assign zero value to participating in even a high-quality contributory pension plan (Galiani and Weinschelbaum 2012; Levy 2008; Levy and Cruces 2021).

For example, noncontributory pensions exist in Brazil, where the monetary values of both systems, contributory and noncontributory, do not differ substantially for low-wage workers. The social pension in Brazil is statutorily set equal to one minimum wage. The contributory pension is 60 percent of the past income bounded to at least one minimum wage, leading to low-wage workers receiving the same pension benefits as people who have not contributed (enough) to the contributory pension system.

The sense of duty and the intrinsic motivation to pay taxes also affect how workers value compliance with regulations and participation in social protection. Tax morale enters the framework, this time along the "valuation" dimension. Defined as the "intrinsic motivation to pay taxes" (OECD 2019), tax morale also extends to payroll contributions. *Tax morale*, defined in greater detail in chapter 7, is taxpayers' willingness to comply with tax and contribution laws and regulations, as well as their sense of the fairness and justice of contributing to public finances through taxation.

Tax morale is a motivation to comply with mandates that is greater than what can be explained by the probability of detection and sanctions. The factors that influence an individual's tax morale include perceptions of government effectiveness and the quality of the services offered, the "fairness" of tax policies—both in fairness toward the government and toward other taxpayers— and the capacity of enforcement mechanisms. Higher tax morale raises the value of social protection coverage and, thus, the likelihood of complying with regulations and participating.

In contrast, workers' valuation may be undermined when overreach and misalignment of government instruments occur. The concept of *overreach* describes the situation when governments intervene when it is not necessary or implement programs that provide more than what households reasonably require. Examples of overreach include pension subsidies for high-income workers, which create budgetary deficits (Perry et al. 2007), or high levels of generosity of government pensions (and by extension, the contribution rate to sustain it), which are set without regard to market-provided old-age savings options. "Misalignment" of instruments occurs when the instruments that are introduced tend to serve more than one purpose or when the wrong risk-sharing instruments are used. Misalignment creates a disconnect between the contribution and the benefit associated with it, which diminishes the valuation of the benefit.

Often, governments use social security for redistribution, breaking the Tinbergen Rule, which states that governments should only use one instrument for one policy objective (Tinbergen 1952). In this case, serving multiple purposes, such as efficient risk management, progressive redistribution, and poverty elimination or economic inclusion, is too much to ask of a single instrument. However, misalignment may also arise when the wrong instrument is used given the size and probability of the potential loss, for example, including high-probability events in a risk-pooling plan or mandating people to save for low-probability events with catastrophic costs (Packard et al. 2019). If governments fail to provide adequate insurance mechanisms, people will place a lower value on the contributions paid toward them. In extreme cases, the overreach and misalignment of instruments may cause substantial budgetary deficits, leading to a decrease in service quality, resulting in even lower valuation by workers of the contributions they are mandated to pay.

Of course, each factor will have different effects on workers' incentives to comply with and participate in the social protection program, depending on their preferences. Standard economic theory predicts that individuals' utility depends on their specific preferences. As Levy (2008) pointed out, differences in preferences occur due to differences in discount rates; risk aversion; and certain life events, such as sickness. Preferences may also be distinct for women and men and for individuals with different household compositions (for example, the presence and number of young children or the presence of an elderly dependent family member). Hence, preferences depend on different sociodemographic and socioeconomic characteristics and may change due to certain events.

The extent to which individuals' preferences are stable or shift over time—and how these impact savings and insurance decisions—is still disputed. Modigliani and Brumberg (1954) claimed in their Life-Cycle Hypothesis that individuals smooth their consumption over time. However, the field of behavioral economics challenges the assumption that people have time-consistent preferences.

Hyperbolic discounting[5] posits that individuals potentially place less value on consumption in the future and more value on present consumption. Hence, they would rather consume today instead of tomorrow. This phenomenon describes the fact that preferences are not constant over time. Hyperbolic discounting is relevant in the context of contributions toward long-term, direct benefits such as retirement pensions. For example, younger workers may prefer to forgo contributing toward retirement benefits in exchange for higher take-home pay in the present (Rabin 1998).

DIMENSION 3. COSTS OF NONCOMPLIANCE

The costs of noncompliance primarily consist of the costs of detection but also potentially include other costs, such as constrained access to finance (Meghir, Narita, and Robin 2015). When firms and workers—even self-employed workers—weigh the costs and benefits of complying with government mandates, the costs of detection play a major role (Levy 2008; Ulyssea 2018). The costs of detection are a function of the probability of detection and the fine incurred if detected. As Levy (2008) pointed out, the costs of detection must be larger than the costs workers and firms save through noncompliance. Ulyssea (2018) discussed that employers in Brazil weigh the costs of noncompliance versus the costs of compliance.

When the perceived probability of being detected is higher, the incentives to comply with regulations are higher. The probability of being detected differs due to factors such as firm size and heterogeneities between workers.

Larger firms are more visible to tax and labor inspection officers and consist of more employees who could potentially file complaints against their employer (Meghir, Narita, and Robin 2015; Ulyssea 2018). This issue also holds for self-employed workers and one-person firms. If they experience revenue growth, they become more visible to the authorities and their competitors and thus also face a rising likelihood of detection as they grow.

In addition, worker heterogeneities may alter the probability of being detected. Ulyssea (2018) pointed out that the probability of inspection potentially varies by workers' skill levels. Workers of different skill levels might have different probabilities of reporting their employer to the authorities. Consequently, the costs of noncompliance can vary based on workforce composition. In addition, under certain circumstances, workers are aware of the viability of their employer. Badaoui and Walsh (2022) found that employees report their employer only if the employer can actually bear the costs of being fined and complying with the labor regulation.

Furthermore, labor inspections and government credibility to execute them are important factors influencing the probability of being detected. The government can actively change the probability of detection by increasing the frequency and efficiency of tax and labor inspections. In addition, technological advancement has the potential to increase the efficiency of inspections (Gallo and Thinyane 2021).

Other factors, such as the employer's risk aversion, influence the perceived probability of detection. In cases in which tax and labor inspections are executed infrequently and thus the likelihood of detection is low, a risk-averse employer or self-employed worker might still conclude that the probability of detection is high. Consequently, for them, the costs of noncompliance are perceived as substantial.

When the pecuniary costs of noncompliance (such as fines) are higher, the incentives to comply with regulations are higher. The government can actively change the costs of noncompliance by increasing the probability of detection and the fines imposed when noncompliant firms and individuals are caught. Empirical evidence has shown that increasing the costs of noncompliance leads to lower levels of noncompliance within compliant firms (Ulyssea 2018, 2020); however, it also increases the number of noncompliant firms, induces dis-employment effects (Almeida and Carneiro 2012), and reduces the stock of formal employment in the longer run (Samaniego de la Parra and Fernández Bujanda 2024).

The nonpecuniary costs of noncompliance (such as lack of access to formal credit) may also influence the incentives to comply with regulations. Noncompliant firms face a greater risk of detection as they grow but continue to evade compliance in their employment practices. In turn, this lowers their access to finance and imposes an additional cost of noncompliance on the firm (Meghir, Narita, and Robin 2015).

OBSERVED EQUILIBRIA

All the factors in the three dimensions—the extent of market competitiveness, workers' valuation of benefits and services, and the perceived and actual costs of noncompliance—influence the outcomes of negotiations between employers and workers (refer to figure 3.3). Government policies shape the "negotiating table" at which employers and workers come to agreements. These negotiations determine the type of employment, the total compensation, and the split between direct and indirect compensation in the remuneration package. These, in turn, affect whether the parties to the negotiation choose to comply partially or fully with the laws and regulations—and, where exemptions exist, whether to participate voluntarily in social protection plans.

When the market is highly competitive—that is, when there is contestability and low levels of market distortions—workers place a high value on benefits, firms perceive the costs of noncompliance as high, and workers and firms will be more likely to comply with regulations or participate voluntarily in social protection. Because in this case employees have greater bargaining power, employer contributions will not be passed through to employees. Therefore, employers will pay the payroll contributions in addition to the wage.

While the interplay of the factors in these three dimensions occurs simultaneously, some authors attribute a certain order to the decision-making process. Workers have a prior-held set of perceptions and beliefs and assign a value to a certain package of contributory benefits. Employers and self-employed individuals expect a certain cost of noncompliance. Subsequently, workers and employers—if an employer is present—bargain over the wage level (Bobba, Flabbi, and Levy 2022) and the extent to which the worker pays for employer contributions through a reduction in take-home pay given the distortions of the market (Bobba et al. 2021).

Limited evidence is available to determine which dimension dominates in the negotiation. Because the evidence behind the multiple factors influencing the incentives to comply with and participate in voluntary schemes is drawn from partial equilibrium analysis, most often there is no clarity on which of the forces will prevail. Moreover, the methodologies used to identify the relative or absolute importance of each factor are different, and hence the ways they impact outcomes and incentives can also differ. Outside the scenario of higher (lower) market competition, workers' valuation, and cost of noncompliance, the effects on incentives will depend on the force of each factor in determining the final level of compliance observed in the labor market and for whom. Chapter 5 introduces the concept of the "formalization tax rate" as a flexible tool—even if it is only an indicator from partial equilibrium analysis—that allows assessing the impact of several factors consistently (even if most of them are in the workers' valuation dimension).

FIGURE 3.3

Likelihood of observing compliance with labor laws and regulations and participation in voluntary insurance schemes

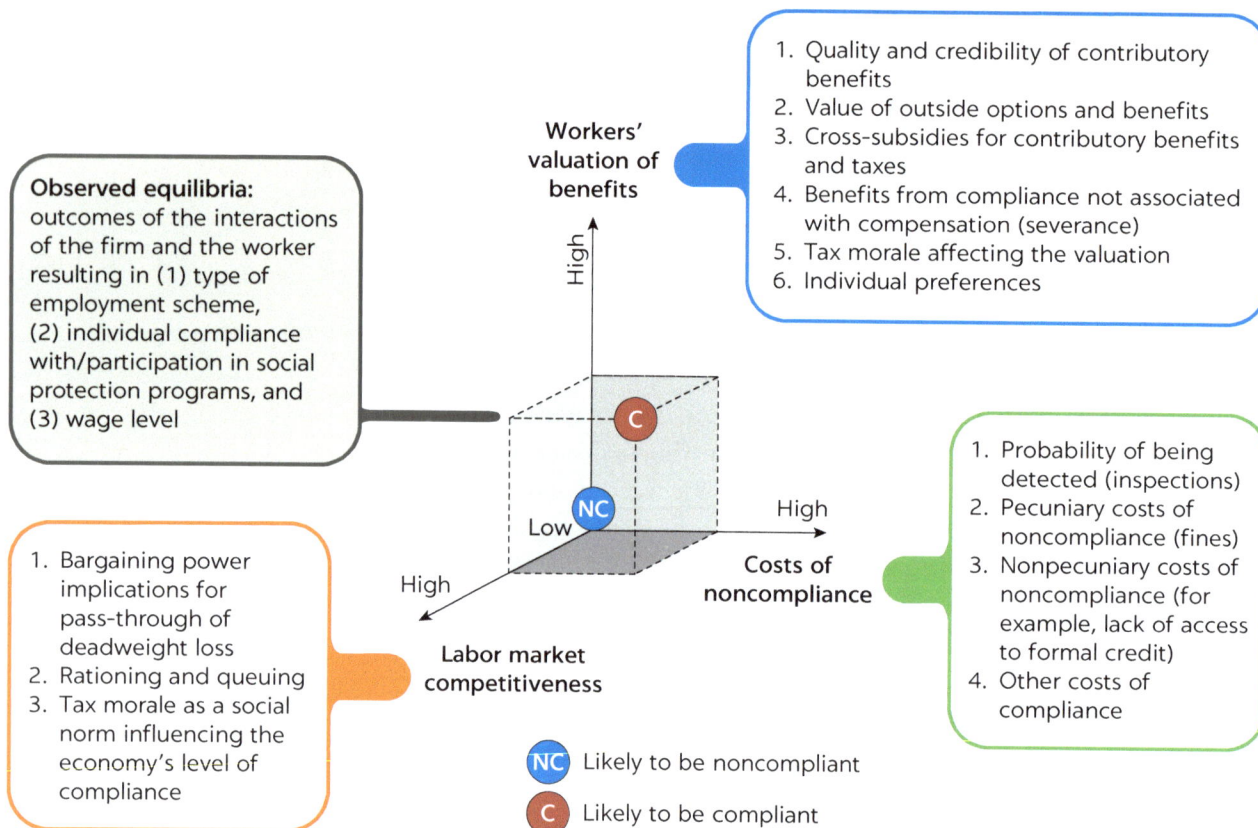

Source: Adapted from Fietz (forthcoming).

The multiplicity and interconnections of factors make charting the position for a few case countries difficult. For example, Brazil has a high level of noncompliance (33.8 percent) and a low level of compliance among the self-employed (1.6 percent). Hence, it is expected that the country has low market competitiveness, costs of noncompliance, and valuation of benefits and services. However, a simple glance at the indicators may not paint such an image.

First, markets may not have been tightening in Brazil in 2022, with unemployment falling sharply after the spike in the wake of COVID-19. Second, the cost of noncompliance might be relatively high compared to other countries, as Brazil has the second highest enforcement index after Jamaica (refer to table 3B.1 in annex 3B). However, valuation may be low for many, because the value of outside options is high and multiple examples of overreach and misalignment exist. The high value of outside options can be seen in the social pension, the Benêficio de Prestação Continuada (Continuous Cash Benefit), which pays a benefit equivalent to the minimum wage. Overreach and misalignment can also be seen in the important cross-subsidization of the pension system (Tsukada and Zviniene 2023).

NOTES

1. The material in this chapter draws on the background paper by Fietz (forthcoming).
2. The empirical evidence varies based on the definition of "covered" and "uncovered." To relate to the framework, the work cited above defines *uncovered workers* as workers in small firms, workers in unregistered firms, or workers without a signed labor card or contract. Other scholars define uncovered workers as those who are self-employed (for example, refer to Ham [2018]).
3. When drawing conclusions on overall impacts on poverty and inequality, all these factors—potential wage increases in the noncompliant sector, effects on noncompliance, and effects on employment types—should be considered together.
4. Exclusion is not necessarily a permanent state. Workers might use noncompliant jobs as an entry point to signal their productivity and potentially transition to compliance after the signaling takes place or their human capital increases sufficiently (Bobba et al. 2021; Maloney 1999).
5. Hyperbolic discounting is also called "present bias."

REFERENCES

Ades, A., and R. Di Tella. 1997. "The New Economics of Corruption: A Survey and Some New Results." *Political Studies* 45 (3): 496–515. https://doi.org/10.1111/1467-9248 .00093.

Almeida, R., and P. Carneiro. 2012. "Enforcement of Labor Regulation and Informality." *American Economic Journal: Applied Economics* 4 (3): 64–89.

Almeida, R., L. Orr, and D. Robalino. 2014. "Wage Subsidies in Developing Countries as a Tool to Build Human Capital: Design and Implementation Issues." *IZA Journal of Labor Policy* 3 (1): 12. https://doi.org/10.1186/2193-9004-3-12.

Altonji, J. G., and C. R. Pierret. 2001. "Employer Learning and Statistical Discrimination." *Quarterly Journal of Economics* 116 (1): 313–50.

Badaoui, E., and F. Walsh. 2022. "Productivity, Non-Compliance and the Minimum Wage." *Journal of Development Economics* 155: 102778. https://doi.org/10.1016/j .jdeveco.2021.102778.

Bardhan, P. 1997. "Corruption and Development: A Review of Issues." *Journal of Economic Literature* 35 (3): 1320–46.

Bell, L. A. 1997. "The Impact of Minimum Wages in Mexico and Colombia." *Journal of Labor Economics* 15 (3): S102–35.

Blanchard, O. J., and P. Diamond. 1994. "Ranking, Unemployment Duration, and Wages." *Review of Economic Studies* 61 (3): 417–34.

Bobba, M., L. Flabbi, and S. Levy. 2022. "Labor Market Search, Informality, and Schooling Investments." *International Economic Review* 63 (1): 211–59. https://doi .org/10.1111/iere.12536.

Bobba, M., L. Flabbi, S. Levy, and M. Tejada. 2021. "Labor Market Search, Informality, and On-the-Job Human Capital Accumulation." *Journal of Econometrics* 223 (2): 433–53. https://doi.org/10.1016/j.jeconom.2019.05.026.

Cahuc, P., F. Postel-Vinay, and J.-M. Robin. 2006. "Wage Bargaining with On-the-Job Search: Theory and Evidence." *Econometrica* 74 (2): 323–64. https://doi.org/10.1111 /j.1468-0262.2006.00665.x.

Cazzuffi, C., M. Pereira-López, I. Rosales, and I. Soloaga. 2023. "Monopsony Power and Labor Income Inequality in Mexico." IDB Working Paper Series No. 1339, Inter-American Development Bank, Washington, DC.

Farber, H. S., and R. Gibbons. 1996. "Learning and Wage Dynamics." *Quarterly Journal of Economics* 111 (4): 1007–47.

Fields, G. 1975. "Rural-Urban Migration, Urban Unemployment and Underemployment, and Job Search Activity in LDCs." *Journal of Development Economics* 2 (2): 165–87.

Fietz, K. Forthcoming. "The multiple roots and causes of informality." PhD thesis, German Insitute for Global and Area Studies, Hamburg, Germany.

Flabbi, L., and M. M. Tejada. 2023. "Are Informal Self-Employment and Informal Employment as Employee Behaviorally Distinct Labor Force States?" *Economics Letters* 231: 111278.

Foguel, M. N., C. H. Corseuil, R. Paes de Barros, and P. G. Leite. 2000. "Uma Avaliação Dos Impactos Do Salário Mínimo Sobre O Nível De Pobreza Metropolitana No Brasil."

Galiani, S., and F. Weinschelbaum. 2012. "Modeling Informality Formally: Households and Firms." *Economic Inquiry* 50 (3): 821–38. https://doi.org/10.1111/j.1465-7295.2011.00413.x.

Gallo, M., and H. Thinyane. 2021. "Supporting Decent Work and the Transition towards Formalization through Technology-Enhanced Labour Inspection." ILO Working Paper No. 41, International Labour Organization, Geneva.

Gindling, T. H., and K. Terrell. 2009. "Minimum Wages, Wages and Employment in Various Sectors in Honduras." *Labour Economics* 16 (3): 291–303. https://doi.org/10.1016/j.labeco.2008.10.001.

Gramlich, E. M., R. J. Flanagan, and M. L. Wachter. 1976. "Impact of Minimum Wages on Other Wages, Employment, and Family Incomes." *Brookings Papers on Economic Activity* 1976 (2): 409. https://doi.org/10.2307/2534380.

Gruber, Jonathan. 1994. "The Incidence of Mandated Maternity Benefits." *American Economic Review* 84 (3): 622–41.

Ham, A. 2018. "The Consequences of Legal Minimum Wages in Honduras." *World Development* 102: 135–57. https://doi.org/10.1016/j.worlddev.2017.09.015.

Harris, J. R., and M. P. Todaro. 1970. "Migration, Unemployment and Development: A Two-Sector Analysis." *American Economic Review* 60 (1): 126–42.

Hashimzade, N., G. D. Myles, and B. Tran-Nam. 2013. "Applications of Behavioural Economics to Tax Evasion." *Journal of Economic Surveys* 27 (5): 941–77. https://doi.org/10.1111/j.1467-6419.2012.00733.x.

Holzmann, R., Y. Pouget, M. Vodopivec, and M. Weber. 2011. "Severance Pay Programs around the World: History, Rationale, Status, and Reforms." Social Protection Discussion Paper SP 1111, World Bank, Washington, DC.

Kanbur, R., and L. Ronconi. 2018. "Enforcement Matters: The Effective Regulation of Labour." *International Labour Review* 157 (3): 331–56.

Koettl-Brodmann, J., C. E. Montenegro, and T. G. Packard. 2012. *In from the Shadow: Integrating Europe's Informal Labor*. Directions in Development: Human Development. Washington, DC: World Bank.

Lemos, S. 2009. "Minimum Wage Effects in a Developing Country." *Labour Economics* 16 (2): 224–37. https://doi.org/10.1016/j.labeco.2008.07.003.

Levy, S. 2008. *Good Intentions, Bad Outcomes: Social Policy, Informality, and Economic Growth in Mexico*. Washington, DC: Brookings Institution. http://choicereviews.org /review/10.5860/CHOICE.46-2199.

Levy, S., and G. Cruces. 2021. "Time for a New Course: An Essay on Social Protection and Growth in Latin America." UNDP LAC Working Paper No. 24, Background Paper for the UNDP LAC 2021 Regional Human Development Report, United Nations Development Programme, New York.

Lotti, G., J. Messina, and L. Nunziata. 2016. "Minimum Wages and Informal Employment in Developing Countries." Jobs and Development Conference Working Paper, World Bank, Washington DC.

Maloney, W. F. 1999. "Does Informality Imply Segmentation in Urban Labor Markets? Evidence from Sectoral Transitions in Mexico." *World Bank Economic Review* 13 (2): 275–302.

Manning, A. 2021. "Monopsony in Labor Markets: A Review." *ILR Review* 74 (1): 3–26. https://doi.org/10.1177/0019793920922499.

Maratou-Kolias, L., K. M. Fietz, M. Weber, and T. Packard. 2020. "Quantifying and Validating the Cliffs of the Labor Market Regulation 'Plateau': A Global Review of Labor Market Institutions." Jobs Group, Social Protection and Jobs Global Practice, World Bank, Washington, DC.

Meghir, C., R. Narita, and J.-M. Robin. 2015. "Wages and Informality in Developing Countries." *American Economic Review* 105 (4): 1509–46. https://doi.org/10.1257 /aer.20121110.

Messina, J., and J. Silva. 2017. *Wage Inequality in Latin America: Understanding the Past to Prepare for the Future*. Latin American Development Forum. Washington, DC: World Bank.

Mincer, J. 1976. "Unemployment Effects of Minimum Wages." *Journal of Political Economy* 84 (4): S87–104.

Modigliani F., and R. Brumberg. 1954. "Utility Analysis and the Consumption Function: An Interpretation of Cross-Section Data." In *Post-Keynesian Economics*, edited by K. K. Kurihara, 419–21. New Brunswick, NJ: Rutgers University Press.

Neri, M., G. Gonzaga, and J. M. Camargo. 2001. "Salário Mínimo, 'Efeito-Farol' e Pobreza." *Brazilian Journal of Political Economy* 21 (2): 263–76. https://doi.org /10.1590/0101-31572001-1264.

OECD (Organisation for Economic Co-operation and Development). 2019. "Tax Morale: What Drives People and Businesses to Pay Tax?" Paris: OECD. https://doi.org/10.1787 /f3d8ea10-en.

Packard, T., U. Gentilini, M. Grosh, P. O'Keefe, R. Palacios, D. Robalino, and I. Santos. 2019. *Protecting All: Risk Sharing for a Diverse and Diversifying World of Work*. Human Development Perspectives. Washington, DC: World Bank. https://openknowledge .worldbank.org/handle/10986/32353.

Packard, T. G., and C. Montenegro. 2017. "Labor Policy and Digital Technology Use: Indicative Evidence from Cross-Country Correlations." Policy Research Working Paper No. 8221. World Bank, Washington, DC.

Perry, G. E., O. Arias, P. Fajnzylber, W. F. Maloney, A. Mason, and J. Saavedra-Chanduvi. 2007. *Informality: Exit and Exclusion*. Washington, DC: World Bank. https://doi .org/10.1596/978-0-8213-7092-6.

Rabin, M. 1998. "Psychology and Economics." *Journal of Economic Literature* 36: 11–46.

Samaniego de la Parra, B., and L. Fernández Bujanda. 2024. "Increasing the Cost of Informal Employment: Evidence from Mexico." *American Economic Journal: Applied Economics* 16 (1): 377–411. https://doi.org/10.1257/app.20200763.

Silva, J., L. D. Sousa, T. G. Packard, and R. Robertson. 2021. *Employment in Crisis: The Path to Better Jobs in a Post-COVID-19 Latin America.* World Bank Latin America and Caribbean Studies. Washington, DC: World Bank.

Stigler, G. J. 1946. "The Economics of Minimum Wage Legislation." *American Economic Review* 36 (3): 358–65.

Summers, L. H. 1989. "Some Simple Economics of Mandated Benefits." *American Economic Review* 79 (2): 177–83.

Tinbergen, J. 1952. *On the Theory of Economic Policy (Contributions to Economic Analysis).* Amsterdam: North-Holland Publishing Company.

Tsukada, R., and A. Zviniene. 2023. "The Brazilian Pension System under an Equity Lens." Technical Note, World Bank, Washington, DC. http://documents.worldbank.org/curated/en/099050324164012038.

Ulyssea, G. 2018. "Firms, Informality, and Development: Theory and Evidence from Brazil." *American Economic Review* 108 (8): 2015–47. https://doi.org/10.1257/aer.20141745.

Ulyssea, G. 2020. "Informality: Causes and Consequences for Development." *Annual Review of Economics* 12 (1): 525–46.

4 Benefits and Costs of Compliance and Participation

THE DE JURE PERSPECTIVE OF WORKERS AND EMPLOYERS

LEGAL AND REGULATORY LANDSCAPE FOR WORKERS

This chapter describes the legal and regulatory "landscape" that working people navigate, shaped by regulations, personal income taxation, and social protection policies. The chapter models the benefits and costs of compliance—or participation among those who are afforded the choice—using the de jure "tax wedge" to compare across profiles of working people and countries. Modeling the de jure parameters of countries' tax and benefit systems enables identifying potential incentive "pressure points," which are intended or unintended cost and benefit "prompts" that encourage or discourage compliance and participation. The de jure modeling presented in this chapter forms an essential foundation for the empirical analysis that follows in chapters 5 and 6 of the report.

The de jure model is used for both country-specific and cross-country comparisons. The first part of the chapter presents an in-depth description of the de jure tax wedge modeling methodology and an initial characterization of the incentives faced by workers in seven country cases—Brazil, Colombia, El Salvador, Jamaica, Mexico, Peru, and Uruguay. It also provides a concise but comprehensive overview of the tax, benefit, and contribution landscape for each country, highlighting potential obstacles, incentives, and disincentives to compliance and participation. This analysis is complemented by a uniform selection of tables and figures from the de jure modeling of the country cases (refer to annexes 4B and 4C). The second part of the chapter leverages the uniform indicators created from the de jure modeling to compare the tax and social protection incentive landscapes across the case studies.

The following are the five main observations from the cross-country de jure comparison:

- Notable differences exist in the intensity with which countries use payroll taxes. Compensation structures, particularly the share of the tax wedge

A reproducibility package is available for this book in the Reproducible Research Repository at https://reproducibility.worldbank.org/catalog/330/.

earmarked for indirect, long-term benefits, contribute significantly to differences in compliance and participation costs. In several countries, generally available benefits (not directly linked to individual contributors or their families) are funded through payroll taxes, with significant cross-country differences in the benefits provided.

• Government-financed, in-work benefits reduce the tax wedge, and their amounts often depend on family composition. Positive incentives to register employment can be created by these in-work benefits, particularly when financed by transfers from general revenues. Countries use this instrument to varying degrees.

• Variations in the tax wedge can also emerge at higher income levels and for different family structures. Many governments offer people earning lower incomes relatively generous exemptions from personal income tax. Where and how intensively personal income tax, social insurance contributions, and other payroll taxes appear in the income distribution create incentives that vary with income level.

• The "discontinuities" in how the tax wedge varies with earned income are few and minor. These discontinuities are created by abrupt changes in tax rates, contributions, or benefits as people move up the earned-income distribution. They can create additional disincentives to program compliance, especially for specific groups of workers. Key factors that contribute to these discontinuities include eligibility rules, benefit withdrawal mechanisms, and the gradient of the tax wedge curve.

• The tax and benefit incentive "landscape" appears differently depending on assumptions about workers' perceived value. A large tax wedge does not always discourage registration if workers view their contributions as valuable investments in future benefits. Workers' perceptions of value—one dimension of the conceptual framework in chapter 3—emerge as a vital determinant of incentives.

DE JURE TAX WEDGE METHODOLOGY

The de jure tax wedge captures several elements of personal income tax and social protection policies that influence incentives. The de jure modeling begins with a deep dive into the legislation and regulation of wages and contracting, personal income taxation, social insurance plans, in-work benefits, and cash transfer programs. This legislation shares similar policy objectives—such as poverty alleviation, protection of people vulnerable to impoverishment, inclusion of historically excluded groups, and employment promotion and protection—in the seven country cases. However, the objectives vary in relative importance and the design of the specific programs through which they are pursued. As a result, the tax and benefit "systems" differ significantly in complexity and scope, leading to interesting variation in how they shape the incentives and, eventually, the choices of workers and firms.

The best-designed tax and social protection systems not only provide essential protection but also create incentives to comply with mandates (and, among exempted workers, to participate in insurance programs). Mapping the taxes, contributions, and benefits of each country into uniform categories allows identification of where the strengths and weaknesses of their design lie. (Chapter 3 discusses how various components of the tax and benefit system influence the levels of compliance and participation.)

The applied de jure methodology follows the Organisation for Economic Co-operation and Development's (OECD's) *Taxing Wages* series (1999–present).[1] The de jure methodology can measure the differences between the total labor cost perceived by employers and the take-home incomes of workers and can explain from what policies and programs those differences arise. The differences represent "distortions" from the textbook assumption of a competitive labor market and the "burden" that the policies introduce on employers and workers. The distortions are usually expressed as percentages of total labor cost.

This report builds on the OECD methodology and makes some adaptations to the context of Latin America and the Caribbean (LAC).[2] As outlined in chapter 3, compliance and participation depend on the payroll contributions. Therefore, this chapter classifies elements that affect disposable income differently into taxes, benefits, and compensation.

In addition, the chapter shows the tax wedges for self-employed workers and microentrepreneurs. By including workers beyond dependent workers, the approach offers an inclusive understanding of labor market dynamics across diverse types of employment. This issue is especially relevant for LAC countries, where, in many cases, more than half of the workforce is independent workers (refer to chapter 2).[3]

The "total tax wedge" measures the share of labor costs that stem from mandates in addition to wage regulations and gives an indication of the costs of complying when contracting an employment relationship. The tax wedge is essentially the difference between what employers spend on labor costs and what employees receive as take-home pay. This difference represents the nonwage costs created by personal income taxes, additional levies on payroll, and statutory social insurance contributions paid by both employees and employers, net of in-work cash benefits. The sum of these costs is presented as a percentage of total labor cost in equation 4.1:

$$\text{Total tax wedge} = \frac{\text{Total payroll taxes} + \text{Total contributions} - \text{In-work benefits}}{\text{Total labor cost}} \quad (4.1)$$

where *total contributions* comprise statutory payments made by workers—and by employers in the name of the people they employ—to secure individual (or household) eligibility for health insurance, retirement pensions, unemployment insurance, and coverage for occupational hazards. *Total payroll taxes* include the personal income tax and levies on payroll that are not individually earmarked to finance benefits and services for the worker. Examples include payments toward an agricultural fund, such as Brazil's Instituto Nacional de Colonização e Reforma Agrária (National Institute for Colonization and Agrarian Reform) and Colombia's Instituto Colombiano de Bienestar Familiar (Colombian Institute of Family Welfare), a provider of early childhood development and other family services. *Total labor cost* is the sum of the previously mentioned nonwage costs and wage costs, including an extra annual payment or holiday bonus, if applicable. *In-work benefits* are cash transfers received while working, such as wage "top-ups" and child allowances paid by the government.

The underlying assumption of the modeling is that, because a larger total tax wedge reduces workers' take-home pay and increases employers' labor costs, it creates disincentives to comply with mandates (or to participate among those for whom take-up is voluntary). The measure can also be applied to independent workers. It is common practice that self-employed workers or microentrepreneurs bear part of the contributions paid by employers in a dependent work relationship. Thus, the total tax wedge for self-employed workers or microentrepreneurs represents the share of total labor costs that are nonwage costs and paid by independent workers (refer to figure 4.1 for the tax wedge of select LAC countries).

FIGURE 4.1

Total augmented tax wedge in select LAC countries, 2013–23

Total augmented tax wedge (%)

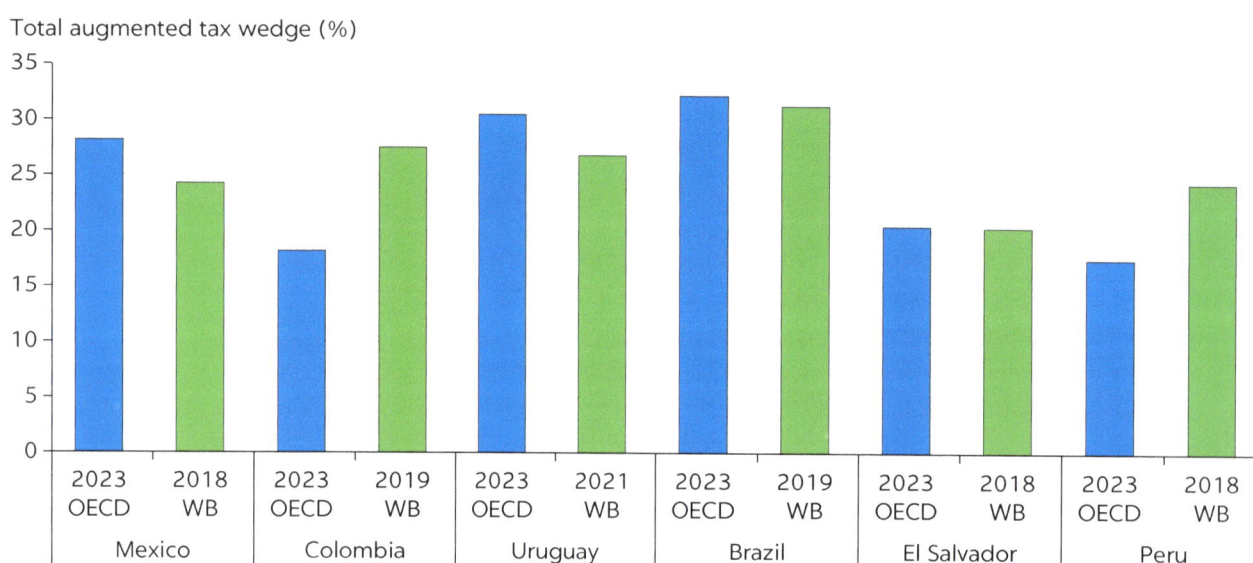

Source: Original figure for this publication.
Note: The figure compares the tax wedge (share of labor costs that are nonwage costs) calculated in this report (WB) and the tax wedge calculated by the OECD (latest year available) for a single-earner household. The main difference arises due to nontax compulsory payments, which are not included in the OECD statistics for Brazil, El Salvador, Peru, and Uruguay but are included in the WB calculations. In addition, differences exist in the definition of wages. The WB calculations always consider annual leave, holidays, and year-end bonuses. For Colombia, the difference arises due to the transport subsidy and consideration of the conditional cash transfer in the WB calculations. The difference in years also explains the difference in the tax wedges. LAC = Latin America and the Caribbean; OECD = Organisation for Economic Co-operation and Development; WB = World Bank.

A detailed accounting of benefits, mandates, and eligibility conditions has been compiled for the seven country case studies. The key policy and program parameters are summarized in table 4.1.[4] These parameters determine total labor cost and take-home income, including all government-paid benefits that vary with employment status and the wage level to capture take-home income. Because these benefits may vary with household composition, they are included in the accounting. The number of dependents, particularly the number of children, can influence the deductions that taxpayers can claim or the benefits they receive.

The modeling also distinguishes between dependent (wage or salaried workers) and independent (self-employed workers) employment status as taxes and social security contributions often vary across these categories. The tax wedge can vary greatly across the ways in which people can be legally employed or self-employed.

The de jure methodology disaggregates labor costs into taxes, compensation, and benefits, providing a detailed framework to analyze how statutory tax and contribution rates, eligibility criteria, and the perceived value of benefits influence workers' and employers' decisions to comply or participate. The components of total labor costs are classified into three main categories: taxes, compensation, and government-financed benefits.

- Taxes, which are paid by the worker or the employer, do not provide direct entitlements to the worker or firm, but they may have indirect benefits, such as funding public goods or improving business conditions.

- Compensation encompasses payments that grant workers direct entitlements to current, future, or contingent benefits, including immediate ("short-term") benefits such as health insurance coverage, "long-term" benefits such as retirement pensions, and "contingent benefits" triggered by specific events, such as unemployment or accidents.

- Government-financed benefits include in-work benefits such as wage subsidies, which are often conditional on workers' characteristics or compliance (for example, Brazil's Abono Salarial [bonus salary] or Peru's family subsidy). Benefits also include social assistance programs that are accessible to both dependent and self-employed workers.

The disaggregation of these labor costs is crucial for analyzing workers' valuation of compliance. By mapping these components systematically, the de jure methodology enables deeper insights into how statutory tax and contribution rates, eligibility requirements, benefit valuation, and wage components influence decisions to comply or participate.

TABLE 4.1 Categories and components of total labor costs

TOTAL LABOR COSTS (L1 + L2 + L3)

NONWAGE COSTS		WAGE COSTS AND TOTAL EARNINGS	BENEFITS (PAID THROUGH THE GOVERNMENT)
Net income related to paid employment (L1 + I3 – SC – PIT)			
Firm (employers' social security expenditure [L2] and other costs [L3])	Worker (employee's compulsory social security contributions and personal income tax)	Gross earnings (L1)	
Other costs: taxes (regarded as labor costs) (L3)	Taxes (regarded as labor costs)	A. Direct wages and salaries	In-work benefits (paid through the government) and employment-related social security benefits (paid through the government) (I3)
Payroll taxes: payment not associated with an individual entitlement • Taxes	Payroll taxes (PIT): payment not associated with an individual entitlement • Taxes	• For example, straight time pay of time-related workers	• Direct, immediate benefits → part of net labor income
Social security expenditure (L2)	Social security contributions (SC)	B. Renumeration for time not working	Social assistance benefits (paid through the government)
Health contributions • Indirect short-term compensation	Health contributions • Indirect short-term compensation	• Annual vacation, other paid leave	• Direct, immediate benefits
Pension contributions • Indirect long-term compensation	Pension contributions • Indirect long-term compensation	C. Bonuses and gratuities • For example, year-end and seasonal bonuses	
Mandatory savings account • Indirect contingent compensation	Mandatory savings account • Indirect contingent compensation	D. Remuneration in kind	
Accident insurance contributions • Indirect contingent compensation	Accident insurance contributions • Indirect contingent compensation	• For example, food, drink, fuel, and other in-kind payments	
Unemployment insurance • Indirect contingent compensation	Unemployment insurance • Indirect contingent compensation	E. Cost of workers' housing borne by employers	
Severance payment		• For example, cost of establishment-owned dwellings	

Source: Original table for this report.

Note: Annex 4A provides further details on the definitions in the table. I3 = in-work benefits and employment-related social security benefits (paid through the government); L1 = gross earnings; L2 = employers' social security expenditure; L3 = other costs (for example, taxes regarded as labor costs); PIT = personal income tax; SC = employee's compulsory social security contributions.

The tax wedge analysis identifies possible de jure pressure points across income levels that could create disincentives to comply or participate. The analysis also reveals how tax wedges evolve with different income levels and across family structures, identifying any discontinuities, such as where sudden changes in tax rates, contributions, or benefit eligibility occur. These incentive "pressure points," such as income thresholds for in-work benefits or eligibility rules for noncontributory or subsidized social insurance, can increase the effective tax burden for certain groups, discouraging compliance among lower income workers or those with fluctuating earnings. Countries that gradually phase in and out the eligibility conditions as well as benefit amounts as earned income changes, rather than abruptly ending them, most likely will not have substantial discontinuities. These countries provide a better landscape of incentives for working people to navigate. The rate of change (or slope) of the tax wedge curve is another indicator of interest in the incentives analysis.

The de jure methodology complements the formalization tax rate analysis in chapter 5 by mapping legal mandates, enabling a comprehensive assessment of compliance incentives, and identifying possible reforms. The de jure methodology serves as a foundational step for policy analysis by offering a clear picture of how tax and benefit policies interact to affect compliance incentives. It shows which elements of the regulatory framework may encourage or hinder participation or compliance. By mapping these costs and incentives consistently across countries, the de jure approach complements the formalization tax rate analysis, which focuses on actual economic impacts by capturing the perceived and realized costs of formalization for workers and employers. While the analysis of the formalization tax rate quantifies these incentives for each respondent in a survey microdata set, the de jure model offers a systematic view of the legal mandates that underpin the responses. Together, these approaches allow a thorough examination of the structural and practical factors influencing labor market compliance and can inform targeted reforms to increase formalization.

KEY OBSERVATIONS FROM THE DE JURE MODELING FOR EACH COUNTRY CASE STUDY

The complete de jure mapping for each country case study is presented in annexes 4A, 4B, and 4C. Annex 4B provides the mapping for all the countries, using the same layout as table 4.1. Annex 4C includes a selection of figures that allow analysis of the tax wedge and total labor costs. Although the figures provide fuller details, the key features of the tax and benefit landscape and their implications for incentives are summarized in the following subsections for each country.

Brazil

In Brazil, the de jure tax and benefit modeling for workers in dependent employment shows an incentive compatible design. Employees face steadily rising pension contribution and personal income tax rates as their income increases. At lower income levels and as earned income rises, there is a gradual withdrawal of the conditional cash transfer Bolsa Familia, which avoids any abrupt increases in the tax wedge. Most contributions that are statutorily assigned to employers and employees are linked to direct (short- or long-term), wholly owned benefits for the workers making the contributions. For this reason, the benefits from these contributions are more likely to be perceived as a part of the employees' compensation package. However, some noteworthy exceptions include contributions toward an agricultural fund, Instituto Nacional de Colonização e Reforma Agrária (National Institute for Colonization and Agrarian Reform), which administers land reform issues that do not directly benefit workers, and an education fund, the Salário Educação.

Nevertheless, a dependent employment relationship is costly relative to other ways of legally contracting people in Brazil. Dependent workers have a tax wedge of 27.5 percent at the statutory minimum wage (MW) and 31 percent at the median wage. Independent workers—especially those in the Individual Microentrepreneur System (MEI)—face a substantially lower tax wedge of 2.4 and 2.7 percent at the MW and median wage, respectively. This leads to the phenomenon of pejotização (reliance on contract workers) as described in box 4.1. Therefore, in Brazil, the incentive compatibility of the design depends heavily on valuation.

Box 4.1

Differing costs of Brazil's multiple options for legal employment

Brazil's self-employment landscape is marked by a variety of employment regimes, making it complex to navigate. These regimes include options such as the "independent worker" (trabalhador autônomo), the Individual Microentrepreneur System (MEI), and the Simplified Tax Regime (SIMPLES) for small businesses (refer to figure B4.1.1). Each system imposes different levels of tax and social security obligations, tailored to the size and nature of the business. For instance, independent workers can choose from various pension contribution plans, while microentrepreneurs benefit from a simplified tax structure with minimal contributions. The SIMPLES regime, in contrast, allows entrepreneurs with higher revenues to consolidate multiple taxes into a single payment, simplifying compliance.

All these self-employment options have a lower tax wedge than the traditional dependent employee contracting modality under the Consolidation of Labor Laws (CLT). However, they also offer a lower degree of protection, particularly pension rights and unemployment benefits. Although these regimes are designed to increase compliance and participation and reduce the tax burden on self-employed individuals, they also create

continued

Box 4.1, Differing costs of Brazil's multiple options for legal employment *(continued)*

opportunities for firms to exploit the system through employment arbitrage. The diversity of employment contracts can lead to unintended consequences, such as firms opting to hire fewer dependent workers and increasingly relying on external contractors operating under the MEI.

With this practice, which is known as pejotização in Brazil, firms favor engaging with microentrepreneurs because doing so is significantly cheaper than hiring employees under standard traditional dependent employee contracts.

FIGURE B4.1.1

Tax wedge at 1 minimum wage in Brazil, by type of employment

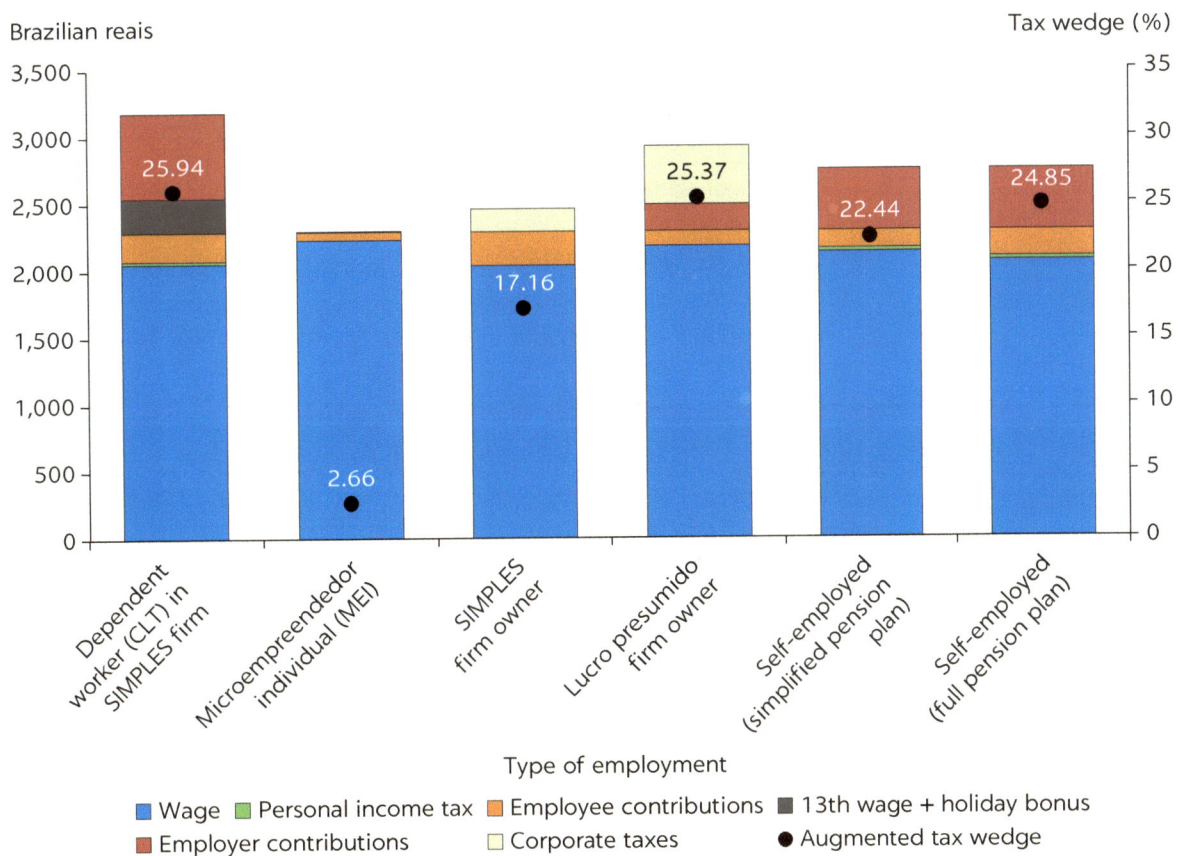

Source: Original figure for this publication.
Note: The figure shows the tax wedge for a single-earner household at the income level of the average worker.
CLT = Consolidation of Labor Laws; PJ = Pessoa Jurídica; MEI = Microentrepreneur System; SIMPLES = Simplified Tax Regime.

If workers value contributions paid as future benefits, the system is highly incentive compatible. Although this is the case for most of the countries in the region, the in-work benefits directed to low-income workers lead to a negative tax wedge under the full valuation assumption.[5] However, if workers do not value their contributions, the system—especially for dependent workers—is expensive and thus provides a disincentive to comply.

Colombia

In Colombia, the social security system is structured around two main regimes, one for dependent workers and one for independent workers. Both are designed primarily for individuals earning above the MW, although in 2019, approximately 46 percent of Colombian workers earned a gross income below this threshold. This discrepancy poses significant challenges, as workers earning below the MW are considered illegal if they are dependent employees, while independent workers earning less than the statutory minimum are not required to contribute to social security.

This lack of coverage under labor legislation has profound implications for social protection, which are partially addressed by a subsidized health system that coexists with contributory social health insurance. These two health coverage plans provide nearly identical benefits, disincentivizing participation in the contributory plan. Long vesting periods for pensions represent a major issue, as fluctuations between formal and informal employment prevent many workers from qualifying for a pension. This issue reinforces the perception of pension contributions as a tax rather than a benefit.

In addition, low-income workers who voluntarily opt into the system face disproportionately high contribution rates relative to their income, further discouraging participation. The issue of disproportionate contributions extends to independent workers earning up to 2.5 MWs, as fixed contributions in this income range disproportionately reduce their available income. Income taxation is levied only on earnings that exceed roughly 4 MWs, a threshold passed by only 6 percent of the working population. Furthermore, various deductions from the personal income tax further narrow the tax base.

In summary, the lack of participation or compliance in Colombia may be attributed to the lack of an effective mechanism to include those earning below the MW, the near-identical coverage of the contributory and subsidized health plans, the low incentives to participate in the pension system, and the disproportionate contribution burden on independent workers earning between 1 and 2.5 MWs.

El Salvador

In El Salvador, the design of the income tax and labor contributions may generate strong disincentives to comply. The country's tax design is progressive, with a tax-exempt bracket for the lowest labor incomes (currently at $472 monthly, approximately 1.3 times the most-common MW) and increasing rates as labor income rises. However, the fixed exemption generates disincentives to comply, as those who earn salaries slightly exceeding the exemption are worse off. They will have to pay income tax of 10 percent on income exceeding the limit and also a fixed amount equivalent to 3.7 percent of the supposedly exempt amount.

Social security contributions are regressive: Workers' monthly contribution is 3 percent of their net salary, but this figure is capped at US$30 per month. That is, workers earning more than 2.7 times the most-common MW pay less than the 3 percent required of others. These designs result in the tax and contribution burden for lower-income workers being close to zero, growing to 13 percent for those earning around 3 MWs, but becoming progressively smaller for those with higher incomes.

However, these nonlinearities in the cost of formality are not reflected in the formality rates, indicating that the complexities of formality go beyond its costs. Most of the contributions paid by lower wage workers and their employers are allocated to funding long-term direct benefits (through a retirement pension), a smaller portion to funding direct short-term benefits (through health insurance), and nothing to funding contingent benefits. This scheme, in which contributions do not translate into concrete benefits, creates disincentives for compliance.

Jamaica

In Jamaica, two notable "kinks" appear in the tax and benefit structure. The first kink is at 4.1 MWs, where the contributions toward the National Insurance scheme and the National Health Fund reach their ceilings, creating a small decline in the wedge. The second kink is at 4.3 MWs, where the personal income tax starts, causing the wedge to rise sharply to 19.4 percent for dependent workers and to 12.6 percent for self-employed workers at 5 MW, eventually reaching 27.3 and 21.4 percent, respectively, at 10 MW.

The payroll components of the National Health Fund, education tax, and Human Employment and Resource Training (HEART) Trust (a training fund) are potential drivers of disincentives toward compliance and participation because they are pure taxes funding universal programs rather than providing direct, wholly owned benefits to contributors. For dependent workers, more than 50 percent of payments on the payroll go to such taxes even at lower income levels—representing a significant disincentive toward compliance, because workers receive no specific program access in return for these substantial mandatory payments.

Mexico

In Mexico, the costs associated with coverage are, in general, higher for lower-income workers because of the relatively high fixed fee that all compliant and participating workers are required to pay for health insurance and social security, regardless of their income level. However, dependent employees are eligible for an employment subsidy that exceeds the personal income tax at very low levels of income, effectively creating an income transfer to such workers. This subsidy phases out completely at 2.6 MW, creating a notable discontinuity. Yet even prior to this point, a key "kink" in the tax wedge appears at 1.3 MW, where dependent employees begin facing the highest tax wedge of all workers.

Some payroll components stand out for their design: For employees, both personal income tax and social insurance contributions increase with income, while self-employed workers face a much-flatter and -lower wedge because their social insurance contributions are levied on a fixed base of 1 MW regardless of actual earnings. This is a notable incentive issue in which low-income workers face disproportionate compliance costs despite the initial subsidy, due to the regressive nature of the fixed health fee. The health insurance component appears to be a pure tax at higher income levels, as the benefits of coverage do not scale with the increasing contributions.

Peru

Peru's tax wedge starts at 24.3 percent at the MW, placing it mid-range among the peer countries analyzed for this report. The tax structure shows no sharp discontinuities or "kinks" that would create clear compliance disincentives at certain wage levels. However, the health and pension contributions are relatively high for low-income workers, creating a regressive effect and, thus, potentially creating disincentives to comply at lower income levels. A small share (0.8 percent) of payroll taxes goes to indirect benefits (a training fund), representing the only "pure tax" without a direct benefit to the contributing worker.

The family subsidy stands out in the model as an employer-funded rather than a government-funded benefit, increasing employer costs and, thus, potentially making employers hesitant to offer compliant employment to workers with children of eligible ages. Because self-employed workers can choose whether to make social insurance contributions, their participation depends on how much they value these benefits. Self-employed workers may exercise their right to opt out if they see little value in participating.

Uruguay

At the MW, the entire tax wedge in Uruguay consists of contributions that link directly to short- and long-term benefits that are wholly owned by contributing workers and their dependents, with only 0.1 percent going to contingent benefits through an education program. Thus, there are no "pure tax" components of the tax wedge. Social insurance contributions paid by employees follow a progressive structure, increasing with income levels—a notable contrast to many regional peers for which these contributions often create regressive effects.

The valuation of the benefits becomes crucial: If workers fully value their benefits, the effective tax wedge drops to zero for both dependent and self-employed workers, as all contributions translate into perceived value. However, without full valuation, compared to dependent workers, self-employed workers face a higher wedge of 29.3 percent at 1 MW. This issue creates a system in which workers' participation likely depends heavily on how much they value the benefits they receive in return for their contributions.

INSIGHTS FROM CROSS-COUNTRY COMPARISONS OF THE FINDINGS FROM THE DE JURE MODELS

The incentives to comply with or participate in social protection programs are shaped by the design of the legal and regulatory framework, which varies significantly across countries. The previous section and the figures in annex 4C are most useful for analysis of the differences between different types of workers in the same country. Analysis of how policy differs across countries shows how the de jure tax wedges differ in size and composition for the same type of worker at similar levels of earned income (in figure 4.2, the green segments below the horizontal access are in-work benefits).

The tax wedge is a measure of the price "distortions" prevalent in the labor market and the incentives to comply with labor regulations. On average, dependent workers face higher tax wedges than independent workers do (25.3 and 21.3 percent for a single worker at 1 MW, respectively). For dependent workers in single-earner households, Colombia has the highest tax wedge (31.2 percent), and Jamaica has the lowest (16.6 percent). Independent workers in Colombia also face a notably high tax wedge (33.7 percent), which is due to the minimum base of the social insurance contribution set at 1 MW. In contrast, independent workers in Jamaica and Peru face relatively low tax wedges compared to their peers (10.0 and 17.2 percent, respectively).

FIGURE 4.2

De jure tax wedges at 1 minimum wage: single-earner households in select LAC countries

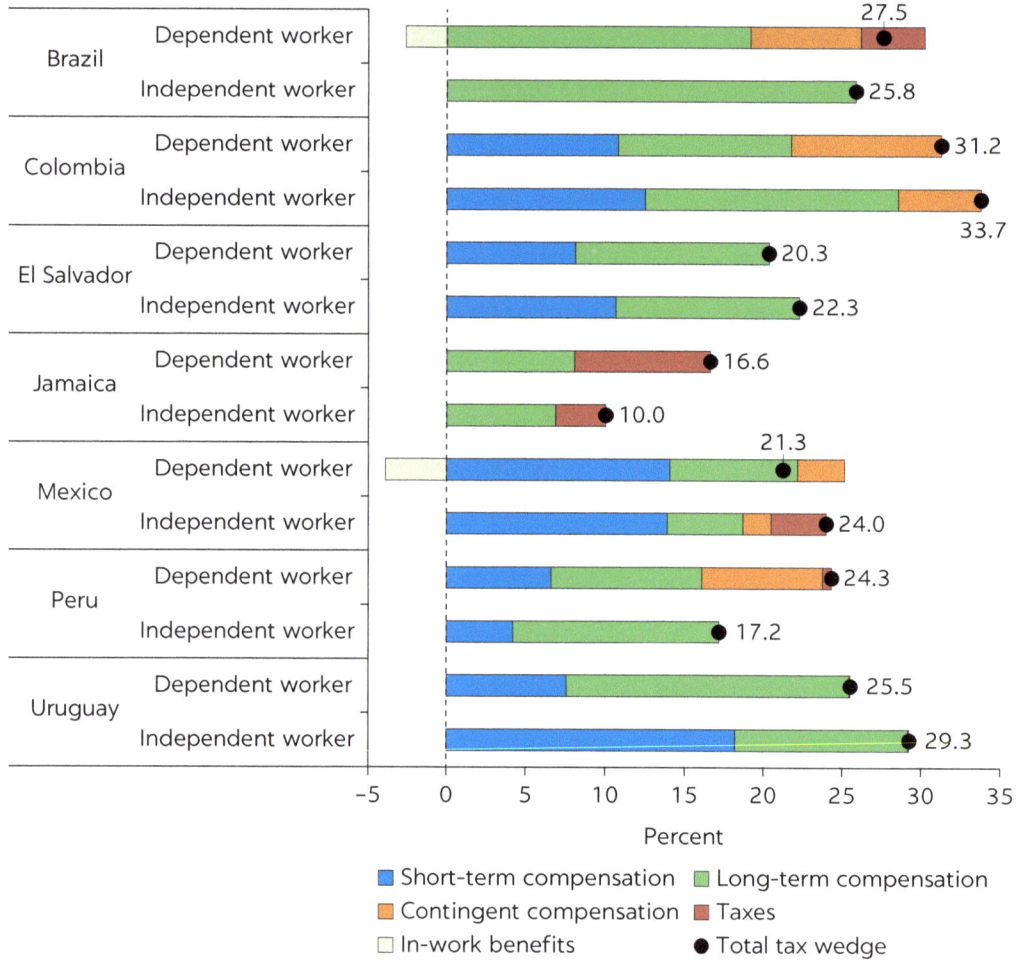

Source: Original figure for this publication.
Note: Calculations are based on data from 2018 for Jamaica, 2021 for Uruguay, and 2019 for the other countries. The figure shows the tax wedge for a single-earner household without children. The tax wedge shown includes nontax compulsory payments, which are compulsory payments that do not meet one of the other two elements in the definition of tax: They are requited or paid to an entity outside the general government (or both) (OECD 2021). Short-term compensation includes contributions toward health insurance. Long-term compensation includes contributions toward pension benefits. Contingent compensation includes contributions toward unemployment insurance, accident insurance, and others. Taxes include personal income tax and other payroll taxes that are not connected to a direct benefit for the worker. Total labor costs include wages and all other compensation. Annex 4A provides more details. LAC = Latin America and the Caribbean; OECD = Organisation for Economic Co-operation and Development.

Variation in the tax wedge at 1 MW across countries and worker types is driven largely by differences in compensation structures. At 1 MW, personal income taxes matter much less than statutory contribution payments because workers at that level of income are expected to pay personal income tax in a few countries (Brazil, Jamaica, and independent workers in Mexico) or receive tax credits (dependent workers in Mexico). In most countries, long-term compensation—mainly contributions to a retirement pension social insurance plan—constitutes the largest portion of the tax wedge. Contingent compensation, such as contributions toward unemployment insurance and occupational hazard insurance, is primarily required for dependent workers. Colombia is an exception, as it is the only country where independent workers also contribute toward insurance for occupational hazards.

Short-term compensation, including health insurance, is provided universally in some countries, like Brazil and El Salvador, and is, therefore, not included in the tax wedge calculation for all countries. In addition, payroll taxes—whether paid by the employer or the employee—are applicable in Brazil, Jamaica, and Mexico at 1 MW. However, in Jamaica in the year of analysis, no short-term or contingent compensation was present, which, in addition to the overall low contribution rates, lowered the tax wedge (refer to figure 4.2, for single-earner households).[6] In Peru, the tax wedge increases for workers with children due to a family subsidy that is paid and financed by the employer. Figure 4.3 shows the de jure tax wedges for households with two adults and two children.

In-work benefits financed directly by the government lower the tax wedge and can vary in amount with family structure. In Brazil and Mexico, in-work benefits for low-wage workers apply. Dependent workers in Mexico who earn less than 2.4 MWs are eligible for a benefit that is intended to cover personal income tax obligations. However, this subsidy may exceed the actual personal income tax due and thus effectively becomes an in-work benefit for low-wage workers. In Brazil, low-wage, dependent workers are eligible to receive two different types of in-work benefits: the Salario Familia (family allowance), which works as a child allowance, and the Abono Salarial (bonus salary), a wage top-up that applies to workers who have low earnings and have had a compliant dependent work contract for at least 5 years. In Brazil, the in-work benefits and, accordingly, the tax wedge change with the child allowance benefit, which increases with the number of children in a family.

The analysis needs to be extended beyond 1 MW, as additional variations in the tax wedge appear at higher levels of earnings and for other family composition structures. Figure 4C.1 in annex 4C illustrates how the tax wedge changes with increasing income for each of the seven country cases. For instance, in Brazil and Uruguay, progressive tax schedules cause the tax wedge to rise continuously with higher levels of income. However, in Colombia, the tax wedge decreases at around 2 MWs due to withdrawal of the employer-paid employment subsidy. In addition, figure 4C.2 shows the tax wedge across the minimum wage distribution grouping taxes and contributions by short-term compensation, long-term compensation, contingent compensation, and taxes.

FIGURE 4.3

De jure tax wedges at 1 minimum wage: households with two adults and two children in select LAC countries

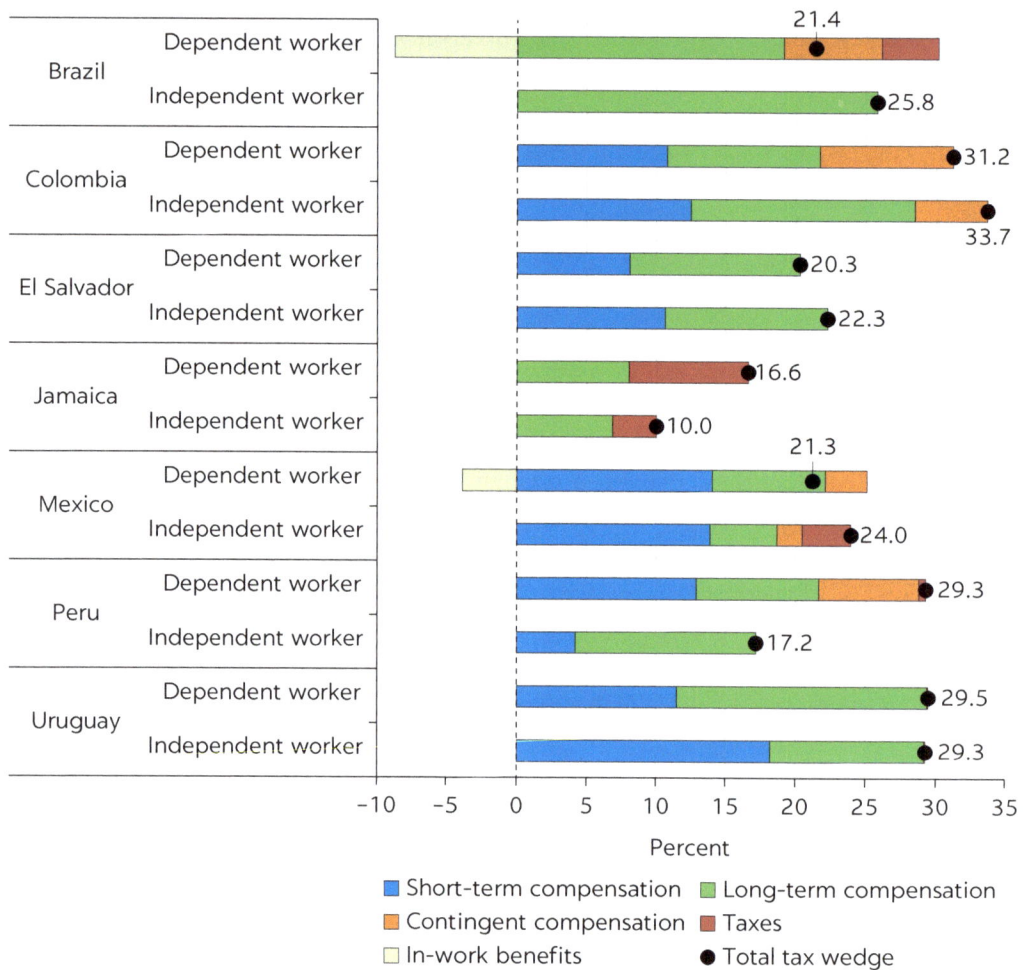

Source: Original figure for this publication.

Note: Calculations are based on data from 2018 for Jamaica, 2021 for Uruguay, and 2019 for the other countries. The figure shows the tax wedge for a family of two adults (one earner) and two children. The tax wedge shown includes nontax compulsory payments, which are compulsory payments that do not meet one of the other two elements in the definition of tax: they are requited or are paid to an entity outside the general government (or both) (OECD 2021). Short-term compensation includes contributions toward health insurance. Long-term compensation includes contributions toward pension benefits. Contingent compensation includes contributions toward unemployment insurance, accident insurance, and others. Taxes include personal income tax and other payroll taxes that are not connected to a direct benefit for the worker. Total labor costs include wages and all other compensation. Annex 4A provides more details. LAC = Latin America and the Caribbean; OECD = Organisation for Economic Co-operation and Development.

Discontinuities in the tax wedge, caused by the abrupt withdrawal or introduction of certain taxes, contributions, and benefits, can create additional disincentives (figure 4C.3 in annex 4C provides an overview of all tax wedges by country). In almost all the case study countries, low-wage workers are exempt from paying personal income taxes under specific rules.[7] However, the way these exemptions are phased out can lead to significant jumps in the tax wedge, potentially discouraging workers from increasing their (compliant) labor supply. For example, in Jamaica, the tax wedge for dependent workers increases sharply from about 7 percent to around 16 percent once personal income taxes become applicable. This sudden increase might incentivize workers to limit their earnings to stay in a lower tax bracket rather than increasing their working hours and wages, which would subject them to a higher tax rate.

The rules for determining eligibility and how benefits are withdrawn are important factors that create discontinuities. In addition to in-work benefits, social assistance benefits and the design of their rules determine the level of disincentives. (In the conceptual framework in chapter 3, these social assistance benefits are referred to as "outside options" because they are outside the employment relationship.) Social assistance benefits might be withdrawn when a worker (or employer) becomes compliant or starts to participate, as the government is able to observe income or higher income.

Although normally those benefits do not depend on compliance or participation status, they may potentially be withdrawn, because "formal" income is more difficult to hide than "informal" income. In addition, as labor income increases, benefits might be withdrawn. The design of the withdrawal rules is important. In Brazil, for example, the conditional cash transfer (in its 2019 rules) was withdrawn gradually and thus did not pose sharp disincentives toward increasing labor supply. In Colombia, in contrast, withdrawal of the transport subsidy decreased the tax wedge (because the subsidy was paid by the employer and, thus, was part of nonlabor costs); however, it also decreased workers' net incomes and, thus, may have discouraged workers from increasing their labor supply.

It is also important to consider the slope of the tax wedge curve. In addition to discontinuities, the rate at which the tax wedge increases is an indicator of both disincentives and equity. A sharply rising tax wedge may discourage workers from complying with tax regulations or participating in the formal labor market at higher levels of income, as the cost of compliance and participation becomes more burdensome. However, this steepness is also linked to distributional objectives. Progressive tax schedules are designed to ensure a degree of redistribution from high- to low-income individuals. Therefore, achieving a balance between minimizing disincentives and promoting equity is essential.

In several countries, general benefits not tied directly to workers' future benefits are financed through payroll taxes, and these benefits vary significantly across countries. As discussed in chapter 3, on the conceptual framework of this report, there is a risk of governments misaligning or overreaching in their tax and benefit policies, leading to low valuation and eventually noncompliance or nonparticipation. This issue occurs when taxes levied on wages are not directly connected to future benefits for the worker or, in the case of dependent employment, for the employer. Such misalignment is observed in Brazil, Colombia, Jamaica, and Peru.

Jamaica represents the most-extreme case, where employers and workers contribute nearly 10 percent of wages toward payments not linked to direct benefits for the workers. These payments fund the National Health Fund, education tax, and HEART Trust. In Brazil, 2.7 percent of wages go toward an agricultural fund and an education fund. In Peru, 0.8 percent is allocated to an industrial training fund (the National Training Service of Industrial Work, SENATI).

Most countries in the LAC region have implemented simplified tax regimes for independent "microentrepreneurs." In Brazil, Colombia, Mexico, and Uruguay, such regimes can streamline tax processes for small firms that fall below a specified size threshold (sometimes defined by income and other times by the number of people they employ), often within particular sectors or types of economic activities. The primary aim of these simplified tax regimes is to lower tax rates and reduce participation costs for microentrepreneurs. Typically, these regimes consolidate income and sales taxes into a single levy. In addition, some of these systems provide subsidies to support social protection for both microentrepreneurs and their potential employees (Azuara et al. 2019).

Although their direct effects on participation and compliance are ambiguous (Bruhn and McKenzie 2014; Fajnzylber, Maloney, and Montes-Rojas 2011; Piza 2018; Rocha, Ulyssea, and Rachter 2018), the systems are used widely (Azuara et al. 2019) and reduce the tax wedge substantially. In Mexico, for example, the Tax Incorporation Regime reduced the tax wedge from about 24 percent (for normal self-employed workers) to about 20 percent at 1 MW.[8] In El Salvador, Jamaica, and Peru, in contrast, no simplified tax systems are in place.

A large tax wedge does not necessarily discourage registration if workers perceive their contributions as valuable future benefits. As discussed in chapter 3, the perceived value of these benefits plays a critical role in compliance and participation. This perception shifts the de jure tax wedge toward the perceived tax wedge, which more accurately reflects workers' views on the benefits associated with their contributions. The key distinction between these concepts lies in how much workers value the benefit package they receive in the short term, long term, or contingent future. Although a high de jure tax wedge may not directly indicate disincentives to compliance, a high perceived tax wedge does suggest such disincentives. Conversely, if workers do not value the future benefits tied to their contributions, a high tax wedge can become a significant barrier to compliance or participation.

Figure 4.4 illustrates the substantial impact that valuation has on the tax wedge at 1 MW. For dependent workers in Brazil, for example, the tax wedge decreases from 27.5 percent to −4.7 percent if all contributions are valued because in-work benefits surpass payroll taxes.

FIGURE 4.4

Tax wedge under the full valuation and no valuation assumptions

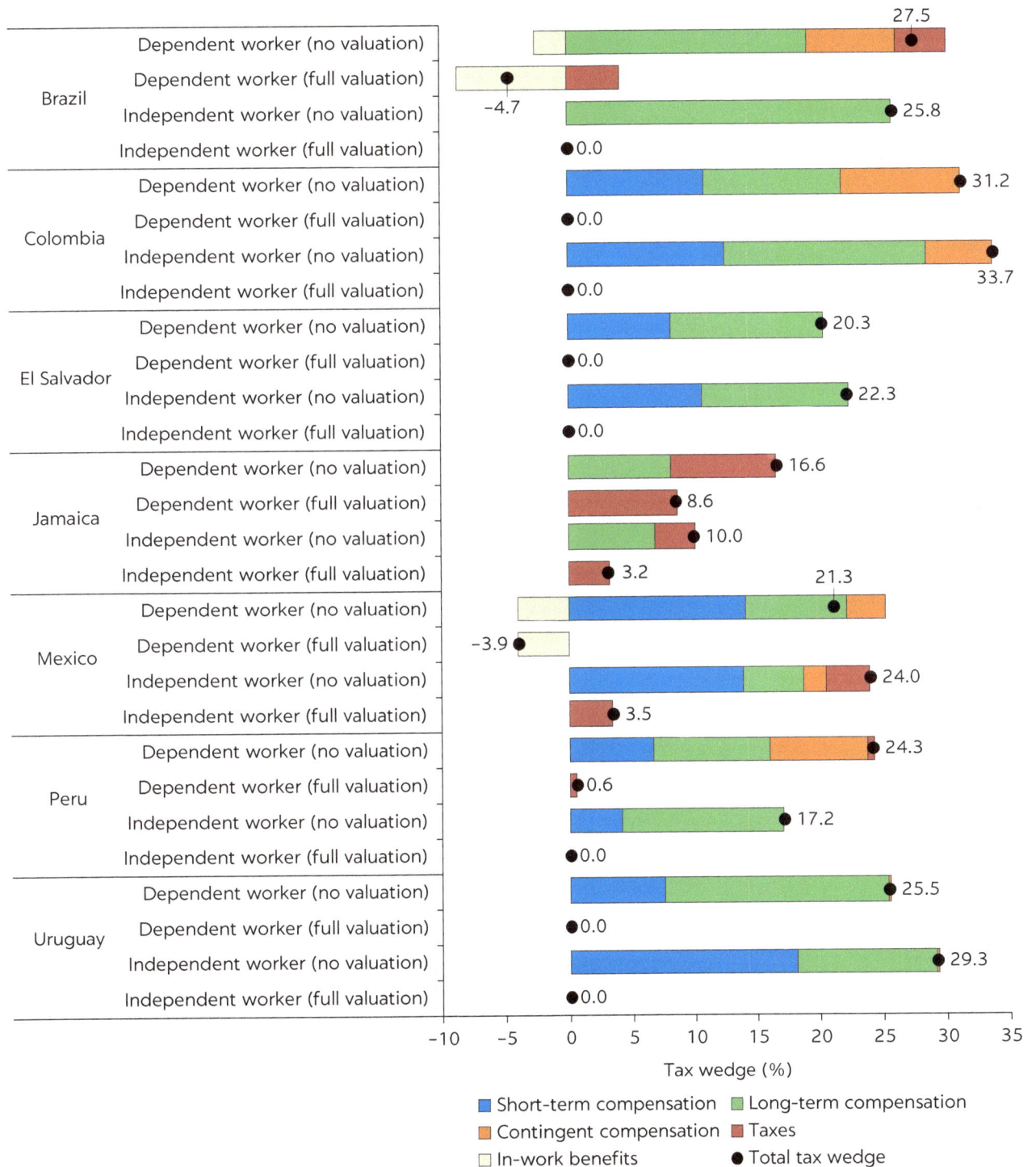

Source: Original figure for this publication.

SUMMARY OF THE DE JURE ANALYSIS

The analysis in this chapter showed the importance of scrutinizing the de jure (dis)incentive "landscape" as a whole. Detailed descriptions and comparisons of the tax and benefit system within a country (comparison of different wage levels, family compositions, and employment contracts), as well as between countries, highlighted potential (dis)incentive "pressure points." In addition, the analysis highlighted that policies and programs need to be analyzed in a specific country context to determine valuation and move from the de jure tax wedge to the perceived tax wedge.

Policy makers aiming for significant improvement in incentives should focus on "incentive pressure points" and prioritize actions that address these areas where most working people are concentrated. Changes to the tax and benefit framework must align with a country's income distribution. For example, smoothing the tax wedge to avoid creating disincentives should be prioritized at points in the income distribution where substantial portions of the population are located. Changes in personal income tax and social protection eligibility, benefit, and contribution policies will have the greatest impact on incentives if they are focused on the points in the earned-income distribution where large segments of the labor force—or groups of particular interest—are observed. Therefore, a detailed mapping of taxes and benefits should be accompanied by an analysis of the labor market and income distribution in the respective country.

Although the de jure analysis offers numerous insights on the design of the tax and benefit landscape, it is important to recognize its limitations. Analysis of the de jure modeling identifies only the theoretical (dis)incentives to comply and participate. The analysis does not account for the distribution of workers across different incentive groups, nor does it fully capture how taxes and benefits influence individual decisions to formalize. Figure 4C.4 in annex 4C shows the distributions of worker types by earned income, as observed in labor force survey data.

However, this is just the first level of empirical validation of the de jure modeling. Factors such as the availability of formal job opportunities, productivity differences between formal and informal ways of organizing production and delivering services, and the many nonwage benefits associated with covered and noncovered ways of working (such as the utility workers may derive from flexibility and autonomy) all play significant roles in these decisions. Therefore, although the de jure analysis offers valuable insights, extensive empirical analysis of microdata showing where and how people with different characteristics and earnings levels are actually working is necessary. This would help to quantify the real-world impacts of taxes and benefits on the costs of compliance and participation, considering the choice to take up a formal job or to work longer in formal work. Chapter 5 presents a deeper level of empirical analysis.

NOTES

1. The OECD publishes the yearly report *Taxing Wages* (1999–present), which analyzes the tax wedges of its member countries. The series was established in 1999, and each edition focuses on one aspect, such as the incentives for second earners in the 2024 edition.
2. This methodology departs in certain aspects from the OECD methodology. First, the OECD classified nonwage costs as the sum of social security contributions, personal income taxes, and payroll taxes minus in-work cash benefits and non-work-related cash benefits paid by the government. Although this report applies the same sum, it only deducts in-work cash benefits and does not deduct non-work-related cash benefits. Second, the OECD distinguishes between the pure and augmented tax wedges. The augmented tax wedge includes so-called *non-tax compulsory payments*, which are "requited and unrequited compulsory payments to privately managed funds, welfare agencies or social insurance schemes outside general governments and to public enterprises" (OECD 2019–present). This report follows the definition of the *augmented tax wedge* and refers to it as the *tax wedge*. In addition, for wages, the report considers components such as annual leave, holiday bonuses, and year-end bonuses.
3. Since 2022, OECD publications also include information on self-employed workers.
4. Tables 4B.1–4B.14 in annex 4B define the policy and program parameters by country.
5. A similar scenario can be observed only in Mexico.
6. Jamaica has since introduced an unemployment income protection plan.
7. An exception is independent workers in Mexico, who must pay personal income tax.
8. The Tax Incorporation Regime system was replaced by the Simplified Trust Regime in 2022.

REFERENCES

Azuara, O., R. Azuero, M. Bosch, and J. Torres. 2019. "Special Tax Regimes in Latin America and the Caribbean: Compliance, Social Protection, and Resource Misallocation." IDB Working Paper 9511, Inter-American Development Bank, Washington, DC.

Bruhn, M., and D. McKenzie. 2014. "Entry Regulation and the Formalization of Microenterprises in Developing Countries." *World Bank Research Observer* 29 (2): 186–201. https://doi.org/10.1093/wbro/lku002.

Fajnzylber, P., W. F. Maloney, and G. V. Montes-Rojas. 2011. "Does Formality Improve Micro-Firm Performance?" *World Development* 39 (9): 1580–93.

OECD (Organisation for Economic Co-operation and Development). 2019. *Taxing Wages*. Paris: OECD. https://www.oecd-ilibrary.org/taxation/taxing-wages_22205578.

OECD (Organisation for Economic Co-operation and Development). 2019–Present. *Taxing Wages*. Paris: OECD. https://www.oecd-ilibrary.org/taxation /taxing-wages_22205578.

OECD (Organisation for Economic Co-opeation and Development). 2021. *Taxing Wages: Non-Tax Compulsory Payments as an Additional Burden on Labour Income in 2021*. Paris: OECD.

OECD (Organisation for Economic Co-operation and Development). 2024. *Taxing Wages: Non-Tax Compulsory Payments as an Additional Burden on Labour Income in 2023*. Paris: OECD.

Piza, C. 2018. "Out of the Shadows? Revisiting the Impact of the Brazilian SIMPLES
    Program on Firms' Formalization Rates." *Journal of Development Economics*
    134: 125–32.

Rocha, R., G. Ulyssea, and L. Rachter. 2018. "Do Lower Taxes Reduce Informality?
    Evidence from Brazil." *Journal of Development Economics* 134: 28–49. https://doi
    .org/10.1016/j.jdeveco.2018.04.003.

5 The "Formalization Tax Rate"
A COMPOSITE MEASURE OF BENEFIT AND TAX INCENTIVES

A MEASURE OF THE COSTS AND BENEFITS OF COMPLIANCE

Quantifying how reforms shape incentives is essential for effective tax and social protection policy making. Derived from the de jure modeling presented in chapter 4 in this report, this chapter uses a single composite measure of the costs and benefits that compliance (and participation where and for whom it is voluntary) imposes on households. The composite measure, known as the *formalization tax rate* (FTR) (Koettl and Weber 2012), is comparable across countries and suitable for distributional policy analysis.

This chapter benchmarks the costs of social protection and personal income taxation across six country cases—Brazil, Colombia, El Salvador, Mexico, Peru, and Uruguay. The chapter also identifies specific segments of the workforce of particular interest and assesses the relative importance of different aspects of the tax–benefit architecture in creating disincentives to compliance and participation. Chapter 6 presents simulations of how policies can affect incentives to comply with labor regulations, demonstrating how the FTR can be used in policy dialogue to evaluate alternative reforms.

The FTR is an integrated measure of the costs and benefits workers and firms incur when complying with tax, social protection, and labor regulations—that is, when "formalizing" the employment relationship. The FTR builds on classic measures of labor supply incentives, where workers aim to maximize the value of their hours worked as described in the conceptual framework presented in chapter 3. The FTR measures the full financial cost of complying with labor regulations, which includes income taxes, social insurance contributions, and any social assistance benefits or mandatory in-work benefits lost by reporting higher income. The elements of the tax–benefit system mapped and modeled in chapter 4 are integrated into a single comprehensive metric that captures their net effect. The FTR is calculated for workers based on their observed work patterns, personal attributes, and household characteristics, allowing for a rich distributional analysis of the impact of changes to the rules. The FTR combines

A reproducibility package is available for this book in the Reproducible Research Repository at https://reproducibility.worldbank.org/catalog/330/.

different aspects of the conceptual framework presented in chapter 3—such as different degrees of valuation or bargaining power.

This chapter uses FTRs to analyze the compliance and participation incentives across the country cases and identifies six principal findings for the crafters of taxation and social protection policy to consider:

- Statutory social insurance contributions are the largest component affecting the FTR. In the Latin American and the Caribbean (LAC) countries analyzed, personal income taxes and social assistance transfers play a minor role.

- Improving workers' perceived value of contributing to social insurance plans can minimize the disincentives to formalization. Priorities should include boosting service quality, improving workers' information and trust in institutions, and designing integrated social protection architectures to prevent noncontributory programs from reducing the perceived value of contributory programs.

- Incentives differ substantially between dependent employment and self-employment. Across the countries analyzed, the costs of compliance faced by dependent workers average between 20 and 40 percent of household income. Self-employed workers typically face lower costs of compliance and participation between 5 and 25 percent of household income.

- Wealthier countries exhibit larger gaps in incentives between dependent and self-employed workers. These gaps create strong financial incentives for firms to circumvent salaried work by hiring self-employed contractors.

- Special tax regimes for self-employed workers may induce formalization by keeping disincentives to a minimum and offering lower levels of social protection. In contrast, traditional self-employment regimes with fixed contribution bases can generate high disincentives at low levels of earnings.

- Incentives to register and comply with labor regulations vary widely across groups within each country's workforce. The FTR indicator can be exploited to identify and target certain groups of workers facing large disincentives.

The FTR presented here builds on previous versions proposed in the literature in several ways. The concept of the FTR was first introduced by Koettl and Weber (2012) and subsequently applied to five countries in Latin America (Bolivia, Colombia, Ecuador, Peru, and the República Bolivariana de Venezuela) by Bargain, Jara, and Rivera (2024) and Jara et al. (2023). In contrast to these studies, this chapter explicitly recognizes that avoiding detection by tax and labor authorities requires employers and employees in dependent work relationships to collude. Therefore, the measure used here encompasses taxes and contributions that the employee is required to pay but also those paid by the employer.

In addition, the analysis allows the worker's valuation of social insurance benefits to impact the incentives to comply and participate. Varying valuation—a crucial aspect of the theoretical framework in chapter 3—allows for simulating the impacts of policies affecting these benefits or workers' perceptions of the probability of receiving them.

Finally, the chapter accounts for the fact that the worker and employer may bargain over the worker's wage, if the employment is registered, to ensure that both parties benefit. Koettl and Weber (2012) assumed that employer contributions are fully passed through to registered workers in the form of lower wages. Instead, based on a simple static bargaining model, this chapter predicts the FTR as a function of the relative bargaining power of both parties and the worker's valuation of social insurance benefits.[1] Box 5.1 describes the strengths and shortcomings of the FTR.

Box 5.1

Strengths and shortcomings of the formalization tax rate

The formalization tax rate (FTR) considers a broader household-level context that influences the registration decision on top of the direct impact of taxes and benefits on a worker's earnings. For example, complying with labor regulations means that labor income becomes directly visible to the state and could cause another family member to lose eligibility for a means-tested benefit. In countries with joint filing, the increase in income taxes paid upon registering would depend on whether the worker's spouse also earns taxable income. Workers who enjoy health insurance coverage from a family member should put a lower value on contributing themselves to social insurance. Therefore, their incentives to register will be lower.

By considering changes in the household's overall income, the FTR captures these important mechanisms. The parameter governing the valuation of social protection benefits can also take different values based on a worker's family composition.

The FTR facilitates cross-country comparisons, emphasizing how differences in institutions and labor force characteristics interact. The distribution of workers across wage levels and dependent versus independent worker status varies widely in the region, and the same policy can have different impacts in different countries. For policy makers, these comparisons are critical, as they can highlight best practices, identify areas where reforms may be needed, and reveal the broader regional dynamics of labor formalization. For example, progressive tax schedules with high exemption levels are potentially inefficient for increasing equity, because large parts of the wage distribution are not affected.

Several limitations of the indicator must be acknowledged and guide its interpretation. For example, because the data do not usually contain firm profit information, they cannot capture the fact that registering a worker can inflate labor costs, thereby reducing declared profits and corporate taxes. This would offset a fraction of the costs of registering a worker but is not captured in the FTR measure.

In addition, calculation of the FTR assumes a specific formalization pathway for each worker, although several pathways may exist. To keep the

continued

Box 5.1 Strengths and shortcomings of the formalization tax rate, *(continued)*

measure transparent, only "in situ" formalization is considered, meaning that only the registration status of the worker changes and everything else is kept constant. This issue is conceptually problematic for employees of unregistered firms because, to formalize the worker, the firm itself would need to register, implying that the FTR underestimates the cost of formalizing for this category of workers. However, this approach is consistent with the focus on costs related to the tax and benefit system.

Another issue arises when workers can choose between several legal tax regimes. For example, in Brazil, some self-employment can be registered as individual microentrepreneurs or self-employed workers, for which different tax and contribution regulations apply. In such situations, the calculation makes assumptions based on the most common formalization pathways in each specific context.

This chapter calculates FTRs only for dependent workers with earnings at or above the minimum wage; therefore, significant segments of the workforce may not be included in the analysis (refer to the discussion in chapter 2). Only those workers are included because unregistered workers earning less than the minimum wage may not be productive enough for their employers to agree to formalize them if this implies raising their wage above the legal minimum. Indeed, studies in the Harris and Todaro (1970) tradition consider that these workers are involuntarily "rationed out" of formal jobs due to high minimum wages and would likely not respond to the kinds of incentives captured by the FTR. An alternative assumption would be to consider that, taking the minimum wage as given, the only pathway for these low-productivity dependent workers to register is by becoming self-employed, and to calculate the FTR based on this hypothetical transition.

FTR DEFINITION AND INTERPRETATION

The FTR measures the monetary costs associated with each worker's registration, including taxes, social insurance contributions, and forgone social benefits. As indicated in the framework in chapter 3, these costs are weighed against many other considerations surrounding the decision to register that are independent of taxes and benefits. Such considerations include the expected cost of penalties incurred by the employer if it is caught hiring unregistered wage workers and the direct cost to unregistered self-employed workers if they operate illegally or evade taxes. Workers may also value having a formal job if it would affect their future employment prospects or access to credit, or if social status is associated with having a formal job.

The direct impact of workers' FTR on their formality status has been established empirically. Koettl and Weber (2012) showed that, for several Eastern European countries, higher FTRs are significantly correlated with the probability of noncompliance. More recently, Bargain, Jara, and Rivera (2024) demonstrated a causal impact of FTRs on formality. They exploited changes in tax and benefit regulation in Bolivia, Colombia, and Ecuador between 2008 and

2019 using a pseudo-panel approach (Blundell, Duncan, and Meghir 1998), showing that changes in formality across different population groups are negatively correlated with changes in formalization incentives as captured by the FTR.

The FTR faced by a worker is defined by equation 5.1:

$$FTR = \frac{\Delta Taxes + \Delta Contributions \times (1 - Valuation) + \Delta Transfers}{Informal\ household\ income}, \qquad (5.1)$$

where

- *ΔTaxes* is the difference in taxes paid by the household if the worker is registered versus unregistered.

- *ΔContributions* is the difference in employer and employee social insurance contributions if the worker is registered versus unregistered.

- *Valuation* is the ratio of the discounted present value of the marginal social protection benefit accrued by an additional contribution and the amount contributed.

- *ΔTransfers* is the difference in social assistance and work benefits received by the household if the worker is unregistered versus registered.

- *Informal household income* is the worker's disposable household income when unregistered.

As governments tend to tax rather than subsidize formal employment, FTRs are typically positive, and a higher FTR reflects a higher disincentive to formalize. The indicator is normalized by the worker's disposable household income rather than by labor costs (as is the case for other labor supply incentive measures). This difference is because the FTR captures how the incomes of other family members can be affected by a worker's registration status, for example, if it causes them to fail a household means test. When employers can lower wages, workers effectively bear the burden of regulation (known as *full pass-through*). In that case, the FTR can be interpreted as "the share of household disposable income taxed away when a worker becomes formal."

The first component of the FTR is income taxes. Wages reported by the employer, usually above a certain threshold, are subject to income taxation. The public goods financed by taxation are enjoyed by both registered and unregistered workers, so paying taxes is not compensated by corresponding benefits from the individual's point of view and, therefore, creates disincentives to formalize the employment relationship. Depending on social norms and individual preferences, workers may have a sense of civic duty and understand the need for public goods and redistribution from which they derive a benefit (for details, refer to chapter 3). This issue is difficult to quantify and is not considered in the baseline indicator. A straightforward extension of the indicator would adjust the tax component to vary with individual- or country-level measures of tax morale (for details on tax morale, refer to chapter 7).

The design of the personal income tax can potentially create disincentives toward registered work, especially for second earners in the case of special rules for joint taxation (OECD 2024). Among the countries considered in this chapter, only Brazil has rules for joint taxation: Married couples can submit a joint personal income tax declaration and declare dependents together. Thus, the disincentives caused by income taxes vary with a worker's family composition and the employment status of family members.

The second component of the FTR is social insurance contributions, which can be offset by the value attached to the corresponding benefits accrued. In a dependent employment relationship, contributions are usually paid in part by employees and in part by employers (as outlined in the figures in chapter 4). In contrast, self-employed workers typically pay the full contributions, although they often face reduced rates (refer to chapter 4). The FTR incorporates both employer and employee contributions because they both create disincentives to formality (refer to box 5.2 for discussion of this point).

Box 5.2

Implementing the formalization tax rate using micro survey data

The calculation of formalization incentives at the individual level leverages microsimulation tools developed for each country to simulate the distributional impacts of policy changes. These tools allow researchers to predict how reforms of, say, taxation or social security could impact economic outcomes, such as the distribution of household incomes, labor supply, or the poverty rate. Microsimulation tools compute how de jure tax and benefit regulations apply to the workers observed in the data, given their reported income, individual characteristics, and household composition. The outputs from the microsimulation tools are the taxes paid, social insurance contributions made, social assistance benefits received by every household in the survey, and the households' disposable income (refer to figure B5.2.1).

For the calculation of the formalization tax rate (FTR), taxes, social security contributions, benefits, and disposable household income are calculated under two scenarios. The worker is assumed to have registered with the social security authority in one scenario but not in the other. Comparing these scenarios produces the difference in taxes, contributions, and benefits for every individual that results from the decision to register (refer to annex 5A for the detailed procedure).

A critical assumption when calculating the FTR has to do with whether the wage paid by the

continued

Box 5.2 Implementing the formalization tax rate using micro survey data, *(continued)*

employer will adjust to the decision of formalizing. Depending on the relative bargaining power of the employer and the worker and the worker's valuation of social insurance benefits, employers may be able to lower the wage upon formalizing to pass through some of the tax and contribution wedge onto the workers. Box 5.3 discusses this point in greater detail.

FIGURE B5.2.1

Steps in the implementation of the FTR

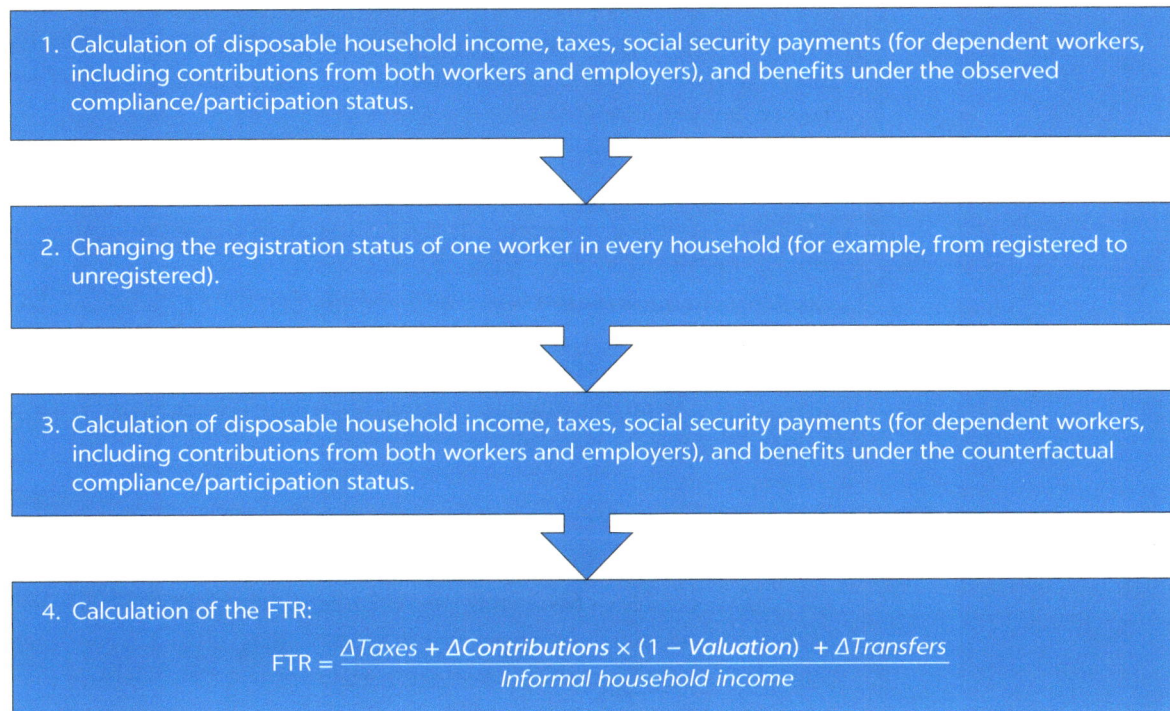

1. Calculation of disposable household income, taxes, social security payments (for dependent workers, including contributions from both workers and employers), and benefits under the observed compliance/participation status.

2. Changing the registration status of one worker in every household (for example, from registered to unregistered).

3. Calculation of disposable household income, taxes, social security payments (for dependent workers, including contributions from both workers and employers), and benefits under the counterfactual compliance/participation status.

4. Calculation of the FTR:

$$FTR = \frac{\Delta Taxes + \Delta Contributions \times (1 - Valuation) + \Delta Transfers}{Informal\ household\ income}$$

Source: Original figure for this publication.

An important consideration is that these contributions are paid in exchange for social insurance benefits. The expected benefits accrued with each additional contribution may be valued below or above the immediate loss of salary, depending on the rules of each social protection program (actuarial fairness); the quality and credibility of institutions; and the perceptions, preferences, and circumstances of each worker. More details are provided on these points in the discussion of the framework for this report in chapters 3 and 7.

This chapter only emphasizes that the FTR explicitly models the extent to which social insurance contributions are perceived as a pure tax or a just payment for future benefits. Under the latter assumption, workers value the benefits at exactly the cost of the contributions, perfectly offsetting the impact of contributions on the decision to register. The analysis here includes the full contributions in the measure of incentives. The last section in this chapter briefly explores how the incentives change as the workers' valuation of social security benefits increases.

The last component of the FTR is government transfers, which may incentivize or disincentivize worker registration. One advantage of the FTR is its ability to incorporate implicit taxes, which arise when social benefits are withdrawn because a worker registers. Most countries in Latin America have conditional cash transfers in place, which aim to reduce poverty and increase human capital through their conditionalities. Although several countries analyzed in this report have complex proxy means-tested eligibility criteria (Colombia, Mexico, Peru, and Uruguay), other countries rely on a pure means-tested eligibility criterion (Brazil).

Eligibility is not generally dependent on registration status, but earned income is easier to hide if workers are not compliant with or do not participate in the system. These considerations are likely to be more relevant in the future. As governments improve their information infrastructure and strengthen processes for interministerial exchange of data, formal income declared to one administration can be used to check households' eligibility for social assistance.

Yet, transfers can also encourage registration, as certain countries offer in-work benefits for low-wage registered workers. For example, in Brazil, compliant low-wage dependent workers receive a wage subsidy[2] or a child allowance.[3] In Mexico, low-wage dependent workers are eligible to receive a tax credit. These considerations will become increasingly significant as social assistance programs continue to expand worldwide. Therefore, the FTR offers a flexible tool and a more-accurate reflection of the total financial burden on workers registering to comply and participate, especially in environments where social benefits play a major role in household income.

The FTR considers the incentives to register employment for both sides of the labor market. Employers and employees often engage in negotiations on wages, where the decision to register the worker to comply and participate with taxation and social insurance plans is a joint one. In many cases, employer contributions to social insurance and other mandated benefits are effectively "passed through" to workers, meaning that these contributions are factored into the overall compensation package. This wage pass-through mechanism matters for the impact of taxes and benefits on workers' take-home pay. Box 5.3 elaborates on these points, as it describes the bargaining model underpinning the incentive indicators.

Box 5.3

A simple static bargaining model of worker registration

The formalization tax rate (FTR) can be grounded in a simple theoretical framework designed to capture the firm's decision to register a worker and the way that wages are affected by this decision.

The FTR involves comparing informal workers' observed situation to a hypothetical scenario in which their employer had decided to register them; or, conversely, comparing formal workers' situation with the scenario in which they had not been registered. Anecdotal evidence from the Latin America and the Caribbean region abounds in which workers and employers collude to avoid paying taxes and social insurance contributions. To make this beneficial for both parties, workers can be compensated for lost benefits in the form of higher wages, and firms can be compensated for the risk of penalties in the form of lower labor costs. These wage adjustments are relevant to understand the impacts of formalization on workers' welfare and firms' profits.

The mechanisms are captured by considering a static version of the model put forward by Bobba et al. (2021), which adapts the classic search-matching-bargaining model (Mortensen and Pissarides 1994) to allow firms to decide whether to register workers. In this simple framework, a firm and a worker meet and jointly generate a certain level of revenue. They bargain over the wage to split this revenue after the firm has decided whether to register the worker. This exercise assumes that the match is permanent so that no dynamic considerations intervene, and it is a one-shot decision.

Formality involves paying taxes and contributions and possibly losing noncontributory benefits.[a] Intuitively, because the bargaining process allows the parties to compensate each other by adjusting the wage level, the only consideration that matters for the registration decision is whether the revenue, net of taxes, benefits, and contributions, is greater under formality or informality.

In a simple case where workers only pay a fixed contribution to formal security C and value the corresponding benefits at B, the firm's profits and workers' utilities under formality and informality are given by equation B5.3.1:

$$\pi_0 = y - w_0$$
$$\pi_1 = y - w_1 + C$$
$$u_0 = W_0$$
$$u_1 = W_1 + B, \qquad \text{(B5.3.1)}$$

where y is the revenue, and W_F is the wage under formality status F.

This yields a total surplus:

$$S_0 = y$$
$$S_1 = y - C + B \qquad \text{(B5.3.2)}$$

The decision to register only depends on whether the total surplus is larger under formality or informality:

$$F = 1 \; \text{if and only if} \; S_1 - S_0 = B - C > 0 \qquad \text{(B5.3.3)}$$

Therefore, while the firm formally decides on the registration outcome, workers and firms are always in agreement about the outcome. In that sense, the FTR captures the perspectives of both the worker and the firm. Another implication is that both employer and employee contributions matter for the decision to formalize. The wage is then determined by Nash bargaining, which implies that the incidence of contributions on the firm and worker will depend on their respective bargaining power α.

The difference in surplus is equal to the nonvalued part of social security contributions $B - C$. The FTR simply captures this "formalization wedge," normalized by the worker's disposable household income.

a. A straightforward extension allows the revenue itself to differ based on the formality status of the worker.

The FTR is calculated using microdata from representative labor force surveys, allowing for distributional policy analysis (refer to box 5.2 for details on the construction of the indicator). The impact of a distortionary tax depends on both the intensity of the distortion (the level of the income tax rate) and the number of workers exposed to that distortion (the tax-benefit). The procedure yields a measure of incentives at the individual level, which allows capturing both dimensions and assessing the distributional impacts of policies. Thus, the analysis can identify specific groups within the population that may be affected by the tax-benefit system. Distributional analyses provide valuable insights into policies' potential equity and efficiency impacts. Thus, such analyses are crucial for understanding the real-world implications of policy decisions for different segments of the workforce and can inform more-targeted and -effective policy interventions.

INCENTIVES FOR FORMALIZATION IN SIX LAC COUNTRIES[4]

This section implements the FTR indicator using survey data from six countries—Brazil, Colombia, El Salvador, Mexico, Peru, and Uruguay. The calculations are based on the de jure tax and benefit mapping presented in chapter 4. Using each country's microsimulation tool, which calculates the taxes and benefits applicable to each household based on its characteristics, the de jure parameters are applied to the household survey from 2019 for the respective country. The year 2019 was chosen to gain insights into the steady-state tax and benefit structure before the global COVID-19 pandemic, during which many emergency benefits were introduced. Whenever possible, reforms of the tax and benefit system that lasted longer than or were introduced after the state of emergency in most countries are reflected in the simulations of the effects of reforms on incentives, which are presented in chapter 6.[5]

Across the countries analyzed, dependent workers face median FTRs between 20 and 40 percent of household income, and self-employed workers typically face lower FTRs, between 5 and 25 percent of household income. Figure 5.1 shows box and whisker plots that represent how FTRs are distributed among the workers in each country. Panel a shows the distributions for dependent workers, and panel b shows the distributions for self-employed workers. The middle bar in each box is the median FTR.

Incentives vary widely within each country, as FTRs can be exploited to identify and focus on specific groups of workers facing greater disincentives. Figure 5.1 shows how widespread FTRs are within each country and group of workers. For example, in Brazil, some workers face almost no cost of formalizing, while others would pay most of their earnings in taxes, contributions, and forgone social assistance transfers if they registered. Contributions and taxes for low-wage dependent earners are almost entirely offset by in-work benefits connected to compliant dependent employment. In addition, the conditional cash transfer can still be received when switching from noncompliance to compliance if the income per capita lies below the cash transfer's threshold.[6]

At the other end of the FTR distribution, workers might be subject to high FTRs due to the withdrawal of benefits (such as social pensions within the family or the conditional cash transfer) that were received because certain parts of the noncompliant income were hidden from the authorities. When switching to compliance, this subterfuge is no longer possible and thus benefit eligibility is lost.

This distributional analysis is possible because FTRs are computed at the individual level. Potential taxes and benefits are simulated based on each worker's income level and household composition. Greater heterogeneity—differences in the valuation of social security benefits by age and family situation, for example—can easily be incorporated into the indicator. Therefore, policy makers can identify which groups of workers face the largest disincentives and simulate solutions that target and reduce them.

FIGURE 5.1

Distribution of formalization incentives, by country and employment status, 2019

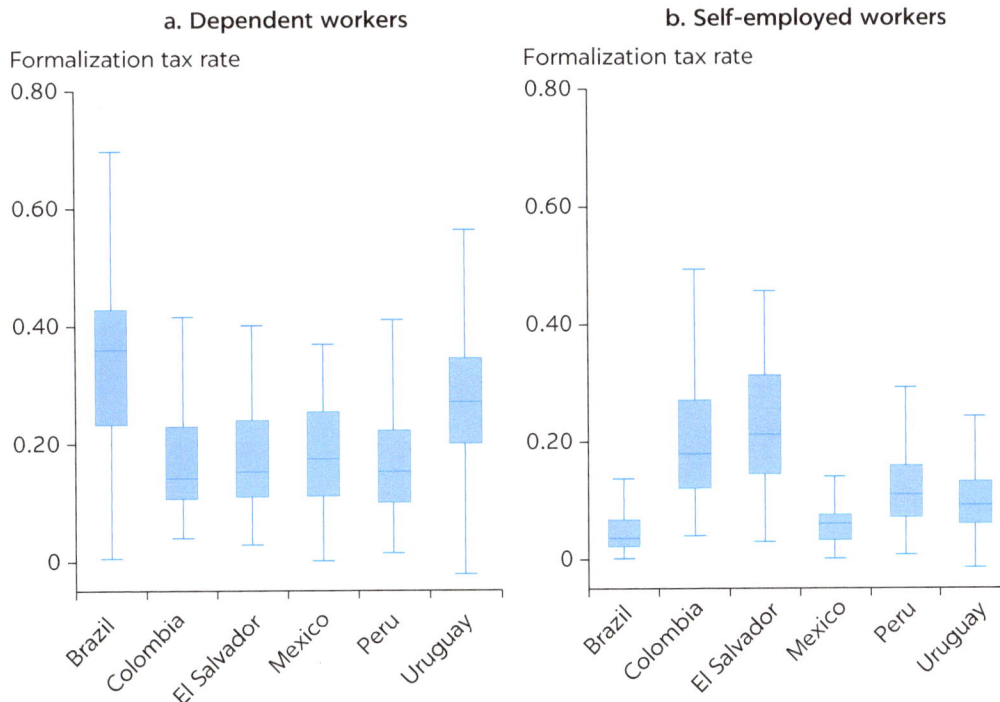

Source: Original figures for this publication, based on microsimulations using data from Brazil's 2019 National Household Sample Survey, Colombia's 2019 Great Integrated Household Survey, El Salvador's 2019 Multipurpose Household Survey, Mexico's 2018 National Survey of Household Income and Expenditure, Peru's 2019 National Household Survey, and Uruguay's 2021 Continuous Household Survey.

Special provisions and simplified tax regimes keep disincentives to a minimum for self-employed workers, while the "mainstream" contributory regimes for self-employment with fixed contribution bases can generate very high disincentives at low levels of earnings. Figure 5.2 shows how FTRs change with workers' earnings, which are expressed as multiples of the applicable minimum wage in each country. The sizes of the spheres are proportional to the number of workers observed at each wage level. In countries with simplified tax regimes for self-employed workers, such as Brazil and Mexico, the median FTR for that group is very low, below 10 percent of household income.

In contrast, the "mainstream" contributory plans can create large disincentives for self-employed workers to participate, due to fixed contribution bases, as described in chapter 4 (refer to figure 5.2, panel b, for Colombia). Due to data limitations, Colombia's simplified tax regime for independent workers is not modeled. Therefore, the strongly decreasing FTR pattern for independent workers in Colombia shows how fixed contribution bases can create high disincentives for low-earning independent workers.

FIGURE 5.2

Formalization incentives, by level of earnings, country, and employment status, 2019

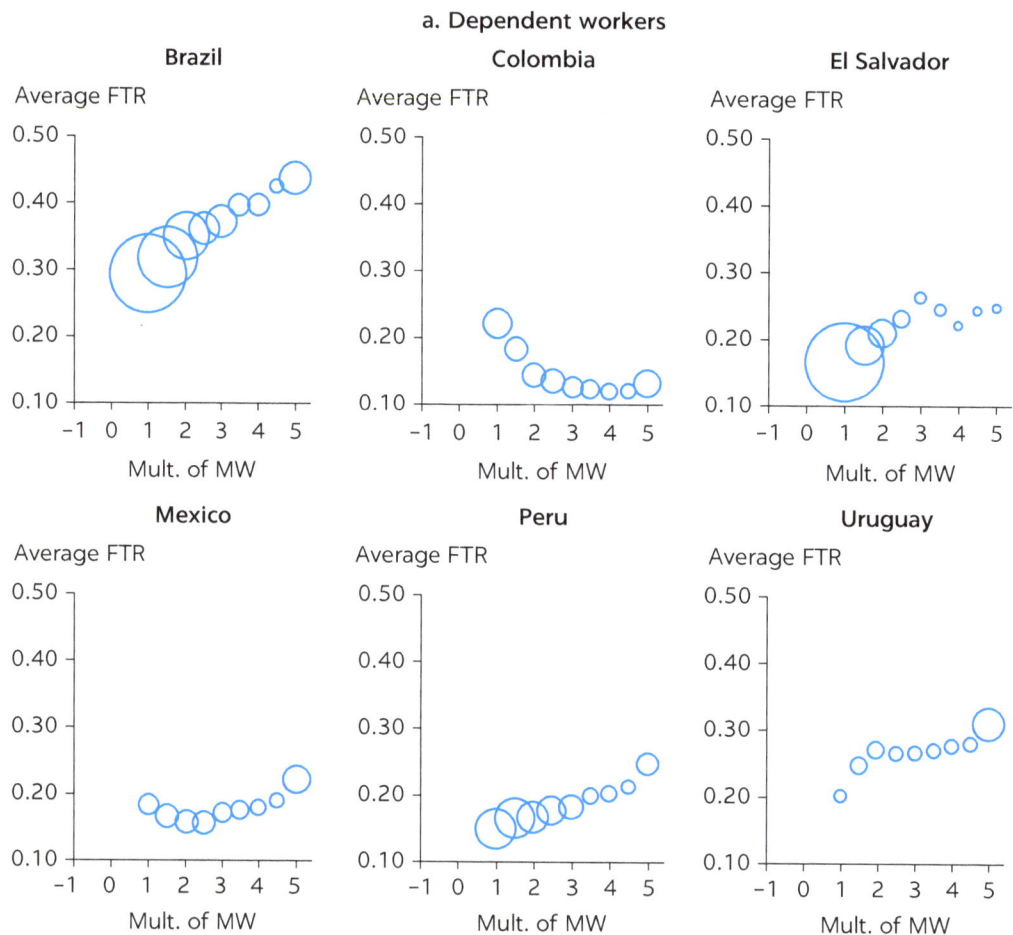

a. Dependent workers

continued

FIGURE 5.2 Formalization incentives, by level of earnings, country, and employment status, 2019, (continued)

b. Self-employed workers

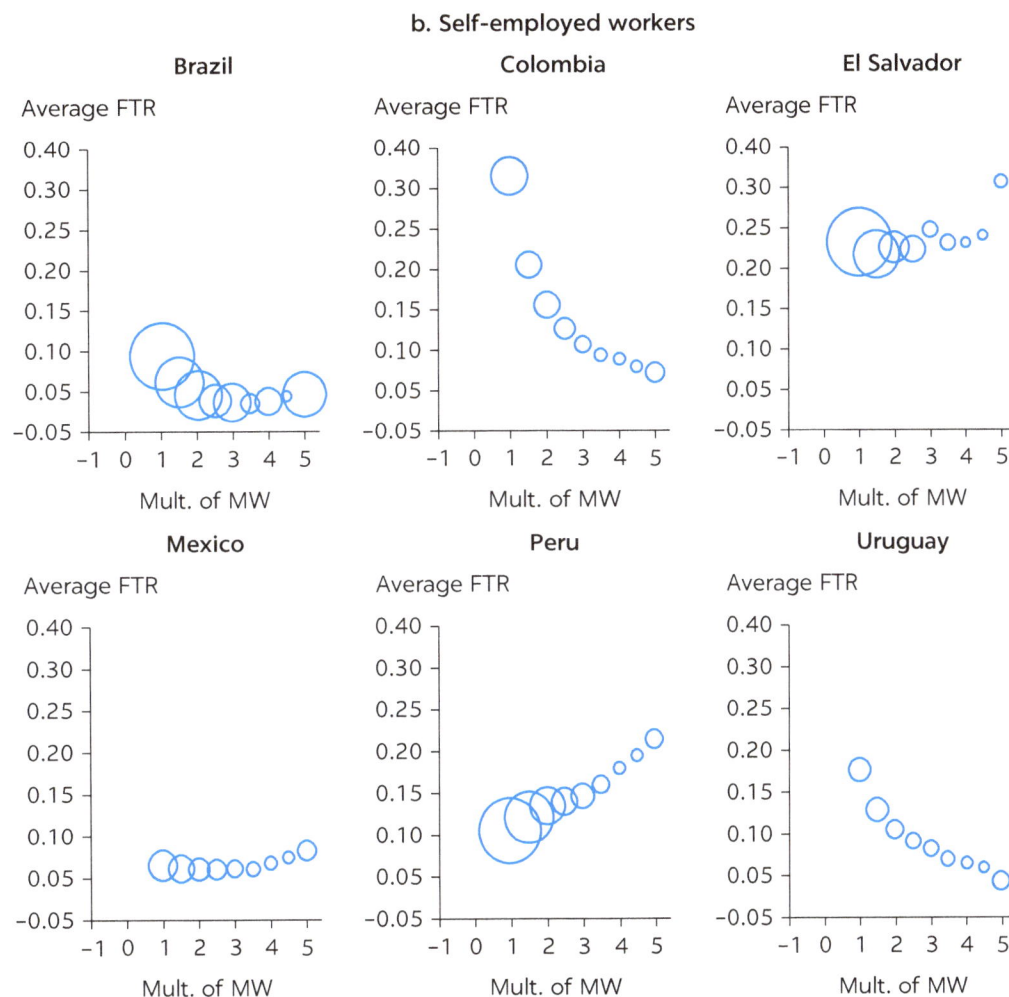

Source: Original figures for this publication, based on microsimulations using data from Brazil's 2019 National Household Sample Survey, Colombia's 2019 Great Integrated Household Survey, El Salvador's 2019 Multipurpose Household Survey, Mexico's 2018 National Survey of Household Income and Expenditure, Peru's 2019 National Household Survey, and Uruguay's 2021 Continuous Household Survey.
Note: FTR = formalization tax rate; Mult. of MW = multiple of the minimum wage.

The relatively wealthier countries tend to exhibit larger differences in formalization costs between dependent and self-employed workers, creating incentives for firms to engage in arbitrage in how they contract workers. For example, Brazil combines a progressive income tax schedule with progressive workers' pension contributions and subsidies for low-earning workers. As a result, FTRs strongly increase with wages and having a large variety of simplified tax systems results in a low FTR for self-employed workers. Anecdotal evidence from Brazil suggests that employers tend to replace dependent workers with microentrepreneurs under the MEI (Microemprendedor Individual) regime to reduce payroll taxation.[7] Such trends show that harmonization of taxation and the level of protection between dependent and self-employed regimes is needed to ensure balanced incentives.

Statutory social insurance contributions account for the largest segment of the FTR. As shown by the de jure analysis in chapter 4, social insurance contributions tend to dwarf other costs of formalization. Figure 5.3 confirms this diagnostic once the distribution of workers' characteristics is considered. For each country and group of workers, the figure shows the breakdown of the average FTR into the components due to taxes, statutory contributions, and transfers. In many countries, most workers are observed below the minimum income threshold to be subject to the income tax, further reducing its impact on formalization decisions. One exception is Mexico, where taxes play a sizable role. Those taxes include personal income tax and a federal tax.

Interestingly, the statutory incidence of contributions differs across countries, with potential impacts on wages. Figure 5.3 also shows that countries differ in who pays for the social insurance contributions—the worker or the firm. Although standard economic theory predicts that only the overall wedge matters and not the statutory split between employees and employers, recent empirical research has shown that the statutory incidence of payroll taxes matters for determining their effective incidence on wages (Benzarti 2024; Bozio et al. 2024).

FIGURE 5.3

Decomposition of formalization disincentives into social security contributions, income taxes, and transfers, by country, 2019

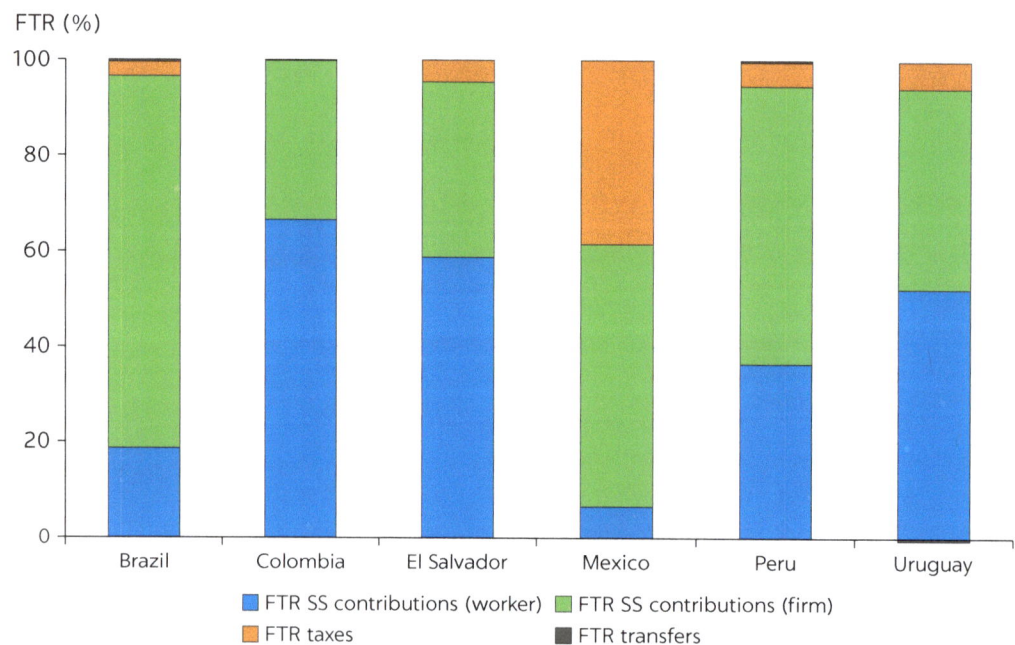

Source: Original figure for this publication, based on microsimulations using data from Brazil's 2019 National Household Sample Survey, Colombia's 2019 Great Integrated Household Survey, El Salvador's 2019 Multipurpose Household Survey, Mexico's 2018 National Survey of Household Income and Expenditure, Peru's 2019 National Household Survey, and Uruguay's 2021 Continuous Household Survey.
Note: FTR = formalization tax rate; SS = social security.

Improving the value that workers perceive in making social insurance contributions would offset most of the disincentives to comply and participate. If workers value social insurance contributions, they may not pose as much of a disincentive to workers registering. At higher levels of perceived value, these contributions instead are considered deferred compensation in the form of future benefits, such as retirement pensions and old-age care.

As discussed in chapter 3, workers' valuation depends on various factors, some of them objective and others purely informational or perceptual. Objective considerations include competition from other pressing needs for liquidity, the quality of services offered, the availability of similar noncontributory benefits, and the misalignment of institutions and individual preferences. In addition, workers may misunderstand or ignore the rights accrued from contributing to social insurance, underestimate the probability of risks covered by social insurance programs, or excessively discount benefits far in the future due to present bias or eroded trust in institutions. Some of these factors are explored in chapter 7. As those factors differ by country and worker, the FTR formula allows the valuation parameter to vary for individuals with different characteristics. For example, box 5.4 shows the correlations between formalization disincentives and workers' gender, age, education, and urban residence.

Box 5.4

Gender dimension of labor supply decisions, taxes, and benefits

The design of the tax and benefit system can impact women and men differently for several reasons. On the one hand, the design of the tax schedule and income tax filing requirements may disincentivize the "second earner" in the household—traditionally a woman—from increasing labor supply at the extensive or intensive margin. On the other hand, the design of social insurance plans might incentivize only a single household member to be registered with the social insurance institution, thereby providing coverage to all household members. Figure B5.4.1 shows the correlations between formalization disincentives and gender, age, education, and urban residence.

Higher formalization tax rates for men can be attributed to several factors related to job characteristics and socioeconomic policies. Women often occupy lower-paying, less-secure jobs, which are typically associated with lower costs of formalization relative to income. Women tend to earn lower wages because they are expected to trade off wages for flexibility, interrupt their careers to care for children and elderly family members, or face pure discrimination in wages and career opportunities. In addition, in some countries, joint taxation and family insurance plans act as disincentives for women's formal employment. Under joint taxation, a second income (usually the woman's) is taxed at a higher marginal rate, reducing the financial benefit of formal employment. Moreover, family insurance plans often cover dependents, including spouses, making formal employment less attractive for women who may already be covered under a spouse's plan, further increasing their relative formalization tax rate.

continued

Box 5.4 Gender dimension of labor supply decisions, taxes, and benefits, *(continued)*

FIGURE B5.4.1

Correlations between formalization disincentives and gender, age, education, and urban residence

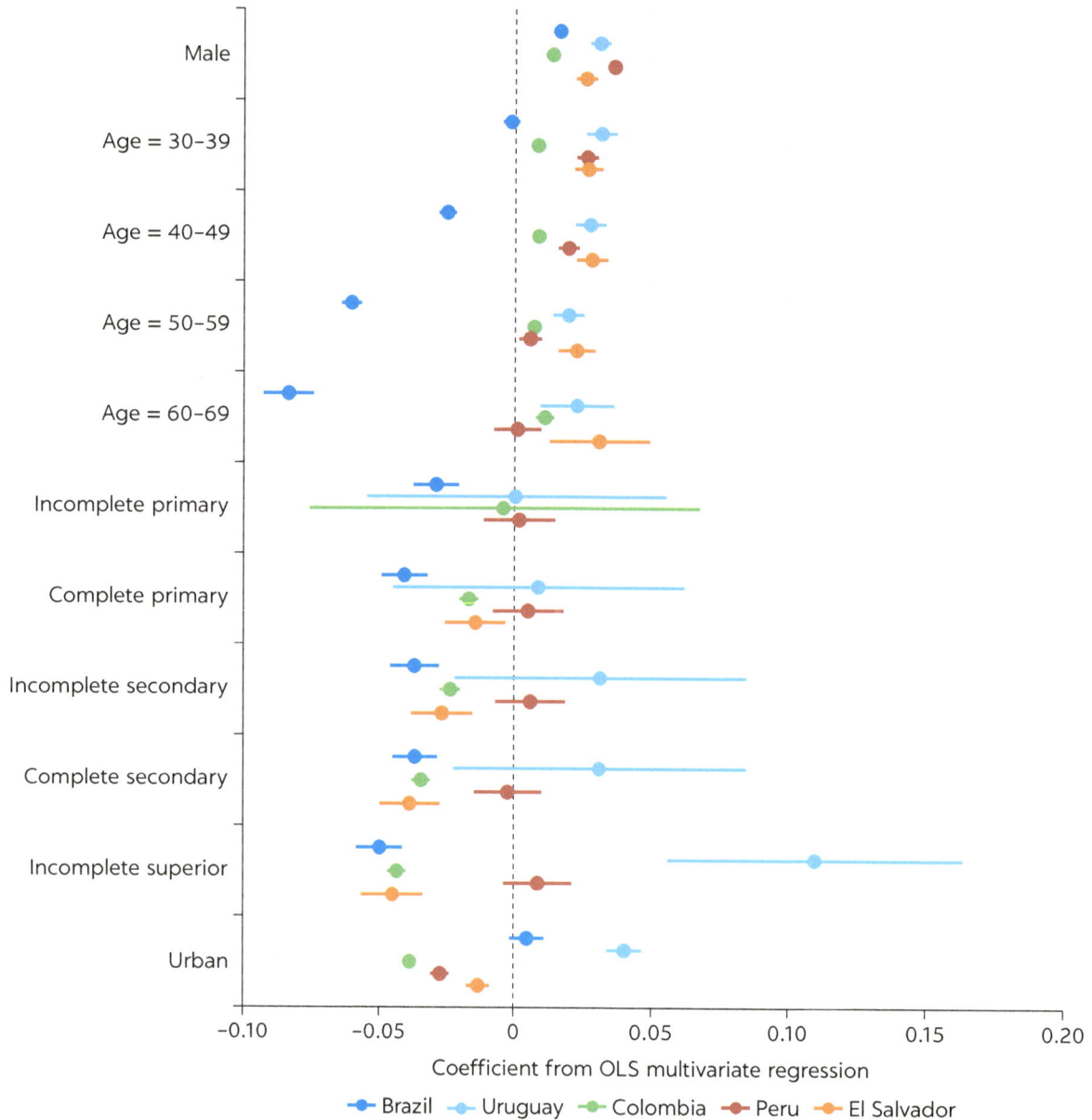

Source: Original figure for this publication, based on microsimulations using data from Brazil's 2019 National Household Sample Survey, Colombia's 2019 Great Integrated Household Survey, El Salvador's 2019 Multipurpose Household Survey, Mexico's 2018 National Survey of Household Income and Expenditure, Peru's 2019 National Household Survey, and Uruguay's 2021 Continuous Household Survey.
Note: The figure shows the effect of gender on formalization disincentives after controlling for other sociodemographic characteristics. OLS = ordinary least squares.

In addition, it is possible to assume that workers with a formally employed spouse discount the value of their own contributions to health insurance because they can benefit from spousal coverage. Similarly, the valuation of health insurance contributions could be lower for workers who may qualify for free health care due to a low household income. It is also possible to analyze the impact of policies that improve the valuation of benefits by simulating FTRs under different valuation parameters. Although performing these analyses is beyond the scope of this chapter, figure 5.4 illustrates the potential of boosting the valuation of benefits to improve formalization incentives. The figure shows how the FTR indicator changes as benefit valuation moves from 0 percent of paid contributions to 100 percent.

FIGURE 5.4

Impact of benefit valuation on formalization incentives

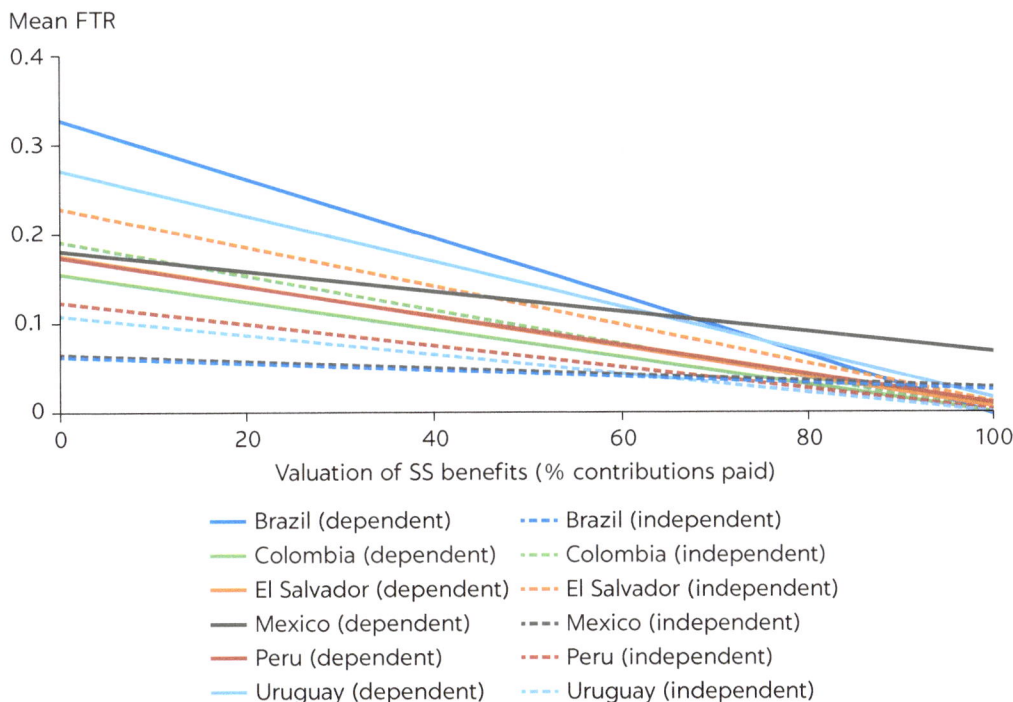

Source: Original figure for this publication, based on microsimulations using data from Brazil's 2019 National Household Sample Survey, Colombia's 2019 Great Integrated Household Survey, El Salvador's 2019 Multipurpose Household Survey, Mexico's 2018 National Survey of Household Income and Expenditure, Peru's 2019 National Household Survey, and Uruguay's 2021 Continuous Household Survey. *Note:* FTR = formalization tax rate; SS = social security.

NOTES

1. The thought experiment corresponding to the assumptions of the model is that the worker becomes registered but stays in the same firm and job. The measure easily extends to workers becoming more productive upon formalizing. However, Ulyssea (2018) showed that the formal-informal wage gap becomes very small once the analysis controls for firm fixed effects.

2. The Abono-Salarial (Salary Bonus) is an in-work benefit granted to low-wage workers who have had a formal dependent work relationship for at least 5 years.
3. The Salario Familia (Family Salary) is a child allowance for low-wage workers.
4. Jamaica is not included in this analysis due to a lack of reliable income data from survey or administrative sources.
5. One exception is Uruguay, which uses 2021 data due to changes in the survey methodology introduced by the National Statistics Office, which impede comparable application of the microsimulation tool for incidence analysis for 2019 or 2020.
6. Changes in the conditional cash transfer since 2019 have changed these results.
7. For example, refer to https://www1.folha.uol.com.br/mercado/2024/07/total -de-meis-cresce-e-pejotizacao-preocupa.shtml.

REFERENCES

Bargain, O., H. X. Jara, and D. Rivera. 2024. "Tax Disincentives to Formal Employment in Latin America." LSE International Inequality Institute Working Paper No. 144, London School of Economics and Political Science, London. https://eprints.lse.ac.uk /125368/1/LSC_III_Working_Papers_144-combined.pdf.

Benzarti, Y. 2024. "Tax Incidence Anomalies." Working Paper 32819, National Bureau of Economic Research, Cambridge, MA. https://doi.org/10.3386/w32819.

Blundell, R., A. Duncan, and C. Meghir. 1998. "Estimating Labor Supply Responses Using Tax Reforms." *Econometrica* 66 (4): 827–61.

Bobba, M., L. Flabbi, S. Levy, and M. Tejada. 2021. "Labor Market Search, Informality, and On-the-Job Human Capital Accumulation." *Journal of Econometrics* 223 (2): 433–53. https://doi.org/10.1016/j.jeconom.2019.05.026.

Bozio, A., T. Breda, J. Grenet, and A. Guillouzouic. 2024. "Does Tax-Benefit Linkage Matter for the Incidence of Payroll Taxes?" PSE Working Paper halshs-02191315, Paris School of Economics, Paris.

Harris, J. R., and M. P. Todaro. 1970. "Migration, Unemployment and Development: A Two-Sector Analysis." *American Economic Review* 60 (1): 126–42.

Jara, H. X., M. C. Deza Delgado, N. Oliva, and J. Torres. 2023. "Financial Disincentives to Formal Employment and Tax-Benefit Systems in Latin America." *International Tax and Public Finance* 30 (1): 69–113. https://doi.org/10.1007/s10797-021-09724-8.

Koettl, J., and M. Weber. 2012. "Does Formal Work Pay? The Role of Labor Taxation and Social Benefit Design in the New EU Member States." *SSRN Electronic Journal.* https://doi.org/10.2139/ssrn.2003626.

Mortensen, D. T., and C. A. Pissarides. 1994. "Job Creation and Job Destruction in the Theory of Unemployment." *Review of Economic Studies* 61 (3): 397–415. https://doi .org/10.2307/2297896.

OECD (Organisation for Economic Co-operation and Development). 2024. *Breaking the Vicious Circles of Informal Employment and Low-Paying Work.* Paris: OECD. https://doi.org/10.1787/f95c5a74-en.

Ulyssea, G. 2018. "Firms, Informality, and Development: Theory and Evidence from Brazil." *American Economic Review* 108 (8): 2015–47.

6 Reforms to Incentives and Their Simulated Importance

A COMMON OBJECTIVE MOTIVATES DIFFERENT REFORMS

The indicators of compliance and participation in tax and formal social protection structures presented in chapter 2 are a clear reminder that, although reducing the size of "economic informality" and the prevalence of informal work is a shared challenge, its features and dimensions vary substantially across countries in Latin America and the Caribbean (LAC). In addition, that job informality is a characteristic of lower-earning workers but not always of higher earners implies different policy prescriptions for Brazil, Colombia, and Uruguay on the one hand and for Peru on the other.

Furthermore, the de jure modeling presented in chapter 4 demonstrates policy and institutional similarities and also tremendous differences. A plausible priority action in Brazil or Uruguay (countries with almost no exemptions from mandatory participation) would probably be less impactful in Peru, where most job informality takes the form of self-employment, which is exempt from many government mandates. Colombia, El Salvador, and Mexico are between these extreme profiles, but, nonetheless, each case deserves closer attention.

Interestingly, the estimates of the formalization tax rates (FTRs) presented in chapter 5 show that higher-income countries tend to tax dependent workers at higher rates compared to self-employed workers. How intensively governments use earmarked payroll taxes to finance "non-Bismarckian" policies and programs (for example, universal "flat" benefits, social inclusion objectives determined beyond the labor market) is also substantially different. Finally, countries vary by the extent to which programs financed by general revenues (for example, targeted and conditional cash transfers, in-work benefits, exemptions from personal income tax, and other subsidies) are focused on workers or households earning certain levels of formal (observed) income. Given the differences in observed compliance and participation, as well as those in the "rules of the game" as captured by the de jure modeling,

A reproducibility package is available for this book in the Reproducible Research Repository at https://reproducibility.worldbank.org/catalog/330/.

it is not surprising that countries' reform priorities—although motivated by the common objective of formalizing a greater share of work—differ substantially.

This chapter analyzes how specific reform measures influence incentives. These reforms were selected from among recent policy actions taken since 2019, governments' stated policy objectives, and ongoing dialogue with counterparts and national experts. Given its importance in the earlier empirical analysis of workers' observed outcomes in chapters 2 and 5, this chapter prioritizes reforms that impact the FTR directly, which are those that alter de jure costs directly. These reforms include measures that alter "market competitiveness"—the left-hand-side horizontal axis of the conceptual framework in figure 3.3 in chapter 3.[1] However, most of the reforms analyzed in this chapter influence how workers value compliance (or participation where they are exempt from government mandates), which are on the vertical axis of the conceptual framework.

This report contributes to emergent literature on changes in social protection parameters leading to improvements in incentives (refer to box 6.1). None of the measures analyzed in this chapter changes the likelihood of being detected or the severity of sanctions for noncompliance. A growing body of empirical literature shows that investments in a government's capacity to monitor and enforce policies and regulations can have a significant, positive impact on compliance (Almeida and Ronconi 2016; Kanbur and Ronconi 2018).

Workers' response to changes in the formalization tax rate: A review of the evidence

The formalization tax rate (FTR) is a composite, synthetic measure of incentives. Yet, do economic incentives, as captured by this synthetic indicator, significantly sway actual formalization decisions? The recent empirical literature provides ample evidence that this is the case.

As this report emphasizes, not all workers face the same formalization incentives and, accordingly, impacts of varying magnitudes can be found in the literature. Research has delineated a consistent range of elasticities of formalization decisions to tax and benefit rules. However, this is not a priori obvious, as

economists have long viewed labor markets in the Latin America and the Caribbean (LAC) region as segmented in the sense that informal sector workers simply did not have access to formal jobs, or the formal-informal wage gap was too large for taxes or benefits to affect formalization decisions.

In a recent study, Bargain, Jara, and Rivera (2024) provided estimates that most directly speak to the relevance of the FTR for formalization decisions. Using microsimulations to compute FTRs in Bolivia, Colombia, and Ecuador at different points in time,

continued

Box 6.1 **Workers' response to changes in the formalization tax rate: A review of the evidence,** *(continued)*

the researchers linked changes in formality with reforms that impacted the FTR differently for various groups. They measured elasticities of formalization in the 0.3–0.5 range. Therefore, increasing the FTR by 10 percent (for example, through a payroll tax increase of about 1 percentage point) decreased formal employment by 3–5 percent. Koettl and Weber (2012), who introduced the concept of the FTR, obtained a larger elasticity of 1.1, but they relied on static cross-country comparisons.

These results are supported by a larger literature that examines the components of the FTR (social insurance contributions, noncontributory benefits, and taxes) in isolation. The evidence is thinnest on income taxes, likely because income tax bases are typically narrow in lower-middle-income countries, so that changes in income tax rates do not affect employment decisions for the bulk of workers. Indeed, as shown in chapter 5, the tax component of the FTR is small in most of the countries examined. Consistently, McKay, Pirttilä, and Schimanski (2019) found little impact of income taxation on formalization decisions in Sub-Saharan Africa.

As shown in chapter 5, the largest component of the FTR is social security contributions, and their importance for formality decisions is evident in the literature. Several studies have considered "natural experiments" involving payroll tax reforms (sometimes through wage subsidies) in the LAC region, as well as in Ethiopia and Türkiye. Those studies used various control groups to isolate reform impacts. Although some studies found no impacts on formal employment and pension participation (Bedi et al. 2022; Cruces, Galiani, and Kidyb 2010; Gruber 1997), others measured elasticities ranging between 0.4 and 1.0 (Aşık et al. 2022; Betcherman, Daysal, and Pagés 2010; Kugler and Kugler 2009; Kugler, Kugler, and Herrera Prada 2017).

The literature emphasizes that these responses will be larger if employers cannot pass higher labor costs on to employees in the form of lower wages. This could happen due to downward wage rigidities such as relatively high, statutory minimum wages or if employees do not value social security benefits. Consistently with the discussion of benefit valuation in chapter 7, the empirical link between contributions and benefits affects the decision to formalize and also whether to underreport earnings when working formally.

Becerra (2024) showed that a 1993 increase in the vesting period necessary to obtain Colombia's minimum pension reduced formality by 2.8 percent. A longer vesting period implies that the money's worth of participating in the pension program decreases for workers who expect to qualify only for the minimum contributory pension. Thus, lower benefit valuation increases disincentives to formalize, as shown in chapter 5. The effect is not limited to being registered but also concerns the fraction of earnings reported. Recent studies in Brazil, Mexico, and Uruguay showed that underreporting is severe at younger ages in defined-benefit systems, because pensions depend on earnings reported late in the worker's career (Feinmann, Hsu Rocha, and Lauletta 2024; Kumler, Verhoogen, and Frías 2020; Lauletta and Bergolo 2023).

The last component of the FTR is noncontributory benefits. If formalization jeopardizes workers' eligibility for cash transfers, they may choose to remain informal. For example, Bergolo and Cruces (2021) found that a means-tested social assistance transfer in Uruguay reduced formal employment by 6 percentage points among beneficiaries (other examples of this effect include De Brauw et al. [2015] and Garganta and Gasparini [2015]). Likewise, guaranteeing social security benefits to workers who do not contribute reduces incentives

continued

Box 6.1 Workers' response to changes in the formalization tax rate: A review of the evidence, *(continued)*

to remain formal. For example, the extension of health insurance coverage to unregistered workers in Mexico (Seguro Popular [Popular Insurance]) reduced social security registrations by 4 percent in smaller firms (Bosch and Campos-Vazquez 2014).

Social pensions can also weaken the link between contributions and benefits. Cabezon (2024) considered Chile's 2008 expansion of its minimum pension, which reduced the

contribution-benefit link by 33 percent, and found that formal earnings declined by 2.9 percent. However, that study also estimated that the stronger insurance provided by the new minimum pension increased welfare overall despite the previously mentioned labor market distortions. Thus, higher formality is a key outcome, but it must sometimes be traded off against other important objectives.

The analysis is presented in the sequence of the three dimensions of the conceptual framework and incentive channel rather than as a complete package of measures for each country. For country policy dialogue, it would make more sense to show the selected reforms by country to assess the power of an integrated reform package. However, in this chapter, the reforms are organized along the incentive channels and dimensions of the conceptual framework to draw inferences about their impacts on compliance and participation incentives.

The chapter starts by detailing the reform measures by country. Table 6.1 describes the reforms analyzed in six country cases—Brazil, Colombia, El Salvador, Mexico, Peru, and Uruguay—and summarizes the policy rationale for each measure. These policies are organized by country (refer to column 1) and by the dimension and specific incentive channel of the conceptual framework through which they operate (refer to column 4).

The reform analysis presented in this chapter answers three questions that are vital to prioritizing measures and crafting a reform strategy:

- How many people are affected by a measure? (For what share of the working population does the reform alter incentives?)

- Who are the people affected by the reform?

- By how much are their incentives changed?

The behavioral responses to these incentive changes are not estimated. The simulation tools are "static" in that subsequent changes in compliance and participation behaviors are not analyzed. This is an important limitation of the scope of the analysis in this report and its value for policy makers seeking specific advice. Follow-up analysis is planned that will provide credible estimates of the likely gains in compliance and participation—formalization of work—that can reasonably be expected from these reforms and others not discussed in this report.

The analysis also does not include scrutiny of each country's public revenue and expenditure position or how they would restructure other taxes to accommodate the reforms. Both are extensions of this regional study that can be pursued through country-level dialogue.

TABLE 6.1 Select reform measures analyzed for their impact on the FTR

COUNTRY	REFORM MEASURE	REFORM DESCRIPTION	RELEVANT DIMENSION AND INCENTIVE CHANNEL
Brazil	Increase in the Bolsa Familia eligibility threshold and generosity	This reform was implemented in 2022. The eligibility threshold increased from R$89 per capita (basic benefit) and R$178 per capita (variable benefit) to a unified threshold of R$218 per capita. The benefit levels increased from R$89 per family to R$142 per household member for the basic benefit and from R$41 to R$150 per child ages 0–6 for the child benefit. Thus, a family must receive at least R$600. If the sum of the benefits is lower, the family receives a top-up to reach R$600.	Valuation dimension: value of outside options and benefits
	Disregard of the social pension benefit Beneficio de Prestação Continuada (Continuous Cash Benefit) in the determination of Bolsa Familia eligibility	A reform recently presented to the Congress proposes to disregard the disability benefit and social pension benefit (equivalent to 1 times the MW) from the family income used to determine eligibility for Bolsa Familia.	Valuation dimension: value of outside options and benefits
	Reduction of payroll taxation by eliminating INCRA and Salario Educação (Education Allowance)	Elimination of the payroll tax for INCRA and Salario Educação would increase the gross wage by about 2.7 percentage points.	Valuation dimension: overreach and misalignment of government instruments
Colombia	Increase in the MW	From 2019 to 2024, the MW increased almost 57 percent in a country with an already-binding statutory wage floor. The analysis isolates the effects on incentives of the MW increase.	Labor market competitiveness: increase in the MW

continued

TABLE 6.1 Select reform measures analyzed for their impact on the FTR, *(continued)*

COUNTRY	REFORM MEASURE	REFORM DESCRIPTION	RELEVANT DIMENSION AND INCENTIVE CHANNEL
	Reduction of payroll taxation, lowering the statutory contribution to the CCF to prioritize job search, income, and other forms of support to unemployed workers	The CCF are complex institutions that finance a range of services. Of the social protection functions delegated to the CCF, income and job search support services are of highest priority for employment and are the least likely to have a viable publicly or privately provided substitute. These components have been found to be underfunded and have not been used by independent workers, for whom CCF are voluntary.	Valuation dimension: reducing the cost of benefits, reducing misalignment, and increasing tax morale
	Reductions of the minimum income used as the lowest permitted base of contributions to social insurance	Lowering the minimum contribution base from 1 MW to 72 percent of the MW, which corresponds to the average income of nonvulnerable workers according to the SISBEN.	Valuation dimension: reducing the cost of benefits, reducing misalignment, and increasing tax morale
El Salvador	Removal of the maximum contributory wage	Social security contributions are regressive, because higher-wage earners pay proportionally less. A more-equitable system could be achieved by converting social security contributions to a more-progressive model.	Valuation dimension: value of outside options and benefits
Mexico	Increase in the MW	Since 2019, the statutory MW in Mexico has more than doubled.[a] This rise was implemented in annual increases between 2019 and 2024. The MW was increased from Mex$88.36 per day to Mex$248.93 per day (in 2018 prices, Mex$193.04 per day).	Labor market competitiveness: rationing and queuing
	"Universalization" of priority health coverage (reducing the IMSS contribution by the cost of providing preventive, primary, and essential health services)	Repeated administrations have committed to implementing the constitutional right to health coverage in Mexico. Given fiscal constraints, a pragmatic step toward delivering on this promise is to make preventative, primary, and priority treatments free at the point of service for all people, reducing statutory contributions by an amount equivalent to the costs of these services.	Valuation dimension: value of outside options and benefits

continued

TABLE 6.1 **Select reform measures analyzed for their impact on the FTR,** *(continued)*

COUNTRY	REFORM MEASURE	REFORM DESCRIPTION	RELEVANT DIMENSION AND INCENTIVE CHANNEL
	"Universalization" of child care services (eliminating the prior contribution requirement, reducing the IMSS contribution by the current statutory rate for child care)	The principal obstacle to women's greater participation in the labor force and their formal employment is the lack of quality child care. As a first step toward a commitment to a National Care System, child care services would be made available to all parents, and statutory contributions would be reduced by the corresponding amount.	Valuation dimension: value of outside options and benefits
Peru	Increase in the progressivity of contributions	Currently, all workers pay the same amount of contributions. To make the system more progressive, firm contributions for health insurance, unemployment insurance, and work accident insurance are made progressive, as well as the pension contributions paid by the worker. Currently, the system offers two extra wages at the end of the year—low-wage workers receive one and high-wage workers receive two.	Valuation: social norms (fairness considerations)
Uruguay	Elimination of the formal income threshold to receive noncontributory family social transfers (AFAM–PE)	Uruguay's main noncontributory transfer program is called AFAM–PE. Households with children (who must be attending school) apply to be tested by a proxy means test, which is also combined with a cap on formal income. In 2022, this cap was eliminated, as it could work as a negative incentive to participation in formal jobs. The effects of the policy change were simulated.	Valuation dimension: value of outside options and benefits
	Increase in the valuation of unemployment benefits for independent workers	The benefits for independent workers were reformed, in particular, unemployment insurance plans.	Valuation dimension: value of outside options and benefits

Source: Original table for this publication.
Note: AFAM–PE = Asignaciones Familiares del Plan de Equidad (Family Allowances–Equity Plan); CCF = Cajas de Compensación Familiar (Family Compensation Funds); FTR = formalization tax rate; IMSS = Mexican Institute of Social Security; INCRA = Instituto Nacional de Colonização e Reforma Agrária (National Institute for Colonization and Agrarian Reform); MW = minimum wage; SISBEN = System of Identification of Social Program Beneficiaries.
a. OECD 2024.

DIMENSION 1: POLICIES AFFECTING LABOR MARKET COMPETITIVENESS

In less-competitive labor markets, employers' bargaining power increases, making it less likely that employment complies with regulations or that wages incentivize participation. As discussed in chapter 3, competitiveness could be curtailed due to the labor market structure (monopsony, with few firms hiring in certain occupations or segments of the labor market) but also due to labor market regulations, especially high minimum wages relative to median earnings. Compared to those in high-income countries, minimum wages relative to the median wage are relatively higher in developing countries, including those examined in this report. This policy has drawn more attention recently given the increases in minimum wages in Costa Rica and Mexico (Maloney et al. 2024).

This section explores how labor market policies may affect the incentives to comply and participate in Mexico and Colombia, which were chosen to showcase the potential effects of minimum wage changes on incentives. Among the country cases, Mexico's minimum wage policy has been the most substantial in recent years. Colombia's national minimum wage has been high and rising relative to median earnings over the longest period and, as shown by the analysis in chapters 4 and 5, the high minimum wage increases the FTR.

The examples of Mexico and Colombia provide a consistent message: Increases in the minimum wage contribute to lower incentives to comply or participate, as the increased wage leads to increased rationing and queuing but also through the valuation channel.[2] As explained in chapter 3, increases in the minimum wage incentivize employers to hire fewer workers who comply with the regulations, resulting in an increase in noncomplying dependent workers and a larger share of workers in self-employment in the tertiary sector, passing the burden of the payments of the contributions for social insurance to self-employed workers.

The FTR analysis also shows that this policy may create important disincentives for self-employed workers to participate in social insurance plans due to the design of the payment system. By tying the payment of the contributions to the statutory minimum wage—by establishing a minimum level of contributions as in Colombia or by making the contributions proportional as in Mexico—self-employed workers may find it too expensive for what they receive or may even find it unaffordable. Simulations of the impact of an increase in the minimum wage on the FTR for all countries are shown in annex 6A.

Increased minimum wage in Mexico

The minimum wage has increased substantially in Mexico since 2018—from Mex$88.36 per day in 2018 to Mex$248.93 per day in 2024, an increase of 118 percent in real terms.[3] An increase of this size affects the formal labor demand for low-wage dependent workers, as well as the incentives to formalize other segments of the labor market, because social insurance contributions for self-employed workers depend on the minimum wage. For example, in Mexico, self-employed workers make payments for disability and life insurance contributions based on the minimum wage. Hence, an increase in the minimum wage increases the costs of compliance and participation.

Using the FTR to examine the indirect effect of the minimum wage on incentives to formalize shows that mainly low-wage self-employed workers are impacted. The simulation exercise analyzes a real minimum wage increase of 118.5 percent. The overall simulated impact on the FTR is significant: It increases the FTR by 3.1 percentage points (p.p.), from 27.9 to 31.0 percent, and the effect is concentrated among self-employed workers (refer to figure 6.1).[4] Additional analysis shows that the effect is larger for those with less schooling, fewer hours of work, lower wages, and larger families (for more details, refer to Avila, Freije-Rodríguez, and Marín 2024).

FIGURE 6.1

Effects on the FTR due to a statutory increase in the minimum wage in Mexico, by worker type, 2018

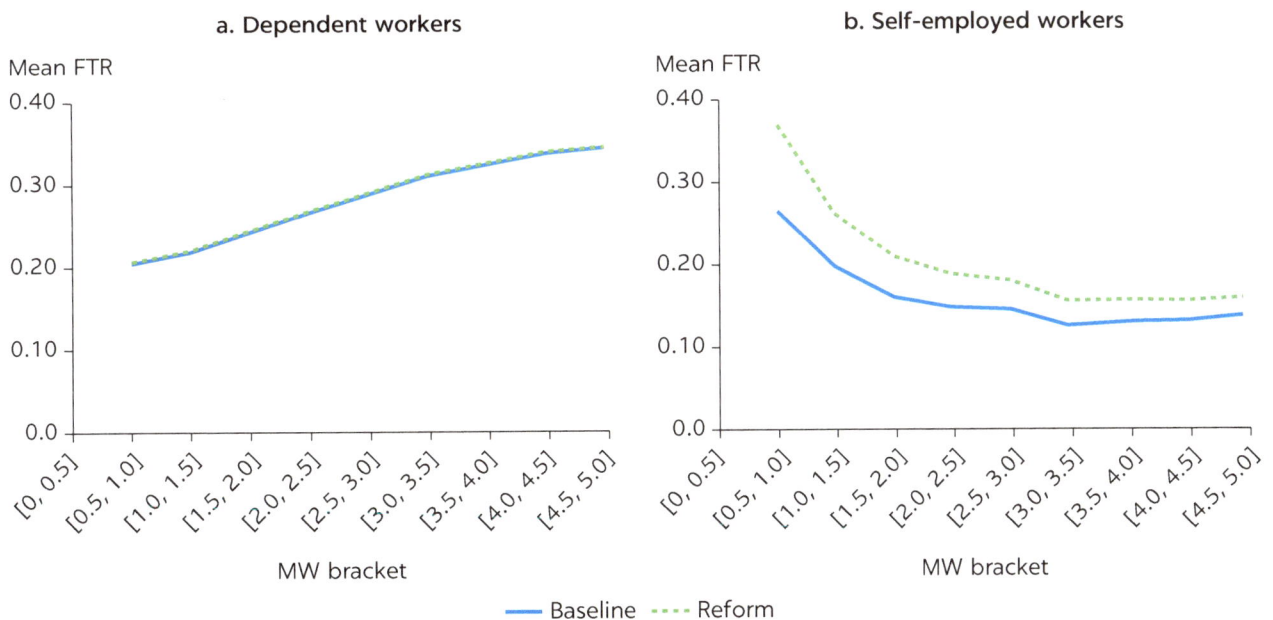

Source: Original figures for this publication using data from Mexico's 2018 National Survey of Household Income and Expenditure.
Note: MW brackets are assigned based on formal earnings. FTR = formalization tax rate; MW = minimum wage.

Increased minimum wage in Colombia

As in Mexico, Colombia has seen substantial increases in the minimum wage over the past 5 years. Between 2019, the baseline year of the simulations, and 2024, Colombia's nominal minimum wage rose by almost 57 percent (corresponding to a real increase of 14 percent), a striking increase for a country already recognized for having a high minimum wage (Col$828,116) relative to the median wage (around Col$400,000). The higher minimum wage drove up the minimum amount required for social insurance contributions. For people earning less than but close to the minimum wage, the increases raised the disincentive to participate.

The increases in the minimum wage in Colombia have created additional disincentives. The simulation illustrates how the statutory real increases in the minimum wage from 2019 to 2024 would have influenced the FTR for Colombian workers in 2019 by raising the cost of compliance and participation. The increases in the minimum wage raised disincentives through two channels: first, by increasing the cost of formal employment and pushing more workers into noncompliant employment or self-employment, and second, by raising the cost of participation for lower-income self-employed workers.

This reform disproportionately affects low-income workers, particularly dependent workers earning below 1 times the minimum wage and independent workers earning up to 2.5 times the minimum wage (refer to figure 6.2). Market competitiveness is hindered by the rising costs of formality driven by minimum

FIGURE 6.2

Effects on the FTR due to statutory increases in the minimum wage in Colombia, by worker type, 2019

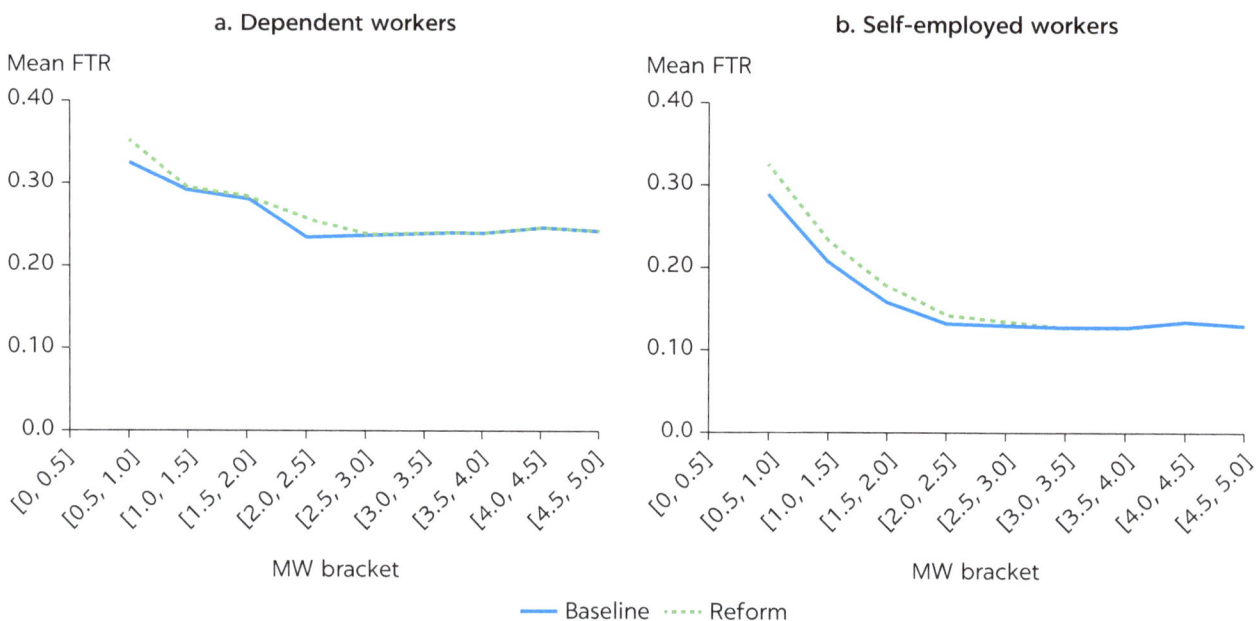

Source: Original figures for this publication using data from the 2019 Colombian National Administrative Department of Statistics Large Integrated Household Survey.
Note: MW brackets are assigned based on formal earnings. FTR = formalization tax rate; MW = minimum wage.

wage increases, as discussed in chapter 3. Dependent workers earning less than the minimum wage are likely to experience higher compliance costs, and some households newly eligible for the country's transportation subsidy may also face increased compliance burdens.

For independent (self-employed) workers, the base for contributions is 40 percent of their labor income, which creates a significant disincentive to formalize. The effect of the increased FTR is to lower wages by 4.2 percent for workers with wages lower than but close to the minimum wage. The effect becomes negligible for dependent workers earning just above 2 times the minimum wage, as the transport subsidy is no longer provided to them. For independent workers earning just above 2.5 times the minimum wage, 40 percent of their labor income reaches 1 times the minimum wage (refer to figure 6.3). These effects are most pronounced among workers with lower

FIGURE 6.3

Changes in the FTR due to the real increase in the minimum wage in Colombia, 2019–24

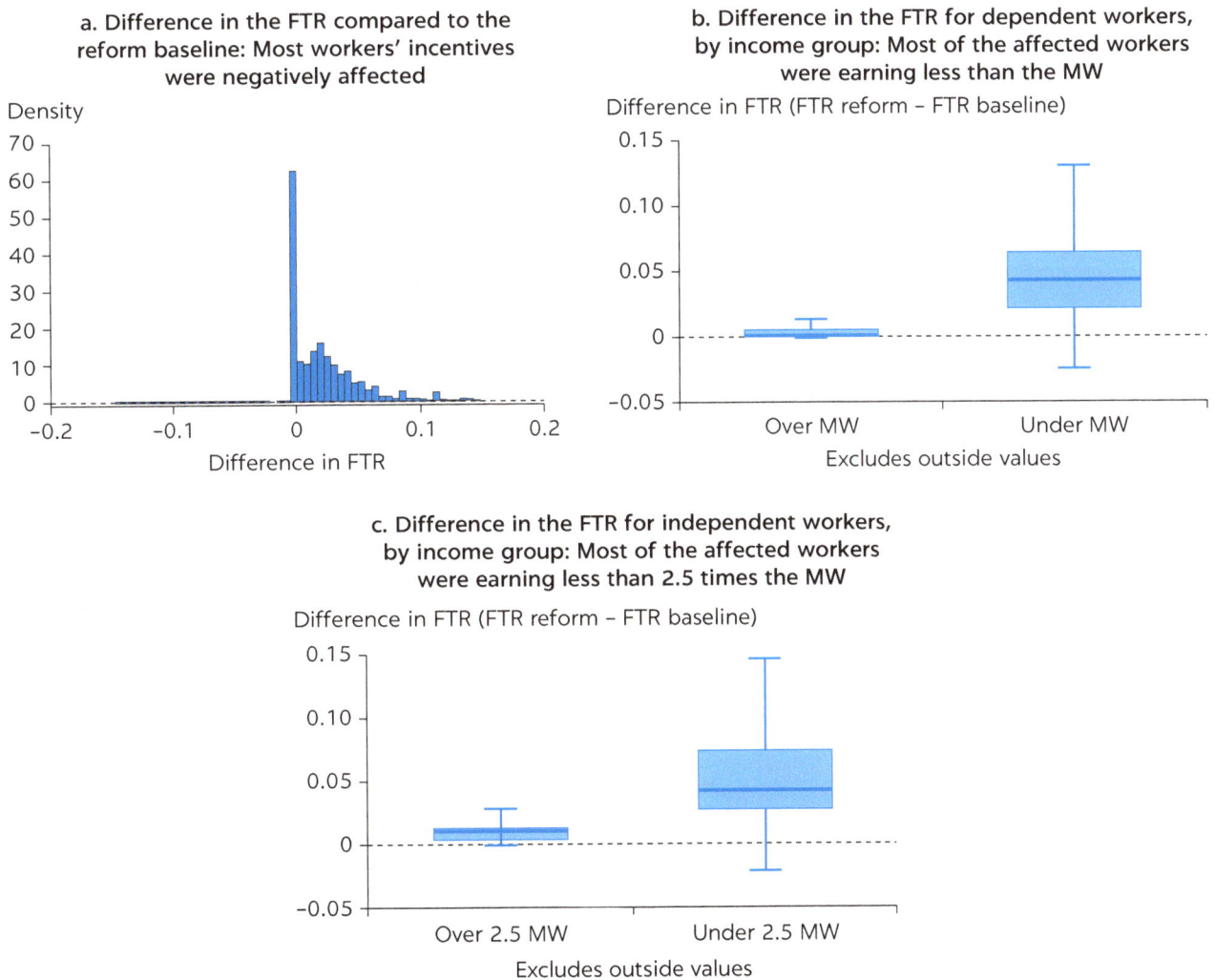

a. Difference in the FTR compared to the reform baseline: Most workers' incentives were negatively affected

b. Difference in the FTR for dependent workers, by income group: Most of the affected workers were earning less than the MW

c. Difference in the FTR for independent workers, by income group: Most of the affected workers were earning less than 2.5 times the MW

Source: Original figures for this publication using data from the 2019 Colombian National Administrative Department of Statistics Large Integrated Household Survey.
Note: FTR = formalization tax rate; MW = minimum wage.

educational attainment (less than tertiary education), rural populations, employees in smaller companies or sectors such as agriculture and wholesale trade, people in households with more members and more children, and the younger population with more working hours.

As the minimum wage continues to climb, its unintended consequence is a reduction in Colombia's market competitiveness. The high wage floor increases the financial burden for employers and raises the barrier for workers to formalize their employment. The result is a labor market where businesses are discouraged from hiring formally, and workers are increasingly pushed into the informal economy to avoid escalating costs. In this context, the simulation makes clear that, although it is well-intentioned, the continuous upward trend of the minimum wage has created a counterproductive dynamic. This dynamic undermines formal employment opportunities, particularly for vulnerable groups, and weakens overall market efficiency.

DIMENSION 2: CHANGES IN WORKERS' PERCEIVED VALUE OF COMPLYING AND PARTICIPATING

Changes in the perceived value of complying with labor regulations influence workers' and employers' decisions to participate in formal employment. While some policies aim to strengthen enforcement or raise awareness, others focus on directly altering the cost-benefit calculation individuals face when deciding whether to formalize. Dimension 2 of the framework examines policies that improve the perceived returns to formal participation. The following subsections analyze reforms that reduce the de jure wedge in absolute terms in Brazil and Mexico; policies directly increasing perceived value by reducing social security contributions or increasing expected future benefits in Mexico, Colombia, Uruguay, El Salvador, and Peru; and policies influencing the value of outside options and benefits in Brazil and Uruguay.

Policies that reduce the de jure wedge in absolute terms

The most direct way to eliminate distortions and incentivize compliance with regulations is to reduce the size of taxes that do not create any value to the worker or the firm. As shown in figure 4.2 in chapter 4, the size of the de jure tax wedge is relatively high for countries in the LAC region. Combined with low tax morale—discussed at greater length in chapter 7—and the overall ineffectiveness of public spending, the large tax wedge reduces the incentive to comply with regulations. This section tests policies to address this: first, elimination of taxes collected through the payroll in Brazil, and second, changes in child care contributions in Mexico.

The simulations of the FTR for Brazil, Colombia, and Mexico confirm that increasing the tax wedge decreases the incentive to comply or participate to a small extent.[5] These simulations call attention to an important trade-off that policy makers often face, between introducing large changes for a small segment of payers or smaller changes for a broader base. Reforms that target the incentives of those at the margin could be more effective, for example, in the case of Mexico. However, failing to account for all the distributional effects may result in more disincentives than the policy intended. Simulations of a reduction in the de jure tax wedge for all the case study countries are shown in annex 6A.

Brazil's elimination of payroll taxes except the personal income tax

Reducing the tax wedge by eliminating nonvalued contributions could increase incentives toward compliance. A potential focus for policy reform could be the removal of employer contributions that neither directly benefit workers nor are valued by employers.[6] This approach aims to increase the valuation of social insurance benefits by reducing the cost of complying and participating without affecting benefit quality.

As shown in chapter 4, several payroll taxes, such as the Salário Educação (Education Allowance) and contributions to the Instituto Nacional de Colonização e Reforma Agrária (National Institute for Colonization and Agrarian Reform, an agricultural fund), are seen as additional costs that do not provide direct benefits to the employees themselves.[7] Therefore, the following simulation explores the impact of removing specific employer payroll taxes. By eliminating those, the policy aims to reduce employer payroll costs by 2.7 p.p. of the total taxes and contributions on gross earnings of 35.8 percent, thus lowering the financial burden on employers.

This type of reform improves the incentives to comply with regulations. On the one hand, the reduction in payroll costs is expected to have a low-intensity impact, given the relatively small decrease in overall contribution rates. Thus, the FTR does not undergo a sizable change compared to other reform simulations for Brazil introduced later in this chapter. On the other hand, the scope of the impact of this reform is large, as all dependent workers would be affected by the same amount (because the payroll tax is reduced for everyone equally). At the margin, the policy could make formal employment more attractive to employers, potentially leading to an increase in the number of formal jobs available in the market (refer to figure 6.4).

FIGURE 6.4

Elimination of payroll taxes and changes in the FTR in Brazil, 2019

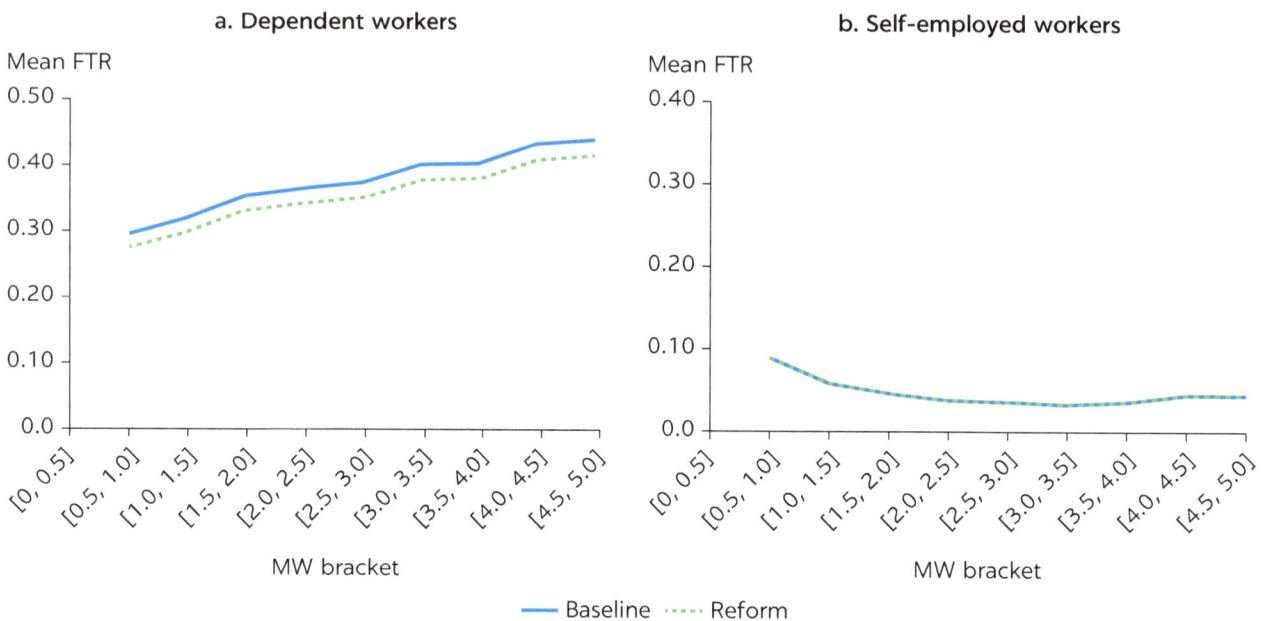

Source: Original figures for this publication using data from Brazil's 2019 National Household Sample Survey.
Note: MW brackets are assigned based on formal earnings. FTR = formalization tax rate; MW = minimum wage.

Mexico's changes in child care contributions

Removing child care contributions shows limited impact on formalization incentives in Mexico. This simulation explores the elimination of the social security contribution for child care centers (guarderías), which currently amounts to 1 percent of the contribution base salary for employees only, as neither employers nor self-employed workers contribute to this benefit.[8] The impact on the FTR is minimal, showing a reduction of only 0.6 p.p., from 27.9 to 27.3 percent. This modest effect is uniformly distributed across workers, with no significant variations by age, education level, wage bracket, or working hours (Avila, Freije-Rodríguez, and Marín 2024).

The limited impact can be attributed to two factors: the small contribution rate (1 percent) and its narrow application only to dependent workers, effectively covering just half of the working population. As illustrated in figure 6.5, the reform shows no effect on employers and self-employed workers, while producing only a marginal reduction in the tax burden for employees.

Policies that increase perceived value by reducing contributions or increasing benefits

Valuation, or the value that workers perceive, is an important channel of influence on incentives. As explained in chapter 3, this channel not only

FIGURE 6.5

Changes in child care contributions and in the FTR in Mexico, 2018

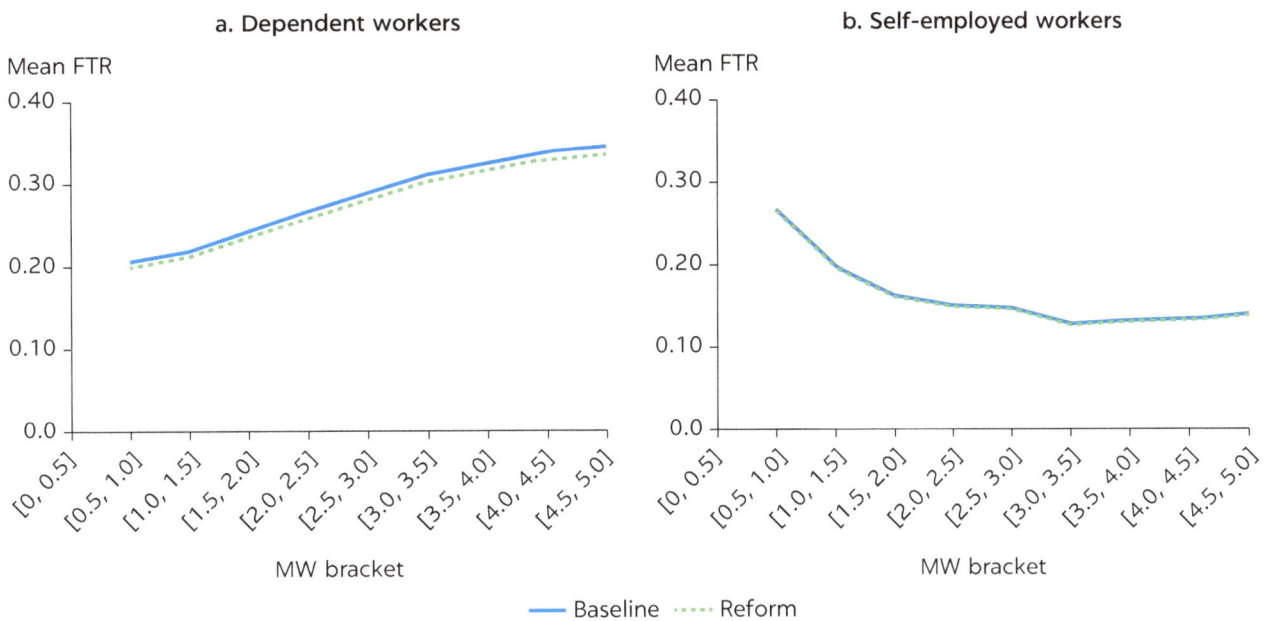

Source: Original figures for this publication using data from Mexico's 2018 National Survey of Household Income and Expenditure.
Note: MW brackets are assigned based on formal earnings. FTR = formalization tax rate; MW = minimum wage.

operates through the contribution payments made for social insurance but also operates through the scheme design, such as the minimum years of contributions for eligibility, quality of the benefit received when the covered risk materializes, and perceived fairness of the system. The analysis in this subsection examines the impacts on the incentives to comply and participate in a set of hypothetical reforms: changes to financial protection from health care costs in Mexico, a reduction in payroll contributions in Colombia, an unemployment insurance benefit in Uruguay, much-broader take up of a lower minimum contribution base in Colombia, a health insurance reform in El Salvador, and a reform of various statutory contributions in Peru. Simulations of changes in valuations for all the countries are shown in annex 6A.

Incentives to formalize can be tackled not only by reducing contributions for social insurance but also by coupling them with highly valued benefits and services. The mix of policies examined through the FTR shows that reductions in contribution payments increase the incentives to comply with the schemes. The impact is usually higher on low-income workers, as these contributions represent a higher cost burden of compliance on their already low wages.

Mexico's changes in financial protection from the cost of health care

Mexico has long sought to provide enhanced financial protection against health care costs to the large segment of its working population and their families that are not currently covered by social insurance. The hypothetical reform simulated here seeks to "universalize" coverage by removing the statutory contribution requirement for a basic package of the most vital health treatments, both preventative and remedial, shifting the financing for these services from payroll contributions to general taxation. This shift would result in reducing the fixed fee (cuota fija) of the Mexican Institute of Social Security (IMSS) health insurance contributions from 20.40 to 9.06 percent of the Unidad de Medida y Actualizacion (UMA; Unit Measure of Adjustment), which is the earnings reference used for calculating contributions. This hypothetical reform would universalize access to health care, possibly through the newly created IMSS–Bienestar but for the whole population, funded through general revenues rather than payroll taxes, making it effectively a noncontributory risk-pooling and redistribution plan.

This reform would impact the incentives for all types of workers similarly (refer to figure 6.6). Namely, it would lead to an important reduction in the FTR for workers earning below the minimum wage (and even for those under the augmented minimum wage). However, the size of the reduction in the FTR tapers off as worker incomes increase. Avila, Freije-Rodríguez, and Marín (2024) showed that the effect, again, is higher for those with less schooling,

FIGURE 6.6

"Universalizing" access to health coverage through reductions in statutory contributions for health in Mexico, 2018

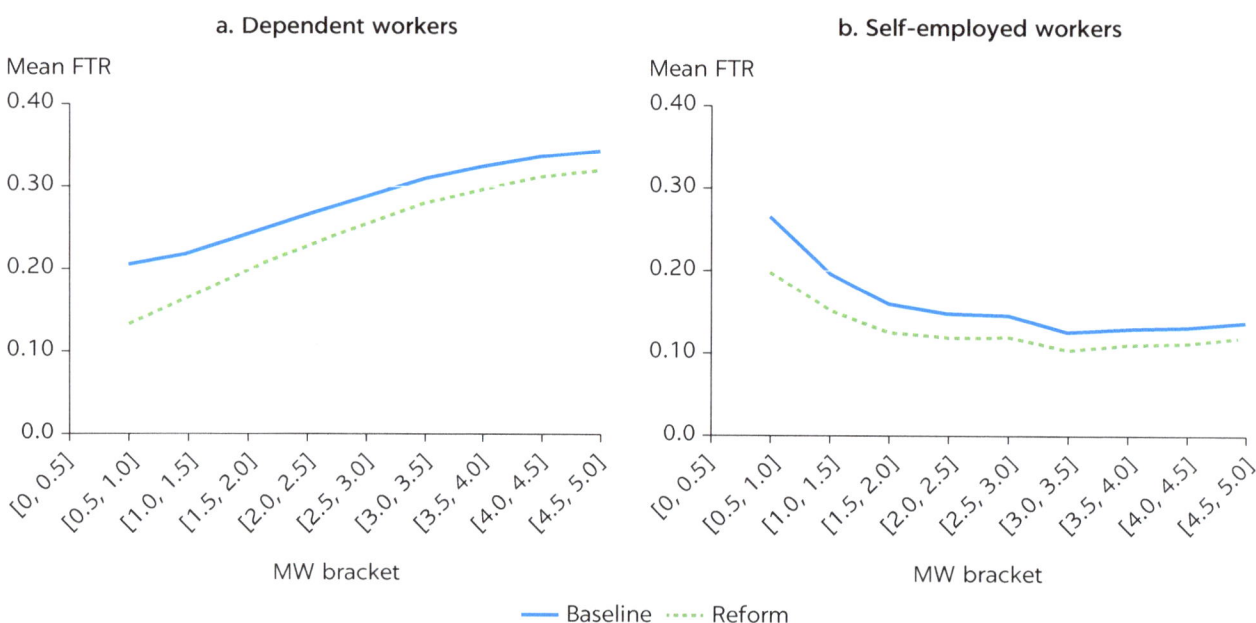

Source: Original figures for this publication using data from Mexico's 2018 National Survey of Household Income and Expenditure.
Note: MW brackets are assigned based on formal earnings. FTR = formalization tax rate; MW = minimum wage.

fewer hours of work, and smaller multiples of the minimum wage. This finding is because, although the reform involves an important reduction in the contribution rate, the base of the contribution (the UMA) is fixed for all workers, so it represents a smaller share of household income for workers with higher earnings.

Colombia's reduced contribution to the Cajas de Compensación Familiar

While the Cajas de Compensación Familiar (CCF; Family Compensation Funds) offer important and valued services, most vulnerable workers do not participate. Of the social protection functions delegated to the CCF, income and job search support for eligible unemployed workers are of highest social priority and the least likely to have publicly or privately provided substitutes. The mandate to contribute to the CCF only applies to dependent workers. Independent workers can choose to contribute voluntarily, although few do so.

To guarantee access to these services for everyone, this contribution can be restructured, making it mandatory for all, allowing a lower rate than the current one, and only funding the social protection for people who have become unemployed. The reform simulated here is a 1 p.p. decrease in the contribution to the CCF, which would be dedicated solely to funding unemployment income support and job search services. The resulting 3 percent contribution would be a level comparable to that for unemployment insurance and job search support in other countries in the region (Alvarado, Meléndez, and Pantoja 2021).

Reducing contributions for dependent workers and extending the mandate to contribute for independent workers could rebalance the system eliminating a cost disincentive to seek dependent work. The reform would result in a slight reduction of approximately 1 percent in the FTR for dependent workers while introducing a modest increase in the FTR for independent workers of just over 1.2 percent. Notably, the effects are larger for lower-income workers, as shown in figure 6.7.

A lower contribution rate for the CCF and elimination of the exemption for independent workers would reduce compliance costs and address the distortion favoring self-employment (refer to figure 6.7). The effects of these changes tend to favor more-educated workers in larger companies, urban areas, and specific regions like Antioquia, and workers with fewer working hours would experience the most-negative impacts. In aggregate, the valuation of dependent work should increase as independent work becomes more expensive and dependent work becomes less costly (refer to figure 6.8). The reform would offer something vital in return, as independent workers would be entitled to unemployment insurance and other social protection services, which could shift their perception of the CCF contributions from an unnecessary tax to a valued safety net.

FIGURE 6.7

FTR simulations of reduced contributions for the CCF in Colombia, 2019

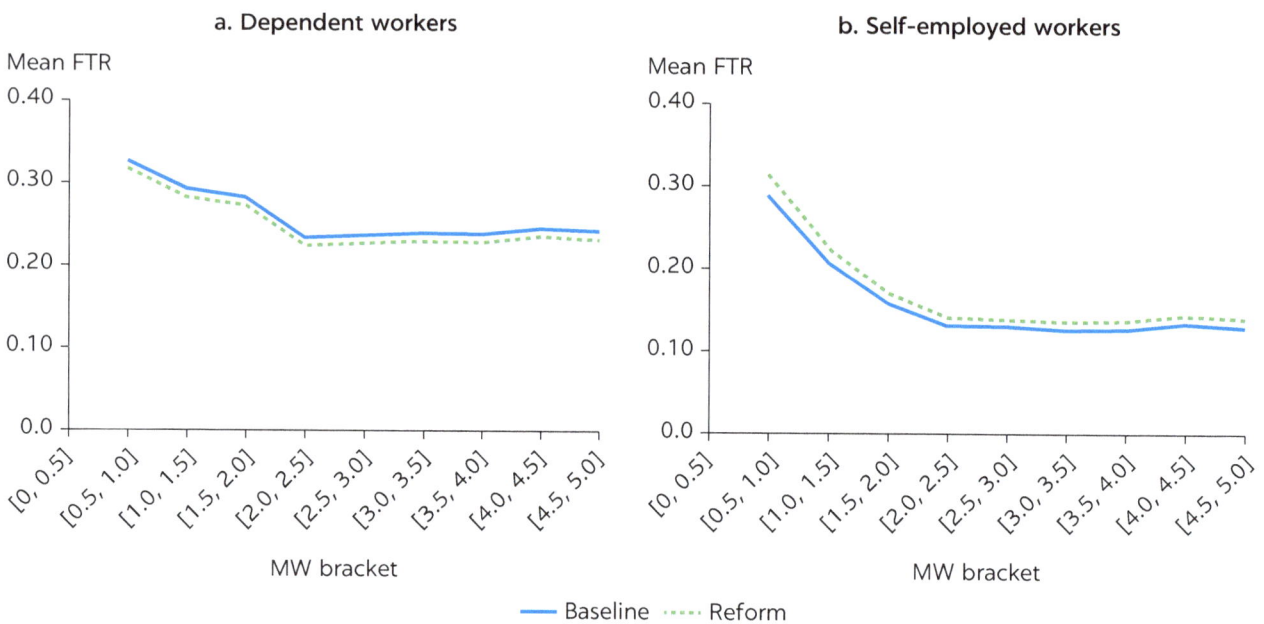

Source: Original figures for this publication using data from the 2019 Colombian National Administrative Department of Statistics Large Integrated Household Survey.
Note: MW brackets are assigned based on formal earnings. CCF = Cajas de Compensación Familiar (Family Compensation Funds); FTR = formalization tax rate; MW = minimum wage.

Incentives could be improved by lowering the costs of CCF coverage and focusing the CCF on supporting unemployed workers. A redefined and streamlined CCF service—focused on delivering unemployment income and job search support—could significantly enhance the way workers value their contributions. Rather than viewing the payments as another payroll tax, both dependent and independent workers could see the CCF as a provider of unemployment protection and job search services that cannot be found elsewhere. Other services provided by the CCF could still be available but funded through voluntary contributions, leaving the core focus on strengthening social protection for all workers.

Uruguay's introduction of an unemployment subsidy for independent workers

Unemployment insurance played a crucial role in mitigating poverty during the COVID-19 crisis in Uruguay. It was estimated that the poverty rate (measured by the national poverty line) would have increased from 8.8 percent in 2019 to 14.1 percent in 2020 in the absence of unemployment insurance and additional support measures. Instead, the poverty rate reached only 11.6 percent (World Bank 2021). However, registered independent workers lacked access to unemployment benefits and were not reached by the emergency policies during the pandemic.

FIGURE 6.8

Changes in the FTR under the proposed changes in contributions for the CCF in Colombia, 2019

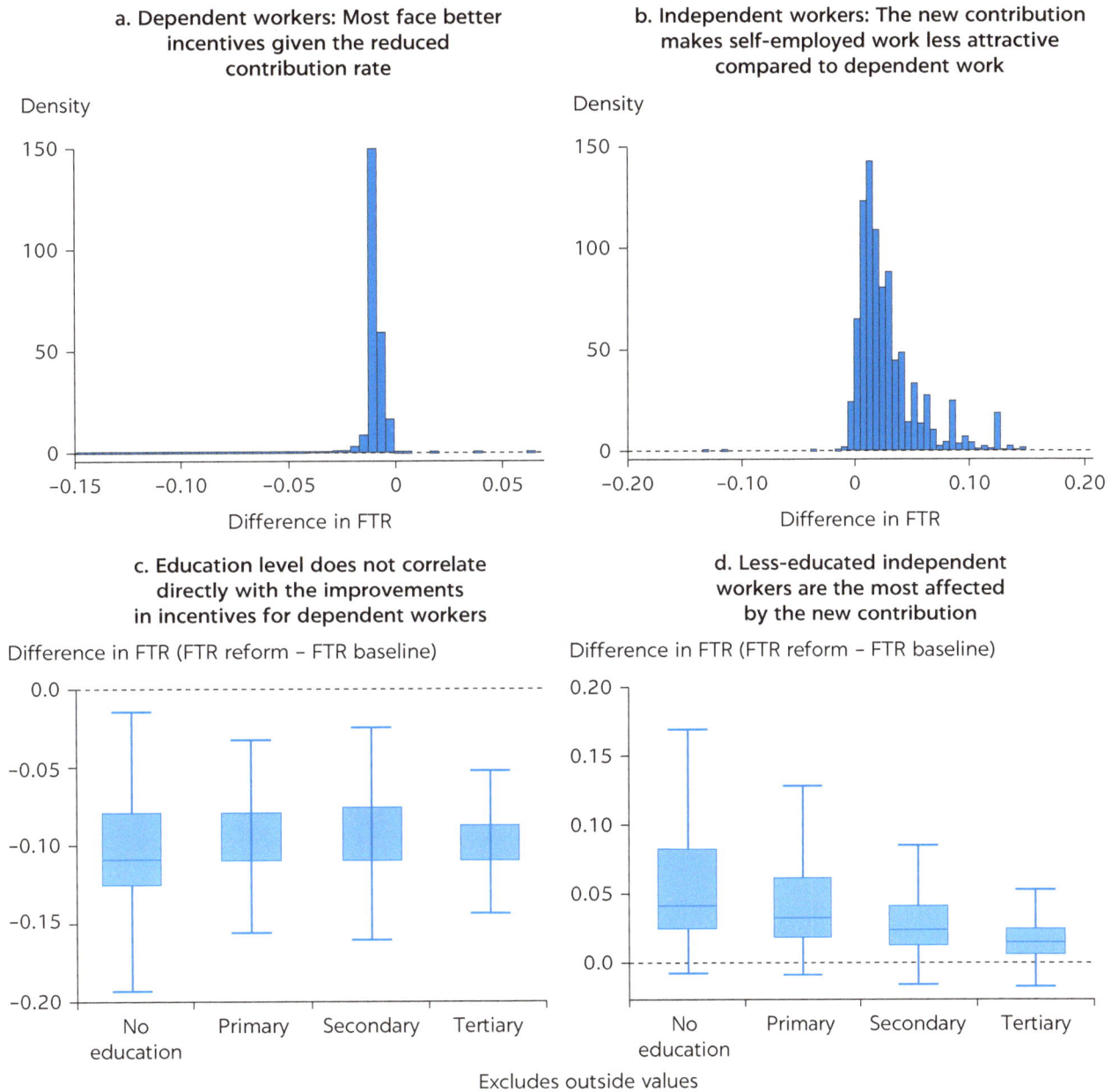

a. Dependent workers: Most face better incentives given the reduced contribution rate

b. Independent workers: The new contribution makes self-employed work less attractive compared to dependent work

c. Education level does not correlate directly with the improvements in incentives for dependent workers

d. Less-educated independent workers are the most affected by the new contribution

Excludes outside values

Source: Original figures for this publication using data from the 2019 Colombian National Administrative Department of Statistics Large Integrated Household Survey.
Note: CCF = Cajas de Compensación Familiar (Family Compensation Funds); FTR = formalization tax rate.

This subsection examines how the expansion of unemployment insurance to cover independent workers would impact the incentives to contribute in the monotributo regime (Uruguay's simplified tax system for small businesses and self-employed individuals). The simulation of an unemployment benefit for independent workers offers up to 3 months of minimum wage payments per year after workers have contributed as monotributistas (the small businesses and self employed workers who elect the simplified, single tax payment program).[9] Similar unemployment assistance exists, for example, in Canada, and it was introduced during the COVID-19 pandemic for self-employed, freelance, contract, and gig workers in the United States (OECD 2023). This policy is modeled as a shift in the valuation of social contributions paid by self-employed workers under monotributo, and the parameter is calculated using the value of the benefit considering the requirement to contribute for a minimum period.

The introduction of this unemployment benefit is estimated to affect the formalization incentives of 1 in 4 workers and more than half of the poor population. As anticipated, the FTR for all the affected workers (all self-employed workers) decreases with the new policy, with the largest impact observed among workers in the lowest percentiles of the distribution of household income per capita (refer to figure 6.9). The effect ranges from an average 16 percent reduction in the FTR for workers in the poorest percentiles to an average 5 percent reduction for workers between the 15th and 25th percentiles, which corresponds to the range of 1.5–2 times the minimum wage.

Colombia's lower minimum statutory contribution base

Reducing the minimum contribution base improves access to social security and incentivizes formalization for low-income workers. Lowering the minimum contribution base from 1 minimum wage to 72 percent of the minimum wage aligns contributions with workers' actual incomes, enabling over half of Colombia's workforce, who earn less than the minimum wage, to participate in the social security system. This reform is expected to reduce the FTR for dependent workers earning close to the minimum wage by approximately 3 percent, while self-employed workers see an even greater improvement of 7.2 percent.[10]

These changes significantly lower the relative cost of participation for low-income workers, particularly those earning below 2.5 times the minimum wage. As a result, the reform encourages compliance among previously excluded groups, addressing the structural barriers to formalization in Colombia (refer to figure 6.10).

The benefits extend to workers with lower education levels, those living in rural areas, and those employed in lower-productivity sectors. Workers who gain the most from this reform include self-employed workers and those in the agriculture, industry, wholesale and trade, and transport sectors. Better-off workers, often younger and working fewer hours, are less affected, ensuring that the reform primarily benefits vulnerable groups. Improved incentives for formalization could positively impact 9.3 percent of dependent workers (approximately 1 million) and 78.6 percent of independent workers (7.3 million) (refer to figure 6.11). These groups will experience reduced costs and easier access to protections like pensions and unemployment insurance.

FIGURE 6.9

Changes in the FTR with the introduction of an unemployment subsidy for independent workers in Uruguay, 2021

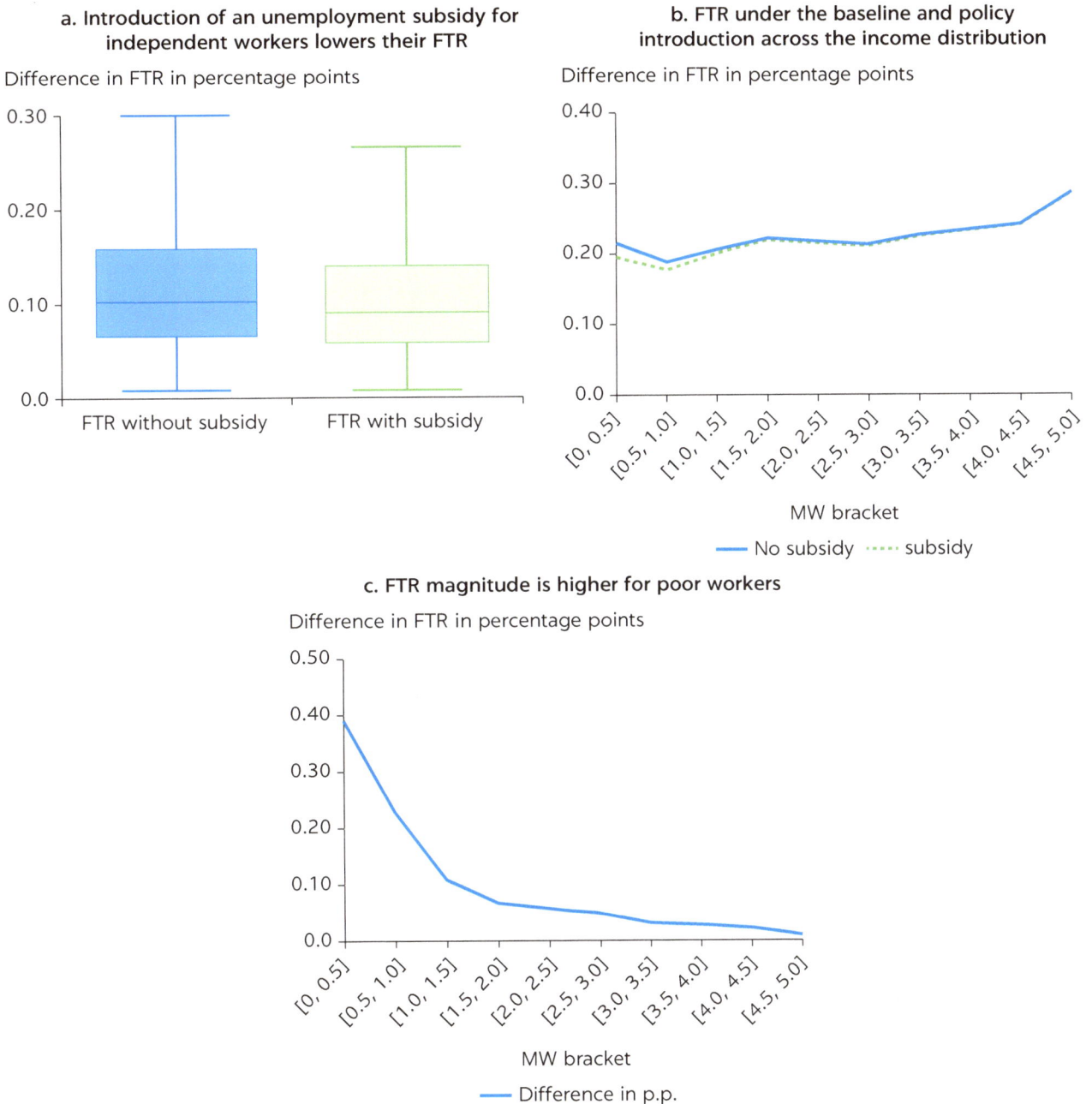

a. Introduction of an unemployment subsidy for independent workers lowers their FTR

Difference in FTR in percentage points

b. FTR under the baseline and policy introduction across the income distribution

Difference in FTR in percentage points

c. FTR magnitude is higher for poor workers

Difference in FTR in percentage points

Source: Original figures for this publication using data from Uruguay's 2021 National Statistics Institute Continuous Household Survey.

Note: MW brackets are assigned based on formal earnings. FTR = formalization tax rate; MW = minimum wage; p.p. = percentage points.

The reform complements ongoing changes to Colombia's statutory pension plans and strengthens the fairness of the social security system. By expanding the reach of the proposed semi-contributory pillar and introducing mechanisms like the Sistema de equivalencias (an eligibility equivalence system, used to convert actual retirement savings into credit toward a full pension annuity), the reform makes

FIGURE 6.10

Lowering the minimum statutory contribution base in Colombia, 2019

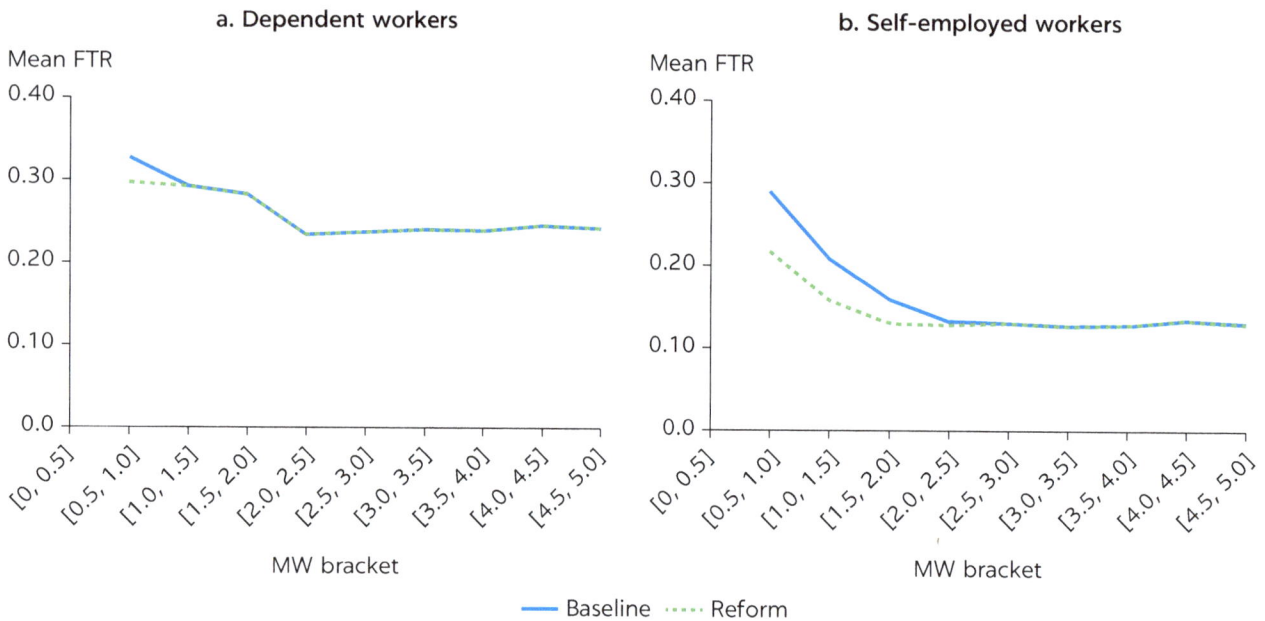

a. Dependent workers

Mean FTR

b. Self-employed workers

Mean FTR

— Baseline ····· Reform

Source: Original figures for this publication using data from the 2019 Colombian National Administrative Department of Statistics Large Integrated Household Survey.
Note: MW brackets are assigned based on formal earnings. FTR = formalization tax rate; MW = minimum wage.

contributing toward a pension more flexible and accessible. Improved monitoring through systems like the Registro Social de Hogares (Social Household Registry) and the Registro Universal de Ingresos (Universal Income Registry) mitigates the risk of misreporting income, ensuring fairness and functionality. While higher earners experience minimal impact, low-income workers see substantial benefits, with contributions better aligned to their incomes. This reform reduces systemic inequities, paving the way for a more-inclusive and more-sustainable social protection model.

El Salvador's change to the health insurance system

A potential policy reform in El Salvador is to restructure health insurance contributions to create a more-progressive system while maintaining overall revenue. Cross-subsidizing health contributions by removing the income ceiling could improve incentives and coverage while maintaining fiscal sustainability. This policy actively affects the aspect of fairness as outlined in chapter 3 on the valuation dimension.

The following simulation explores implementing a dual approach: eliminating the income ceiling for contributions for high-income workers while reducing contribution rates for minimum wage workers. Currently, health contributions are capped at salaries of US$1,000 per month, limiting the redistributive capacity of the system. By removing this ceiling while simultaneously lowering contribution rates for minimum wage workers to 3.5 percent (2.5 percent paid

FIGURE 6.11

Changes in the FTR under a lower minimum statutory contribution base in Colombia, 2019

a. Most workers will not be affected, as the general rules will not change, and those who are affected are mostly affected positively

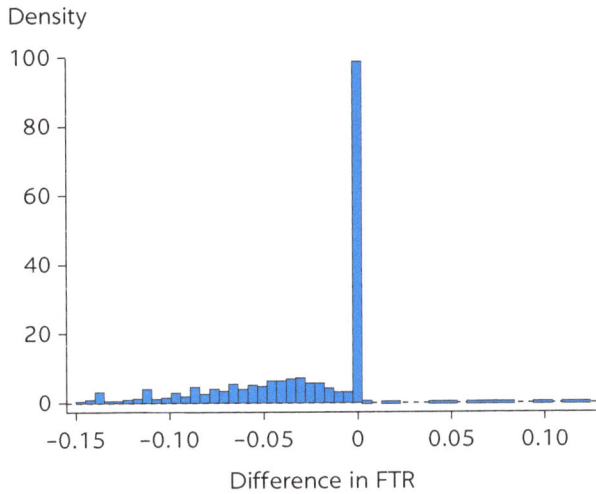

b. Dependent workers under the minimum wage would experience an improvement in their incentives

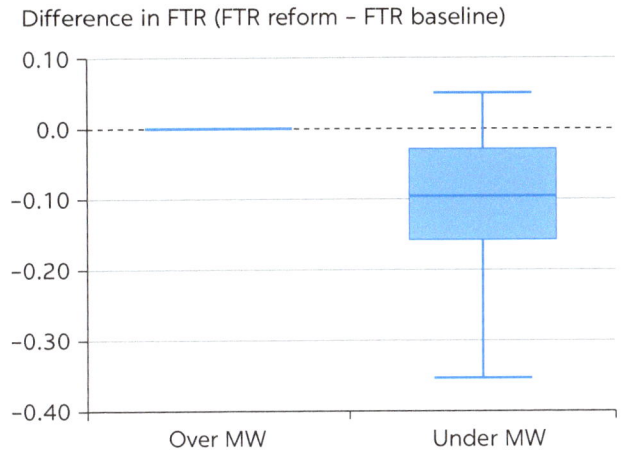

c. Most independent workers under 2.5 MW would have improved incentives toward participation and complying

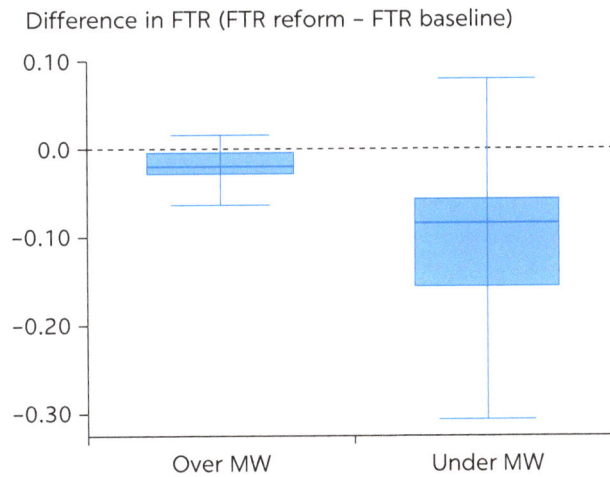

Source: Original figures for this publication using data from the 2019 Colombian National Administrative Department of Statistics Large Integrated Household Survey.
Note: FTR = formalization tax rate; MW = minimum wage.

by the employer and 1.0 percent paid by the employee), the reform aims to reduce the financial burden on lower-income workers while maintaining system sustainability through increased contributions from higher earners.[11]

The proposed policy decreases the FTR for low-income workers and increases the FTR for high-income workers (refer to figure 6.12). The simulation results show that the reform has differential impacts across the wage distribution, but only for dependent workers. For workers earning below the minimum wage, the FTR decreases from around 15 to 11 percent, reflecting the reduced health

FIGURE 6.12

FTR simulations of changes in health insurance in El Salvador, 2019

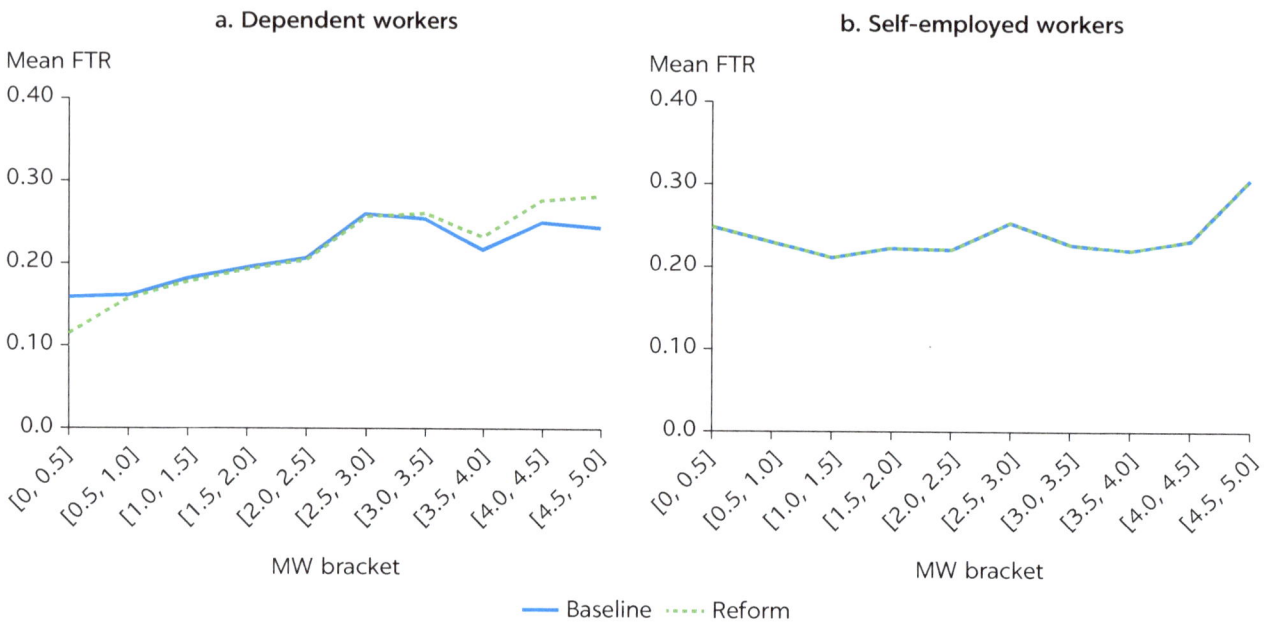

Source: Original figures for this publication using data from El Salvador's 2019 Encuesta de Hogares de Proposites Multiples (Multiple Purpose Household Survey).
Note: MW brackets are assigned based on formal earnings. FTR = formalization tax rate; MW = minimum wage.

contribution rates for low-income workers. The policy's impact is relatively neutral for middle-income workers earning between 1 and 3 times the minimum wage. However, for high-income workers (those earning above 4.5 times the minimum wage), the FTR increases by approximately 5 p.p., reaching nearly 28 percent, due to the elimination of the income ceiling. In contrast, the reform shows—as expected—no impact on self-employed workers.

Peru's facilitation of social security contributions

Peru faces challenges with high social security contributions disproportionately affecting low-income workers, potentially leading to informal employment arrangements in which both employers and employees opt out of pension and health care plans. To address this issue, a proposed reform would introduce a progressive social security contribution structure based on workers' income rather than firm size, featuring three brackets with varying contribution levels. The lowest bracket (under S/.1,500 per month) would have minimal pension contributions and access to noncontributory health care, the middle bracket would introduce increased pension contributions and employer-provided health care, and the highest bracket would maintain standard contribution rates (for details, refer to table 6.2). This approach aims to encourage formalization and firm growth while remaining fiscally neutral, following similar successful reforms in other countries.

TABLE 6.2 Proposed social security reform in Peru

			PROPOSED REGIME		
		CURRENT REGIME	FROM MW TO S/.1,500/ MONTH	FROM S/.1,500/ MONTH TO PIT THRESHOLD	MORE THAN PIT THRESHOLD
Firm contributions	Family subsidy (% MW)	10	10	10	10
	Health contribution (%)	9	0	6	9
	Unemployment insurance (%)	8.60	4.2	4.2	8.3
	Accident insurance (%)	1.90	1.90	1.90	1.90
Worker contributions	Pension contributions (%)	13	7	9	13

Source: Original table for this publication.
Note: MW = minimum wage; PIT = personal income tax.

The simulation results demonstrate that the proposed social security reform would reduce the FTR by 5.6 p.p. overall, from 15.1 to 9.5 percent, with similar impacts across dependent workers (–5.9 p.p.) and self-employed workers (–5.3 p.p.). The impact is most pronounced among low-wage workers, particularly those in the lowest income bracket, where the FTR drops by 8 p.p., from 14.0 to 6.1 percent, compared to reductions of 5.5 p.p. in the second bracket and only 0.4 p.p. in the top bracket (refer to figure 6.13). However, workers earning below the minimum wage would see more-modest benefits due to pension contribution constraints. These results indicate that the reform successfully achieves a more-progressive system than the current one.

FIGURE 6.13

FTR simulations of changes in contributions in Peru, 2019

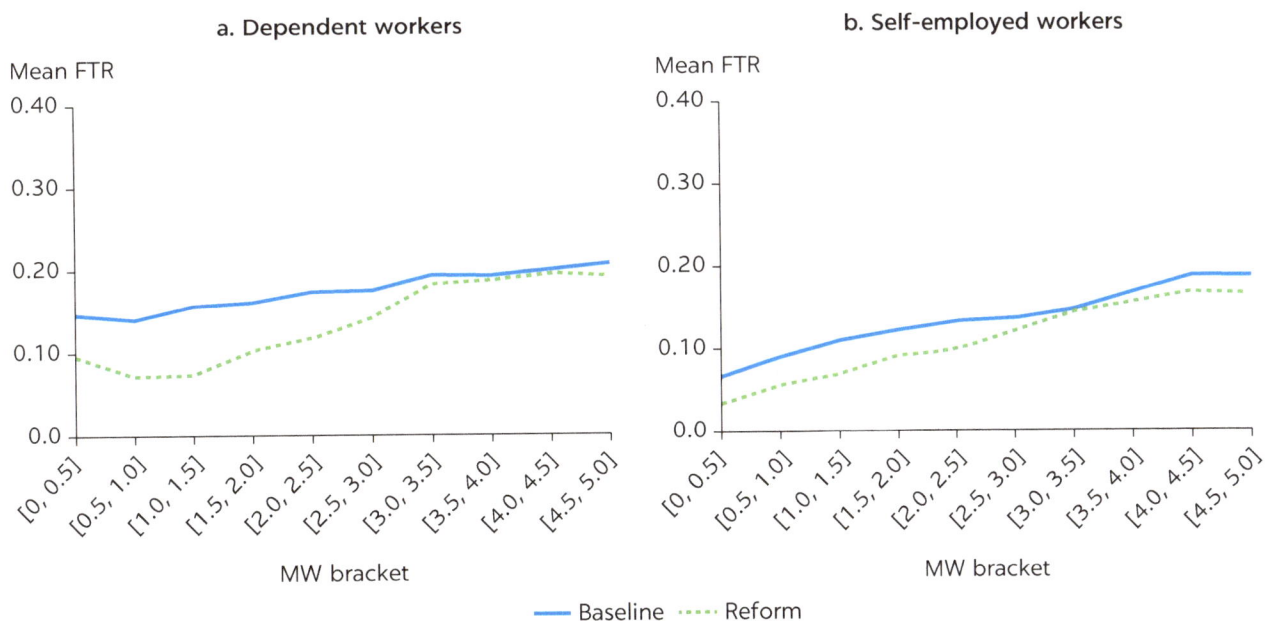

Source: Original figures for this publication using data from Peru's 2019 Encuesta Nacional de Hogares (National Household Survey).
Note: MW brackets are assigned based on formal earnings. FTR = formalization tax rate; MW = minimum wage.

Policies influencing the value of outside options and benefits

Social protection systems are consolidated in many countries in the LAC region and, hence, are perceived as a reliable source of income for some families. This situation regularly raises the question whether the systems are adequately designed to protect families from shocks and poverty while incentivizing formal employment. Most LAC countries have a conditional cash transfer program or an unconditional cash transfer program. The seven country cases in this report have mature cash transfer programs complemented by other social assistance services (including social pensions) and in-work benefits.[12] On the whole, these programs have good coverage and adequate benefits.

The countries' governments are constantly monitoring the programs to adjust to the changing needs of vulnerable groups given the economic cycle and to ensure that the programs promote incentives to work. The following subsections show how incentives to comply with regulations might have changed with recently introduced reforms or might change with other reforms being considered, as well as whose incentives are more likely to be affected.[13]

Brazil's Bolsa Familia's generosity increased with improved targeting

In 2022, the Government of Brazil substantially changed the rules of the country's conditional cash transfer program, Bolsa Familia. This reform changed the parameter of the outside options in the valuation dimension of the conceptual framework. Before the change, families were entitled to two types of benefits: the basic benefit and the variable benefit (conditional on having children). If families had a per capita income below R$89, they were entitled to the basic benefit, which amounted to R$89 per family. If the family still did not reach R$89 per capita, a top-up benefit was provided to guarantee at least R$89 per capita. Families with children and a per capita income below R$41 were eligible to receive an additional variable benefit of R$41 per child.

As described in chapter 4, this reform did not pose strong disincentives toward formality. After the reform, the benefit generosity was increased substantially (refer to table 6.3). After several reforms during the COVID-19 pandemic, including the introduction and phase out of temporary programs, families now receive increased financial support relative to the prepandemic levels. The basic benefit has been raised to R$142 for each family member, ensuring that no family receives less than R$600. Moreover, the eligibility criteria have been expanded, allowing more families to access assistance, for those with per capita income up to R$218. In addition, alterations have been made to the assistance for children: those up to age 6 years receive R$150, and those ages 7–18 receive R$50. Families can receive this support if their per capita income does not exceed R$218 per person.

TABLE 6.3 Bolsa Familia rules in Brazil, 2019 and 2024

	RULES AS OF 2019	RULES AS OF 2024
Eligibility	• Basic benefit: Income per capita < R$89 • Variable benefit: Income per capita < R$178	• Basic benefit: Income per capita < R$218 • Variable benefit: Income per capita < R$218
Generosity	• Basic benefit: R$89 (including top-up to guarantee R$89 per capita) • Variable benefit: R$41 per child	• Basic benefit: R$142 per household member (including top-up to guarantee R$600 per household) • Child benefit: R$150 per child for children up to age 6 years • Youth benefit: R$50 per child for children ages 7–18 years

Source: Original table for this publication.

Increasing the value of outside options increases the incentives to avoid compliance with regulations for those who qualify for the benefit. Counterfactual simulations of the FTR show that,[14] although only 16 percent of workers currently receive Bolsa Familia, the reform's impact extends to 42 percent of the workforce, affecting the incentives to comply with regulations of a significantly larger portion than the direct beneficiaries (refer to figure 6.14).

This issue suggests that the reform influences the behavior of more workers than those directly enrolled in the program. This situation exists because nonqualifying formal workers could theoretically become eligible by transitioning to informal employment and hiding their income. It underscores the importance of effective enforcement mechanisms and the discoverability of informal income to maintain the effectiveness of social welfare programs like Bolsa Familia. The impact is strongest for low-wage workers (75 percent of low-wage workers are impacted) and less strong for high-wage workers (70 percent of high-wage workers are not impacted), with no notable differences by gender.

Uruguay's elimination of a formal income threshold for receiving noncontributory family social transfers

In 2022, the Uruguayan government reformed the family allowance program by eliminating the income cap on formal income. The Asignaciones Familiares–Plan de Equidad (AFAM–PE) (Family Allowance and Equity Plan) program is a targeted cash transfer aimed at low-income families with children to reduce poverty and inequality. Before the 2022 reform, eligibility for the program was based on means-tested criteria that focused on the household's overall economic vulnerability and included an income cap on formal income designed to target the assistance toward families with low and vulnerable income levels, specifically those below a given formal earnings threshold. If a family's income from formal employment rose above the cap, the family was disqualified from receiving the cash transfer.

FIGURE 6.14

Distribution of the FTR in Brazil, 2019

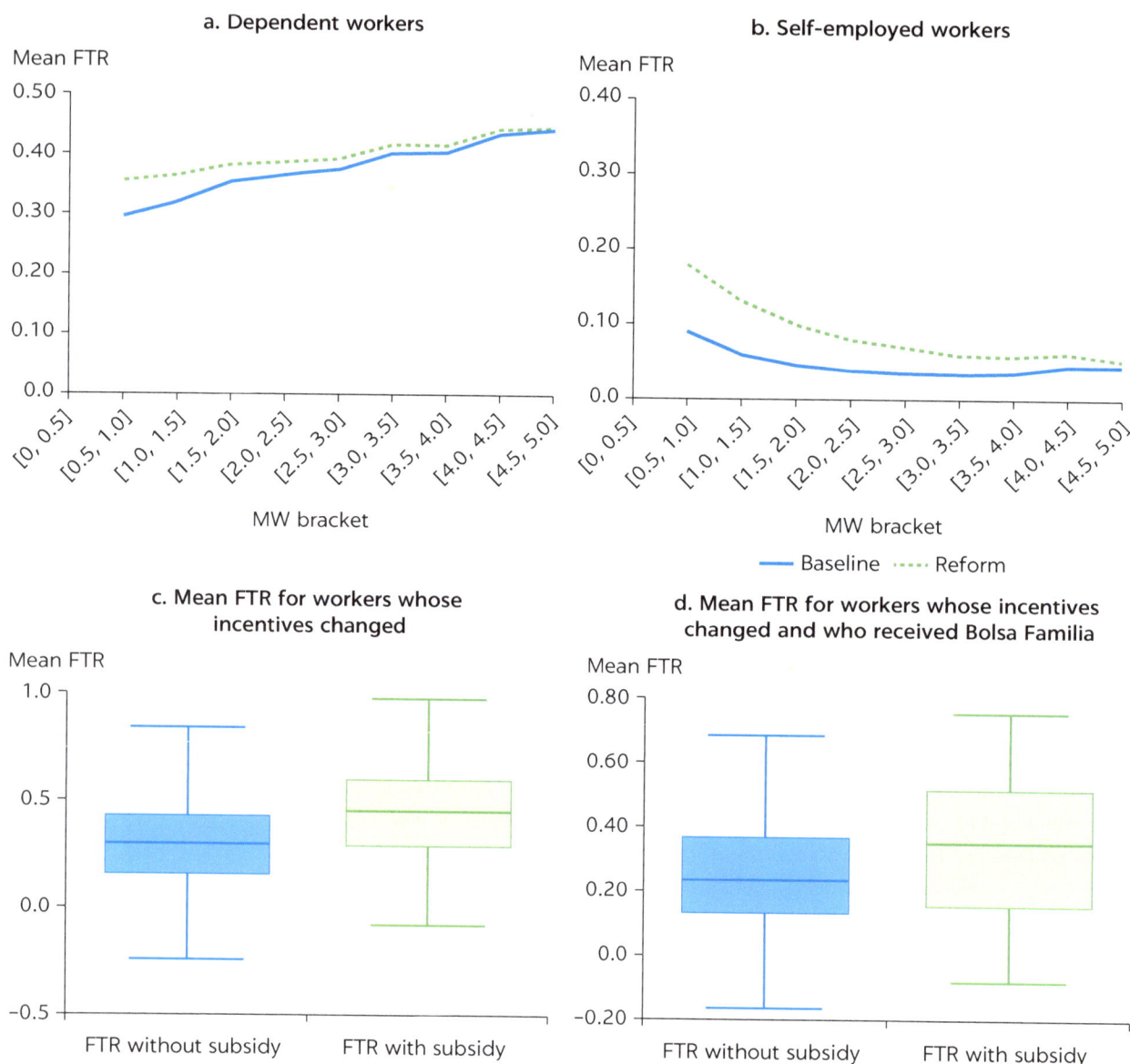

Sources: Original figures for this publication using data from Brazil's 2019 National Household Sample Survey and BraSim 2019.
Note: MW brackets are assigned based on formal earnings. In panels c and d, the figures exclude outliers. FTR = formalization tax rate; MW = minimum wage.

Although it was not a key aspect of formalization issues in Uruguay, this cap could create a disincentive to increase formal employment or declare formal income, as beneficiaries risked losing the benefit if they surpassed the threshold.[15] According to the Government of Uruguay, the reform measure allowed 21,000 additional families to access the transfer.[16]

Thus, elimination of the formal income cap reduced the value of the outside option for formal workers, as now they can access the cash transfer program. The policy affects 1.5 percent of total workers with a calculated FTR and almost no poor workers.[17] Although the policy change affects a limited number of workers and does not seem to change the average FTR with all workers included, the FTR for those affected decreased by 20.6 percent on average (refer to figure 6.15).

Given the high proportion of independent workers in the informal sector and the well-targeted cash transfer program, the policy change appears to address disincentives at the margin for those subject to the original income cap. The impact is more pronounced for the poorest households, except those in households earning below 1 times the minimum wage. Households led by a single mother are disproportionately represented among the affected households (21.7 percent compared to 7.6 percent of all households with children in the FTR sample). In addition, almost all the affected households rely on a single source of labor income (97.8 percent compared to 40.1 percent of all households with children in the FTR sample). Furthermore, other incentives, such as those related to labor force participation at both the extensive and intensive margins, could also be affected but are not modeled in this analysis.

Brazil's Increase in Bolsa Familia's coverage

In Brazil, debate is ongoing about disregarding the Beneficio de Prestação Continuada (BPC; Continuous Cash Benefit) when calculating eligibility for Bolsa Familia, again linking to the valuation dimension of the conceptual framework. Bill 3619, introduced in 2023, seeks to amend article 4 of Law 14,601, dated June 19, 2023, to exclude the BPC from the calculation of monthly per capita family income used to determine eligibility for Bolsa Familia. This proposed change aims to address issues related to the inclusion of BPC as income, which some argue unfairly penalizes families by inflating their income and thereby denying them access to social assistance programs.

If passed, the bill will likely significantly affect the number of households eligible for Bolsa Familia, the budget required to include all eligible households, and the incentives for formal employment. By excluding BPC from income calculations, more families could qualify for Bolsa Familia, increasing the program's coverage and potentially necessitating a higher budget allocation to accommodate the additional beneficiaries.

The rationale behind the bill is that BPC should be seen as a benefit rather than labor income. Treating BPC as income can artificially increase a family's reported income, thereby excluding them from receiving necessary social benefits. This issue is problematic for families with higher health care costs due to elderly or disabled members, who rely heavily on such assistance. In addition, including BPC as income could undermine the benefits of Bolsa Familia by not accounting for the financial disparities faced by these vulnerable groups.

FIGURE 6.15

Changes in the FTR with the elimination of the formal income cap in Uruguay, 2021

a. The average change in FTR with
the policy change was minimal

b. Among those affected by the policy,
the average effect was a reduction
of 33 percent in the FTR

c. FTR under baseline and policy change
dropping the formal income cap
for cash transfer eligibility

d. The magnitude difference
in scenarios (p.p.)

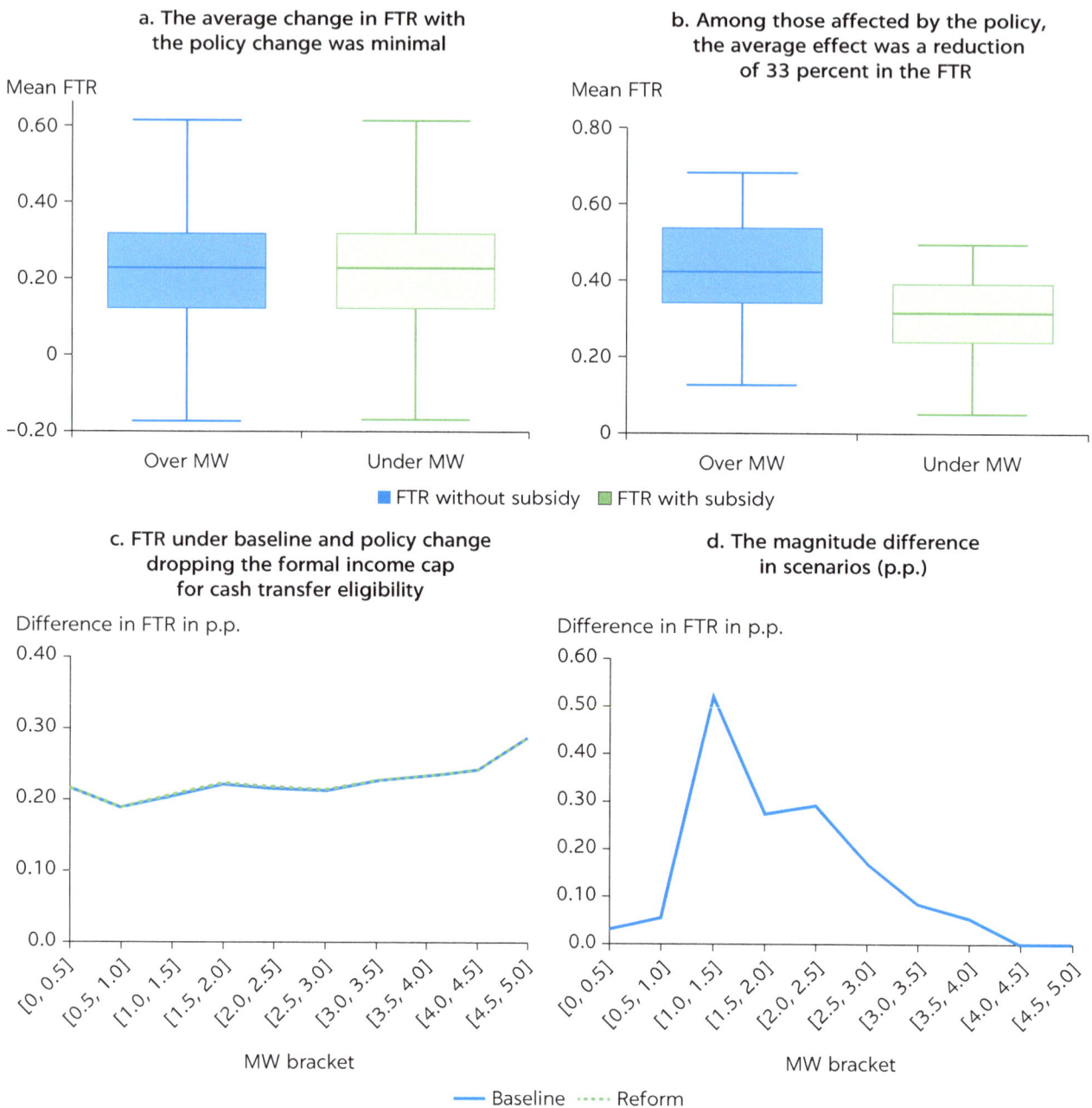

Source: Original figures for this publication using data from Uruguay's 2021 National Statistics Institute Continuous Household Survey.
Note: MW is assigned based on formal earnings. FTR = formalization tax rate; MW = minimum wage; p.p. = percentage points.

However, simulation results of the proposed amendment indicate that it would impact incentives toward working formally among low-income workers with BPC beneficiaries at home. The effects of this policy shift are twofold. Families that become eligible for Bolsa Família after the BPC discount will have less incentive to underreport their income and may be more inclined toward formal employment. Conversely, families closer to the eligibility threshold after the reform may be more likely to underreport informal income and pursue informal

FIGURE 6.16

Results from the simulation of increasing the Bolsa Familia benefit in Brazil, 2019

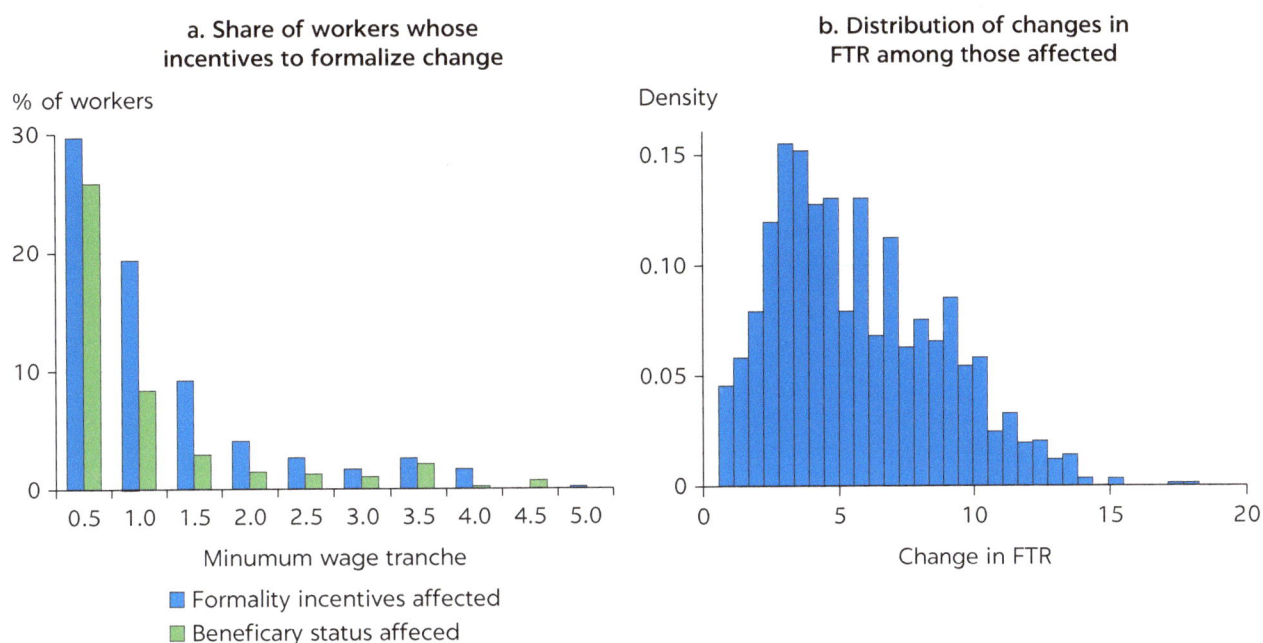

a. Share of workers whose incentives to formalize change

b. Distribution of changes in FTR among those affected

■ Formality incentives affected
■ Beneficary status affeced

Sources: Original figures for this publication using data from Brazil's 2019 National Household Sample Survey and BraSim 2019.
Note: Minimum wage brackets are assigned based on formal earnings. FTR = formalization tax rate.

work to remain eligible for benefits. Figure 6.16, panel a, shows that the share of workers whose incentives would be affected surpasses the number of workers who would actually become eligible after the reform.

The impact of these changes strongly depends on assumptions about the detection of informal income. If informal income is not accurately discovered, families may manipulate their income reporting to gain or maintain eligibility for Bolsa Familia. The simulations show that the FTR increases by an average of 7.7 percent for those who experienced a change in incentives due to the policy adjustment (refer to figure 6.16, panel b).

WHAT DO CHANGES IN INCENTIVES MEAN FOR EMPLOYMENT OUTCOMES?

The analysis of hypothetical reforms and their simulated impacts on incentives calls for humility in making policy recommendations. This chapter presented analysis of how incentives to (in)formalizing work can be altered by reforms, but it did not attempt to quantify what the response to these changes might be. While further work to take this important additional step is planned as part of the World Bank's country policy dialogue, it falls outside the parameters of this regional study. However, analyses undertaken by others of earlier reform measures in the region indicate that, although they are helpful, changes that directly lower the costs of formalizing are not sufficient to result in a substantially altered share of people complying with mandates and choosing to participate in the tax and benefit systems.

A tax reform in Colombia, designed to improve incentives by lowering nonwage costs, demonstrates the importance of managing expectations. In 2012, the Government of Colombia passed an ambitious reform that lowered the statutory contributions and other payroll tax obligations on formal employment relationships by 13.5 p.p. By many rigorous estimates, this reform led to an increase in formal employment of 3–4.5 percent (refer to box 6.2). Although it was a significant increase, this outcome disappointed many observers given the size of the reduction in payroll taxes. The reduction in the tax wedge was an important reform but not a proverbial "silver bullet" against informal employment as the persistently high levels of noncompliance in Colombia today attest.

Box 6.2

Impact of tax and social protection reforms on (dis)incentives to formalize work in Colombia

The Government of Colombia passed an ambitious tax reform in December 2012 aimed at improving equity, promoting hiring in the formal sector, and simplifying the tax system to improve compliance. Statutory payroll taxes were lowered by 13.5 percentage points for workers earning up to 10 times the minimum wage. To compensate for the revenue lost from payroll taxes, a new tax, the Contribución Empresarial para la Equidad (CREE; Business Contribution for Equity) tax, was created. The CREE was effectively equivalent to a corporate income tax (CIT) of 8 percent. To avoid increasing the tax burden on firms, the actual CIT was simultaneously decreased from 33 to 25 percent.

To simulate the impact of the reform, Anton (2014) calibrated a general equilibrium model for the Colombian economy. The simulation results suggested that the reform would have a positive but small effect on total employment, increasing it by 0.3–0.5 percent compared to the prereform scenario. However, the simulation showed that formal employment as a share of total employment would increase by 3.4–3.7 percent, while informality would decrease by 2.9–3.4 percent. Notably, the model predicted a 4.9 percent increase in the formal wage rate, net of taxes and transfers. The simulations suggested that formal workers might bear a significant share of the tax burden imposed by nonwage labor costs through lower wages.

In the years that followed, many researchers have studied the impact of the reform using several analytical techniques. For example, Fernandez and Villar (2017) used difference-in-differences and kernel propensity score matching applied to household survey microdata from 2008 to 2015. Echoing Anton's (2014) simulation results, Fernandez and Villar (2017) found that the 2012 reform led to a significant reduction in the informality rate. Two years after the reform, the informality rate had diminished by about 4.0 percentage points. Despite a substantial increase in the minimum wage during the same period, the reform resulted in a decrease in informality, suggesting that the reform's impact

continued

Box 6.2 Impact of tax and social protection reforms on (dis)incentives to formalize work in Colombia, *(continued)*

was strong enough to counteract the effects of the minimum wage increase.

Morales and Medina (2017) focused on the intensity of the treatment, which they measured by the potential savings for firms resulting from the tax reform. These researchers used a dynamic panel framework with a linear regression strategy, utilizing longitudinal data from all the formal firms in Colombia. The results showed a significant and positive effect of the tax reform on employment at both the firm and economic sector–municipality levels. The impact was heterogeneous across firm sizes, with larger firms exhibiting higher elasticities and contributing more to overall job creation. The results showed that the reform led to an increase in employment, particularly for larger firms. This study suggests that the reduction in payroll taxes had a substantial positive impact on formal employment in Colombia, particularly for larger firms.

Bernal et al. (2017) used detailed firm-level administrative data covering all formal employment in Colombia before and after the reform. Their analysis focused on firms, as their hiring and wage policies are directly affected by payroll taxes. The study utilized a difference-in-differences approach, taking

advantage of the fact that not-for-profit firms, many of which are de facto for profit, were exempt from the reform. The average firm in sectors affected by the reform increased its formal employment by about 4.3 percent and its average wage by 2.7 percent in the first 5 months after the reform came into full effect, compared to the average firm in unaffected sectors.

Collectively, these studies generally support efforts to increase formal employment by reducing payroll taxes.

Finally, Pfutze and Rodriguez-Castelan (2019) analyzed the introduction of the Colombia Mayor program, a noncontributory cash transfer to older workers. This program provided the researchers with an ideal scenario in which to test the program's impact on labor supply, finding that the benefit increased labor force participation among beneficiaries younger than age 70. For men, this effect was noticeable in self-employment and the cultivation of agricultural land. Women were more likely to move into formal employment as a result of the benefit. The study's findings challenge the common assumption that noncontributory pensions incentivize recipients to leave the labor force.

Substantial, lasting improvements in levels of compliance and participation require governments to act on all the incentive dimensions of the conceptual framework in chapter 3. No measure analyzed in this chapter is as ambitious as Colombia's 2012 tax reform. In the tax and social protection policy arena, few governments in the LAC region today are willing to attempt such deep and controversial reforms. Indeed, few governments anywhere in the world are willing to take such dramatic measures. However, even a package of reforms that lowers costs and improves incentives enough to bring working people to a "point of indifference" between complying and not complying will need further measures to "nudge" them past indifference to compliance.

Policy makers should remember that improvement of de jure incentives is necessary but may not be a sufficient reform strategy. Rather, real progress in reducing noncompliance and gains in participation are likely to come only from concerted action along all three dimensions of the conceptual framework (and probably others not in the scope of this report). Chapter 7 discusses the more-abstract concepts of the popular and personal perceptions that determine outcomes through people's "tax morale."

NOTES

1. Using the FTR and other assumptions, in principle, changes in the pass-through could be modeled. However, doing so would rely heavily on assumptions and would not be aligned with the current criteria for policy selection.
2. Simulations of minimum wage changes in all countries are presented in figure 6A.1 in annex 6A.
3. The minimum wage per day in 2018 prices would be Mex$193.04, meaning that the minimum wage increased in real terms by 118 percent in 6 years.
4. Employers (not shown here) also see an impact.
5. Simulations of payroll tax changes in Brazil, Colombia, El Salvador, Mexico, and Peru are presented in figure 6A.2 in annex 6A.
6. Anecdotal evidence from Brazil indicates that, while contributions that are directed toward professional training are potentially not valued by the employee, employers value those contributions. Therefore, the current policy experiment does not propose eliminating those contributions.
7. Although Sistema S (a training institution) does not provide direct benefits to workers, it potentially benefits employers, and, thus, they might value it.
8. This contribution can be considered a nonvalued payroll tax, as workers may not receive direct benefits from their contributions, particularly those workers without children who do not require child care services.
9. To avoid perverse incentives, the policy should consider eligibility after at least 1 year of monotributo or at least 3 years as formal dependent workers. However, it was not possible to introduce these features in the simulated scenarios with the available data.
10. This reform proposal builds on two existing mechanisms of Colombia's pension framework—the semi-contributory pillar introduced by the 2024 Pension Reform (Pilar semicontributivo) and the Sistema de Equivalencias, which associates voluntary BEPS (Beneficios Económicos Periódicos Sociales) pension savings to contributory weeks. Our adaptation would extend the semi-contributory pillar to cover individuals earning below one minimum wage—who today are ineligible—and to ensure compatibility with the pension system, route their lower-base contributions through the Equivalencias mechanism. Unlike the other simulated reforms, both instruments are already operative in Colombia, and here we model their integration into a unified, mainstream administrative process that systematically articulates these existing tools to boost coverage.
11. The proposed changes would maintain the current combined 10.5 percent contribution rate (7.5 percent employer and 3.0 percent employee) for workers earning between the minimum wage and US$1,000, while extending these same rates to all earnings above US$1,000. This reform acknowledges the sectoral variation in minimum wages across El Salvador, with rates in the maquila (foreign-owned factories) (98.4 percent), sugar cane harvesting (74.7 percent), and agriculture (66.6 percent) sectors set as percentages of the standard minimum wage in trade, services, and industry.
12. The seven country case studies are Brazil, Colombia, El Salvador, Jamaica, Mexico, Peru, and Uruguay. Due to data constraints, Jamaica is not included in this chapter.

13. Simulations of changes in the countries' noncontributory benefits are presented in figure 6A.3 in annex 6A.

14. The simulation assumes that not all informal labor income is reported. Thus, although Bolsa Familia is means tested and is not automatically lost when moving to formality, the risk of losing Bolsa Familia increases, because underreporting of labor income is less feasible for formal (versus informal) workers.

15. Failache, Giaccobasso, and Ramirez (2013) found evidence of higher informality as a consequence of the existence of the income cap to access the program.

16. Refer to Rendición de Cuentas y Balance de Ejecución Presupuestal del Ejercicio. 2023. Exposición de Motivos. https://www.gub.uy/ministerio-economia-finanzas /politicas-y-gestion/rendicion-cuentas-balance-ejecucion-presupuestal-ejercicio -2023.

17. AFAM–PE affects only vulnerable dependent households with children, and the elimination of the income cap affects those above the income threshold. Independent workers are not affected, as they are either informal or contributing under monotributo, and their formal income would not be observable to the social security authority.

REFERENCES

Almeida, R., and L. Ronconi. 2016. "Labor Inspections in the Developing World: Stylized Facts from the Enterprise Survey." *Industrial Relations* 55 (3): 468–89. https://doi.org /10.1111/irel.12146.

Alvarado, F., M. Meléndez, and M. Pantoja. 2021. "Mercados laborales fragmentados y el Sistema de Protección Social en Colombia." UNDP LAC Working Paper No. 14. Documento de Antecedentes para el Informe Regional de Desarrollo Humano 2021 de PNUD ALC. United Nations Development Programme, New York.

Anton, A. 2014. "The Effect of Payroll Taxes on Employment and Wages Under High Labor Informality." *IZA Journal of Labor and Development* 3: 20.

Aşık, G., L. L. Y. Bossavie, J. Kluve, S. E. Nas Ozen, M. Nebiler, and A. M. Oviedo Silva. 2022. "The Effects of Subsidizing Social Security Contributions: Job Creation or Informality Reduction?" Policy Research Working Paper 9904, World Bank, Washington, DC.

Avila, C., S. Freije-Rodríguez, and F. Marín. 2024. "Microsimulations of Policy Changes Affecting Formalization Tax Rate in Mexico." Washington, DC.

Bargain, O., H. X. Jara, and D. Rivera. 2024. "Tax Disincentives to Formal Employment in Latin America." LSE International Inequality Institute Working Paper No. 144, London School of Economics and Political Science, London, UK. http://eprints.lse.ac .uk/125368/1/LSC_III_Working_Papers_144-combined.pdf.

Becerra, O. 2024. "The Effect of Future Pension Benefits on Labor Supply in a Developing Economy." *Economic Development and Cultural Change* 72 (3): 1527–66.

Bedi, A. S., A. Shiferaw, M. Söderbom, and G. A. Zewdu. 2022. "Social Insurance Reform and Workers' Compensation." *Labour Economics* 78 (October).

Bergolo, M., and G. Cruces. 2021. "The Anatomy of Behavioral Responses to Social Assistance When Informal Employment Is High." *Journal of Public Economics* 193 (January).

Bernal, R., M. Eslava, M. Melendez, and A. Pizon. 2017. "Switching from Payroll Taxes to Corporate Income Taxes: Firms' Employment and Wages after the 2012 Colombian Tax Reform." *Economia* 19 (1): 41–74.

Betcherman, G., N. M. Daysal, and C. Pagés. 2010. "Do Employment Subsidies Work? Evidence from Regionally Targeted Subsidies in Turkey." *Labour Economics* 17 (4): 710–22.

Bosch, M., and R. Campos-Vazquez. 2014. "The Trade-Offs of Welfare Policies in Labor Markets with Informal Jobs: The Case of the 'Seguro Popular' Program in Mexico." *American Economic Journal: Economic Policy* 6 (4): 71–99. doi:10.1257/pol.6.4.71.

Cabezon, F. 2024. "The Unequal Protection of Social Security in the Presence of Informality: Theory and Evidence from Chile."

Cruces, G., S. Galiani, and S. Kidyb. 2010. "Payroll Taxes, Wages and Employment: Identification through Policy Changes." *Labour Economics* 17: 743–49.

De Brauw, A., D. O. Gilligan, J. Hoddinott, and S. Roy. 2015. "Bolsa Familia and Household Labor Supply in Brazil." *World Development* 70: 69–81.

Failache, E., M. Giaccobasso, and L. Ramirez. 2013. "Transferencias de Ingresos y Mercado de Trabajo. Evaluación de Impacto de Asignaciones Familiares Plan de Equidad sobre la informalidad laboral." Thesis, Universidad de la República, Montevideo, Uruguay.

Feinmann, J., R. Hsu Rocha, and M. Lauletta. 2024. "Payments Under the Table: Employer-Employee Collusion in Brazil." https://papers.ssrn.com/sol3/papers.cfm?abstract_id=4270665.

Fernandez, C., and L. Villar. 2017. "The Impact of Lowering the Payroll Tax on Informality in Colombia." *Economia* 18 (1): 125–55.

Garganta, S., and L. Gasparini. 2015. "The Impact of Social Protection Programs on Labor Informality: Evidence from Argentina's Asignacion Universal por Hijo." *Journal of Development Economics* 115: 99–110.

Gruber, J. 1997. "The Consumption Smoothing Benefits of Unemployment Insurance." *American Economic Review* 87 (1): 192–205.

Kanbur, R., and L. Ronconi. 2018. "Enforcement Matters: The Effective Regulation of Labour." *International Labour Review* 157 (3): 331–56.

Koettl, J., and M. Weber. 2012. "Does Formal Work Pay? The Role of Labor Taxation and Social Benefit Design in the New EU Member States." SSRN Electronic Journal. https://doi.org/10.2139/ssrn.2003626.

Kugler, A., and M. Kugler. 2009. "Labor Market Effects of Payroll Taxes in Developing Countries: Evidence from Colombia." *Economic Development and Cultural Change* 57 (2): 335–58.

Kugler, A., M. Kugler, and L. O. Herrera Prada. 2017. "Do Payroll Tax Breaks Stimulate Formality? Evidence from Colombia's Reform." Working Paper 23308, National Bureau of Economic Research, Cambridge, MA.

Kumler, T., E. Verhoogen, and J. Frías. 2020. "Enlisting Employees in Improving Payroll-Tax Compliance: Evidence from Mexico." *Review of Economics and Statistics* 102: 1–45.

Lauletta, M., and M. Bergolo. 2023. "Pension Privatization, Behavioral Responses, and Income in Old Age: Evidence form a Cohort-Based Reform." Technical Report, University of California, Berkeley, CA.

Maloney, W., P. Garriga, M. Meléndez, R. Morales, C. Jooste, J. Sampi, J. Thompson Araujo, and E. Vostroknutova. 2024. *Competition: The Missing Ingredient for Growth? Latin America and the Caribbean Economic Review*. Washington, DC: World Bank.

McKay, A., J. Pirttilä, and C. Schimanski. 2019. "The Tax Elasticity of Formal Work in African Countries." WIDER Working Paper Series wp-2019–69, World Institute for Development Economics Research, Helsinki, Finland.

Morales, L. F., and C. Medina. 2017. "Assessing the Effect of Payroll Taxes on Formal Employment: The Case of the 2012 Tax Reform in Colombia." *Economia* 18 (1): 75–124.

OECD (Organisation for Economic Co-operation and Development). 2023. "Benefit Reforms for Inclusive Societies in the United States: Income Security During Joblessness." OECD, Paris.

OECD (Organisation for Economic Co-operation and Development). 2024. *OECD Employment Outlook 2024: Country Notes: Mexico*. Paris: OECD. https://www.oecd.org/en/publications/oecd-employment-outlook-2024-country-notes_d6c84475-en/mexico_6ff7c0af-en.html#:~:text=In%20May%202024%2C%20the%20real,(in%20relation%20to%202023).

Pfutze, T., and C. Rodriguez-Castelan. 2019. "Can a Small Social Pension Promote Labor Force Participation? Evidence from the Colombia Mayor Program." *Economia* 20 (1): 111–54.

World Bank. 2021. "Uruguay Public Expenditure Review: Recent Fiscal and Distributional Trends in the Context of the COVID-19 Shock." World Bank, Washinton, DC.

7 Good Governance, Perceived Value, and Tax Morale

MORE THAN THE TAX WEDGE?

The tax wedge in most countries in the Latin America and the Caribbean (LAC) region is substantial but lower than that in many high-income countries (HICs). This chapter replicates estimates of the de jure tax wedge (described in chapter 4 of this report) and extends the estimates to HICs. While the tax wedge is high in many LAC countries, it is higher in Germany, Greece, Italy, and Spain. Indeed, among the countries included in figure 7.1, the labor tax wedge is highest in Germany, a country with low levels of avoidance and evasion. This observation presents a paradox: If the tax wedge and resulting formalization tax rates (FTRs) are lower in LAC countries than in many countries of the Organisation for Economic Co-operation and Development (OECD), why are the rates of informal employment in LAC countries so much higher?

What is the role of trust in government and social norms in shaping incentives to work formally?, Tommasi and Saavedra-Chanduvi (2007) explored institutional and political motivations for people to work informally. They posited that informality in Latin America is "a reflection of dysfunctional interactions between individuals and the State and of the latter's inability to perform adequately in regard to redistribution and the provision of public goods and services" (Tommasi and Saavedra-Chanduvi 2007, 1). The authors argued that this translates into low rates of social insurance compliance and coverage; pervasive evasion of tax, labor, and business regulations; and low levels of tax collection, law enforcement, and trust in the state. The challenge for these countries, then, is to build more-inclusive social contracts underpinned by realistic domestic consensus, accounting for country-specific institutional background and prevailing social norms. These incentive channels are discussed in this chapter.

A reproducibility package is available for this book in the Reproducible Research Repository at https://reproducibility.worldbank.org/catalog/330/.

FIGURE 7.1

Estimates of the augmented de jure tax wedge in LAC and OECD countries, 2019 and 2023

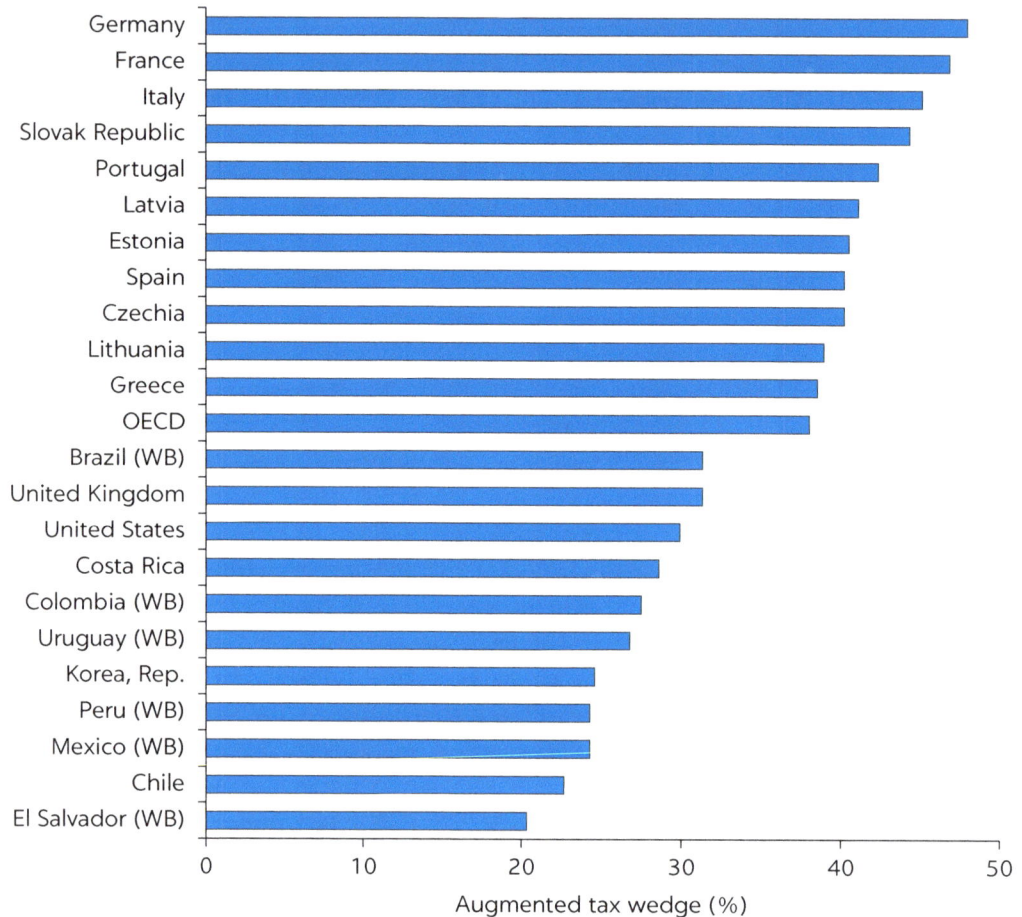

Sources: Original figure for this publication using calculations from U.S. legislation and country tax and benefit reports from the World Bank for 2017 and the OECD for 2023. *Note:* The figure compares the *tax wedges* (the shares of labor costs that are nonwage costs) in the countries analyzed in this report and in select OECD countries. Minor differences exist in the calculation of the tax wedge. First, differences arise in the definition of wages: World Bank calculations always include annual leave, holiday pay, and end-of-year bonuses. Second, minor differences exist in the inclusion of nontax compulsory payments. LAC = Latin America and the Caribbean; OECD = Organisation for Economic Co-operation and Development; WB = World Bank.

The incentives of employers and workers are also shaped by prevailing perceptions of the government's credibility. The analysis in chapters 3–5 of this report showed how the extent to which mandated benefits and contributions are a deterrent to "formalizing" work is tightly linked to the value individuals place on coverage. The report's conceptual framework distinguishes between an individual's valuation—shaped by the quality and reliability of social insurance coverage relative to that of alternative forms of saving and insuring, time and risk preferences, advantages of registered employment such as job security, and so forth—and the role that markets and other contextual factors—such as institutional credibility, the quality of governance, and social norms regarding compliance—play in creating a collective narrative about the value of coverage. Thus, while individual perceptions of value are important to individuals' considerations, so, too, can the collective narrative—and the resulting share of other market participants who are complying or evading—shape decisions at the margin.

Do these perceptions influence individuals' and firms' choices to be compliant? This chapter compares how the simulated benefits and costs to individuals of contributing to social insurance pension plans vary in select countries for which data on individuals' contribution histories are available. The chapter compares the estimated net benefits received or net taxes paid by individuals with different employment, income, and contribution histories. The simulations discussed in chapter 6 indicated that, given the now-ubiquitous noncontributory pension benefit programs, for many lower-earning workers, contributions to social insurance pension plans have a large tax component.

This chapter examines the relationship between the extent of noncompliant work and an indicator of "tax morale" that accounts for people's perceptions of political stability, the rule of law, and political corruption. The large-sample, cross-country multivariate correlation analysis controls for other contextual factors: the stringency of employment protection legislation, the level of the statutory minimum wage, and total labor taxes including social insurance contributions. Although the findings show that policy and regulatory factors are significantly associated with the share of people working informally, one of the strongest correlates is the augmented indicator of tax morale.

INSTITUTIONAL CREDIBILITY AND TRUST: KEY ASPECTS OF REDUCING THE "WEDGE"

Market participants' perceptions of governance, institutional credibility, and social norms are important for increasing compliance and participation. Most literature on the determinants of job informality places the greatest weight on policy design, regulation, and structural factors. Other studies emphasize the quality and credibility of governance institutions. Although it may be necessary to minimize the structural distortions caused by taxation and social protection policies, good policy design alone may not be a sufficient condition to formalize a significant share of informal work. Market participants' perceptions of governance and institutional credibility, as well as social norms, must be factored into the discussion to arrive at effective policy solutions that will bring more people into—and increase their hours of—formal work. These segments of the literature overlap and complement each other.

Shifting government-mandated pension plans from a risk-pooling system to individual savings well illustrates this complementarity. The predicted impact on incentives to become compliant or participate from shifting a social insurance pension plan from a pure risk-pooling ("defined benefit") arrangement to one based primarily on individual savings ("defined contribution"), whether actual or notional, reveals this overlap. The standard two-sector labor pricing model predicts that, at the margin, a higher statutory contribution rate for social insurance distorts labor allocation decisions when benefits are only loosely related to contributions, as with many defined-benefit formulas that redistribute income as well as risk. For retirement pensions in which the payoff for workers' "investment" in the plan lies far in the future, the distortion is even greater if preferences for consumption today are felt more keenly due to limited access to credit.

A direct link between contributions and benefits will lower distortion and increase participants' valuation of contributions. The conventional two-sector model predicts that linking benefits closely with contributions (a parametric change in defined-benefit formulas or an outright structural shift to individual savings) will lower distortions, as a larger share of contributions is perceived as fully owned deferred wages (as described in chapter 3). Regardless of whether an actual reduction in statutory contributions exists, the tighter link between contributions and benefits lowers the "pure tax" element of the mandate. Distortions in the contract between employers and workers should also be reduced, assuming that employers can "pass through" the costs of statutory contributions to workers in the form of lower take-home pay. As discussed in earlier chapters, a binding statutory minimum wage constrains employers' ability to pass through these costs.

The perceived credibility of the tax and social insurance systems is an important driver of workers' valuation. Even with the best-designed, actuarially fair pension plan, the behavioral response to the shift to a direct link between contributions and benefits depends critically on whether workers perceive that the link between contributions today and benefits far in the future is "credible" (refer to chapter 3). In many low- and middle-income countries, both public and private institutions struggle to maintain such credibility over short periods, much less the long span of a working life in social insurance contracts. In these relatively fragile institutional settings, workers might heavily discount that they will receive a pension at all, increasing the perceived tax burden of mandatory contributions and employers' ability to treat these as deferred wages, no matter how tight the link to benefits is on paper.

Not only distortions but also the nature of governance, institutional credibility, and social norms matter when aiming to increase compliance and participation. The previously mentioned points are the conceptual arguments that lead to the broader conclusion that, although it may be necessary to minimize structural distortions caused by the poor design of taxation, factor market regulation, and social protection policy, it is not sufficient for substantial gains in compliance or participation. The nature of governance, institutional credibility, and social norms of compliance must be factored into the discussion for effective policy solutions that will help formalize a larger share of work (refer to chapter 3). In this vein, Perry et al. (2007, 19) concluded that, for many countries in Latin America, "informality is a canary in the coal mine—the symptom of poor policies and, more profoundly, a lack of confidence in the state and perhaps in our fellow citizens."

SIMULATING THE VALUE OF PARTICIPATION: CONTRIBUTORS' "SOCIAL SECURITY WEALTH"

Are social insurance pension plans a good deal for workers? It is unrealistic to expect most working people to determine the actuarial value of their compliance or voluntary participation in what are, in many instances, opaque social insurance benefit parameters. It is an unreasonable expectation from most working people about the "fairness" of social health insurance benefits relative to their actual risk profiles (for this reason, this section focuses narrowly on old-age pensions). However, it is worth scrutinizing these parameters, along with income and work history data, to establish an objective measure of value. Recent analysis by Apella and Zunino (2025) did just this, using relatively rare data from social insurance administrators, which were made available only for Argentina, Mexico, Peru, and Uruguay (refer to table 7.1).[1] Apella and Zunino focused on social insurance pension plans, as these are typically the largest segment of the total package of social insurance coverage and are relatively intuitively easier than other social insurance plans.

Many workers in select LAC countries fail to meet the minimum contribution history to receive a contributory pension. The main challenge of simulating the value proposition for workers of participating in a social insurance pension plan is the limited portion of their observed employment histories during which individuals have contributed (their "contribution density"). As might be expected, in each of the four countries for which administrative data were made available, the contribution density of working women is lower than that of working men (as shown by the higher bars on the left side of the graphs in figure 7.2). Other than in the social sectors and public administration, women are significantly less likely to hold compliant jobs or participate, and, by extension, women are less likely to contribute to social insurance. However, although the distribution of men is more uniform, many achieve lower contribution densities than required to meet the vesting requirements for minimum contributory pensions.

FIGURE 7.2

Observed contribution density: Portion of working life making contributions to social insurance

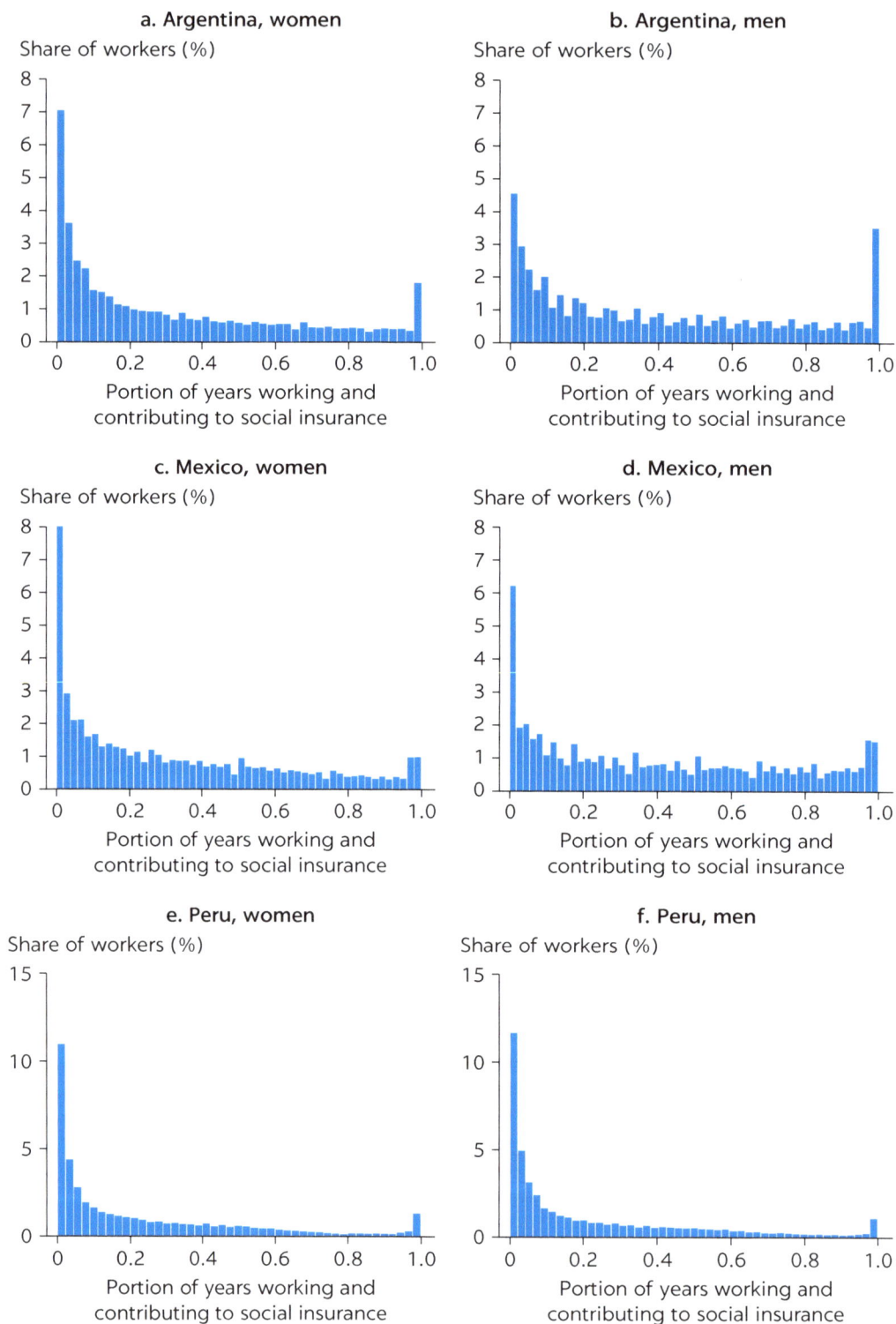

a. Argentina, women

Share of workers (%)

Portion of years working and contributing to social insurance

b. Argentina, men

Share of workers (%)

Portion of years working and contributing to social insurance

c. Mexico, women

Share of workers (%)

Portion of years working and contributing to social insurance

d. Mexico, men

Share of workers (%)

Portion of years working and contributing to social insurance

e. Peru, women

Share of workers (%)

Portion of years working and contributing to social insurance

f. Peru, men

Share of workers (%)

Portion of years working and contributing to social insurance

continued

Figure 7.2 Observed contribution density: Portion of working life making contributions to social insurance, (continued)

g. Uruguay, women

Share of workers (%)

h. Uruguay, men

Share of workers (%)

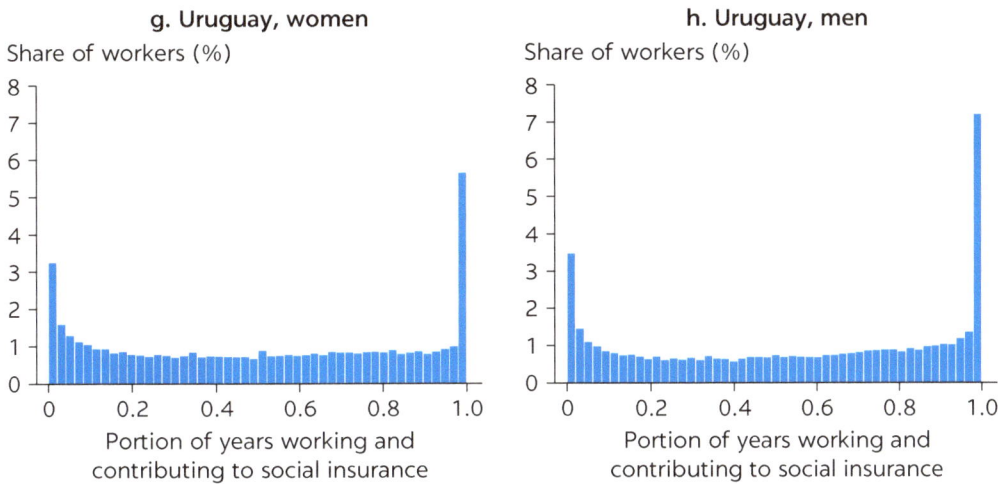

Sources: Reprinted with permission from Apella and Zunino 2025.
Note: The figures use administrative data on employment spells and contribution history.

Social security wealth (SSW) indicators were derived from actual and estimated pension contributions and expected retirement income. To overcome the limitations mentioned earlier, Apella and Zunino (2025) followed a three-step process. First, they obtained a set of simulated labor histories using the contribution histories observed in administrative data and econometric hazard models with labor force survey data to simulate probable "exits," "entries," and the implied contribution histories over each worker's complete working life. Second, the different levels of contributions that these individuals would have to make during their working lives were computed for the simulated employment and contribution histories, as well as the retirement income they would expect to receive. Third, the authors defined a synthetic indicator that summarizes the actuarial relationship between the contributions individuals are likely to make and the retirement income they can expect to receive: their SSW.[2] Based on this indicator, Apella and Zunino drew conclusions as to whether (1) the pension plans were actuarially neutral for individuals or the expected benefits included a net subsidy or net tax, and (2) the correlation between the generosity of the pension plan and contribution density presented incentives to participate (to formalize employment and contribute).

TABLE 7.1 Pension plans for Argentina, Mexico, Peru, and Uruguay

TYPE OF PLAN	ARGENTINA DEFINED BENEFIT	MEXICO DEFINED CONTRIBUTION	PERU DEFINED BENEFIT	URUGUAY MIXED
Generalized noncontributory pension	Yes	Yes	No	Yes
Minimum retirement age, years	65 for men, 60 for women	60	65 for men, 60 for women	65
Contributions required for a contributory benefit	30 years	1,250 weeks	10 years	25 years (age 65) 23 years (age 66) 21 years (age 67) 19 years (age 68) 17 years (age 69) 15 years (ages 70 or older)
Calculation of the pension	PBU + PAP	Maximum between calculation based on the Accumulated Savings Fund and PMG	$250 (10–15 years of contributions) $350 (15–20 years of contributions) Variable calculation as a percentage of the SR (20+ years of contributions)	TA × Cont. × SR

Source: Reprinted with permission from Apella and Zunino 2025.
Note: The PBU is a fixed amount. PAP is a variable benefit of 1.5 percent of the SR (in Argentina, it corresponds to the last 10 years of contributions) multiplied by the number of years of service. In Mexico, the PMG is a fixed amount in the ISSSTE and an increasing amount with the average salary contributed to the IMSS. In Peru, it corresponds to the last 5 years of contributions. In Uruguay, it corresponds to the last 20 years of contributions. Cont. = years of contributions; IMSS = Mexican Social Security Institute; ISSSTE = Institute for Social Security and Services for State Workers in Mexico; PAP = Second Pillar Pension Benefit; PBU = Universal Basic Pension; PMG = Guaranteed Minimum Pension; SR = reference salary; TA = acquisition rate, which varies with age.

Based on the value of SSW, conclusions can be drawn on whether pension plans are neutral, favorable, or unfavorable for the worker. By definition, a value of the SSW indicator equal to zero indicates that the pension plan is actuarially neutral, that is, the present value of contributions is identical to the present value of what workers can expect to receive as retirement pensions. In the case of "actuarial neutrality," the pension plan only alters the temporal pattern of individuals' income throughout their life cycle, without changing the total amount of income. Thus, according to Burkhauser and Warlick's (1981) classification, the pension plan is considered simply a savings and insurance program, without any net transfers or intragenerational redistribution.

A value of SSW greater (less) than zero indicates an actuarially favorable (unfavorable) situation for individuals insofar as they would receive (make) a net transfer for their participation in the pension plan. In this case, the pension plan is considered a joint insurance and transfer program and involves both redistribution of income and risk.

Figure 7.3 shows the average SSW results for workers in each decile of contribution density. The SSW indicator is presented for the contributory and noncontributory streams of benefits together and for only the contributory benefits. For the prospective participants in all four countries' social insurance pension plans, the simulation results indicate that minimum periods of contributions to become vested are a powerful deterrent. This is noticeable in Argentina, where, if it were not for noncontributory benefits, negative values of SSW would be obtained for all but the workers with the

FIGURE 7.3

Estimates of social security wealth from social insurance pension plans in Argentina, Mexico, Peru, and Uruguay

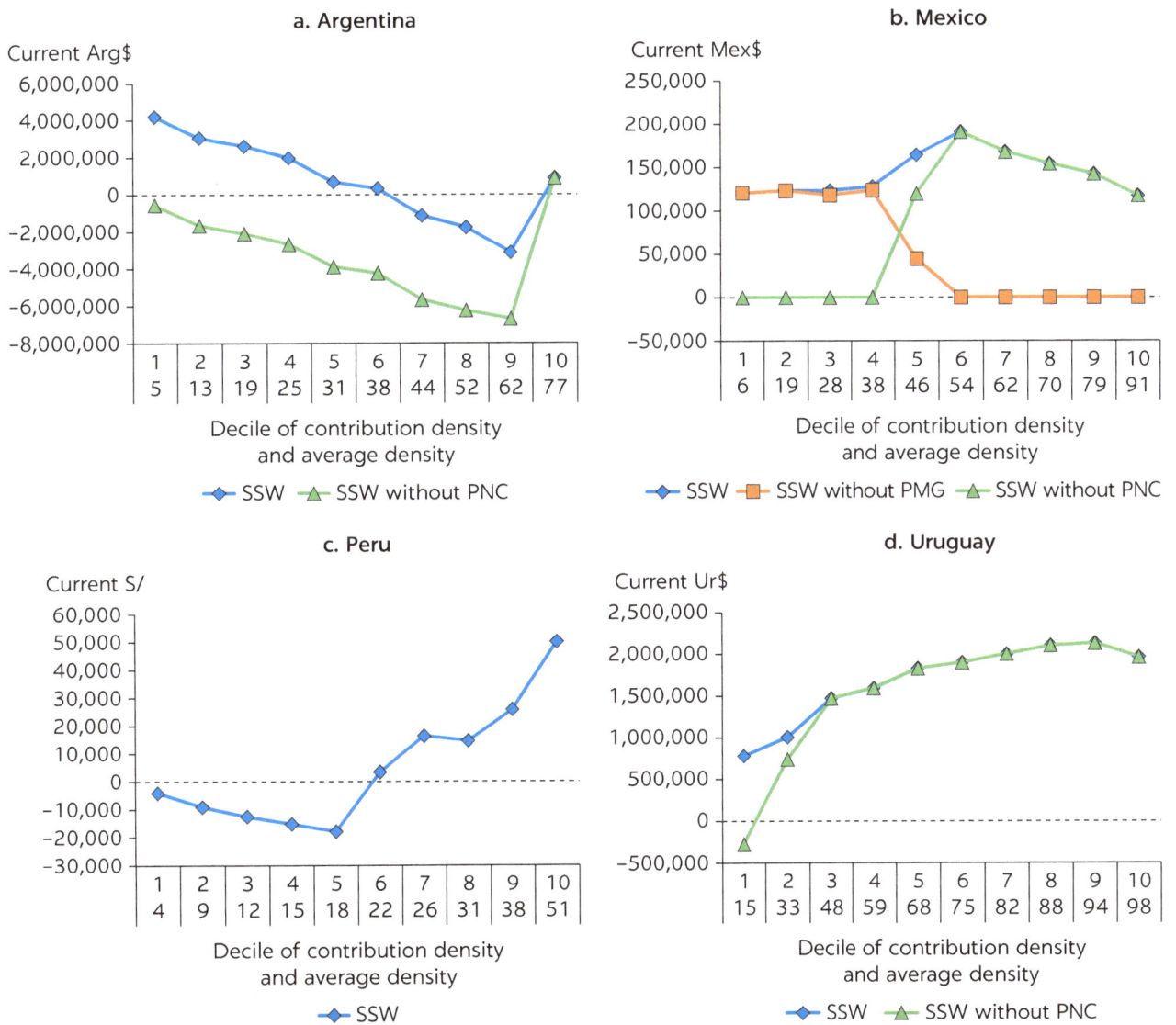

Source: Reprinted with permission from Apella and Zunino 2025.
Note: PMG = Guaranteed Minimum Pension; PNC = noncontributory pension; SSW = total social security wealth.

highest levels of contribution density (contribution density deciles 9 and 10). Although they are less exclusionary in the other three countries, requirements for minimum contribution periods make contributions a pure tax for more than half of the workers in Peru (which does not have a guaranteed minimum contributory benefit and has only a small noncontributory pension program). The minimum contribution requirement is the least exclusionary in Uruguay.

Because the principal segment of the pension plan offered by the Mexican Social Security Institute (IMSS) is an individual-owned savings plan, participants get back their accumulated savings even if they do not meet the minimum density to become vested for the minimum contributory pension (in Mexico's IMSS, SSW is zero—actuarially fair—even for participants with the lowest density of contributions). In the other countries, minimum required contribution periods appear to be a disincentive to participation. If workers are unlikely to meet the minimum contribution requirements (those with low contribution densities), their contributions are a pure tax. If a noncontributory benefit is available, the rational strategy for most workers is to minimize their contributions, as their SSW can be made up almost entirely by subsidies from the noncontributory program.

In the case of Mexico's IMSS, the contributory minimum pension guarantee generates implicit subsidies that fall with the level of contribution density (positively correlated with income) for two reasons: (1) As income grows, the proportion of cases in which a minimum pension guarantee is not relevant rises, and (2) as income grows, the difference between the Guaranteed Minimum Pension (PMG) and the benefit that corresponds to that of the individual savings pillar is smaller (lower subsidy).

This situation explains the downward trend in SSW between deciles 6 and 10 in Mexico. However, in all the density deciles, the average SSW is greater than zero, which denotes that, for some individuals, the PMG determines their retirement income. Among people who would not meet the participation requirement for a contributory pension, from the point of view of workers, the return of their individual savings ensures that the contributions made do not end up as a tax transfer to the system. In turn, among those who have access to a contributory pension, although the generosity of the system, summarized in the SSW indicator, decreases with the level of contributions, a greater history of contributions is associated with higher benefits; therefore, at the margin, the pension plan encourages participation.

THE PUZZLE OF COMPLIANCE

An inscription over the entrance to the U.S. Internal Revenue Service building declares, "Taxes are the price we pay for a civilized society," attributed to Oliver Wendell Holmes, Jr. The important policy question this inscription provokes is, to what extent are individuals willing to pay this price? (Adams 1993; Torgler 2007, 2012). In answer to this question, a growing literature is fast converging on an important conclusion: The traditional cost-benefit approach economists have taken to examine tax compliance is inadequate as a framework for understanding why people pay taxes. Rather, the basic economic model of individual choice must be expanded by introducing aspects of behavior and motivation (Torgler 2012).

In Becker's (1968) crime and punishment model, a rational individual maximizes the expected utility of a tax evasion gamble by weighing the benefits of successful cheating against the risky prospect of detection and punishment. This model, which was first applied to tax compliance by Allingham and Sandmo (1972), is used as a basic theoretical framework in nearly all research on tax compliance. Individuals pay taxes because they are afraid of getting caught and penalized if they do not report all their income. The obvious policy implication is that enforcement matters because it affects the financial considerations that motivate, at least in part, an individual's compliance choices: Enforcement creates deterrence. However, this approach also concludes that an individual pays taxes because—and *only* because—of the economic consequences of detection and punishment. The obvious implication is that governments can encourage greater tax compliance by increasing deterrence through higher audit rates and steeper penalties.

This may be true; however, it is not the full story. A growing body of evidence shows that the levels of compliance observed, especially those determined by enforcement, cannot be explained entirely by pure financial considerations. Taxpayer audits are a central feature of the voluntary compliance system in all countries, largely because more-frequent audits are thought to reduce tax evasion. However, the percentage of individual income tax returns subject to a thorough tax audit is small in most countries, typically less than 1 percent of all returns (Torgler 2007). Similarly, sanctions are low. The penalty even for fraudulent evasion seldom exceeds more than the amount of unpaid taxes, and these penalties are infrequently imposed.

Therefore, a purely probabilistic simulation of the evasion gamble suggests that most rational individuals should underreport income or overclaim deductions not subject to independent verification, because it is unlikely that their cheating will be detected and penalized (Alm and Martinez-Vazquez 2003; Alm, Martinez-Vazquez, and Torgler 2010). Yet, even in the least-compliant countries, evasion never rises to the levels predicted by the conventional model. Indeed, often substantial numbers of individuals apparently pay all or most of their taxes all or most of the time, regardless of the financial incentives they face from the enforcement regime. The basic model of individual compliance behavior, therefore, implies that rational individuals should report virtually no income. Although compliance varies significantly across countries and tax regimes and is often low, it seldom falls to the level predicted by the standard model. Enforcement alone cannot account for observed levels of compliance (Kirchler 2007; Slemrod 1992; Torgler 2007).

INSTITUTIONAL CREDIBILITY: THE KEY TO BUILDING AND MAINTAINING TAX MORALE

What is behind this apparent puzzle of tax compliance? The social norm of compliance or "tax morale"[3] may help explain why people willingly conform. If tax morale is a key determinant in enhancing compliance, policies aside from enforcement would help reduce avoidance and evasion. Deterrence is just one instrument to increase compliance. Improving knowledge about the causes and consequences of tax morale could lead to better tax policy through better voluntary compliance.

Studies have shown a simple but strong inverse relationship between tax morale and the size of the informal economy (Alm and Torgler 2006; Torgler 2005). Moreover, tax morale can explain more than 30 percent of the total variance across countries in the size of the informal economy. The relationship has been confirmed by multivariate analysis that indicates that tax morale has a strong impact on the size of the informal economy, using cross-sectional and panel approaches (Torgler and Schneider 2007, 2009). In an extensive review of tax compliance in OECD countries, Feld and Schneider (2011) found that, when compared to the impact of tax morale, the quantitative impact of deterrence is far less important.

To reduce tax avoidance and evasion, an effective monitoring and enforcement structure is necessary, of course, but is not sufficient. Indeed, extreme penalties can backfire, particularly where institutions are weak, by creating a setting in which bribery and corruption are more prevalent, and the end result may be a general loss of trust. Designing effective policies for reducing tax evasion requires an understanding of the behavioral aspects of the tax compliance decision. If individuals' attitudes toward compliance are a function of social and cultural norms, measures to enhance these norms are an essential complement to the usual enforcement instruments.

Social norms of compliance are shaped by a country's institutions. In representative democracies, taxation and public finance matters are agreed through these institutions (Bird, Martinez-Vazquez, and Torgler 2008). A key driver of avoidance and evasion in Latin America is that most countries for many years lacked a social contract between government and the population (Lledo, Schneider, and Moore 2004). State legitimacy rests to a considerable extent on citizens' "quasi-voluntary" compliance (Levi 1988).

Taxes are considered the "price paid" for government services and, for this reason, taxpayers are sensitive to the way the government uses tax revenues:

Taxpayers perceive their relationship with the state not only as a relationship of coercion and obligation but, more importantly, also as one of exchange. Individuals will feel cheated if taxes are not spent efficiently. Inversely, if citizens believe that their interests and preferences are properly represented in political institutions and they receive an adequate supply of public goods, their identification with the state increases and so, too, does their willingness to contribute.

An inefficient state where corruption is rampant will lower citizens' trust in authority and their incentive to cooperate and contribute. A more-legitimate state increases citizens' willingness to contribute. Many studies have shown that state legitimacy and credibility can increase taxpayers' positive attitudes and commitment to the tax system, with an accompanying positive effect on compliance (Hayoz and Hug 2007; Smith 1992).

Institutional instability, lack of transparency, and weakness in the rule of law undermine the willingness of citizens to be active in the formal economy. A sustainable tax system is based on taxation that is generally seen as "fair" and government that is considered "responsive." This is achieved when people see a strong connection between tax payments and the supply of public goods (Bird, Martinez-Vazquez, and Torgler 2006; Martinez-Vazquez 2001). However, in places where political elites, the public administration, and legislators wield considerable discretionary power; where institutions are neither credible nor working well; and where formal channels of accountability and recourse are missing or weak, citizens quickly lose trust in the authority and credibility of the state.

For these reasons, in countries where corruption is systemic, people begin to feel justified in evading taxes, which can quickly become an accepted social norm. Citizens who pay taxes will feel cheated if they believe that corruption is widespread, their tax burden is not spent well, and they cannot hold their governments accountable for results.

The greatest danger is when a critical mass of tax avoiders and evaders forms, which raises the marginal cost of compliance to such an extent that following the rules becomes unviable. The more widespread the knowledge that others are not paying their taxes, the more noncompliance increases (Adamam and Mumcu 2020; Torgler 2012). As Bergman (2002, 13) stated, "Nobody likes to pay taxes, but what they dislike even more is feeling like a sucker, knowing they are the only one paying taxes."

HOW IMPORTANT IS TAX MORALE? CROSS-COUNTRY CORRELATION ANALYSIS

This section presents the results of a large-sample, multivariate correlation analysis on country-level data. The share of people working informally (presented and explained in figure 2.1 in chapter 2) is regressed on an expanded indicator of tax morale and structural and policy control variables. As these variables rarely change over time, the greater inferential value of this exercise comes from variation in the data across countries. The sample size differs across the correlations, but all the variables included are available for a sample of 875 observations, for 103 countries, over 2008–19. The sample includes 158 observations from LAC, covering 12 countries in the region.

The main variable of interest is tax morale. The usual measure, which is collected by the periodic World Values Survey (WVS) every 4 years (Torgler et al. 2008), yields only a small sample of observations. To increase the number of observations, the analysis here uses additional variables from the World Governance Indicators, constructed by the World Bank, and the Quality of Governance data set from the University of Gothenburg. The additional variables are highly correlated with the WVS tax morale indicator, namely "political stability," "rule of law," and "political corruption." A composite indicator is constructed from these three variables, using principal component analysis.[4] Table 7.2 explains the other variables included in the exercise. Correlation coefficients and their statistical significance are presented in table 7.3. The full set of variables is included in the final specification (refer to column 6). The relationships between each variable and the share of unregistered workers make intuitive sense. The extent of unregistered work falls with a country's level of income per capita, confirming the commonly found inverse relationship between the level of development and various indicators of unregistered work and the size of the informal economy (Ohnsorge and Yu 2022).

Control variables for the stringency of labor market regulation and countries' total payroll taxes show a significant positive association with the extent of unregistered work. The more restrictive a country's employment protection

TABLE 7.2 Country-level variables used in the multivariate correlation analysis

VARIABLE	EXPLANATION	SOURCE
GDP	Log GDP per capita, PPP, constant 2017 international dollars	WDI, World Bank
Tax morale	PCA composite of "political stability," "rule of law," and "political corruption"	WGI, World Bank QoG, University of Gothenburg
epl_db	Employment protection legislation, PCA composite of "restrictions on hiring," "dismissal procedures," and "cost of dismissal" indicators	Employing Workers, Doing Business, World Bank
MW	Statutory MW as a share of value added per worker	ILO and WDI, World Bank
ictd_tapaywf	Total payroll taxes × value added per worker	

Source: Original table for this publication.
Note: GDP = gross domestic product; ILO = International Labour Organization; MW = minimum wage; PCA = principal component analysis; PPP = purchasing power parity; QoG = Quality of Government Institute; WDI = World Development Indicators; WGI = Worldwide Governance Indicators.

TABLE 7.3 Share of people working informally: Cross-country, multivariate correlation analysis

VARIABLE	DEPENDENT VARIABLE: SHARE OF WORKING PEOPLE WORKING INFORMALLY					
	(1)	**(2)**	**(3)**	**(4)**	**(5)**	**(6)**
GDP	−0.000872***	−0.000588***	−0.000883***	−0.000930***	−0.000867***	−0.000512***
	(−47.72)	(−19.93)	(−38.97)	(−33.45)	(−41.23)	(−11.38)
Tax morale		−5.782***				−6.724***
		(−14.94)				(−10.24)
epl_db			2.145***			1.140***
			(7.709)			(3.123)
MW				7.771***		7.619**
				(2.700)		(2.317)
ictd_tapaywf					−0	0**
					(−0.253)	(2.330)
Constant	57.59***	55.63***	59.76***	57.86***	57.04***	50.63***
	(104.9)	(82.57)	(84.54)	(42.20)	(85.55)	(31.28)
No. of observations	2,935	2,260	1,766	1,248	2,057	875
R squared	0.437	0.528	0.516	0.511	0.465	0.600

Source: Original table for this publication.
Note: "Tax morale" and "employment protection" (epl_db) were constructed using PCA. *t* statistics are in parentheses. Refer to table 7.2 for definitions of the variables. epl_db = employment protection legislation; GDP = gross domestic product; ictd_tapaywf = total payroll taxes times value added per worker; MW = minimum wage; PCA = principal components analysis.
***$p < .01$; **$p < .05$.

legislation—measured here by a composite variable constructed from the Doing Business and Employing Workers indicators—the larger the share of people working informally. The level of a country's statutory minimum wage (relative to output per worker) shows the strongest correlation among all the variables—a higher minimum wage is associated with a larger share of people working informally, consistent with the prediction of standard two-sector models and with the importance of the level of the wage floor in the deterrent effect of the FTR. Total payroll taxes have only a weak association with the share of people working informally, largely validating the microdata analysis of the FTR, which accounts for how the burden of payroll taxes varies across different types of workers.

The variable of greatest interest, "tax morale," given the questions posed in this chapter, has a strong inverse relationship with the share of people working informally. Indeed, among the variables included in this analysis, tax morale is surpassed in importance only by the level of the minimum wage, although tax morale has a higher level of statistical significance. Perceptions of political stability, rule of law, and political corruption—all determinants of social norms about compliance—are highly correlated with the share of unregistered workers. Countries with higher levels of tax morale have a smaller share of people working informally. Marginal correlations are plotted in figure 7.4.

FIGURE 7.4

Marginal correlations of the share of people working informally and income, tax morale, employment protection, minimum wages, and total payroll taxes in Argentina

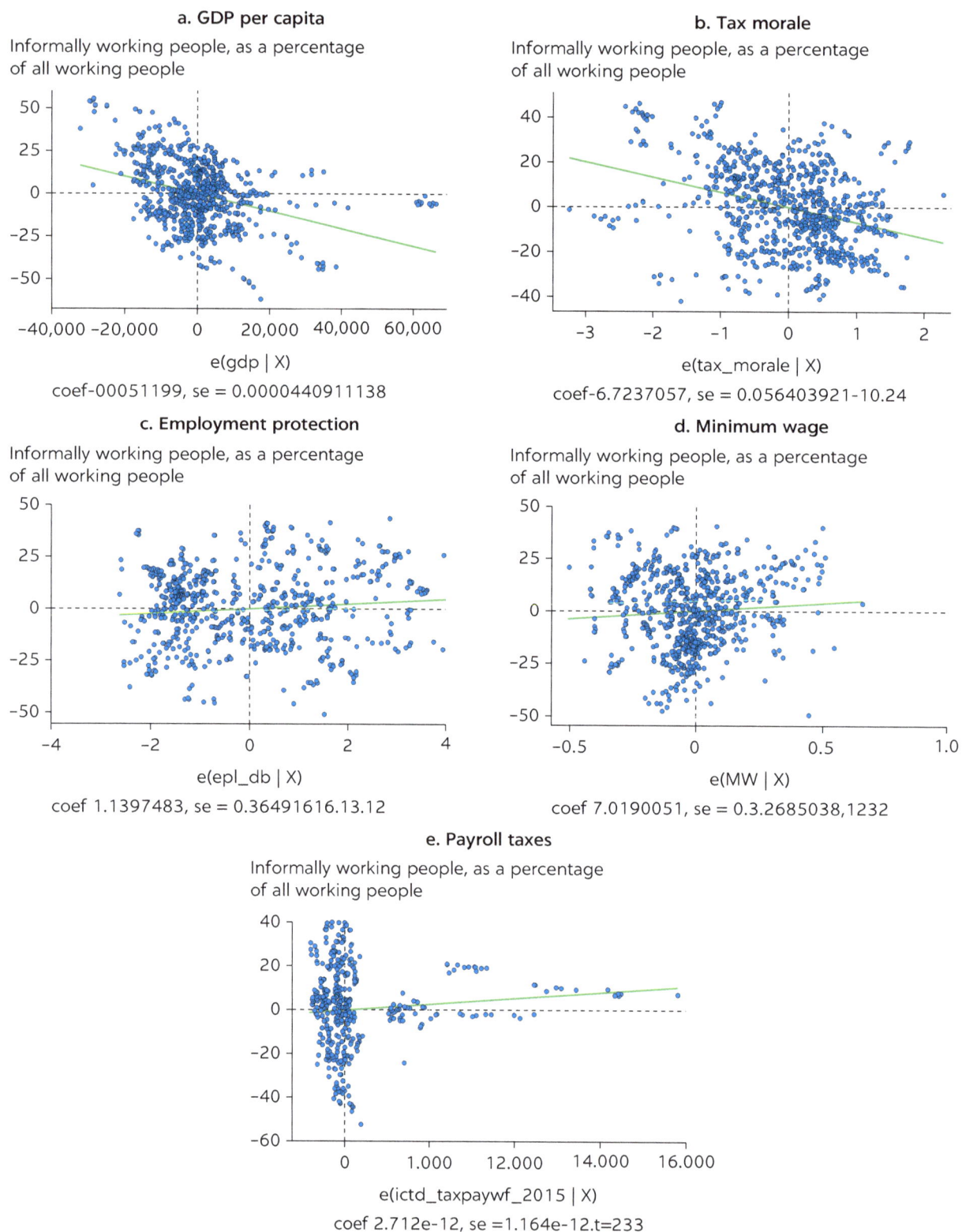

a. GDP per capita

Informally working people, as a percentage of all working people

e(gdp | X)

coef-00051199, se = 0.0000440911138

b. Tax morale

Informally working people, as a percentage of all working people

e(tax_morale | X)

coef-6.7237057, se = 0.056403921-10.24

c. Employment protection

Informally working people, as a percentage of all working people

e(epl_db | X)

coef 1.1397483, se = 0.36491616.13.12

d. Minimum wage

Informally working people, as a percentage of all working people

e(MW | X)

coef 7.0190051, se = 0.3.2685038,1232

e. Payroll taxes

Informally working people, as a percentage of all working people

e(ictd_taxpaywf_2015 | X)

coef 2.712e-12, se =1.164e-12.t=233

Source: Original figures for this publication using data from ILO, QoG, WDI, and WGIs.

Note: Refer to table 7.2 for definitions of the variables. epl_db = employment protection legislation; gdp = gross domestic product; ictd_tapaywf = total payroll taxes times value added per worker; MW = minimum wage. The observations included in each panel are for 103 countries over the years 2008–19.

PRINCIPLES AND PRACTICES TO IMPROVE TAX MORALE

Much of the policy literature on how to improve and sustain tax morale has suggested starting with a shift in how taxation is conducted (Smith 2002). Frey and Feld (2002) argued that tax morale rises when tax officials treat taxpayers with respect. The inverse is also true: Tax morale falls when tax administrators treat taxpayers as suspicious and requiring coercion to pay taxes. Suspicion, control, and coercion on the part of the tax administration can crowd out people's intrinsic motivation to act as good citizens. If tax administrators start with a presumption of trust and good citizenship and establish transparent payment procedures, taxpayers are more likely to respond positively (Torgler 2005, 2012).

Hence, the more that regulatory interactions are based on trust, the more likely that regulators will be able to nurture the development of reciprocal trust relationships (Batrancea et al. 2019). Frey and Feld (2002) empirically showed that a change in treatment improves tax morale and compliance. A shift in the orientation of taxation was key in raising tax morale and compliance in today's HICs.

Where citizens hold positive attitudes toward the tax authority and the tax system, tax morale and collection are significantly greater. Respectful and fair treatment of taxpayers induces respect for the tax system and leads to cooperation. In contrast, opacity, inefficiency, and unfairness in interactions between the tax administration and taxpayers erode the intrinsic motivation to pay taxes (Slemrod and Yitzhaki 2000). Evidence from several countries also shows that, instead of a heavy focus on compliance management, risk control, and enforcement, better results are likely when the tax administration becomes more focused on service, customers, quality, transparency, and making the process of compliance as painless as possible (Vuletin 2024). Where the tax administration tries to be honest, fair, informative, and helpful, acting as a service institution and thus treating taxpayers as partners and not inferiors in a hierarchical relationship, tax morale increases and taxpayers have stronger incentives to pay taxes honestly (Torgler 2005, 2012).

Control and elimination of corruption are also critical to improving tax morale. In countries where corruption is systemic, the obligation to pay taxes quickly vanishes as a social norm. Corruption generally undermines the tax morale of citizens, who feel cheated if they perceive that the public finances are being squandered or used for ill-gotten gains. At the extreme, people can feel strongly entitled to evade taxes and the structures of the formal economy.

NOTES

1. Although it was not one of the countries analyzed in depth for this report, Argentina is included here for comparison value. Limited access to data for Colombia was granted, but the data were not available in time to be included in this report.

2. Following the seminal work of Burkhauser and Warlick (1981) and Forteza and Mussio (2012), lifetime SSW is calculated as the difference between the current expected values at the start of an individual's working life of contributions made and expected retirement income. SSW represents the expected amount of net transfers the pension plan will make to the individual at the end of the life cycle. This indicator has been widely used in the social security literature to quantify transfers (for example, refer to Brown, Coronado, and Fullerton 2009; Gruber and Wise 1999, 2004; Liebman 2001; Zunino et al. 2022).

3. Tax morale is most widely measured using responses to the following World Values Survey (and European Values Survey) question: "Please tell me for each of the following statements whether you think it can always be justified, never be justified, or something in between: … Cheating on tax if you have the chance." The question leads to a 10-scale index of tax morale with the two extreme points "never justified" and "always justified" (Torgler 2007, 2012).

4. In the principal component analysis, the first component, "political stability," contains 85.5 percent of the total information in the three variables.

REFERENCES

Adamam, F., and A. Mumcu. 2020. "Perceptions on Governance Effectiveness and Informality: A Self-fulfilling Equilibrium." Working Paper No. 2010/05, Department of Economics, Bogazici University, Bebek, Istanbul, Türkiye.

Adams, C. 1993. *For Good and Evil: The Impact of Taxes on the Course of Civilization.* London: Madison Books.

Allingham, M. G., and A. Sandmo. 1972. "Income Tax Evasion: A Theoretical Analysis." *Journal of Public Economics* 1: 323–38.

Alm, J., and J. Martinez-Vazquez. 2003. "Institutions, Paradigms, and Tax Evasion in Developing and Transition Countries." In *Public Finance in Developing and Transitional Countries: Essays in Honor of Richard Bird*, edited by J. Martinez-Vazquez and J. Alm, 146–78. Cheltenham, UK: Edward Elgar.

Alm, J., J. Martinez-Vazquez, and B. Torgler, eds. 2010. *Developing Alternative Frameworks for Explaining Tax Compliance.* London: Routledge.

Alm, J., and B. Torgler. 2006. "Culture Difference and Tax Morale in Europe and the United States." *Journal of Economic Psychology* 27 (2): 224–46.

Apella, I., and G. Zunino. 2025. "Trade-off entre los objetivos de los sistemas de pensiones en contextos de baja densidad de cotización. Un análisis de diseños alternativos en cuatro países de América Latina." Serie de Documentos de Trabajo 01/2025, CINVE, Montevideo, Uruguay. https://cinve.org.uy/wp-content/uploads /2024/07/DT-2025-01-ApellaZunino.pdf.

Batrancea, L., A. Nichita, J. Olsen, C. Kogler, E. Kirchler, E. Hoelzl, A. Weiss, et al. 2019. "Trust and Power as Determinants of Tax Compliance across 44 Nations." *Journal of Economic Psychology* 74: 102191. https://doi.org/10.1016/j.joep.2019.102191.

Becker, G. S. 1968. "Crime and Punishment: An Economic Approach." *Journal of Political Economy* 76: 169–217.

Bergman, M. 2002. "Who Pays for Social Policy? A Study on Taxes and Trust." *Journal of Social Policy* 31 (2): 289–305.

Bird, R., J. Martinez-Vazquez, and B. Torgler. 2006. "Societal Institutions and Tax Effort in Developing Countries." In *The Challenges of Tax Reform in the Global Economy*, edited by J. Alm, J. Martinez-Vazquez, and M. Rider, 283–338. New York: Springer.

Bird, R. M., J. Martinez-Vazquez, and B. Torgler. 2008. "Tax Effort in Developing Countries and High-Income Countries: The Impact of Corruption, Voice and Accountability." *Economic Analysis & Policy* 38: 55–71.

Brown, J. R., J. L. Coronado, and D. Fullerton. 2009. "Is Social Security Part of the Social Safety Net?" NBER Working Paper 15070, National Bureau of Economic Research, Cambridge, MA.

Burkhauser, R. V., and J. L. Warlick. 1981. "Disentangling the Annuity from the Redistributive Aspects of Social Security in the United States." *Review of Income and Wealth* 27 (4): 401–21.

Feld, L. P., and F. Schneider. 2011. "Survey on the Shadow Economy and Undeclared Work in OECD Countries." In *Handbook on the Shadow Economy*, edited by F. Schneider. Cheltenham, UK: Edward Elgar.

Forteza, A., and I. Mussio. 2012. "Assessing Redistribution in the Uruguayan Social Security System." *Journal of Income Distribution* 21 (1): 65–87.

Frey, B. S., and L. P. Feld. 2002. "Deterrence and Morale in Taxation: An Empirical Analysis." Available at SSRN: https://ssrn.com/abstract=341380 or http://dx.doi .org/10.2139/ssrn.341380.

Gruber, J., and D. Wise. 1999. *Social Security and Retirement around the World*. Chicago and London: The University of Chicago Press.

Gruber, J., and D. Wise. 2004. *Social Security and Retirement around the World: Microestimations*. Chicago and London: The University of Chicago Press.

Hayoz, N., and S. Hug, eds. 2007. *Tax Evasion, Trust, and State Capacities: How Good Is Tax Morale in Central and Eastern Europe?* Bern: Peter Lang.

ILO (International Labor Organization). n.d. ILOSTAT, Geneva, Switzerland. https://ilostat.ilo.org.

Kirchler, E. 2007. *The Economic Psychology of Tax Behaviour*. Cambridge, UK: Cambridge University Press.

Levi, M. 1988. *Rules and Revenue*. Berkeley, CA: University of California Press.

Liebman, J. 2001. "Redistribution in the Current US Social Security System." NBER Working Paper 8625, National Bureau of Economic Research, Cambridge, MA.

Lledo, V., A. Schneider, and M. Moore. 2004. "Pro-Poor Tax Reform in Latin America: A Critical Survey and Policy Recommendations." IDS Working Paper 230, Institute of Development Studies, Brighton, Sussex, England.

Martinez-Vazquez, J. 2001. "Mexico: An Evaluation of the Main Features of the Tax System." International Studies Program Working Paper 01-12, Andrew Young School of Policy Studies, Atlanta, GA.

Ohnsorge, F., and S. Yu. 2022. *The Long Shadow of Informality: Challenges and Policies*. Washington, DC: World Bank.

Perry, G. E., W. F. Maloney, O. S. Arias, P. Fajnzylber, A. D. Mason, J. Saavedra-Chanduvi, and O. Arias. 2007. *Informality: Exit and Exclusion*. World Bank Latin American and Caribbean Studies. Washington, DC: World Bank. http://hdl.handle.net/10986/6730.

QoG (Quality of Governance Standard Dataset). n.d. The QoG Institute, University of Gothenburg, Göteborg. https://www.gu.se/en/quality-government/qog-data.

Slemrod, J., ed. 1992. *Why People Pay Taxes: Tax Compliance and Enforcement*. Ann Arbor, MI: University of Michigan Press.

Slemrod, J., and S. Yitzhaki. 2000. "Tax Avoidance, Evasion and Administration." NBER Working Paper W7473, National Bureau of Economic Research, Cambridge, MA.

Smith, K. W. 1992. "Reciprocity and Fairness: Positive Incentives for Tax Compliance." In *Why People Pay Taxes: Tax Compliance and Enforcement*, edited by J. Slemrod, 223–58. Ann Arbor, MI: University of Michigan Press.

Smith, R. S. 2002. "The Underground Economy: Guidance for Policy Makers." *Canadian Tax Journal* 50 (5): 1655–61.

Tommasi, M., and J. Saavedra-Chanduvi. 2007. "Informality, the State and the Social Contract in Latin America: A Preliminary Exploration." *International Labour Review* 146 (3–4): 279–309.

Torgler, B. 2005. "Tax Morale in Latin America." *Public Choice* 122: 133–57. https://doi.org/10.1007/s11127-005-5790-4.

Torgler, B. 2007. *Tax Compliance and Tax Morale: A Theoretical and Empirical Analysis.* Cheltenham, UK: Edward Elgar.

Torgler, B. 2012. "Tax Morale, Eastern Europe and European Enlargement." *Communist and Post-Communist Studies* 45 (1–2): 11–25.

Torgler, B., I. C. Demir, A. Macintyre, and M. Schaffner. 2008. "Causes and Consequences of Tax Morale: An Empirical Investigation." *Economic Analysis & Policy* 38: 313–39.

Torgler, B., and F. Schneider. 2007. "Shadow Economy, Tax Morale, Governance and Institutional Quality: A Panel Analysis." IZA Discussion Papers 2563, Institute of Labor Economics, Bonn, Germany.

Torgler, B., and F. Schneider. 2009. "The Impact of Tax Morale and Institutional Quality on the Shadow Economy." *Journal of Economic Psychology* 30: 228–45.

Vuletin, G. 2024. "Progressive Taxation for Growth in LAC." Draft Regional Study for the Office of the Chief Economist, Latin America and Caribbean Regional Office, World Bank, Washington, DC.

WDI (World Development Indicators dataset). 2023. World Bank, Washington, DC. https://databank.worldbank.org/source/world-development-indicators.

WGI (World Governance Indicators dataset). 2023. World Bank, Washington, DC. Accessed June 3, 2025. https://info.worldbank.org/governance/wgi/.

Zunino, G., J. Pessina, M. Pereira, and L. Parrilla. 2022. "Cobertura, suficiencia e impactos distributivos del proyecto de reforma de la Seguridad Social." Centro de Investigaciones Económicas (CINVE), Montevideo, Uruguay.

8 A Reform Roadmap
GUIDING PRINCIPLES, OBJECTIVES, AND MILESTONES ON THE PATH TO IMPROVED INCENTIVES

NOT A BLUEPRINT, BUT A ROADMAP

This chapter concludes the report with reform recommendations in the form of a "roadmap." The roadmap metaphor was chosen to acknowledge that the policy reform process is rarely linear or otherwise orderly—often it is circumstantially random and opportunistic. With a good notion of their destination and the right navigational tools, policy makers can turn circumstances and opportunities to their advantage and stay on track.

As shown in the previous chapters, country contexts vary enormously, as do the measures their governments are likely to prioritize and the impacts these will have on the incentive to (in)formalize work. The conceptual framework presented in chapter 3 recognizes not only that the challenge facing policy makers is multidimensional but also that the current situation (or "equilibrium") is a point at the intersection of (at least) three axes.

The steps that governments in the region can take next will depend on how far along they are on the path of institutional and economic development. Policy makers may not always be able to choose when to take the next steps, but with the benefit of a metaphorical reform roadmap, at least the steps can be taken in a consistent direction.

This chapter sets out the common overarching principles and approaches to reforming taxes and benefits that are likely to lead to wider compliance and greater participation, as well as identifies intermediate objectives and a set of "milestones" to mark progress along the way.

A reproducibility package is available for this book in the Reproducible Research Repository at https://reproducibility.worldbank.org/catalog/330/.

FIVE GUIDING PRINCIPLES FOR DESIGNING AND NAVIGATING A REFORM ROADMAP

What is the destination? Growing economies with robust markets that continuously offer more people better jobs—platforms of opportunity to pursue their aspirations safely and sustainably.

1. Job creation and greater productivity are the priority means to achieve sustained reduction of poverty and inequality

This principle entails reforms that move tax and social protection systems in a direction that matches the evolution of the labor market. Income earned through market work is consistently found to be the strongest, most-effective instrument for helping people overcome and stay out of poverty.

For countries in a region as vulnerable to shocks as Latin America and the Caribbean (LAC), slowing and lowering the churn of households in and out of poverty is foundational for achieving shared prosperity. Governments interested in eradicating poverty should release the labor market mechanism to work as freely as possible to create jobs and growth. Yet, as is the case in most markets, the market for labor is rife with failures. Those most germane to this report include the uneven distribution of bargaining power among employers and job-seekers, information asymmetries, and missing or inadequate insurance instruments.

These market failures are the primary motivation for labor and social insurance policies. Hence, these policies should be remedies that improve job quality and help people manage risks. The policies are not ends in themselves; rather, they are subordinate to the objectives of creating better jobs for more people, raising productivity, and propelling inclusive economic growth. Therefore, policies—whether institutions, regulations, or interventions— must evolve as societies, economies, and the nature of risks in the world of work evolve (Packard et al. 2019).

2. A neutral policy stance on how people earn their living is paramount

Borrowed from the taxation principle of avoiding favorable treatment of income from one source over another (Acosta-Ormaechea, Pienknagura, and Pizzinelli 2022; Furman 2008; Musgrave 1959; Picketty and Saez 2012), *neutrality* should also apply to the design and deployment of mandates on how, where, when, and with what level of protections market work takes place. Although the specifics are still a matter of debate, the rationale for having a mandate to guide people's saving and insurance choices is widely accepted.

What is difficult to defend is the notion that this rationale no longer applies if a person moves from one form of working to another. It is also difficult to argue that individuals somehow overcome myopia and other cognitive limitations when they move from subordinated, dependent employment to working for themselves. It has been argued that self-employed workers have an intrinsically higher tolerance for risk that is integral to the process of creative destruction (Cho, Robalino, and Watson 2014). The empirical evidence to prove or disprove this hypothesis varies by context (Alvarez 2024; Autor and Houseman 2005; Barr and Packard 2002, 2003).

In LAC economies, individuals move in and out of work and across ways of working, and these dynamics frustrate workers' ability to achieve minimum contribution requirements. If a mandate to save and insure is legitimate, it should be so for all working people. Similarly, the arguments for fetishizing certain sectors or ways of working—with special tax treatment and exemptions—over others are growing stale as work in the service sectors grows to be as productive as—or more productive than—manufacturing jobs (Nayyar and Cruz 2018; Nayyar and Davies 2023).

Special regimes—like the Monotributo (the simplified tax system for small businesses and self-employed individuals) in Uruguay or the SIMPLES (Simplified Tax Regime) and MEI (Individual Micro-Entrepreneur System) in Brazil—have opened the doors of social insurance to many self-employed workers. Overnight elimination of such special regimes would be rash, yet ensuring that the application of mandates and taxes is consistent and equitable across the ways people work would remove incentives to avoid and evade. A careful analysis of special regimes and reforms to ensure proportionality— steps toward consistency and eventual convergence—could eliminate incentives for strategic gaming, which often takes the form of firms and workers "disguising" their employment as self-employment or abusing regulations by outsourcing and subcontracting.

3. The structure of program financing should follow best taxation practices

Put another way, the costs of diverging from best taxation practices will accumulate more rapidly than they have in the past. When program financing departs from best practices, the inefficiencies caused by misalignment raise compliance costs and lower the perceived value of benefits. Accumulated legacy liabilities and rising demands on governments combine with population aging to create an imperative to raise public revenue. To address the increased liabilities and demands without impairing productivity and growth, more intensive taxation must adhere to best practices. Although the debate over earmarking taxes is ongoing, sufficient consensus exists on aspects that are core to social protection financing.

These aspects include reserving the use of statutory, individualized payroll taxes for programs that cover losses arising in the labor market and that are influenced by the parties to employment contracts. Examples include the risk of work-related injuries, termination of employment, and loss of the ability to earn due to disability or aging. These losses have few or no *externalities*—the costs imposed on others from leaving these risks uncovered are null or minimal. The coverage entitlements and benefits conferred are wholly owned by contributing individuals and their household dependents.

Social inclusion and equity objectives—such as poverty alleviation and poverty prevention among those living close to the poverty line, the welfare of historically disenfranchised groups, and income redistribution—are laudable but should be financed by general revenues. As a corollary to this argument, if a program is so important for social welfare—in other words, the social costs and consequences of people going without it are so great that it hinders the well-being of others—why make eligibility for coverage and its financing reliant on the good behavior of employers and workers? Reserving the use of payroll taxes strictly for individual (including dependent family) coverage and entitlements would dramatically lower the *perceived* tax element of mandates to save and insure (refer to Palacios and Robalino 2020). Furthermore, this approach would increase the value that working people place on complying and participating (Friedman 1962; Summers 1989).

With a few exceptions, the policies and programs for which a new financing model would be required if governments followed this advice serve important ends. It is not within the scope of this report to present specific proposals for how they should be financed in lieu of payroll taxes, although recent World Bank reports present the broad principles that can guide structural reforms (for example, Packard et al. 2019), as summarized in box 8.1. Rather, the analysis presented in this report adds to the growing number of arguments for governments in the LAC region to broaden their tax bases and pursue a more-balanced deployment of revenue instruments (for example, refer to Vuletin 2024).

4. Purely administrative changes and enhancements yield substantial gains in perceived value

This insight rises to the level of a policy principle, as it points to several measures that can have powerful, positive impacts and yet may not require politically difficult legislative action. Administrative and enforcement capacity needs to be modernized, strengthened, and sustained. The dangers of moral hazard and the temptations for people to "free ride" can be minimized with better-designed policies and programs. Yet, these behaviors are predictably and persistently human reactions to the availability of risk pooling and other collective goods, and, as such, they cannot be eliminated entirely.

Box 8.1

Policy recommendations from a social protection white paper on risk sharing

In September 2019, the World Bank published a white paper that presented a vision for risk-sharing policy, given the impact on labor markets of so-called "global megatrends"—technological, demographic, social, and climate change—all of which diversify the ways in which people work. The white paper concluded that greater access to publicly organized "risk pools"—the unalienable essence of social insurance—financed from taxes with the broadest possible base, should underpin the foundation of any new risk-sharing model in a national social protection system.

The key point of departure from previous studies was the principle that poverty prevention and other inclusion or income redistribution objectives (that is, *vertical redistribution*) should be explicitly and transparently pursued with instruments financed from broad-based taxes. Statutory employer and employee contributions are a financing instrument that should be reserved to finance consumption-smoothing instruments with actuarially fair parameters (that is, *horizontal redistribution*). By following this principle and with more-accessible, more-effective national-level *insurance assistance* in place to help people manage risk and uncertainty, governments would no longer need to rely as heavily on firm-based, employer-provided protections. There would be greater room to loosen restrictions on firms' contracting and dismissal decisions and shift government attention and resources to reemployment services and support for other market transitions.

The fiscal implications seem daunting. However, many countries could finance the proposed protections by reallocating existing expenditures and redeploying resources spent on energy price subsidies or other broad price subsidies. Other countries might need increased revenues. In some countries, governments might be unable to provide sufficient resources for fully realizing optimal risk sharing. Yet, the objective is consistent with the policy agenda to which most governments have already committed—increasing the effectiveness of taxation.

Technological change, one global megatrend noted in the white paper, also offers opportunities for governments to transition away from—or leapfrog over—prevailing industrial era policies and offer more-effective risk sharing to citizens and residents. Faced with an imperative to adopt new policy models, the countries with the lowest incomes might hold an advantage. Low effective coverage of industrial era risk-sharing policies means that acquired rights and other legacy costs that make the transition challenging are lower and opportunities to leapfrog are easier to grasp. Admittedly, the task for governments in Latin America and the Caribbean is more daunting, given higher numbers of benefit recipients, implicit pension liabilities that rival those of European countries, and rapid population aging.

The ultimate administrative asset governments can build for effective risk sharing is more-progressive national tax systems (refer to figure B8.1.1). Along with the proposed new packages of protection, building such a system should be the guiding institutional aspiration of risk-sharing policy.

continued

Box 8.1 Policy recommendations from a social protection white paper on risk sharing, *(continued)*

FIGURE B8.1.1

Optimal risk sharing in a national social protection system

Policy package of protection

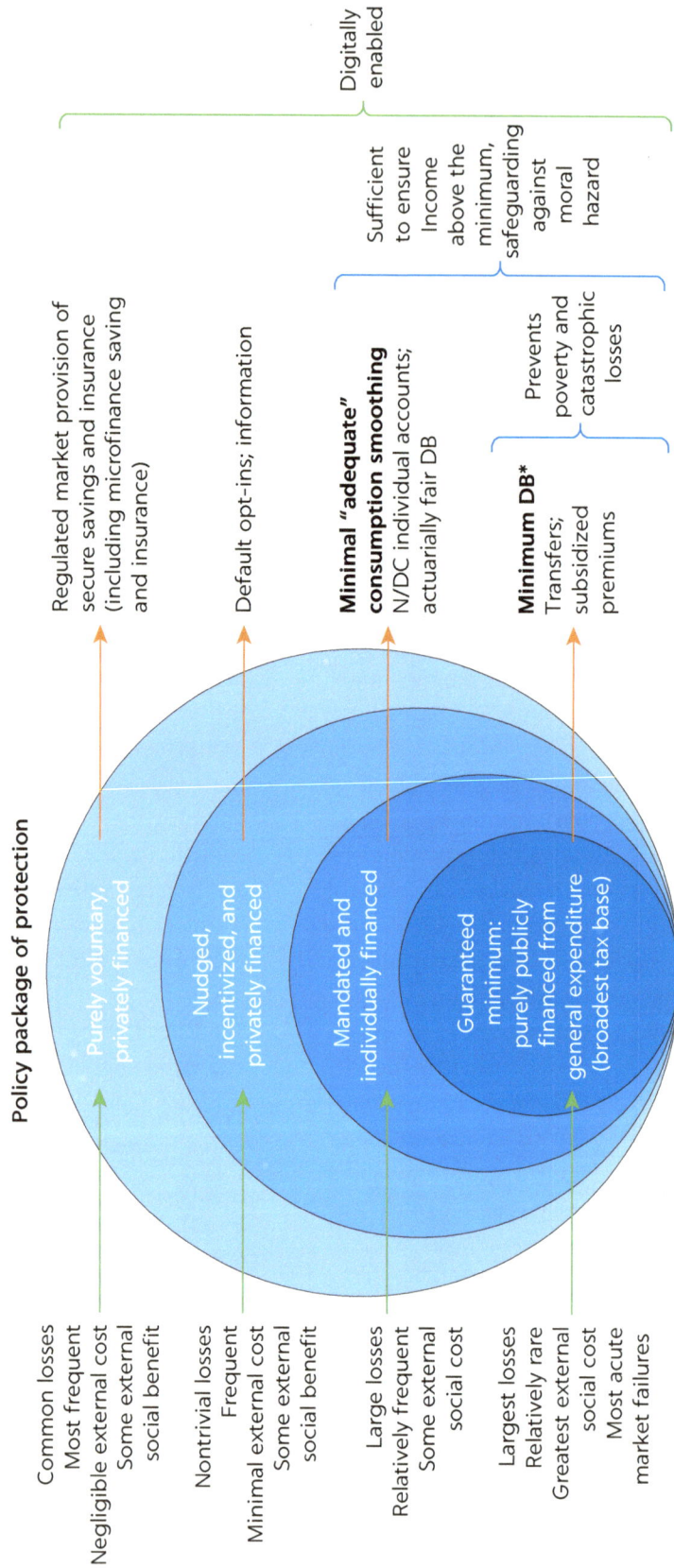

Regulated market provision of secure savings and insurance (including microfinance saving and insurance)

Default opt-ins; information

Minimal "adequate" consumption smoothing N/DC individual accounts; actuarially fair DB

Minimum DB* Transfers; subsidized premiums

Digitally enabled

Sufficient to ensure Income above the minimum, safeguarding against moral hazard

Prevents poverty and catastrophic losses

Purely voluntary, privately financed

Nudged, incentivized, and privately financed

Mandated and individually financed

Guaranteed minimum: purely publicly financed from general expenditure (broadest tax base)

Common losses Most frequent Negligible external cost Some external social benefit

Nontrivial losses Frequent Minimal external cost Some external social benefit

Large losses Relatively frequent Some external social cost

Largest losses Relatively rare Greatest external social cost Most acute market failures

Source: Packard et al. 2019.

Note: DB = defined benefit; N/DC = notional/defined contributions. *The minimum DB replaces contributory minimum guarantees and tax incentives.

Mitigating these behavioral risks requires investing in governments' monitoring and enforcement capacities, making full use of data, using digital technologies, and applying the growing predictive power of machine learning (Zaber, Casu, and Brodersohn 2024). These types of investments can also lower the transaction costs of compliance and participation to more-reasonable levels. The increasing focus on digitization, "human-centered" or "beneficiary-centered" design of administrative procedures, and other improvements in service delivery are steps in the right direction.

Some of the region's innovations in the delivery of social assistance provide the best examples of the path to follow, such as registration and delivery procedures designed around the way people live and work rather than for the convenience of administrators, replacement of proxy measures of household means with systems that observe actual incomes, and interoperability of administrative data sets to lighten the burden on households of identification and validation of their eligibility. By using data and digital technologies more intensively to modernize and augment administrative capacity, outdated design features and procedural practices that create disincentives to registration and participation can be eliminated—for example, the assumed earned income base set equal to multiples of the minimum wage and long minimum contribution requirements to become vested for full, effective social insurance coverage.

5. Trust in policy promises and the government's credibility to follow through are vital determinants of incentives and can be rebuilt

Governments in LAC have provided social protection directly or through para-governmental institutions for a sufficiently long period to have well-documented and known track records. Somewhat paradoxically, although these institutions have stood the test of time and are among the strongest in LAC countries, whether due to inflation, administrative incompetence, or corruption, many citizens view them with cynicism and distrust. These perceptions erode the perceived value of registering work and participating fully in social protection and other forms of taxation (Tommasi and Saavedra-Chanduvi 2007). When a sufficiently large proportion of the population shares these perceptions, it is even more difficult for a single worker or firm sitting on the margin between the formal and informal economies to comply (refer to Packard, Koettl, and Montenegro 2012).

This is a key insight into the nature of compliance: The importance of perceived fairness in tax systems—the psychological and social aspects of taxation—suggests that people are more willing to comply with mandates and pay taxes when they believe others are also paying their fair share (Bergman 2002). The positive message for policy makers is that governments in countries with similar track records have been able to shift these perceptions positively—most notably among the countries in Southern and Central Europe—thus raising trust in institutions, tax morale, and people's compliance with state mandates (Packard, Koettl, and Montenegro 2012; Torgler 2012). Again, the abundance of data and increasing application of digital technology in public administration and service delivery offer yet untapped opportunities for better governance (Santini et al. 2024) and to improve outcomes sufficiently to win back public confidence.

THREE INTERMEDIATE POLICY OBJECTIVES AND STEPS ALONG THE ROAD TO GREATER COMPLIANCE AND PARTICIPATION

With a clearly defined destination, reformers' primary objective should be to ensure that households are lifted out of poverty and protected from systemic or idiosyncratic impoverishing shocks. Achieving this objective requires greater levels of inclusion than what personal taxation and social protection currently achieve, and it would result in greater equity in finding and holding on to formal work. Although greater formality—compliance, participation, and broader coverage of risk-sharing programs—in the world of work is no guarantee of increased productivity and higher growth, it is likely a strong enabling condition.

In a recent review of policy actions to extend social protection to people working informally, Ghorpade, Franco Restrepo, and Castellanos (2024) argued persuasively that, when the principal objective of governments' actions is to expand access to effective protection, gains in other aspects of formalization—such as access to credit, modernization of business practices, and opportunities to scale economic activities—and increases in productivity are likely to follow. Therefore, policy makers should not aim to formalize for the sake of formalizing. If this were the case, introducing changes in regulation that create basic, inexpensive ways of contracting people legally would be sufficient. However, the resulting "tiered" formality could create distortion, exclusion, and inequity, which would be as detrimental to productivity, growth, and social development as the simple textbook dichotomy of "formal" and "informal" employment, as demonstrated by Gatti, Goraus, and Morgandi (2014) for Poland.

The three intermediate policy objectives to increase compliance and participation in social protection and taxation are to raise the value of participating, enhance workers' bargaining power, and increase the government's capacity and responsiveness.

Raise the value of participating in social protection and taxation relative to alternative savings and insurance strategies

This policy objective should be the result of making social protection foundational and complementary to taxation. It is foundational because the social protection and taxation system provides the primary inclusion, redistribution, and risk-sharing functions that informal networks and markets are unable to provide and minimizes the expectation that factor markets are responsible for these functions (refer to box 8.1).

The following are the steps and milestones along the path of increasing the perceived value of taxes and social protection:

- Further expand the coverage of minimum "safety net" structures for poverty elimination, inclusion, and redistribution. With a proper safety net in place, some of the payroll taxation could be eliminated, directly reducing the cost of labor formality. This step should also include expanding the tax base that finances the safety net.

- Reserve earmarked payroll taxation to finance coverage for risks that arise in the labor market and the workplace (for example, work injury, unemployment, loss of earning ability due to disability or age), prioritizing horizontal redistribution of risk and leaving the financing of broader social objectives—including "vertical" redistribution of income—to general revenues.

- Adjust the parameters of social insurance plans so that the link between benefits and mandatory contributions is direct and clear for people to understand, so that "discontinuities" in the proportionality of the benefits of coverage to its costs to the contributor are minimal. This step would increase the likelihood that workers would value mandatory contributions as part of overall remuneration, despite the mandate to participate.

- Make mandates uniform (or at least proportionally consistent) across segments of the labor force. Mandating consumption of a good or service is a powerful policy tool to safeguard public goods from adverse selection. A role for selective or targeted mandates may remain; however, when the selection and targeting process becomes complex and convoluted, the mandate itself should be scrutinized or extended to all neutrally with respect to how people work, whether for themselves or for someone else.

- Minimize the use and duration of *vesting requirements* (the number or periods of prior contributions required for eligibility for full effective coverage) for the social insurance plans for which moral hazard is greatest—unemployment insurance and disability coverage. Design plans with a default to and to reward the return to work.

- Ensure that publicly provided savings and insurance instruments complement—rather than crowd out—the instruments provided by markets. The private financial services sector—including not-for-profit financial cooperatives and microfinance service providers—should grow in transparency, safety, variety, and sophistication. With adequate regulation, the private sector should provide a wider range of competitively priced products. Therefore, the need for publicly provided or mandated individual savings and insurance instruments should abate. In most countries, it would be unlikely that the public policy function would disappear altogether, as there will be losses that risk markets will never cover if simply left unimpeded. Furthermore, the state's intervention cannot realistically be limited to a regulatory role. This situation is demonstrated by new forms of direct provision of financial services in some of the most-sophisticated markets (for example, for health and the cost of health care in almost all high-income countries and for old age and life insurance as in New Zealand's KiwiSaver and the United Kingdom's National Employment Savings Trust).

Sustainably enhance workers' bargaining power

Even if workers and job-seekers recognize and fully value contributory benefits, those with aptitudes and preferences for dependent employment must also contend with employers' preferences. Minimizing the burden of inclusion, redistribution, and risk sharing on factor markets is necessary but insufficient to improve the outcomes of the employment bargain. In many LAC labor markets, the scales are tipped in favor of employers, particularly in monopsonistic or oligopsonistic markets. All the governments in the LAC region deploy labor market regulations enthusiastically for just this reason; however, without actions to spur competition in product and service markets, these regulations often do as much harm as good (Carranza, Saliola, and Packard 2025; Messina and Silva 2018; Silva et al. 2021). Greater investment in building institutions to monitor the competitiveness and contestability of product and factor markets is an important policy agenda that is still pending across the region (refer to Maloney et al. 2024).

The following are the steps and milestones along the path of improving workers' bargaining position:

- Strengthen the capacity of market competition authorities to shift the balance of market power in the direction of workers and job-seekers. Deploying better policies and resources to increase the contestability and competition of product markets as well as factor markets is a priority (Vostroknutova et al. 2025), including to improve labor market outcomes (Carranza, Saliola, and Packard 2025).

- Invest in stronger, more-transparent, and more-representative labor market governance structures, starting with collective-bargaining institutions.

- Implement moderate increases in the statutory wage floor to reflect changes in workers' productivity. As the ratios of statutory wages to median wages in figure 8.1 show, the level at which wage floors are set can quickly overtake actual earnings outcomes in the economy, raising the risks to sustainability and market efficiency.

FIGURE 8.1

Changes in the level of the statutory minimum wage relative to the median wage, select LAC countries, 1990–2022

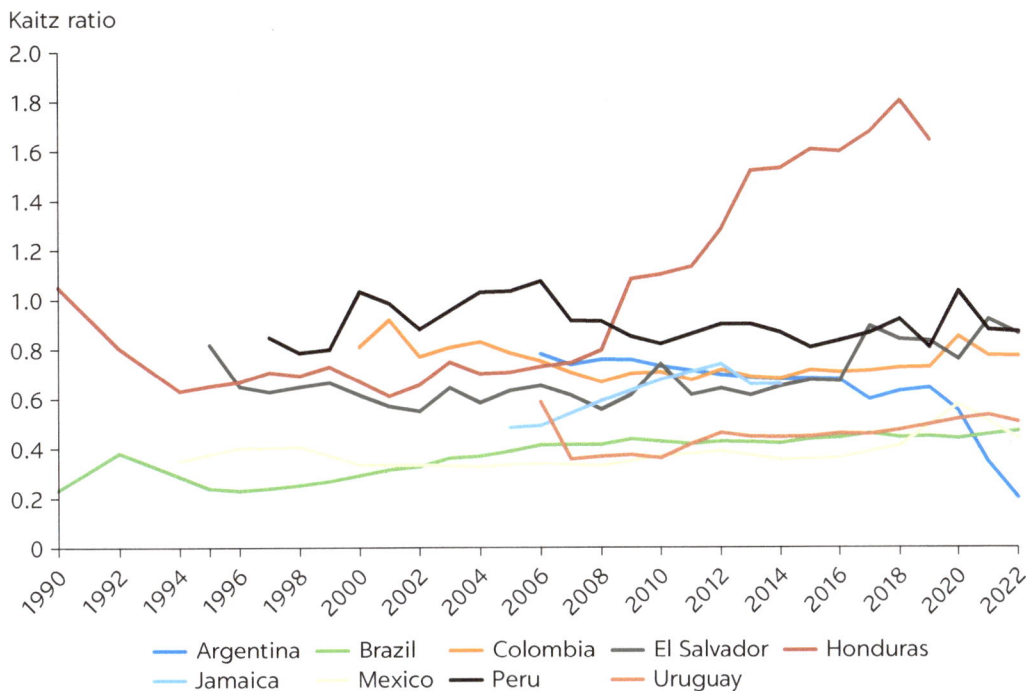

Kaitz ratio

Source: Information System on Labor Markets and Social Security, Inter-American Development Bank.
Note: The *Kaitz ratio* is the level of the statutory minimum wage divided by the economywide median wage.

- Strengthen income support plans to provide faster, more-reliable support for people who lose employment, as well as job search support, to improve the quality of new employment matches. Reserve the use of severance pay for cases of abusive employer practices.

- Use the "space" created by more-reliable support for unemployment and job search benefits to loosen regulatory restrictions on cyclical and reorganizational dismissals.

Increase the government's capacity and responsiveness

The government's capacity and responsiveness must be increased, both in its role as service provider and as that of guarantor and enforcer of the rules. It will be most important to strengthen the government's ability to observe economic activity to gather and maintain administrative data about when and where employment relationships start, earnings and other agreed parameters of employment, and when employment relationships end and under what circumstances. Advances in digital technologies and how they are deployed for the implementation of public policy and administration of programs have been made in countries around the world. India's "Stack" is a prime example of applying digital technology and government data to create a digital public administration infrastructure that has not only improved the efficiency and effectiveness of tax and social policies but also loosened many analogue constraints on productivity (Sahasranamam and Prabhu 2024).

Designing policies and programs that are perceived as valuable and that incentivize participation is important; however, investments to make compliance easier and ensure effective monitoring and enforcement are essential. Investment in digitization, management information systems (MISs), and technology can help improve responsiveness, but it is critical to ensure coherence, consistency, and interoperability when these investments are made (Lindert et al. 2020). In this area, LAC countries are more advanced than most other countries in using data and digital technologies and in building government "analytics ecosystems" (refer to box 8.2).

Box 8.2

The untapped potential of data and digital technology for better governance

In a recent regional study, *Data for Better Governance*, Santini et al. (2024) presented an extensive analysis of how governments in the Latin America and the Caribbean (LAC) region have implemented information systems to digitize, automate, and simplify core government functions. Extensive use of administrative data and adoption of digital management information systems (MISs) have made LAC a global leader in information system coverage.

By 2022, every country in the region had both a public financial MIS and a tax MIS. In addition, 91 percent of the countries in LAC had a human resources MIS, and 84 percent had an e-procurement system. These MISs cover government functions that account for an average of 79 percent of total revenue and grants and at least 40 percent of total spending at the central government level.

However, despite these investments, there is still much untapped potential. Administrative data have been used mainly to produce descriptive analytics for operational and transactional

purposes, like monitoring and accountability. Santini et al. (2024) argued that governments are not taking advantage of opportunities to use advanced analytics to improve decision-making, design more-effective and more-efficient public policies, and strengthen public sector functioning and service delivery.

The study highlighted the need for governments to complete the digitalization of their MISs. Two-thirds of the experts surveyed for the study reported that their systems were not fully digitalized. Levels of digitalization varied substantially across government functions: Information systems for taxation and public financial management were highly digitalized, while MISs in the social sectors had the lowest levels of digitalization.

Incomplete digitalization results in data infrastructure problems that prevent governments from fully leveraging their administrative data to improve policy design and implementation. High-quality, integrated data are essential to analytics, but data fragmentation and

continued

Box 8.2 **The untapped potential of data and digital technology for better governance,** *(continued)*

isolated information systems constrain digitalization. Outdated or inadequate data infrastructure limits the quality and accessibility of administrative data, making it difficult for organizations to use these data for analytics and policy making.

The study also emphasized the importance of data quality and interoperability. Governments must ensure the quality of the data contained in their information systems. Only 25 percent of LAC countries have implemented a data quality framework. When data quality controls are not integrated into an MIS, each team using the system's data must conduct its own quality control process, resulting in inefficiencies. Moreover, the lack of systematic controls can undermine the accuracy, reliability, and replicability of the analytics.

Improving data accessibility and system interoperability should be a governmentwide effort. Less than 35 percent of LAC countries have implemented a government interoperability framework that allows for efficient and secure information exchange between government systems and organizations. Sharing information enables new and innovative analytical applications.

By strengthening their analytical capabilities and data infrastructure, LAC governments can unlock the full potential of their administrative data and create a more-efficient, more-effective public administration. Government analytics can provide policy makers with the evidence needed to make informed decisions, address governance and development challenges, and build citizens' trust in public institutions.

Source: Adapted from Santini et al. (2024).

Even the best-designed policies, regulations, and administrative systems require consistent follow-up. Most low- and middle-income governments, including those in the LAC region, should invest more in the means—reliable data, person power, and systems—to enforce the laws and regulations that have for years been on the statute books (Kanbur and Ronconi 2018). When regulation is unreasonable or outdated, this lack of capacity might have an upside. However, in the long term, when the law is "toothless" because of a lack of monitoring and enforcement capacity, perceived government credibility and tax morale are threatened.

The following are the steps and milestones along the path to increasing government capacity:

- Extend the population coverage (both citizens and residents) of unique, single, personal identification numbers, and use these in administrative data, social registers, and other MISs.

- Ensure interoperability and regular cross-checks of MISs. Even the most-advanced systems are compromised by fragmentation: the inability of administrative data sets to interact in real time. Interoperability of administrative data sets across service delivery, regulatory, and taxation agencies can provide governments with simple but powerful tools to incentivize participation and compliance.

- Deploy digital technologies to modernize and lower the transaction costs of citizen and resident interactions with government agencies (refer to box 8.3). Some of the strongest incentives to evade and avoid arise from the transaction costs of compliance. In fast-evolving societies and markets, the direct and opportunity costs of daily interactions with public agencies that have not been updated can rise steeply, discouraging employers and households with the best intentions.

- Increase the speed and quality of service delivery, including responses to individual and household grievances. Part of the value proposition for households of mandates and social protection programs is knowing that they will receive high-quality services quickly and be treated fairly.

- Use swift action against corruption to improve tax morale. In countries where corruption is systemic, the obligation of paying taxes quickly vanishes as a social norm. Corruption generally undermines citizens' tax morale, and they feel cheated if they perceive that public finances are being squandered or used for ill-gotten gains. At the extreme, people can feel strongly entitled to evade taxes and the structures of the formal economy.

- Develop channels for regular communication with stakeholders, not least of which are the working people in whose names statutory contributions are made.

Box 8.3

Applications of AI in social protection and social insurance administration

Social insurance institutions have increasingly adopted artificial intelligence (AI) to enhance their services and administrative processes. Although most AI applications are universally applicable, specific AI innovations can be observed in various branches of social insurance, particularly in pensions and health plans.

The use of AI in social insurance administration has surged since 2018, with more than half of the observed applications increasing significantly since 2020. Although intelligent chatbots were the predominant AI solution before 2020, a broader range of AI tools, including machine learning and generative AI, have proliferated since then.

AI applications have been instrumental in strengthening administrative capacity in five key areas:

- *Service delivery.* AI enables institutions to improve services by providing better, more-accessible information through various channels.
- *Automation and case management.* AI automates case processing and provides better grievance management support for individuals.
- *Prospective and proactive social insurance.* AI provides institutions with tools for gaining insights and conducting prospective analysis to identify potential outcomes and proactively improve the lives of individuals and cohorts.

continued

Box 8.3 **Applications of AI in social protection and social insurance administration,** *(continued)*

- *Risk management and prevention.* AI supports institutions in identifying and mitigating risks, analyzing member information, and providing better services.
- *Equality and fairness.* AI helps to evaluate AI solutions, programs, and responses to ensure that they uphold the principles of fairness and equity.

The following are examples of AI applications in social insurance:

- *Intelligent chatbots.* Intelligent chatbots have been widely implemented to unburden call centers and leverage digital channels. The surge in demand for services during the COVID-19 crisis further accelerated their adoption.
- *Machine learning for improved health services and well-being.* AI applications leverage large data sets to categorize and identify individuals with potential illnesses, enabling preemptive health services. Examples include the National Health Insurance Service in the Republic of Korea's response to the COVID-19 crisis and

eHealth NSW's sepsis detection prototype in Australia.
- *Leveraging AI to ensure proper use of resources and mitigate fraud.* AI-based fraud detection systems have been implemented by institutions like the Social Security Administering Body for the Health Sector in Indonesia and the National Social Security Fund of Uganda.
- *Leveraging AI to streamline claims management processes.* AI-based systems have been implemented to automate claims processing and match claims with doctors, reducing processing times and improving efficiency. Examples include Austria's Federation of Social Insurances and the openIMIS project implemented through the German Society for International Cooperation.

The increased adoption of AI in social insurance highlights the need for capacity building to leverage the growing number of AI tools and techniques. Data quality is crucial for the responsible application of AI, and data scientists have become increasingly indispensable for the future of social insurance.

Source: Adapted from Zaber, Casu, and Brodersohn (2024).

Substantial, lasting improvement in compliance and participation requires governments to act on all the dimensions of incentives. As chapter 6 in this report concluded from a review of the empirical analysis of Colombia's 2012 tax reform, just lowering the size of the tax wedge is probably insufficient. Even a package of reforms that lowers costs and improves incentives enough to bring people to their "point of indifference" between complying and not complying will need further measures to "nudge" them past indifference to compliance.

This is an important caveat for policy makers to consider: An improvement in de jure incentives is necessary but may not be sufficient as a reform strategy. Instead, real progress in reducing noncompliance and increasing participation is likely to come only from concerted action along all three dimensions of the conceptual framework (refer to chapter 3). Governments are working against strong headwinds, both political and demographic.

REFORMS OF SOCIAL INSURANCE THAT HAVE IMPROVED INCENTIVES

The political obstacles and transition costs of reform can be daunting, yet examples of success exist. Brazil's transition from an employment-based health insurance model to the Sistema Único de Saúde (SUS; Unified Health System) represents a significant social insurance reform in the LAC region and the world. Prior to this fundamental shift in 1988, Brazil operated a highly segmented health system, which provided protection from the impoverishing costs of health care depending on where people worked. Coverage and the quality of care and protection varied substantially. However, even with the Ministry of Health providing a care safety net, the employment-linked social health insurance model left 30–40 million Brazilians—about one-third of the population—without any health coverage.

The transition to universal coverage began with Brazil's 1988 Constitution, which established health as a right of all citizens and a duty of the state. Implementation took place in several phases: the passage of regulations and transfer of responsibilities to states and municipalities in the first half of the 1990s, expansion of services that prioritized primary and preventative care, and the progressive increase in covered services. Particularly for the initial expansion of primary and preventative services, financing came from general federal, state, and municipal taxation, effectively removing obstacles to preventative care and increasing access to a growing package of priority treatments. Perennial quality and cost problems still exist—public health spending as a percentage of gross domestic product (GDP) rose from approximately 2.5–3.0 percent before SUS to 3.5–4.5 percent in the decades since. However, Brazil's transition from an occupation-based to a "universal" model of risk sharing created one of the largest public health systems in the world, covering more than 200 million people (Baeza and Packard 2006; Couttolenc, Gragnolati, and Lindelow 2013; Pestel and Sommer 2017).

More-recent reforms have been designed with the objective of improving incentives to work formally. For example, a reform of Türkiye's Social Insurance and General Health Insurance Law (No. 5510), which came into effect in October 2008, unified previously fragmented social security institutions under a single Social Security Institution. The reform expanded health insurance coverage to aim for universal coverage, tightened the link between pension benefits and contributions, and standardized eligibility conditions and benefit calculations across different occupational groups.

Türkiye's social insurance reform has had several measurable impacts (refer to Acar and Tansel 2019). The share of the population with health coverage increased from approximately 70 percent before the reform to more than 95 percent in the years following implementation. Administrative costs decreased due to the unification of the three previous social security institutions, creating operational efficiencies (official estimates show a 15–20 percent reduction in administrative overhead following the unification of the three prereform social insurance institutions). Although evidence of some reduction in informal employment exists, the effect was modest and uneven across sectors.

Some studies have shown a 2–4 percentage point (p.p.) reduction in informality rates in certain industries (the manufacturing labor force saw a 5–6 p.p. reduction in informality), including among working women, although outcomes for women continue to lag those for men (Özdamar, Giovanis, and Özdaş 2019; World Bank 2013). However, informal work has persisted among self-employed and agricultural workers. Furthermore, despite the reform's intention to improve fiscal sustainability, after the social insurance deficits initially declined, they eventually stabilized and required a transfer from general revenues of 3–4 percent of GDP. Independent assessments of projected costs show a substantial improvement in the long-term fiscal outlook compared with the prereform trajectory (Bump, Sparkes, and Mehtap Tatar 2014).

In addition to Brazil and Türkiye, some of Latin America's institutional forebears have made a similar switch. The reform experiences described earlier required bold, controversial actions; long transitions; and increased spending from general revenues. Yet, the increased spending finances a more-accessible model of protection from the most-impoverishing costs and threats to households' well-being. From a position of greater effective coverage of their populations and improved incentives, these countries have improved jobs and growth prospects.

The reform path chosen by Brazil and Türkiye has been well-trodden. From 1986 to 1990, Spain transitioned away from an employment-based social health insurance system, and by 1999, about 90 percent of the country's public health care was funded through general taxation and accessible by previously excluded segments of the population. From 1978 through the 1980s, Italy replaced a segmented model of occupation-based protection with a model that provides universal coverage regardless of labor market status. Over the same period, Portugal transitioned from employment-based social insurance to broadly accessible financial protection and quality health care. These transitions shared common elements with Brazil's SUS reform, although each country's implementation path reflected its unique political, economic, and social contexts. All these countries face challenges of fiscal sustainability, quality disparities, and the continued existence of parallel private systems despite the public, universal coverage mandate. However, the countries are facing these challenges from a much stronger economic and fiscal position (Busse, Gericke, and Schreyogg 2007; Chawla 2007).

THE POLITICS AND PERSISTENCE OF PAYROLL TAXES

A country's public finance system is the largest, most-efficient mechanism the government can offer to households to redistribute risks, manage uncertainty, and pursue greater equity. Statutory earmarked employer and worker contributions have an important role, but one that is more limited than the role they are assigned in the prevailing employment-based "contributory" social insurance model.

The so-called "Bismarckian" approach to risk sharing in many countries has, over the years, been distorted almost beyond recognition. As discussed in chapter 1, whereas the original approach combined payroll "contribution" financing with proportional benefits designed principally to redistribute risk rather than income, the Bismarckian mechanism has evolved into an instrument for "vertical" as well as "horizontal" redistribution—to redistribute wealth within and between generations as well as redistribute risks and uncertainty (Esping-Andersen 1990). Packard et al. (2019) argued that, for the purposes of wealth redistribution and other inclusion and equity objectives, this distortion of the Bismarckian model leaves households with a relatively inefficient and ineffective instrument where and when a superior alternative is on offer: the larger risk pool financed by a wide and balanced array of tax instruments with a much broader base.

Greater "observability" of household incomes and economic activities *should* offer policy makers more options than payroll taxes. Traditional social insurance plans were designed to take advantage of the relative observability of wages and salaries and use the workplace as a platform for collecting information and contributions. However, the essence of informality is the "unobservability" of income and the workplace. The shortcomings of using a workplace-related contribution mechanism are becoming a problem not only for informally employed individuals but also for nonsalaried workers operating within the framework of the law.

As social insurance plans financed by payroll contributions mature and covered populations age, the statutory rates can rise, reaching high and damaging levels. The rates have reached double digits in most countries in Europe and Latin America and often exceed 20 p.p. At these levels, and when combined with overly stringent labor market regulations like a binding minimum wage, payroll taxes have a negative impact on formal sector employment. The result is a vicious circle in which rates increase, firms and workers have greater incentive to evade contributing, and the tax base narrows.

General revenue is more efficient and the most-equitable financing mechanism for risk pooling with poverty prevention and other social inclusion objectives, assuming progressivity of tax collection instruments and subsequent public spending (Mossialos et al. 2002; Savedoff 2004). The most-important gain from financing minimum risk pooling through general tax revenues is that the risk of losses is effectively pooled across the entire taxpaying population—a larger share of the population than might otherwise be the case, particularly where employers and workers can evade payroll contributions. Shifting to general revenue financing can also be less regressive if revenues from rents, capital gains, and profits are taxed. Of all the sources of financing, general taxation entails the lowest transaction costs for allocating equity subsidies for a given level of risk-pool fragmentation because the entire society becomes a single risk pool (Savedoff 2004).

Yet, despite clear advantages, most policy makers, administrators of social insurance agencies, leaders of labor unions, and even affiliated workers often resist efforts to move away from statutory contributions structured as a payroll tax. Three main arguments are typically made against a shift to general tax financing. First, the providers of employment-based social insurance consider that the payroll tax is a more-independent, more-secure revenue source that is safe from annual political budget discussions. Second, the payroll tax is perceived to be less cyclical than general revenue sources. Third, payroll tax financing makes it more difficult for governments to cut benefits because the statutory nature of the contribution gives workers a sense of entitlement that they will defend and that creates a powerful political deterrent.

Strong political pressures exist not only to keep but to expand the use of statutory contributions. The existing structure of government finances contributes to the politics of payroll taxes. Manow (2010) identified structural differences in the political consequences of financing reforms, which depend on the extent to which statutory social insurance contributions dominate in "welfare state financing," focusing on select European countries. The intensity with which statutory social insurance contributions are used over other taxes is a distinguishing feature between Central and Southern European countries and Nordic countries. Manow framed the analysis as the politician's strategic choice among three alternative responses to an economic slowdown or downturn: cut benefits, raise revenue, or issue debt. Manow charted the political incentive structure according to the power of stakeholders and governance of decision making, the broader budget-setting process, and the strength and independence of a country's monetary authority.

Although no politicians are keen to cut social benefits, those in countries that already use statutory contributions intensively will always have a stronger incentive to raise these even to levels that are prejudicial to job outcomes (Manow 2010). First, people's tolerance for increased contributions is greater than for rises in other taxes, because of their perception of these contributions as part of a personalized contract between themselves and the state to deliver a specific package of services. Second, because decisions about statutory contributions are often directly and disproportionately influenced by worker and employer representatives relative to other taxes, a narrower set of concerns and interests prevails than when decisions are made about other areas of government spending and revenue. Third, a strong and independent monetary authority can constrain the extent to which governments can issue debt rather than raise contributions or cut benefits. Finally, these three factors make statutory contributions attractive to politicians seeking robust financing for their preferred policies and programs. This point explains why the set of social programs financed from payroll taxes has grown (Manow 2010).

Yet, counterarguments to the expanding use of payroll taxes have strengthened. Although independent, earmarked sources of revenue like a statutory payroll tax can provide considerable autonomy to social insurance institutes, those sources of revenue can limit the extent to which these bodies must respond to public questioning of their performance. Furthermore, while all public expenditure can come under pressure during economic downturns that lower governments' overall revenue, financing through payroll contributions and employment can result in a more-severe procyclical pattern—particularly for employment in sectors that comply with the mandate to contribute.

Finally, although payroll taxes confer a strong sense of entitlement and a political deterrent to cuts in services, in a weaker governance context, this may translate into capture by elites rather than protection of services, particularly for the most-vulnerable people. A better "entitlement" that could create the same political deterrent—desirable even on pure efficiency grounds—would be a clearly defined, guaranteed minimum, with fiscal allocations indexed to its costs. The vital element in safeguarding individuals' rights to protection is good governance.

THE CRISIS NOT YET AVERTED: CONSEQUENCES OF INACTION

More than their peers in other mainly middle-income country regions, governments in the LAC region have actively reformed social protection. Changes in demography and the structure of the global economy threatened the coverage, adequacy, and sustainability of past social protection policies and their outcomes. Although the severest coverage gaps have been closed by governments' actions, the challenges of adequacy and sustainability are large. Population aging will raise public spending and liabilities further. Many LAC countries are already spending as much on social protection, including health, as high-income countries that are demographically much "older."

FIGURE 8.2

Social spending and the dependent population in LAC countries, 2020

Public social spending (% of GDP)

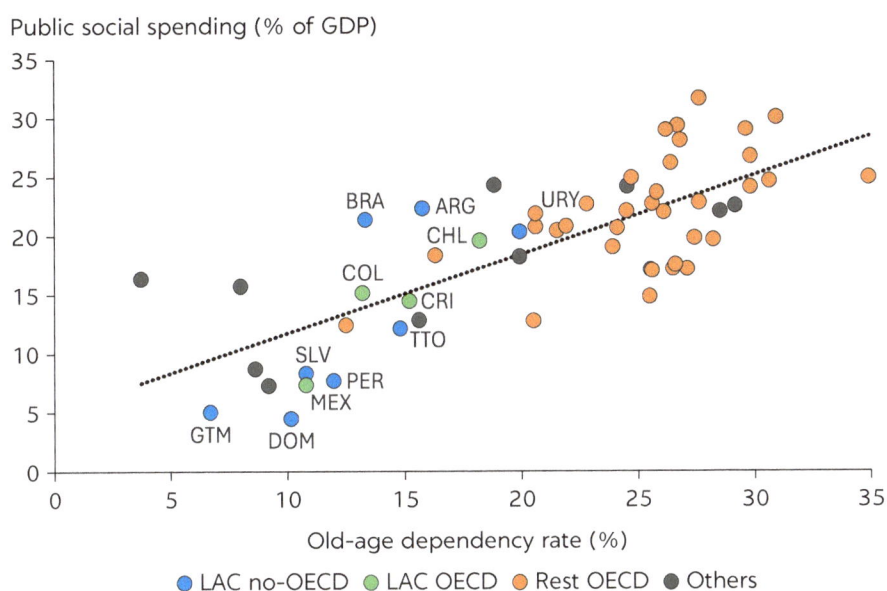

Sources: ECLAC 2024; OECD 2024; WHO 2024.
Note: Social spending is the sum of all public expenditure on social protection (including pensions), health, and education. The old-age dependency rate is population ages 60 years or older / population ages 20–59 years. For a list of country codes, refer to https://www.iso.org/obp/ui/#search. GDP = gross domestic product; LAC = Latin America and the Caribbean; OECD = Organisation for Economic Co-operation and Development.

Design of reform strategies is especially challenging due to the unprecedented speed of aging. By 2045, most LAC countries will share the demographic characteristics of today's Organisation for Economic Co-operation and Development countries, with life expectancy in the 80s and fertility rates below two births per woman (Rofman and Apella 2020). Furthermore, as shown in figure 8.2, old-age dependency rates in the LAC region in 2020 are similar to European dependency rates in 1950. By 2045, LAC dependency rates will be similar to today's European dependency rates. Thus, the aging that took Europe 70 years to accomplish will take LAC only 25 years, or almost three times as fast.

This reality means that LAC, unlike Europe in previous decades, might not have the luxury of time to legislate its tax and social insurance reforms with long transitions. Most European reforms began in the 1980s or slightly earlier, and some are still in progress even now, 40 years later. Latin American systems will have to accomplish these changes three times as fast (refer to figure 8.3).

FIGURE 8.3

LAC countries have had far less time to contain fiscal costs than European countries have had, 1950–2100

Old-age dependency rate (%)

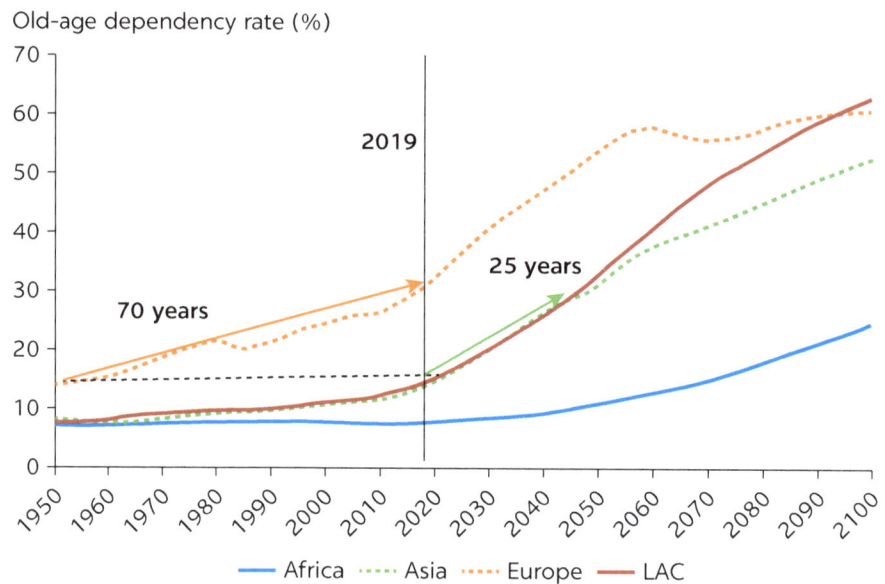

Source: Rofman and Apella 2020.
Note: The old-age dependency rate is population ages 65 years and older / population ages 20–64 years. LAC = Latin America and the Caribbean.

Keep Georgia on your mind: A collapse of "contributory" social insurance

The Republic of Georgia provides sobering lessons on the consequences of ignoring the status quo in LAC countries. During the Soviet era, Georgia, like other Soviet republics, had a pay-as-you-go pension plan fully funded by the state. This system provided universal coverage and was integrated with other social welfare programs. When Georgia gained independence in 1991, it inherited this pension plan. However, the collapse of the Soviet Union and the subsequent economic crisis severely strained Georgia's ability to maintain this pension plan. The early 1990s were marked by hyperinflation, economic collapse, and civil unrest, which made it nearly impossible for the Georgian government to fulfill its pension obligations.

The post-Soviet period was a time of intense reform, including to the public pension system. By the mid-1990s, Georgia needed to reform its pension plan to ensure its sustainability. In 1995, the country introduced its first post-Soviet pension law, which maintained the defined benefit but gradually increased retirement ages and imposed a minimum period of contributions. In 2003, another significant reform was introduced, creating a two-tier pension system. The first tier was a flat rate, universal old-age pension (often referred to as the "basic pension" or "social pension"). This noncontributory benefit was funded from general tax revenues and provided a minimal level of support to all elderly citizens. The second tier was an earnings-related contributory pension designed to provide additional income based on an individual's work history and contributions. However, political pressures gradually raised the level of the noncontributory benefit close to the level of the minimum contributory benefit.

In 2005, the Government of Georgia effectively abandoned the contributory second tier of the pension system for several reasons. First, the compliance rates were low, with employers and employees evading contributions, undermining the system's financial viability. Second, the government lacked the capacity to manage effectively and enforce the contributory system. As a result, the pension system was de facto consolidated into a single-tier noncontributory system. The universal basic pension became the primary form of old-age support, funded entirely from general tax revenues. This change was part of a broader reform of the tax system, which saw the abolition of separate social insurance contributions and their integration into the general income tax.

While this simplification had some advantages, like reducing administrative costs and eliminating evasion of pension contributions, it also had significant drawbacks. These included inadequate benefits, with the flat rate pension set at a very low level, barely enough to cover basic subsistence needs; ineffective consumption smoothing, as the system no longer provided a link between individuals' work history and their pension benefits; and threats to fiscal sustainability, as public pensions were funded entirely from general revenues, which presented risks to long-term affordability, especially given Georgia's aging population.

The disorderly de facto collapse of the contributory pension plan into the noncontributory plan dealt a blow to institutional credibility. In 2018, the Georgian Parliament passed the Law on Funded Pensions, which introduced a new funded pension component to complement the existing universal basic pension. This reform was accompanied by a well-targeted cash transfer program. The reform effectively reestablished a multipillar pension system in Georgia: the existing universal basic pension, funded from general tax revenues; a new mandatory defined contribution system for employed individuals; and a voluntary private pension savings component (which had existed in a limited form since 1998 but had low participation rates).

As of 2024, it was still too early to assess the reform's long-term impacts. However, years of policy changes and the effective abandonment of the old contributory system had eroded public trust in state-managed pension plans. The government has had to work hard to build confidence in the new system.

Mind your mandates: What is the role of the state in enabling optimal insurance?

The main lesson to draw from Georgia's experience is that incentives matter most when designing the interaction between the pure poverty prevention, essential "safety net" and the mandated "consumption-smoothing" coverage over and above the safety net. In Georgia, a noncontributory "social pension" and the contributory "minimum pension guarantee" quickly converged to similar benefit levels, eliminating the incentive to contribute. Convergence between the levels of noncontributory and contributory benefits is apparent in several LAC countries. Policy makers must distinguish between the adequacy of a safety net and the adequacy of coverage that the state mandates to protect people from their limited information, myopia, other cognitive limitations, and constraints on real-world decision making.

The "adequacy" of the safety net can be assessed with reference to a poverty line or other socially accepted absolute measure of avoidable deprivation. However, policy makers around the world have not answered the following question: What is an "adequate" level of additional coverage for the government's mandate? The answer is vital, as it determines all the parameters of protection policies and programs analyzed in this report and, along with analysis of basic needs over the life cycle, is urgent. The present ambiguity may feel politically safe but is not sustainable (refer to figure 8.4). To realize pension promises at current dependency ratios, governments must substantially raise retirement ages.

A fraying social contract?

Households in LAC are increasingly paying out of pocket for vital social services. Observed rates of noncompliance and people choosing not to participate in social protection programs have been discussed at length in earlier chapters. Mirroring these "opt-out" rates and reflecting a growing preference for market provision or that private services are the only option for many, out-of-pocket spending on health and education in many LAC countries is high (refer to figure 8.5).

The terms of the social contract must be renegotiated urgently. If evasion, avoidance, and rates of opting out of tax and social protection mandates are considered alongside the out-of-pocket spending for key social services, a worrying, vicious cycle becomes apparent. Disincentivized, dissatisfied people are turning away from publicly provided services, feeling justified in withholding their contributions to sustain these services, and opting for private provision instead. While a renegotiation of what households should expect from government is probably overdue, policy makers still have time to approach this intentionally and methodically. As the Georgia example demonstrates,

FIGURE 8.4

Given the rising costs of aging, what does social insurance aim to achieve in LAC countries?

a. Public spending on current
and projected pensions,
2015 and 2045

b. "New 65": Retirement age required
to maintain pension plan dependency
ratios, 2040 and 2060

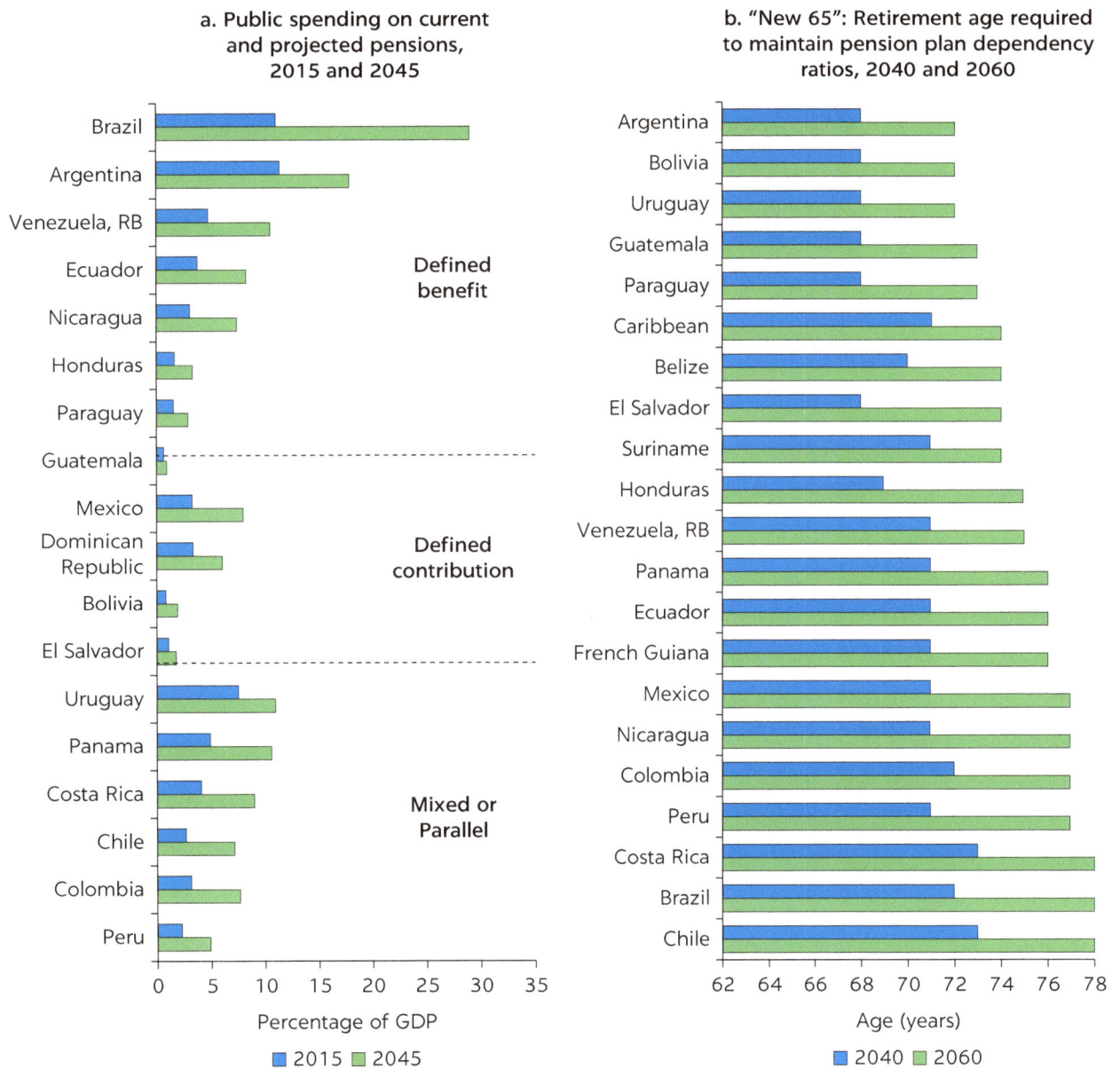

Source: Rofman and Apella 2020.
Note: GDP = gross domestic product; LAC = Latin America and the Caribbean.

the alternative to an intentional, methodical process of renegotiating the social contract is to allow the current clauses of the contract simply to fall away. However, that scenario could entail costs that most people in the LAC region would rather avoid.

FIGURE 8.5

Households' out-of-pocket payments for health and education in LAC countries, 2023

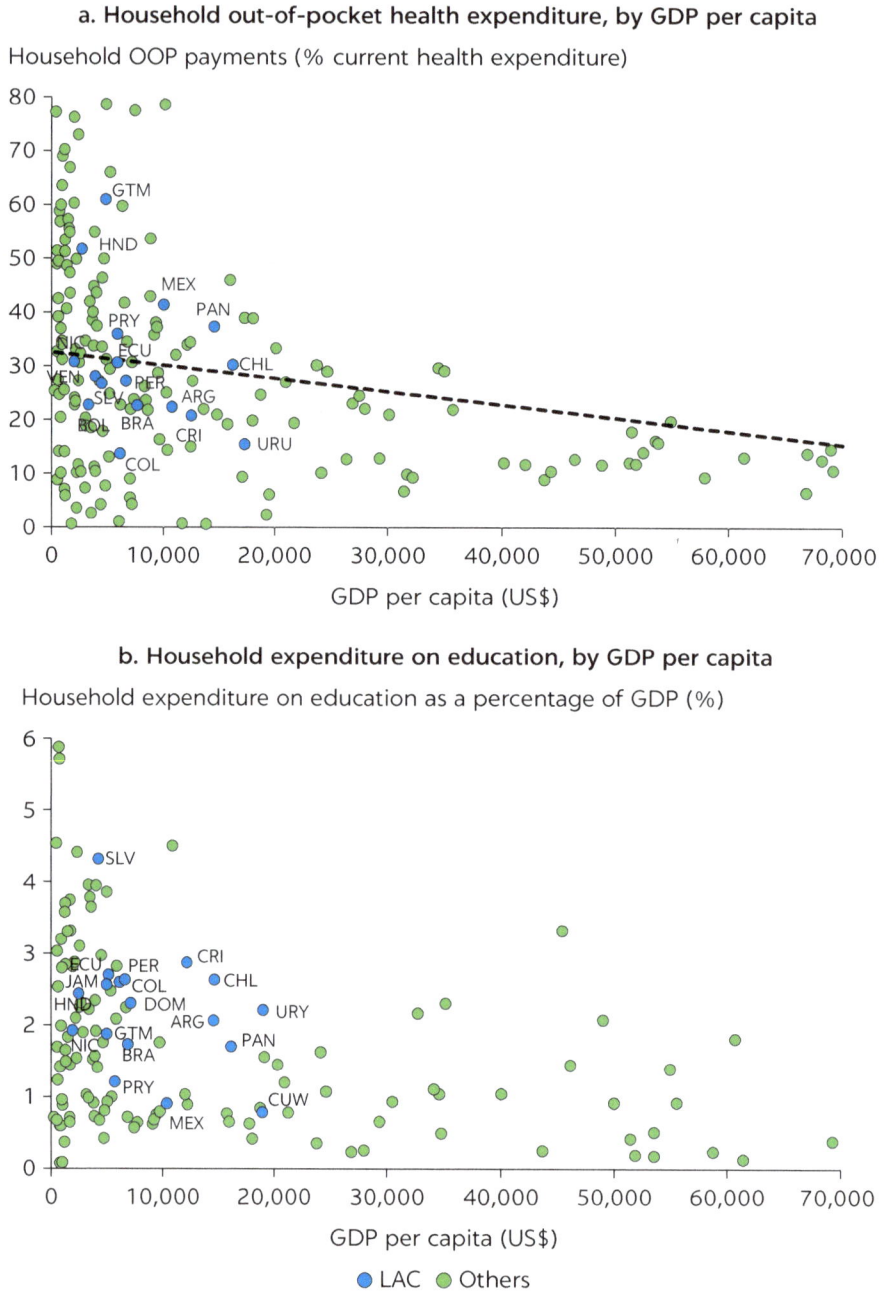

a. Household out-of-pocket health expenditure, by GDP per capita

Household OOP payments (% current health expenditure)

GDP per capita (US$)

b. Household expenditure on education, by GDP per capita

Household expenditure on education as a percentage of GDP (%)

GDP per capita (US$)

● LAC   ● Others

Sources: For panel a: Global Health Expenditure Database, World Health Organization, https://apps.who.int/nha/database/Select/Indicators/en. For panel b: World Bank and UNESCO 2024.
Note: For a list of country codes, refer to https://www.iso.org/obp/ui/#search.
GDP = gross domestic product; LAC = Latin America and the Caribbean; OOP = out of pocket.

REFERENCES

Acar, E., and A. Tansel. 2019. "Analyzing Informality: A Cross-Country Comparison of Informality Rates in Turkey." Working Paper, Turkish Economic Association, Ankara, Türkiye.

Acosta-Ormaechea, S., S. Pienknagura, and C. Pizzinelli. 2022. *Tax Policy for Inclusive Growth in Latin America and the Caribbean.* Washington, DC: International Monetary Fund.

Alvarez, B. 2024. "Shifting Paradigms: The Consequences of Misclassifying Employees as Entrepreneurs." Available at SSRN: https://ssrn.com/abstract=4598482 or http://dx.doi.org/10.2139/ssrn.4598482.

Autor, D., and S. Houseman. 2005. "Temporary Agency Employment as a Way out of Poverty?" NBER Working Paper 11742, National Bureau of Economic Research, Cambridge, MA.

Baeza, C., and T. Packard. 2006. *Beyond Survival: Protecting Households from Health Shocks in Latin America.* Washington, DC: World Bank and Stanford University Press.

Barr, A., and T. Packard. 2002. "Revealed Preference and Self-Insurance: Can We Learn from the Self-Employed in Chile?" Policy Research Working Paper 2754, World Bank, Washington, DC. http://hdl.handle.net/10986/15756.

Barr, A., and T. Packard. 2003. "Preferences, Constraints, and Substitutes for Coverage under Peru's Pension System." Office of the Chief Economist for Latin America and the Caribbean, World Bank, Washington, DC.

Bergman, M. 2002. "Who Pays for Social Policy? A Study on Taxes and Trust." *Journal of Social Policy* 31 (2): 289–305.

Bump, J., S. Sparkes, and C. Mehtap Tatar. 2014. "Turkey on the Way of Universal Health Coverage through the Health Transformation Program." Discussion Paper 91326, World Bank, Washington, DC.

Busse, R., C. Gericke, and J. Schreyogg. 2007. "Analyzing Changes in Health Financing Arrangements in High-Income Countries: A Comprehensive Framework Approach." Working Paper 39913, World Bank, Washington, DC.

Carranza, E., F. Saliola, and T. Packard. 2025. "Regulating Markets So More People Find Better Jobs." Social Protection and Jobs Discussion Paper 2502, World Bank, Washington, DC. http://hdl.handle.net/10986/42833.

Chawla, M. 2007. *Health Care Spending in the New EU Member States: Controlling Costs and Improving Quality.* Washington, DC: World Bank.

Cho, Y., D. Robalino, and S. Watson. 2014. "Supporting Self-Employment and Small-Scale Entrepreneurship: Potential Programs to Improve Livelihoods for Vulnerable Workers." Working Paper 92629, World Bank, Washington, DC.

Couttolenc, B. F., M. Gragnolati, and M. Lindelow. 2013. *Twenty Years of Health System Reform in Brazil: An Assessment of the Sistema Unico de Saude.* Washington, DC: World Bank.

ECLAC (United Nations Economic Commission for Latin America and the Caribbean). 2024. "Public Expenditure in Latin America and the Caribbean." ECLAC, Santiago, Chile.

Esping-Andersen, G. 1990. *The Three Worlds of Welfare Capitalism.* Princeton, NJ: Princeton University Press.

Friedman, M. 1962. *Capitalism and Freedom.* Chicago, IL: University of Chicago Press.

Furman, J. 2008. "The Concept of Neutrality in Tax Policy." Brookings Institution, Washington, DC.

Gatti, R., K. Goraus, and M. Morgandi. 2014. "Balancing Flexibility and Worker Protection: Understanding Labor Market Duality in Poland." Working Paper 98274, Social Protection and Jobs, World Bank, Washington, DC.

Ghorpade, Y., C. Franco Restrepo, and L. E. Castellanos Rodriguez. 2024. "Social Protection and Labor Market Policies for the Informally Employed: A Review of Evidence from Low- and Middle-Income Countries." Social Protection and Jobs Discussion Paper 2403, World Bank, Washington, DC. http://hdl.handle.net/10986/41328.

Kanbur, R., and L. Ronconi. 2018. "Enforcement Matters: The Effective Regulation of Labour." *International Labour Review* 157 (3): 331–56.

Lindert, K., T. George Karippacheril, I. Rodriguez Caillava, and K. Nishikawa Chavez. 2020. *Sourcebook on the Foundations of Social Protection Delivery Systems.* Washington, DC: World Bank. http://hdl.handle.net/10986/34044.

Maloney, W., P. Garriga, M. Meléndez, R. Morales, C. Jooste, J. Sampi, J. Araujo, and E. Vostroknutova. 2024. *Competition: The Missing Ingredient for Growth? Latin America and the Caribbean Economic Review.* Washington, DC: World Bank. http://hdl.handle.net/10986/41230.

Manow, P. 2010. "Trajectories of Fiscal Adjustment in Bismarckian Welfare Systems." In *A Long Goodbye to Bismarck? The Politics of Welfare Reform in Continental Europe,* edited by B. Palier, 279–300. Amsterdam, The Netherlands: Amsterdam University Press.

Messina, J., and J. Silva. 2018. *Wage Inequality in Latin America: Understanding the Past to Prepare for the Future.* Latin American Development Forum. Washington, DC: World Bank. http://hdl.handle.net/10986/28682.

Mossialos, E., A. Dixon, J. Figueras, and J. Kutzin. 2002. *Funding Health Care: Options for Europe.* European Observatory on Health Care Systems Series, World Health Organization. Buckingham, UK: Open University Press.

Musgrave, R. A. 1959. *The Theory of Public Finance: A Study in Public Economy.* New York: McGraw-Hill.

Nayyar, G., and M. Cruz. 2018. "Developing Countries and Services in the New Industrial Paradigm." Policy Research Working Paper 8659, World Bank, Washington, DC. http://hdl.handle.net/10986/30981.

Nayyar, G., and E. Davies. 2023. "Services-Led Growth: Better Prospects after the Pandemic?" Policy Research Working Paper 10382, World Bank, Washington, DC. http://hdl.handle.net/10986/39609.

OECD (Organisation for Economic Co-operation and Development). 2024. *Taxing Wages 2024: Tax and Gender through the Lens of the Second Earner.* Paris: OECD. https://doi.org/10.1787/dbcbac85-en.

Özdamar, Ö., E. Giovanis, and B. Özdaş. 2019. "The Effect of Unemployment Benefits on Health and Living Standards in Turkey: Evidence from Structural Equation Modelling and Regression Discontinuity Design." Available at SSRN: 10.2139/ssrn.3574286.

Packard, T., U. Gentilini, M. Grosh, P. O'Keefe, R. Palacios, D. Robalino, and I. Santos. 2019. *Protecting All: Risk Sharing for a Diverse and Diversifying World of Work.* Washington, DC: World Bank.

Packard, T., J. Koettl, and C. E. Montenegro. 2012. *In From the Shadow: Integrating Europe's Informal Labor*. Directions in Development: Human Development. Washington, DC: World Bank. http://hdl.handle.net/10986/9377.

Palacios, R., and D. Robalino. 2020. "Integrating Social Insurance and Social Assistance Programs for the Future World of Labor." IZA DP No. 13258, Institute of Labor Economics, Bonn, Germany.

Pestel, N., and E. Sommer. 2017. "Shifting Taxes from Labor to Consumption: More Employment and More Inequality?" *Review of Income and Wealth* 63 (3): 542–63.

Picketty, T., and E. Saez. 2012. "A Theory of Optimal Capital Taxation." NBER Working Paper 17989, National Bureau of Economic Research, Cambridge, MA.

Rofman, R., and I. Apella. 2020. *When We're Sixty-Four: Opportunities and Challenges for Public Policies in a Population-Aging Context in Latin America*. International Development in Focus. Washington, DC: World Bank. http://hdl.handle.net/10986/34562.

Sahasranamam, S., and J. Prabhu. 2024. "Digital Public Infrastructure for the Developing World." *Stanford Social Innovation Review* (March), Stanford Center on Philanthropy and Civil Society, Stanford University, Stanford, CA. doi:10.48558/xdtx-pw77.

Santini, J., F. Capurro, D. Rogger, T. Lundy, G. Kim, J. Miranda, S. Cocciolo, and C. Casanova. 2024. *Data for Better Governance: Building Government Analytics Ecosystems in Latin America and the Caribbean*. Washington, DC: World Bank.

Savedoff, W. 2004. "Tax-Based Financing for Health Systems: Options and Experiences." Discussion Paper No. 4, Health System Financing, Expenditure, and Resource Allocation Department, Evidence and Information for Policy Cluster, World Health Organization, Geneva.

Silva, J., L. Sousa, T. Packard, and R. Robertson. 2021. *Employment in Crisis: The Path to Better Jobs in a Post-COVID-19 Latin America*. Latin America and Caribbean Studies. Washington, DC: World Bank. http://hdl.handle.net/10986/35549.

Summers, L. H. 1989. "Some Simple Economics of Mandated Benefits." *American Economic Review* 79 (2), *Papers and Proceedings of the Hundred and First Annual Meeting of the American Economic Association* (May): 177–83.

Tommasi, M., and J. Saavedra-Chanduvi. 2007. "Informality, the State and the Social Contract in Latin America: A Preliminary Exploration." *International Labour Review* 146 (3–4): 279–309.

Torgler, B. 2012. "Tax Morale, Eastern Europe and European Enlargement." *Communist and Post-Communist Studies* 45 (1–2): 11–25.

Vostroknutova, E., J. Sampi, C. Jooste, and J. T. Araujo. 2025. *Competition and Productivity Growth in Latin America and the Caribbean*. Washington, DC: World Bank. http://hdl.handle.net/10986/42869.

Vuletin, G. 2024. "Progressive Taxation for Growth in LAC." Draft Regional Study for the Office of the Chief Economist, Latin America and Caribbean Regional Office, World Bank, Washington, DC.

WHO (World Health Organization). 2024. *Global Spending on Health: Emerging from the Pandemic*. Geneva: World Health Organization. https://iris.who.int/handle/10665/379750.

World Bank. 2013. "Turkey: Managing Labor Markets through the Economic Cycle." Report 70130-TR, World Bank, Washington, DC.

World Bank and UNESCO (United Nations Educational, Scientific and Cultural Organization). 2024. *Education Finance Watch 2024*. Washington, DC, and Paris: World Bank and UNESCO.

Zaber, M., O. Casu, and E. Brodersohn. 2024. *Artificial Intelligence in Social Security Organizations*. Geneva: International Social Security Association.

CHAPTER ANNEXES

Informality in 2019

Analyzing informality in 2019 reveals a similar picture to that observed in 2022. To complement the analysis, the results for 2019 are included here (refer to tables 2A.1 and 2A.2). Compared to 2022, few changes are observed. In 2022, for Colombia, El Salvador, and Uruguay, a higher percentage of complying workers is observed, and for Peru, the percentage of nonparticipating workers is higher (compare figure 2A.1 to figure 2.4 in the main text). The comparison also shows that noncomplying workers are mainly self-employed in Brazil and Uruguay; are private salaried workers in Colombia, El Salvador, and Mexico; and are public salaried workers in Peru. Nonparticipating workers are mainly nonsalaried workers in Brazil and Uruguay and are self-employed workers in Colombia, El Salvador, Mexico, and Peru. Both types of noncovered workers are found mainly in the service sector and employed in small firms. In addition, in Brazil, El Salvador, and Uruguay, noncomplying workers are mostly men, and nonparticipating workers are mostly women. Furthermore, both types of noncovered workers are mainly ages 25–49 years and located in urban areas.

In the lower income deciles, complying and participating workers are almost nonexistent (refer to figure 2A.2). As observed in 2022, the lower deciles of per capita household income have the lowest percentage of complying or participating workers. The percentage of complying workers increases as the income level rises. Similarly, noncomplying and nonparticipating workers earn lower incomes compared to their counterparts. The average earnings of complying workers are twice as high as those of noncomplying and nonparticipating workers.

The shares of labor income, the distributions of the informality categories, and the average labor incomes by category have remained relatively stable over the short term (refer to figures 2A.3, 2A.4, and 2A.5, respectively, compared to figures 2.7, 2.8, and 2.9 in the main text). Labor market conditions are not driving more people into formality or informality. In other words, the informal employment dynamics have remained consistent, which may reflect a lack of opportunities in the formal sector or resistance to changes in labor regulations.

FIGURE 2A.1

Distribution of workers in select LAC countries, by informality category and country, circa 2019

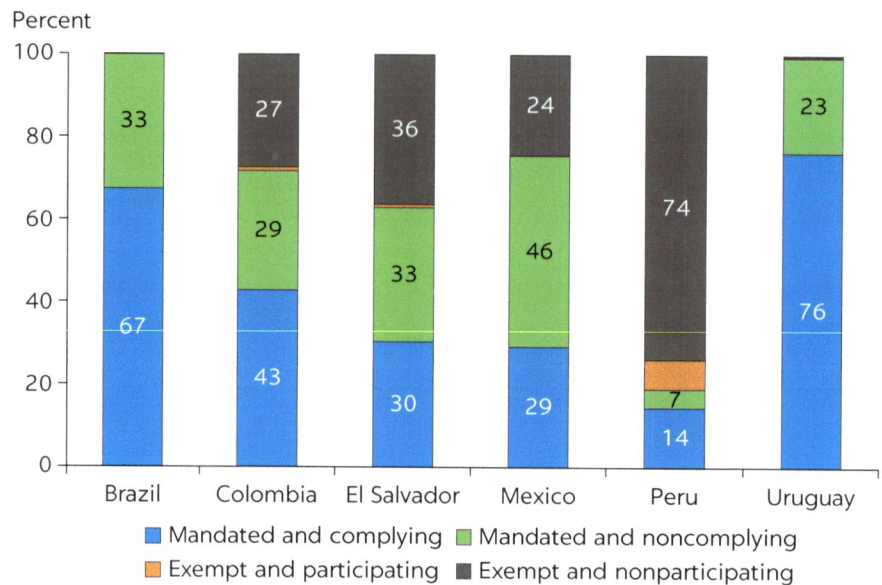

Sources: Original figure for this publication, using data from SEDLAC 2018, 2019.
Note: LAC = Latin America and the Caribbean.

TABLE 2A.1 **Profile of workers in select LAC countries, by (in)formality category and job characteristics, circa 2019**

	MANDATED %	BRAZIL		COLOMBIA		EL SALVADOR		MEXICO		PERU		URUGUAY	
		M AND C	M AND NC	M AND C	M AND NC	M AND C	M AND NC	M AND C	M AND NC	M AND C	M AND NC	M AND C	M AND NC
Type of workers	Employer	5	4	2	7	0	0	0	0	0	0	4	1
	Salaried private	66	43	78	63	75	98	79	93	52	45	65	34
	Salaried public	18	3	10	0	25	2	21	7	48	55	21	0
	Self-employed	12	50	10	30	0	0	0	0	0	0	10	64
	Unsalaried worker	0	0	0	0	0	0	0	0	0	0	0	0
Sector	Agriculture	5	14	5	18	2	22	2	12	6	5	8	9
	Industry	20	22	23	22	26	26	33	26	17	15	15	24
	Services	75	65	72	60	72	52	65	62	77	81	77	67
Firm size	Large	56	15	77	23	73	34	70	37	49	42	56	10
	Small	26	82	13	77	3	65	8	56	0	0	24	90
	Public	18	3	10	0	25	2	21	7	51	58	21	0

	EXEMPT, %	BRAZIL		COLOMBIA		EL SALVADOR		MEXICO		PERU		URUGUAY	
		E AND P	E AND NP	E AND P	E AND NP	E AND P	E AND NP	E AND P	E AND NP	E AND P	E AND NP	E AND P	E AND NP
Type of workers	Employer	0	0	9	3	43	11	—	31	6	5	0	0
	Salaried private	0	0	0	0	0	0	—	0	86	33	0	0
	Salaried public	0	0	0	0	0	0	—	0	0	0	0	0
	Self-employed	0	0	84	84	51	73	—	51	8	48	0	0
	Unsalaried worker	100	100	7	14	6	17	—	18	0	14	100	100
Sector	Agriculture	5	59	7	29	7	21	—	28	6	31	58	29
	Industry	26	0	15	17	23	18	—	16	23	16	7	14
	Services	69	41	78	54	71	61	—	56	71	54	35	57
Firm size	Large	34	8	16	3	24	2	—	5	77	14	9	4
	Small	66	92	84	97	75	98	—	95	23	86	91	96
	Public	0	0	0	0	0	0	—	0	0	0	0	0

Sources: Original table for this publication, using data from SEDLAC 2018, 2019.

Note: E and NP = exempt and nonparticipating; E and P = exempt and participating; LAC = Latin America and the Caribbean; M and C = mandated and complying; M and NC = mandated and noncomplying; — = not available.

TABLE 2A.2 Profile of workers in select LAC countries, by (in)formality category and individuals' characteristics, circa 2019

	MANDATED, %	BRAZIL M AND C	BRAZIL M AND NC	COLOMBIA M AND C	COLOMBIA M AND NC	EL SALVADOR M AND C	EL SALVADOR M AND NC	MEXICO M AND C	MEXICO M AND NC	PERU M AND C	PERU M AND NC	URUGUAY M AND C	URUGUAY M AND NC
Gender	Female	44	40	41	33	38	35	39	38	41	46	46	42
	Male	56	60	59	67	62	65	61	62	59	54	54	58
Age (years)	15–24	13	19	12	19	15	29	13	25	10	19	10	19
	25–49	68	60	71	60	67	57	69	57	61	61	64	55
	50–65	20	21	17	21	18	15	18	18	29	20	26	27
Area	Urban	91	82	64	61	40	36	79	63	54	55	49	65
	Rural	7	17	8	24	18	42	8	22	5	10	5	5
	Capital city	2	1	28	16	42	22	13	15	41	35	46	29
Level of education	Less than primary	15	37	3	16	14	54	2	12	2	4	2	7
	Primary	12	19	14	35	25	27	36	56	5	11	52	78
	Secondary	47	36	53	42	43	17	32	21	35	44	27	12
	Tertiary	25	8	30	7	18	2	30	11	58	41	19	2

	EXEMPT, %	BRAZIL E AND P	BRAZIL E AND NP	COLOMBIA E AND P	COLOMBIA E AND NP	EL SALVADOR E AND P	EL SALVADOR E AND NP	MEXICO E AND P	MEXICO E AND NP	PERU E AND P	PERU E AND NP	URUGUAY E AND P	URUGUAY E AND NP
Gender	Female	100	66	41	38	37	52	—	50	38	49	85	57
	Male	0	34	59	62	63	48	—	50	62	51	15	43
Age (years)	15–24	0	24	3	18	1	14	—	12	10	18	3	34
	25–49	92	66	53	54	50	55	—	55	67	53	58	40
	50–65	8	10	44	28	48	30	—	33	23	29	39	26
Area	Urban	87	50	66	56	58	38	—	53	39	46	30	46
	Rural	13	50	9	35	9	38	—	36	4	28	50	24
	Capital city	0	0	25	9	33	24	—	11	57	27	21	30
Level of education	Less than primary	5	25	8	26	13	55	—	19	3	17	2	6
	Primary	0	25	26	39	12	23	—	53	9	30	67	75
	Secondary	20	32	46	32	34	19	—	18	43	41	25	16
	Tertiary	75	18	19	3	41	3	—	10	45	12	7	3

Sources: Original table for this publication, using data from SEDLAC 2018, 2019.

Note: E and NP = exempt and nonparticipating; E and P = exempt and participating; LAC = Latin America and the Caribbean; M and C = mandated and complying; M and NC = mandated and noncomplying; — = not available.

FIGURE 2A.2

Formality rate among complying and participating workers in select LAC countries, by (in)formality category and per capita household income decile, circa 2019

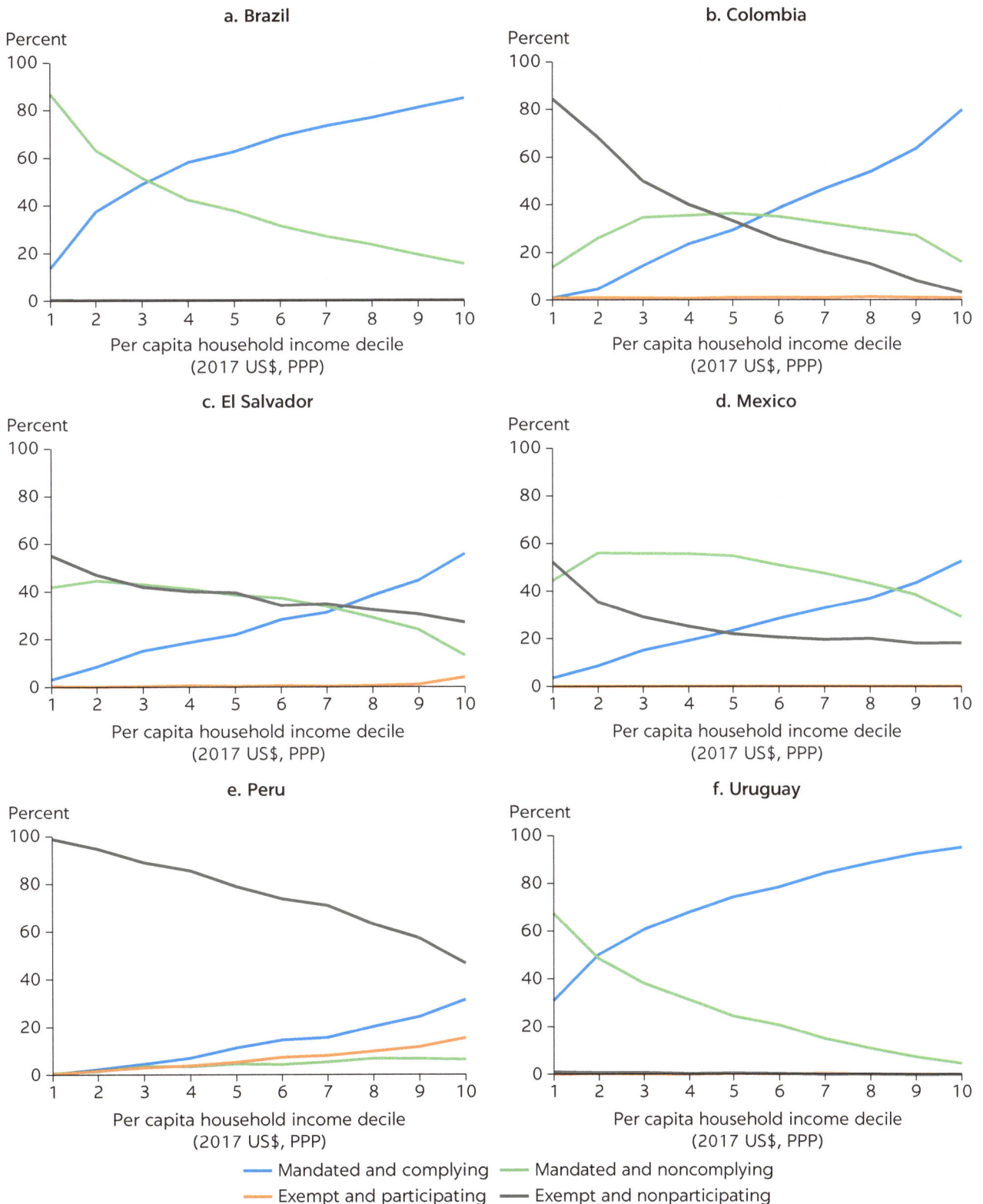

a. Brazil

b. Colombia

c. El Salvador

d. Mexico

e. Peru

f. Uruguay

— Mandated and complying — Mandated and noncomplying
— Exempt and participating — Exempt and nonparticipating

Sources: Original figures for this publication, using data from SEDLAC 2018, 2019.
Note: LAC = Latin America and the Caribbean; PPP = purchasing power parity.

FIGURE 2A.3

Share of total labor income in select LAC countries, by (in)formality category and per capita household income decile, circa 2019

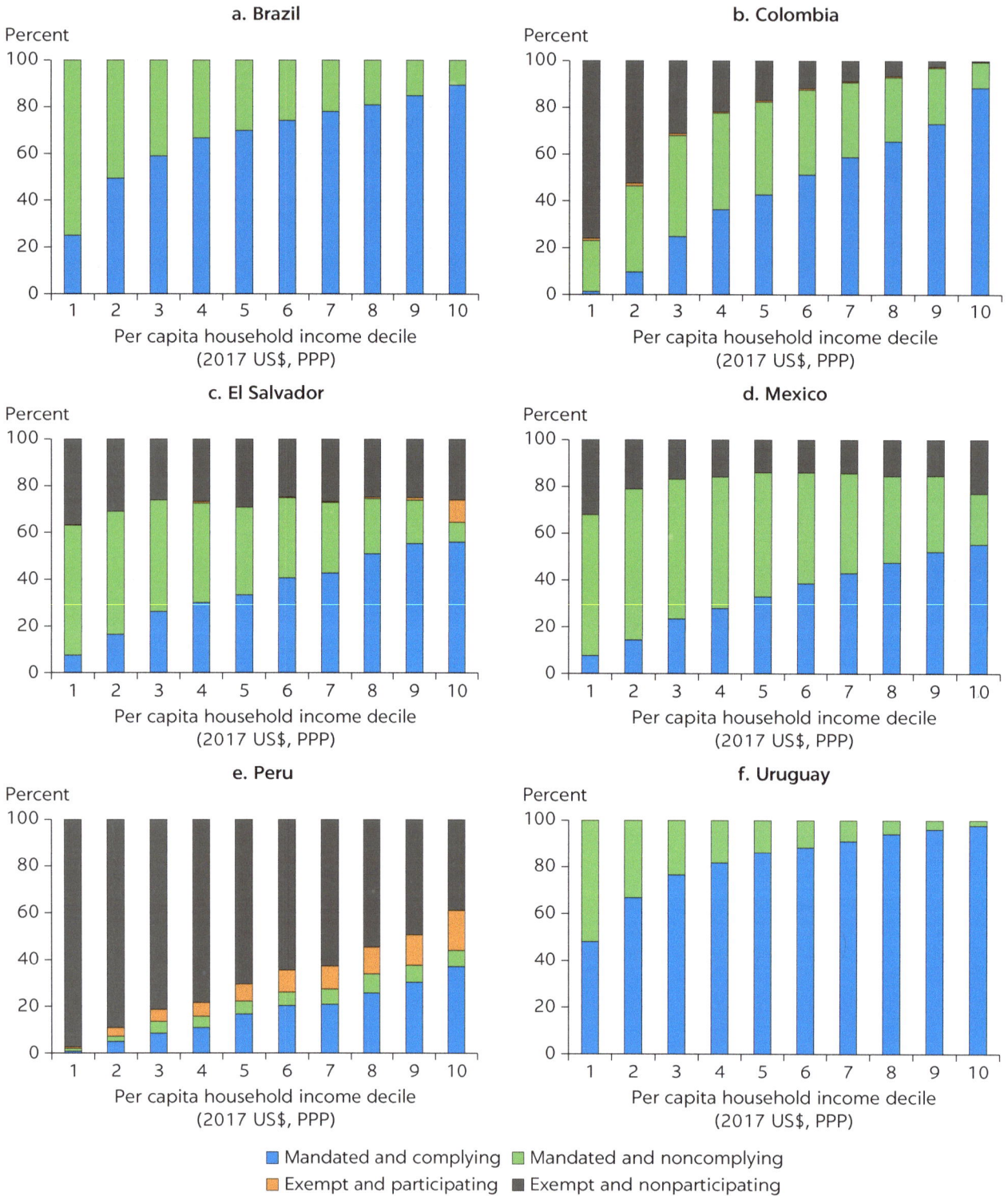

a. Brazil

b. Colombia

c. El Salvador

d. Mexico

e. Peru

f. Uruguay

■ Mandated and complying ■ Mandated and noncomplying
■ Exempt and participating ■ Exempt and nonparticipating

Sources: Original figures for this publication, using data from SEDLAC 2018, 2019.
Note: LAC = Latin America and the Caribbean; PPP = purchasing power parity.

FIGURE 2A.4

Distribution of labor income in select LAC countries, by (in)formality category, circa 2019

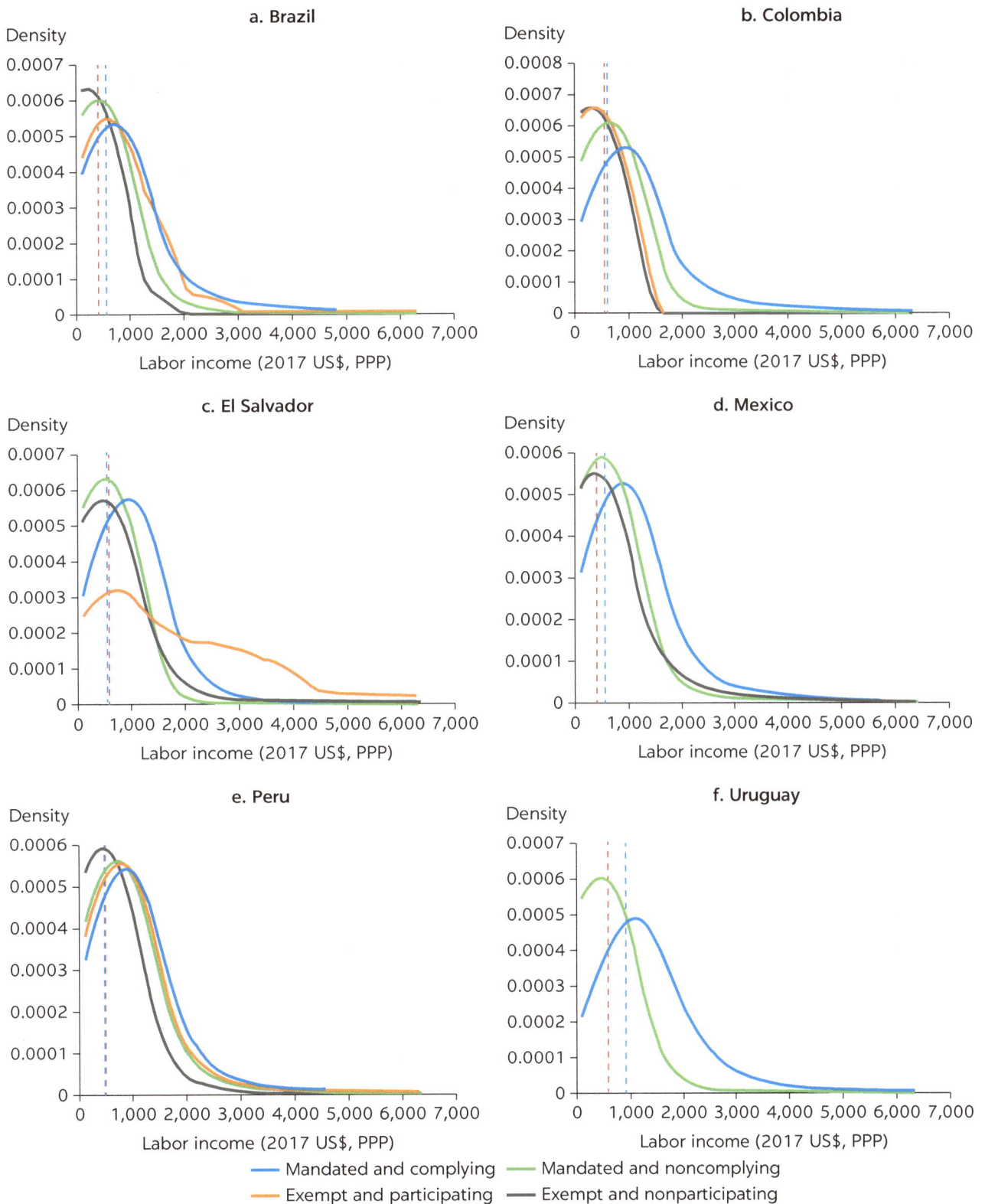

Sources: Original figures for this publication, using data from SEDLAC 2018, 2019.

Note: The red dashed line represents the minimum wage, and the blue dashed line represents the median labor income.

LAC = Latin America and the Caribbean; PPP = purchasing power parity.

FIGURE 2A.5

Average labor income in select LAC countries, by (in)formality category and per capita household income decile, circa 2019

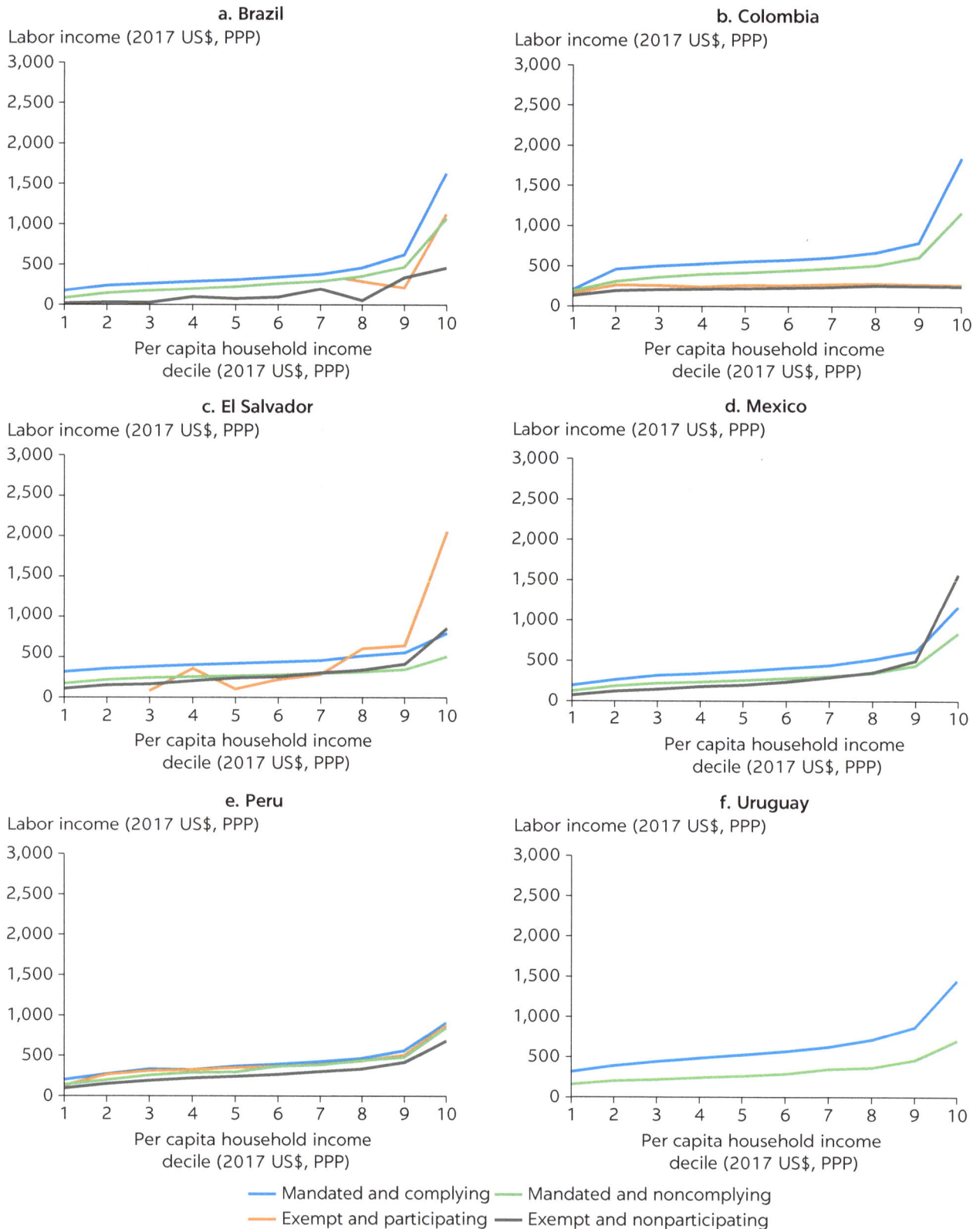

a. Brazil

Labor income (2017 US$, PPP)

Per capita household income decile (2017 US$, PPP)

b. Colombia

Labor income (2017 US$, PPP)

Per capita household income decile (2017 US$, PPP)

c. El Salvador

Labor income (2017 US$, PPP)

Per capita household income decile (2017 US$, PPP)

d. Mexico

Labor income (2017 US$, PPP)

Per capita household income decile (2017 US$, PPP)

e. Peru

Labor income (2017 US$, PPP)

Per capita household income decile (2017 US$, PPP)

f. Uruguay

Labor income (2017 US$, PPP)

Per capita household income decile (2017 US$, PPP)

— Mandated and complying — Mandated and noncomplying
— Exempt and participating — Exempt and nonparticipating

Sources: Original figures for this publication, using data from SEDLAC 2018, 2019.
Note: LAC = Latin America and the Caribbean; PPP = purchasing power parity.

Framework for Self-Employed Workers

The framework could be adjusted to show which factors are relevant for self-employed workers. Depending on the regime of each country, some elements may be regulated with separate taxes, labor regulations, or even firm regulations. Figure 3A.1 shows which factors are likely to be relevant for self-employed workers.

FIGURE 3A.1

Framework for the incentives for the self-employed to formalize

…and some dimensions shut off **for self-employed workers**

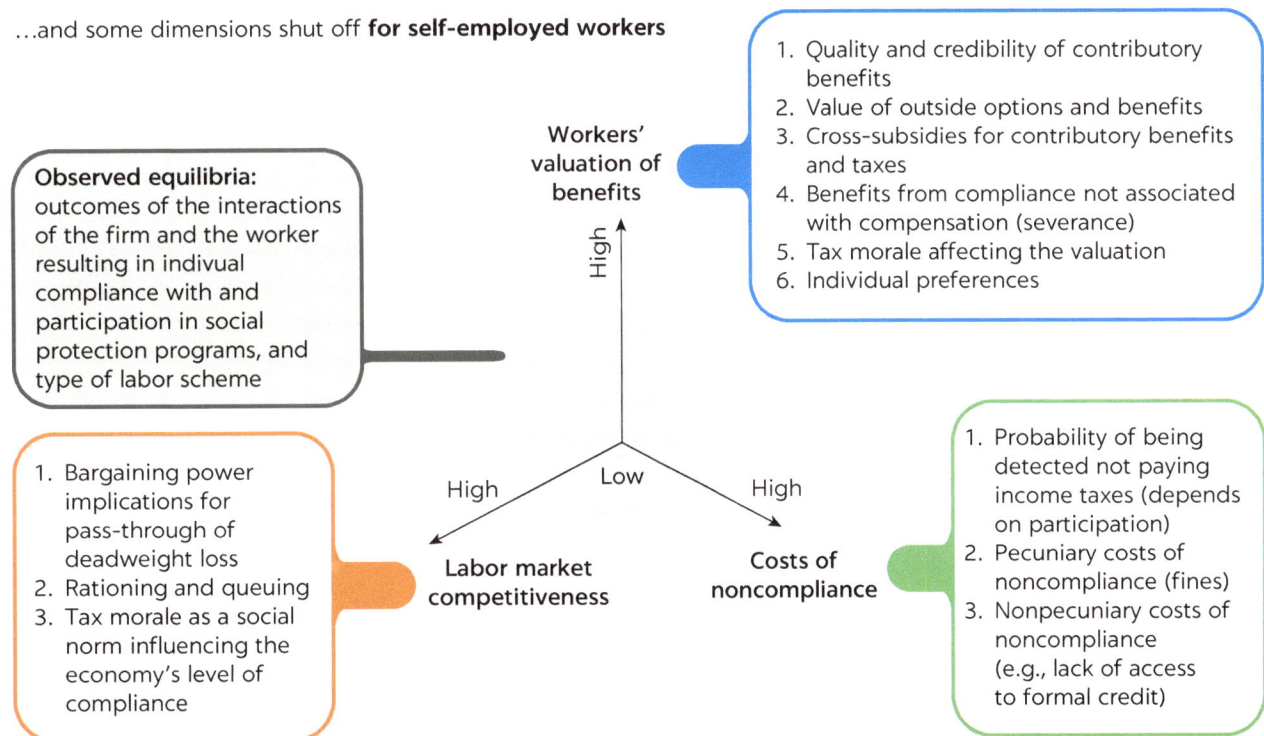

Observed equilibria: outcomes of the interactions of the firm and the worker resulting in indivual compliance with and participation in social protection programs, and type of labor scheme

Workers' valuation of benefits

High

1. Quality and credibility of contributory benefits
2. Value of outside options and benefits
3. Cross-subsidies for contributory benefits and taxes
4. Benefits from compliance not associated with compensation (severance)
5. Tax morale affecting the valuation
6. Individual preferences

High   Low

1. Bargaining power implications for pass-through of deadweight loss
2. Rationing and queuing
3. Tax morale as a social norm influencing the economy's level of compliance

Labor market competitiveness

High

Costs of noncompliance

1. Probability of being detected not paying income taxes (depends on participation)
2. Pecuniary costs of noncompliance (fines)
3. Nonpecuniary costs of noncompliance (e.g., lack of access to formal credit)

Source: Adapted from Fietz (forthcoming).

Enforcement Index

While the evidence is still scarce on the costs and benefits for firms and workers of not complying with regulations, Kanbur and Ronconi (2018) built an index based on observed objective indicators, such as the number of inspectors and trust in courts, for selected countries in the region.
The enforcement index considers the following measures:

- *Inspections.* The first measure is the ratio of the number of labor inspectors to the size of the labor force in each country. The labor inspector is a public official responsible for securing the enforcement of the legal provisions related to wages, safety and health, hours of work, employment of children, and other connected matters. The second measure is the ratio of the number of labor inspections conducted each year to the size of the labor force in each country.

- *Penalties.* Measures of penalties specified in law for low, medium, and high penalty cases are constructed, and criminal penalties are converted into a money metric by assuming that the cost to an employer of serving 1 year in prison equals 10 times the gross domestic product per worker. The low total penalty case assumes a 10 percent probability of receiving the minimum financial fine and a 5 percent probability of receiving the minimum term in prison. The medium total penalty case assumes a 50 percent probability of receiving a medium financial fine and a 25 percent probability of receiving the medium term in prison. Finally, the high total penalty case assumes a 100 percent probability of receiving the maximum financial fine and a 50 percent probability of serving 50 percent of the maximum term in prison.

- *Courts.* Trust in courts is defined as the share of the population that reports having a great deal of confidence in the courts, based on data from the World Values Survey (refer to https://www.worldvaluessurvey.org).

TABLE 3B.1 Enforcement index: Average of the normalized variables, medium total penalty, number of inspectors, and trust in courts

COUNTRY	ENFORCEMENT INDEX
Peru	.0029690
El Salvador	.0073783
Colombia	.0131914
Uruguay	.0134345
Brazil	.0160629
Jamaica	.0521164

Source: Adapted from Kanbur and Ronconi 2018.

Note: The enforcement index considers inspections, penalties, and courts. It uses observations from 2000–12 (although for most countries, observations are available only for 2010–12).

Mapping Methodology for the De Jure Tax and Benefit Modeling

The methodology used in this report for mapping taxes and benefits is closely aligned with the Organisation for Economic Co-operation and Development's *Taxing Wages* series. For each country, a detailed overview of nonwage and wage costs has been established. These costs are classified into categories in table 4.1 in the main text. First, workers must pay personal income taxes and, in some cases, additional taxes on their wages. These taxes are classified as pure taxes because they are not connected to any direct (short- or long-term) benefit to the worker. Second, workers must pay contributions from their wages. The contributions are directed toward health benefits, which can be seen as an indirect, short-term compensation; pension contributions, which can be seen as an indirect long-term compensation; and accident insurance and unemployment insurance, which can be seen as indirect contingent compensation.

If the worker is employed by a firm, the employer may be mandated to pay the same types of taxes and contributions. If self-employed, the individual is responsible for the taxes and contributions of both the worker and the firm because they cannot be passed on to any employer.

Wage costs encompass the monthly wage and, in the case of dependent workers, a 13th month of salary and a holiday bonus. In addition, certain components, such as bonuses and gratuities, in-kind remuneration, and costs of worker housing, might be considered. Finally, workers are entitled to certain benefits. In-work benefits paid through the general government are mainly paid to dependent workers and are conditional on their formality status, while social assistance benefits may be received by both dependent and self-employed workers, whether informal or formal, in most cases. Tables 4A.1–4A.3 explain each component in detail.

Taxes and benefits differ by household composition, labor contract, and wage level. Therefore, the mapping of taxes and benefits is done for several family compositions (such as a single-earner household or a household with 2 adults and 2 children), various forms of employment (such as dependent workers, self-employed individuals, or single-person firms), and multiple levels of labor income. This comprehensive approach ensures that the impacts of taxes and benefits on different types of households and employment situations are accurately captured and analyzed.

TABLE 4A.1 Overview of tax, contribution, and benefit classifications

TOTAL LABOR COSTS (L1 + L2 + L3)			
NONWAGE COSTS		WAGE COSTS / TOTAL EARNINGS	BENEFITS (PAID THROUGH THE GOVERNMENT)
Gross earnings (L1)			
Firm (employers' social security expenditure [L2] and other costs [L3])	Worker (employee's compulsory social security contributions [SC] and personal income tax)		
Other costs: taxes (regarded as labor costs) (L3) Payroll taxes: payment not associated with an individual entitlement • Taxes	Taxes (regarded as labor costs) Payroll taxes (personal income tax): payment not associated with an individual entitlement • Taxes	A. Direct wages and salaries • For example, straight-time pay of time-related workers	In-work benefits (paid through the government) / employment-related social security benefits (paid through the government) Direct immediate benefits → part of net labor income
Social security expenditure (L2) Health contributions • Indirect short-term compensation Pension contributions • Indirect long-term compensation Mandatory savings account • Indirect contingent compensation Accident insurance contributions • Indirect contingent compensation Unemployment insurance • Indirect contingent compensation Severance payment	Social security contributions (SC) Health contributions • Indirect short-term compensation Pension contributions • Indirect long-term compensation Mandatory savings account • Indirect contingent compensation Accident insurance contributions • Indirect contingent compensation Unemployment insurance • Indirect contingent compensation	B. Renumeration for time not working • Annual vacation, other paid leave C. Bonuses and gratuities • For example, year-end and seasonal bonuses D. Remuneration in kind • For example, food, drink, fuel, and other in-kind payments that can be monetarized E. Cost of workers' housing borne by employers • For example, cost of establishment-owned dwellings, other housing costs	Social assistance benefits (paid through the government) • Direct immediate benefits

Source: Original table for this publication.
Note: L1 = gross earnings; L2 = employers' social security expenditure; L3 = other costs (for example, taxes regarded as labor costs); SC = employee's compulsory social security contributions.

Based on the detailed mapping of taxes and benefits, certain indicators might be calculated. Table 4A.2 shows how the following indicators are calculated: total labor costs, net take-home pay, tax wedge, pure tax wedge, and average personal tax rate. Table 4A.3 explains the categories in Table 4A.2.

TABLE 4A.2 Overview of tax and benefit indicators

Labor costs
5 + 1 + 4
Net take-home pay
5 – 3 – 2 + 6
Tax wedge
(1 + 2 + 3 + 4 – 6) / labor costs
Pure tax wedge
(3 + 4) / labor costs
Personal average tax rate (tax burden)
(2 + 3 – 6 – 7) / 5
1 = Social security contributions, employer
2 = Social security contributions, employee
3 = Personal income tax
4 = Non–social insurance payroll taxes
5 = Gross earnings
6 = In-work cash benefits / wage subsidies
7 = Non-work-related cash benefits

Source: Original table for this publication.

TABLE 4A.3 Detailed explanation of the categories in table 4A.2

Dependent workers
From the employer's perspective
Total labor costs (L1 + L2 + L3)
L1. Gross wages/earnings
Total wages/earnings before deductions by the employer for taxes, and before employees' contributions to social security, pensions, union dues, and so forth.
A. Direct wages and salaries *Straight-time pay for time-rated workers; incentive pay for time-rated workers; earnings for piece-rate workers (excluding overtime premiums); and premium pay for overtime, late shifts, and holiday work*
B. Remuneration for time not working *Annual vacation, other paid leave, public holidays and other holidays, other time off granted with pay (union activities, birth or death of family members, marriage, and so forth), severance, and termination pay where it is not regarded as a social security expenditure*

continued

TABLE 4A.3 Detailed explanation of the categories in table 4A.2, *(continued)*

Dependent workers

C. Bonuses and gratuities

Year-end and seasonal bonuses; profit-sharing bonuses; additional payments for vacations, supplementary to normal vacation pay; and other bonuses

D. Remuneration in kind

Food, drink, fuel, and other in-kind payments

E. Cost of workers' housing borne by employers

Cost of establishment-owned dwellings, other housing costs

L2. Employers' social security expenditures

F. Statutory social security contributions

Compulsory payments paid to the general government or designated entities that confer entitlement to receive a (contingent) future social benefit. The payments include unemployment insurance benefits and supplements; accident, injury, and sickness benefits; old-age, disability, and survivors' pensions; family allowances; and reimbursements for medical and hospital expenses or provision of hospital or medical services. Here only contributions levied on employers are considered.

Classification of contributions:
- Indirect short-term compensation: health insurance contributions
- Indirect long-term compensation: pension contributions
- Indirect contingent compensation: accident insurance, unemployment insurance

G. Collectively agreed, contractual insurances

H. Direct payments to employees in respect of absence from work due to sickness, maternity, or employment injury, to compensate for loss of earnings

I. Other direct payments to employees regarded as social security benefits

J. Cost of medical care and health services

K. Severance and termination pay where regarded as social security expenditure

L3. Other costs

L. Cost of vocational training

M. Cost of welfare services
Cost of cafeteria and other food services

N. Cost of education, cultural, recreational, and related family services

O. Grants to credit unions and cost of related services for employees

P. Labor cost not elsewhere classified

Q. Taxes regarded as labor cost

For example, taxes on employment or payroll, included on a net basis, after deduction of allowances or rebates made by the state

Contribution toward indirect benefit

From the dependent worker's perspective

NI. Net income related to paid employment (L1 + I1 + I2 + I3 − SC − PLIT + TA)

L1. Gross wages/earnings

Total wage/earnings before deductions by employer for taxes and before contributions of employees to social security, pensions, union dues, and so forth.

TABLE 4A.3 Detailed explanation of the categories in table 4A.2, *(continued)*

Dependent workers

A. Direct wages and salaries

Straight-time pay for time-rated workers; incentive pay for time-rated workers; earnings of piece-rate workers (excluding overtime premiums); and premium pay for overtime, late shifts, and holiday work

B. Remuneration for time not working

Annual vacation, other paid leave, public holidays and other holidays, other time off granted with pay (union activities, birth or death of family members, marriage, and so forth), severance, and termination pay where not regarded as social security expenditure

C. Bonuses and gratuities

Year-end and seasonal bonuses, profit-sharing bonuses, additional payments for vacations supplementary to normal vacation pay, and other bonuses

D. Remuneration in kind

Food, drink, fuel, and other in-kind payments

E. Cost of workers' housing borne by employers

Cost of establishment-owned dwellings, other housing costs

I1. Other income related to paid employment received from employer

L. Vocational training

M. Welfare services
Cost of cafeteria and other food services, gym, and so forth

N. Educational, cultural, recreational, and related family services

I2. Other income related to paid employment not received from employer

R. Cash, tips, gratuities

I3. Employment-related social security benefits

Social security and assimilated payments for which employment status is a condition of receipt

S. Current employment-related social security benefits received from social security or compulsory insurance schemes or the state

Payments for absence from work due to sickness, maternity, paternity, or occupational injury or disease; payments in respect of temporary or partial lay-off; compensation for medical expenditures; and provision of free health care and other social security and assimilated payments for which employment status is a condition of receipt

SC. Employee's compulsory social security contributions

Compulsory payments paid to general government that confer entitlement to receive a (contingent) future social benefit. These payments include unemployment insurance benefits and supplements; accident, injury, and sickness benefits; old-age, disability, and survivors' pensions; family allowances; and reimbursements for medical and hospital expenses or provision of hospital or medical services. Here only contributions levied on employees are considered.

PLIT. Personal direct taxes on income

Tax on personal income is defined as the taxes levied on the net income (gross income minus allowable tax reliefs)

TA. Tax allowances

Deductions for social security contributions and income taxes, deductible work-related expenses

continued

TABLE 4A.3 Detailed explanation of the categories in table 4A.2, *(continued)*

Dependent workers
Self-employed workers
NI. Net income related to self-employment (SEL1 – SESC – PLIT + TA)
SEL1. Gross income related to self-employment

T. Profit (share of profit) generated by the self-employment activity

U. Where relevant, remuneration received by the owner-manager of a corporation or quasi-corporation

V. Employment-related social security benefits received by the self-employed

   Benefits paid through schemes organized by social security, compulsory insurance institutions, or the state, which recognize the status of employment as a specific condition

SC. Self-employment social security contributions

Compulsory payments paid to government that confer entitlement to receive a (contingent) future social benefit. These payments include unemployment insurance benefits and supplements; accident, injury, and sickness benefits; old-age, disability, and survivors' pensions; family allowances; and reimbursements for medical and hospital expenses or provision of hospital or medical services. Here only contributions levied on employees are considered.

PLIT. Personal direct taxes on income

Tax on personal direct income received is defined as the taxes levied on net income (gross income minus allowable tax reliefs)

TA. Tax allowances

Deductions for social security contributions and income taxes, deductible self-employment-related expenses

Source: Original table for this publication.
Note: I1 = other income related to paid employment received from employer; I2 = other income related to paid employment not received from employer; I3 = employment-related social security benefits; L1 = gross earnings; L2 = employers' social security expenditure; L3 = other costs (for example, taxes regarded as labor costs); NI = net income related to self-employment (SEL1 – SESC – PLIT + TA); PLIT = personal direct taxes on income; SC = employee's compulsory social security contributions; SEL1 = gross income related to self-employment; SESC = self-employment social security contributions; TA = tax allowances.

De Jure Mapping Tables

Tables 4B.1–4B.14 show the key policy and program parameters that determine total labor cost and take-home income by country (Brazil, Colombia, El Salvador, Jamaica, Mexico, Peru, and Uruguay) and worker status (dependent worker or self-employed worker). The tables extend table 4.1 in the main text, which shows all the policy and program parameters, and provide a granular country analysis.

BRAZIL

TABLE 4B.1 De jure mapping for dependent workers in Brazil

TOTAL LABOR COSTS (L1 + L2 + L3)			
NONWAGE COSTS		**WAGE COSTS / TOTAL EARNINGS**	**BENEFITS (PAID THROUGH THE GOVERNMENT)**
		Net income related to paid employment (L1 + I3 – SC – PIT)	
Firm (L2 + L3)	**Worker (PIT + SC)**	**Gross earnings (L1)**	
Taxes (L3)	**Taxes (regarded as labor costs)**	**A. Direct wages and salaries**	**In-work/social security benefits paid through the government**
Payroll taxes (5.8%)	PIT (7.5%–27.5%) Payroll taxes	• For example, straight-time pay of time-related workers	• Direct immediate benefits → part of net labor income (Abono Salarial [bonus salary] and Salario Familia [family allowance])

continued

TABLE 4B.1 De jure mapping for dependent workers in Brazil, *(continued)*

TOTAL LABOR COSTS (L1 + L2 + L3)

NONWAGE COSTS		WAGE COSTS / TOTAL EARNINGS	BENEFITS (PAID THROUGH THE GOVERNMENT)
Social security expenditure (L2)	Social security contributions (SC)	B. Renumeration for time not working	Social assistance benefits (paid through the government)
Health contributions	Health contributions	• Annual vacation, other paid leave	• Direct immediate benefits (Bolsa Familia)
• Indirect short-term compensation	• Indirect short-term compensation		
Pension contributions (20%)	Pension contributions (7.5%–14%)	**C. Bonuses and gratuities**	
• Indirect long-term compensation	• Indirect long-term compensation	• For example, year-end and seasonal bonuses	
Mandatory savings account (8%)	Mandatory savings account		
• Indirect contingent compensation	• Indirect contingent compensation	**D. Remuneration in kind**	
Accident insurance contributions (2%)	Accident insurance contributions	• For example, food, drink, fuel, and other in-kind payments	
• Indirect contingent compensation	• Indirect contingent compensation		
Unemployment insurance	Unemployment insurance	**E. Cost of workers' housing borne by employers**	
• Indirect contingent compensation	• Indirect contingent compensation	• For example, cost of establishment-owned dwellings	
Severance payment (40% of mandatory savings account)			

Source: Original table for this publication.

Note: Text in blue indicates information specific to Brazil. Text in light gray indicates categories of general total labor cost that are not present in Brazil. I3 = in-work benefits and employment-related social security benefits (paid through the government); L1 = gross earnings; L2 = employers' social security expenditure; L3 = other costs (for example, taxes regarded as labor costs); PIT = personal income tax; SC = employee's compulsory social security contributions.

TABLE 4B.2 De jure mapping for independent workers in Brazil

TOTAL LABOR COSTS (L1 + L2 + L3)			
NONWAGE COSTS		**WAGE COSTS / TOTAL EARNINGS**	**BENEFITS (PAID THROUGH THE GOVERNMENT)**
Net income related to paid employment (L1 + I3 – SC – PIT)			
Firm (L2 + L3)	**Worker (PIT + SC)**	**Gross earnings (L1)**	
Taxes (L3)	**Taxes (regarded as labor costs)**	**A. Direct wages and salaries**	**In-work/social security benefits paid through the government**
Payroll taxes	PIT (7.5%–27.5%)	• For example, straight-time pay of time-related workers	• Direct immediate benefits → part of net labor income
Social security expenditure (L2)	**Social security contributions (SC)**	**B. Renumeration for time not working**	**Social assistance benefits (paid through the government)**
Health contributions • Indirect short-term compensation	Health contributions • Indirect short-term compensation	• Annual vacation, other paid leave	• Direct immediate benefits
Pension contributions • Indirect long-term compensation	Pension contributions (11%–20%) • Indirect long-term compensation	**C. Bonuses and gratuities**	
Mandatory savings account • Indirect contingent compensation	Mandatory savings account • Indirect contingent compensation	• For example, year-end and seasonal bonuses	
Accident insurance contributions • Indirect contingent compensation	Accident insurance contributions • Indirect contingent compensation	**D. Remuneration in kind** • For example, food, drink, fuel, and other in-kind payments	
Unemployment insurance	Unemployment insurance	**E. Cost of workers' housing borne by employers**	
• Indirect contingent compensation Severance payment	• Indirect contingent compensation	• For example, cost of establishment-owned dwellings	

Source: Original table for this publication.
Note: Text in blue indicates information specific to Brazil. Text in light gray indicates categories of general total labor cost that are not present in Brazil. I3 = in-work benefits and employment-related social security benefits (paid through the government); L1 = gross earnings; L2 = employers' social security expenditure; L3 = other costs (for example, taxes regarded as labor costs); PIT = personal income tax; SC = employee's compulsory social security contributions.

COLOMBIA

TABLE 4B.3 De jure mapping for dependent workers in Colombia

TOTAL LABOR COSTS (L1 + L2 + L3)

NONWAGE COSTS		WAGE COSTS / TOTAL EARNINGS	BENEFITS (PAID THROUGH THE GOVERNMENT)
Net income related to paid employment (L1 + I3 – SC – PIT)			
Firm (L2 + L3)	Worker (PIT + SC)	Gross earnings (L1)	
Taxes (L3)	Taxes (regarded as labor costs)	A. Direct wages and salaries	In-work/social security benefits paid through the government
Payroll taxes (4%–9%)	PIT (19%–39%) Payroll taxes (1%–2%)	• For example, straight-time pay of time-related workers	• Direct immediate benefits → part of net labor income
Social security expenditure (L2)	Social security contributions (SC)	B. Renumeration for time not working	Social assistance benefits (paid through the government)
Health contributions (8.5%)	Health contributions (4%)	• Annual vacation, other paid leave	• Direct immediate benefits
• Indirect short-term compensation	• Indirect short-term compensation		
Pension contributions (12%)	Pension contributions (4%)	C. Bonuses and gratuities	
• Indirect long-term compensation	• Indirect long-term compensation	• For example, year-end and seasonal bonuses	
Mandatory savings account	Mandatory savings account		
• Indirect contingent compensation	• Indirect contingent compensation	D. Remuneration in kind	
Accident insurance contributions (0.52%–6.96%)	Accident insurance contributions	• For example, food, drink, fuel, and other in-kind payments	
• Indirect contingent compensation	• Indirect contingent compensation		
Unemployment insurance	Unemployment insurance	E. Cost of workers' housing borne by employers	
• Indirect contingent compensation	• Indirect contingent compensation	• For example, cost of establishment-owned dwellings	
Severance payment			

Source: Original table for this publication.
Note: Text in blue indicates information specific to Colombia. Text in light gray indicates categories of general total labor cost that are not present in Colombia. I3 = in-work benefits and employment-related social security benefits (paid through the government); L1 = gross earnings; L2 = employers' social security expenditure; L3 = other costs (for example, taxes regarded as labor costs); PIT = personal income tax; SC = employee's compulsory social security contributions.

TABLE 4B.4 De jure mapping for independent workers in Colombia

TOTAL LABOR COSTS (L1 + L2 + L3)

NONWAGE COSTS		WAGE COSTS / TOTAL EARNINGS	BENEFITS (PAID THROUGH THE GOVERNMENT)
		Net income related to paid employment (L1 + I3 – SC – PIT)	
Firm (L2 + L3)	Worker (PIT + SC)	Gross earnings (L1)	
Taxes (L3)	**Taxes (regarded as labor costs)**	**A. Direct wages and salaries**	In-work/social security benefits paid through the government
Payroll taxes	PIT (19%–39%)	• For example, straight-time pay of time-related workers	• Direct immediate benefits → part of net labor income
Social security expenditure (L2)	**Social security contributions (SC)**	B. Renumeration for time not working	**Social assistance benefits (paid through the government)**
Health contributions	Health contributions (12.5%)	• Annual vacation, other paid leave	• Direct immediate benefits
• Indirect short-term compensation	• Indirect short-term compensation		
Pension contributions	Pension contributions (16%)	**C. Bonuses and gratuities**	
• Indirect long-term compensation	• Indirect long-term compensation	• For example, year-end and seasonal bonuses	
Mandatory savings account	Mandatory savings account		
• Indirect contingent compensation	• Indirect contingent compensation	**D. Remuneration in kind**	
Accident insurance contributions	Accident insurance contributions (0.52%–6.96%)	• For example, food, drink, fuel, and other in-kind payments	
• Indirect contingent compensation	• Indirect contingent compensation		
Unemployment insurance	Unemployment insurance	**E. Cost of workers' housing borne by employers**	
• Indirect contingent compensation	• Indirect contingent compensation	• For example, cost of establishment-owned dwellings	
Severance payment			

Source: Original table for this publication.
Note: Text in blue indicates information specific to Colombia. Text in light gray indicates categories of general total labor cost that are not present in Colombia. I3 = in-work benefits and employment-related social security benefits (paid through the government); L1 = gross earnings; L2 = employers' social security expenditure; L3 = other costs (for example, taxes regarded as labor costs); PIT = personal income tax; SC = employee's compulsory social security contributions.

JAMAICA

TABLE 4B.5 De jure mapping for dependent workers in Jamaica

TOTAL LABOR COSTS (L1 + L2 + L3)

NONWAGE COSTS		WAGE COSTS / TOTAL EARNINGS	BENEFITS (PAID THROUGH THE GOVERNMENT)
Net income related to paid employment (L1 + I3 – SC – PIT)			
Firm (L2 + L3)	Worker (PIT + SC)	Gross earnings (L1)	
Taxes (L3)	Taxes (regarded as labor costs)	A. Direct wages and salaries	In-work/social security benefits paid through the government
Payroll taxes: education tax, 3.5%; HEART contribution, 3%; NHF contribution, 0.5%	PIT (0%/25%/30%) Payroll taxes: education tax, 2.25%; NHF contribution, 0.5%	• For example, straight-time pay of time-related workers	• Direct immediate benefits → part of net labor income
Social security expenditure (L2)	Social security contributions (SC)	B. Renumeration for time not working	Social assistance benefits (paid through the government)
Health contributions, pension contributions, accident insurance contributions: NIS (2%) • Indirect short-term compensation	Health contributions, pension contributions, accident insurance: NIS (2%) • Indirect short-term compensation	• Annual vacation, other paid leave	• Direct immediate benefits: PATH (not modeled)
Mandatory savings account • Indirect contingent compensation	Mandatory savings account • Indirect contingent compensation	C. Bonuses and gratuities • For example, year-end and seasonal bonuses D. Remuneration in kind • For example, food, drink, fuel, and other in-kind payments	

continued

TABLE 4B.5 De jure mapping for dependent workers in Jamaica *(continued)*

TOTAL LABOR COSTS (L1 + L2 + L3)

NONWAGE COSTS		WAGE COSTS / TOTAL EARNINGS	BENEFITS (PAID THROUGH THE GOVERNMENT)
Unemployment insurance	Unemployment insurance	**E. Cost of workers' housing borne by employers**	
• Indirect contingent compensation	• Indirect contingent compensation	• For example, cost of establishment-owned dwellings	
Housing contribution: NHT (3%)	Housing contribution: NHT (2%)		
• Indirect contingent compensation	• Indirect contingent compensation		
Severance payment			

Source: Original table for this publication.

Note: Text in blue indicates information specific to Jamaica. Text in light gray indicates categories of general total labor cost that are not present in Jamaica. HEART = Human Employment and Resource Training; I3 = in-work benefits and employment-related social security benefits (paid through the government); L1 = gross earnings; L2 = employers' social security expenditure; L3 = other costs (for example, taxes regarded as labor costs); NHF = National Health Fund; NHT = National Housing Trust; NIS = National Insurance Scheme; PATH = Programme of Advancement Through Health and Education; PIT = personal income tax; SC = employee's compulsory social security contributions.

TABLE 4B.6 De jure mapping for independent workers in Jamaica

TOTAL LABOR COSTS (L1 + L2 + L3)

NONWAGE COSTS		WAGE COSTS / TOTAL EARNINGS	BENEFITS (PAID THROUGH THE GOVERNMENT)
		Net income related to paid employment (L1 + I3 – SC – PIT)	
Firm (L2 + L3)	Worker (PIT + SC)	Gross earnings (L1)	
Taxes (L3)	**Taxes (regarded as labor costs)**	**A. Direct wages and salaries**	**In-work/social security benefits paid through the government**
Payroll taxes	Payroll taxes: education tax (2.25%); NHF contribution (1%) PIT (0%/25%/30%)	• For example, straight-time pay of time-related workers	• Direct immediate benefits → part of net labor income

continued

TABLE 4B.6 De jure mapping for independent workers in Jamaica, *(continued)*

TOTAL LABOR COSTS (L1 + L2 + L3)

NONWAGE COSTS		WAGE COSTS / TOTAL EARNINGS	BENEFITS (PAID THROUGH THE GOVERNMENT)
Social security expenditure (L2)	Social security contributions (SC)	B. Renumeration for time not working	Social assistance benefits (paid through the government)
Health contributions	Health contributions, pension contributions, accident insurance contributions (4%)	• Annual vacation, other paid leave	• Direct immediate benefits: PATH (not modeled)
• Indirect short-term compensation	• Indirect short-term compensation		
Pension contributions		**C. Bonuses and gratuities**	
• Indirect long-term compensation		• For example, year-end and seasonal bonuses	
Mandatory savings account	Mandatory savings account		
• Indirect contingent compensation	• Indirect contingent compensation	**D. Remuneration in kind**	
Accident insurance contributions		• For example, food, drink, fuel, and other in-kind payments	
• Indirect contingent compensation			
Unemployment insurance	Unemployment insurance	**E. Cost of workers' housing borne by employers**	
• Indirect contingent compensation	• Indirect contingent compensation	• For example, cost of establishment-owned dwellings	
Severance payment	Housing contribution: NHT (3%)		
	• Indirect contingent compensation		

Source: Original table for this publication.

Note: Text in blue indicates information specific to Jamaica. Text in light gray indicates categories of general total labor cost that are not present in Jamaica. I3 = in-work benefits and employment-related social security benefits (paid through the government); L1 = gross earnings; L2 = employers' social security expenditure; L3 = other costs (for example, taxes regarded as labor costs); NHF = National Health Fund; NHT = National Housing Trust; PATH = Programme of Advancement Through Health and Education; PIT = personal income tax; SC = employee's compulsory social security contributions.

MEXICO

TABLE 4B.7 De jure mapping for dependent workers in Mexico

TOTAL LABOR COSTS (L1 + L2 + L3)			
NONWAGE COSTS	WAGE COSTS / TOTAL EARNINGS	BENEFITS (PAID THROUGH THE GOVERNMENT)	
	Net income related to paid employment (L1 + I3 – SC – PIT)		
Firm (L2 + L3)	Worker (PIT + SC)	Gross earnings (L1)	
Taxes (L3)	Taxes (regarded as labor costs)	A. Direct wages and salaries	In-work/social security benefits paid through the government
Payroll tax (2.4%), national average	PIT (1.9%–35%) Payroll taxes	• For example, straight-time pay of time-related workers	• Direct immediate benefits Employment subsidy (discount applicable to PIT) Other discounts applicable to PIT (on C. Bonuses and gratuities + deduction of personal expenses to taxable income)
Social security expenditure (L2)	Social security contributions (SC)	B. Renumeration for time not working	Social assistance benefits (paid through the government)
Health contributions, pension contribution, accident insurance contribution, occupation hazard contribution, child care contribution, housing contribution (16.6%) • Indirect short-term compensation	Health contributions, pension contribution, accident insurance (2.6%) • Indirect short-term compensation Mandatory savings account	• Annual vacation, other paid leave 6 days wages (mapped but not incorporated in the model) **C. Bonuses and gratuities** • For example, year-end and seasonal bonuses Christmas bonus (13th month of salary) + Holiday bonus + Profit sharing	• Direct immediate benefits (old-age noncontributory pension, BBJ scholarships, Seguro Popular → mapped but not incorporated in the model)

continued

TABLE 4B.7 De jure mapping for dependent workers in Mexico, *(continued)*

TOTAL LABOR COSTS (L1 + L2 + L3)

NONWAGE COSTS	WAGE COSTS / TOTAL EARNINGS	BENEFITS (PAID THROUGH THE GOVERNMENT)
	• Indirect contingent compensation	**D. Remuneration in kind** • For example, food, drink, fuel, and other in-kind payments
Unemployment insurance	Unemployment insurance	**E. Cost of workers' housing borne by employers**
• Indirect contingent compensation Severance payment	• Indirect contingent compensation	• For example, cost of establishment-owned dwellings

Source: Original table for this publication.
Note: Text in blue indicates information specific to Mexico. Text in light gray indicates categories of general total labor cost that are not present in Mexico. BBJ = Becas Benito Juárez; I3 = in-work benefits and employment-related social security benefits (paid through the government); L1 = gross earnings; L2 = employers' social security expenditure; L3 = other costs (for example, taxes regarded as labor costs); PIT = personal income tax; SC = employee's compulsory social security contributions.

TABLE 4B.8 De jure mapping for independent workers in Mexico

TOTAL LABOR COSTS (L1 + L2 + L3)

NONWAGE COSTS	WAGE COSTS / TOTAL EARNINGS		BENEFITS (PAID THROUGH THE GOVERNMENT)
	Net income related to paid employment (L1 + I3 − SC − PIT)		
Firm (L2 + L3)	Worker (PIT + SC)	Gross earnings (L1)	
Taxes (L3)	Taxes (regarded as labor costs)	A. Direct wages and salaries	In-work/social security benefits paid through the government
Payroll taxes	PIT (1.9%–35%)	• For example, straight-time pay of time-related workers	• Direct immediate benefits Discounts applicable to PIT (deduction of personal expenses to taxable income)

continued

TABLE 4B.8 De jure mapping for independent workers in Mexico, *(continued)*

TOTAL LABOR COSTS (L1 + L2 + L3)

NONWAGE COSTS		WAGE COSTS / TOTAL EARNINGS	BENEFITS (PAID THROUGH THE GOVERNMENT)
Social security expenditure (L2)	**Social security contributions (SC)**	**B. Renumeration for time not working**	**Social assistance benefits (paid through the government)**
Health contributions	Social security contributions (voluntary social security regime), contribution base fixed to 1 MW Health contributions Pension contributions Accident insurance contributions (off the workplace)	• Annual vacation, other paid leave	• Direct immediate benefits (old-age noncontributory pension, BBJ scholarships, Seguro Popular → mapped but not incorporated in the model)
• Indirect short-term compensation			
Pension contributions		**C. Bonuses and gratuities**	
• Indirect long-term compensation		• For example, year-end and seasonal bonuses	
Mandatory savings account			
• Indirect contingent compensation		**D. Remuneration in kind**	
Accident insurance contributions		• For example, food, drink, fuel, and other in-kind payments	
• Indirect contingent compensation			
Unemployment insurance	Unemployment insurance	**E. Cost of workers' housing borne by employers**	
• Indirect contingent compensation	• Indirect contingent compensation	• For example, cost of establishment-owned dwellings	
Severance payment			

Source: Original table for this publication.
Note: Text in blue indicates information specific to Mexico. Text in light gray indicates categories of general total labor cost that are not present in Mexico. BBJ = Becas Benito Juárez; I3 = in-work benefits and employment-related social security benefits (paid through the government); L1 = gross earnings; L2 = employers' social security expenditure; L3 = other costs (for example, taxes regarded as labor costs); MW = minimum wage; PIT = personal income tax; SC = employee's compulsory social security contributions.

PERU

TABLE 4B.9 De jure mapping for dependent workers in Peru

TOTAL LABOR COSTS (L1 + L2 + L3)			
NONWAGE COSTS		**WAGE COSTS / TOTAL EARNINGS**	**BENEFITS (PAID THROUGH THE GOVERNMENT)**
Net income related to paid employment (L1 + I3 – SC – PIT)			
Firm (L2 + L3)	Worker (PIT + SC)	Gross earnings (L1)	
Taxes (L3)	Taxes (regarded as labor costs)	A. Direct wages and salaries	In-work/social security benefits paid through the government
Payroll taxes (0.8%)	PIT (8%–30%) Payroll taxes	• For example, straight-time pay of time-related workers	• Direct immediate benefits → part of net labor income
Social security expenditure (L2)	**Social security contributions (SC)**	**B. Renumeration for time not working**	**Social assistance benefits (paid through the government)**
Health contributions (9%) • Indirect short-term compensation	Health contributions • Indirect short-term compensation	• Annual vacation, other paid leave	• Direct immediate benefits (Juntos + Pensión 65)
Pension contributions (12%) • Indirect long-term compensation	Pension contributions (13%) • Indirect long-term compensation	**C. Bonuses and gratuities** • For example, year-end and seasonal bonuses	
Mandatory savings account • Indirect contingent compensation	Mandatory savings account • Indirect contingent compensation	**D. Remuneration in kind**	
Accident insurance contributions (0.6%–1.3%) • Indirect contingent compensation	Accident insurance contributions • Indirect contingent compensation	• For example, Food, drink, fuel, and other in-kind payments	
Unemployment insurance (8.6%) • Indirect contingent compensation	Unemployment insurance • Indirect contingent compensation	**E. Cost of workers' housing borne by employers**	
Family subsidy (10% of MW) • Indirect short-term compensation		• For example, cost of establishment-owned dwellings	
Severance payment			

Source: Original table for this publication.

Note: Text in blue indicates information specific to Peru. Text in light gray indicates categories of general total labor cost that are not present in Peru. I3 = in-work benefits and employment-related social security benefits (paid through the government); L1 = gross earnings; L2 = employers' social security expenditure; L3 = other costs (for example, taxes regarded as labor costs); MW = minimum wage; PIT = personal income tax; SC = employee's compulsory social security contributions.

TABLE 4B.10 De jure mapping for independent workers in Peru

TOTAL LABOR COSTS (L1 + L2 + L3)

NONWAGE COSTS		WAGE COSTS / TOTAL EARNINGS	BENEFITS (PAID THROUGH THE GOVERNMENT)
		Net income related to paid employment (L1 + I3 – SC – PIT)	
Firm (L2 + L3)	Worker (PIT + SC)	Gross earnings (L1)	
Taxes (L3)	**Taxes (regarded as labor costs)**	**A. Direct wages and salaries**	**In-work/social security benefits paid through the government**
Payroll taxes	PIT (8%–30%)	• For example, straight-time pay of time-related workers	• Direct immediate benefits → part of net labor income
Social security expenditure (L2)	**Social security contributions (SC)**	**B. Renumeration for time not working**	**Social assistance benefits (paid through the government)**
Health contributions	Health contributions	• Annual vacation, other paid leave	• Direct immediate benefits (Juntos + Pensión 65)
• Indirect short-term compensation	• Indirect short-term compensation		
Pension contributions	Pension contributions (voluntary) (13%)	**C. Bonuses and gratuities**	
• Indirect long-term compensation	• Indirect long-term compensation	• For example, year-end and seasonal bonuses	
Mandatory savings account	Mandatory savings account		
• Indirect contingent compensation	• Indirect contingent compensation	**D. Remuneration in kind**	
Accident insurance contributions	Accident insurance contributions	• For example, food, drink, fuel, and other in-kind payments	
• Indirect contingent compensation	• Indirect contingent compensation		
Unemployment insurance	Unemployment insurance	**E. Cost of workers' housing borne by employers**	
• Indirect contingent compensation	• Indirect contingent compensation	• For example, cost of establishment-owned dwellings	
Severance payment			

Source: Original table for this publication.
Note: Text in blue indicates information specific to Peru. Text in light gray indicates categories of general total labor cost that are not present in Peru. I3 = in-work benefits and employment-related social security benefits (paid through the government); L1 = gross earnings; L2 = employers' social security expenditure; L3 = other costs (for example, taxes regarded as labor costs); PIT = personal income tax; SC = employee's compulsory social security contributions.

EL SALVADOR

TABLE 4B.11 **De jure mapping for dependent workers in El Salvador**

TOTAL LABOR COSTS (L1 + L2 + L3)			
NONWAGE COSTS		WAGE COSTS / TOTAL EARNINGS	BENEFITS (PAID THROUGH THE GOVERNMENT)
Net income related to paid employment (L1 + I3 – SC – PIT)			
Firm (L2 + L3)	Worker (PIT + SC)	Gross earnings (L1)	
Taxes (L3)	Taxes (regarded as labor costs)	A. Direct wages and salaries	In-work/social security benefits paid through the government
Payroll taxes (0.1%)	PIT (0%–30%) Payroll taxes	• For example, straight-time pay of time-related workers	• Direct immediate benefits → part of net labor income
Social security expenditure (L2)	Social security contributions (SC)	B. Renumeration for time not working	Social assistance benefits (paid through the government)
Health contributions (7.5%, but US$1,000 maximum quotable wage)	Health contributions (3%, but US$1,000 maximum quotable wage) (ISSS)	• Annual vacation, other paid leave	• Direct immediate benefits (only subsidies at the household level [electricity, gas, water] and not tied to the employment or income status of any of the household members, therefore not included in the mapping)
• Indirect short-term compensation	• Indirect short-term compensation		
Pension contributions (7.75%)	Pension contributions (7.25%) (AFP)	C. Bonuses and gratuities	
• Indirect long-term compensation	• Indirect long-term compensation	• For example, year-end and seasonal bonuses	
Mandatory savings account	Mandatory savings account		
• Indirect contingent compensation	• Indirect contingent compensation	D. Remuneration in kind	
Accident insurance contributions	Accident insurance contributions	• For example, food, drink, fuel, and other in-kind payments	
• Indirect contingent compensation	• Indirect contingent compensation		

continued

TABLE 4B.11 **De jure mapping for dependent workers in El Salvador,** *(continued)*

TOTAL LABOR COSTS (L1 + L2 + L3)

NONWAGE COSTS		WAGE COSTS / TOTAL EARNINGS	BENEFITS (PAID THROUGH THE GOVERNMENT)
Unemployment insurance	Unemployment insurance	**E. Cost of workers' housing borne by employers**	
• Indirect contingent compensation	• Indirect contingent compensation	• For example, cost of establishment-owned dwellings	
Severance payment (100% of one month's salary for each year worked, but the annual severance payment cannot exceed four months of salary)			

Source: Original table for this publication.
Note: Text in blue indicates information specific to El Salvador. Text in light gray indicates categories of general total labor cost that are not present in El Salvador. AFP = Administradora de Fondos de Pensiones; I3 = in-work benefits and employment-related social security benefits (paid through the government); ISSS = Instituto Salvadoreño del Seguro Social; L1 = gross earnings; L2 = employers' social security expenditure; L3 = other costs (for example, taxes regarded as labor costs); PIT = personal income tax; SC = employee's compulsory social security contributions.

TABLE 4B.12 **De jure mapping for independent workers in El Salvador**

TOTAL LABOR COSTS (L1 + L2 + L3)

NONWAGE COSTS		WAGE COSTS / TOTAL EARNINGS	BENEFITS (PAID THROUGH THE GOVERNMENT)
		Net income related to paid employment (L1 + I3 – SC – PIT)	
Firm (L2 + L3)	**Worker (PIT + SC)**	**Gross earnings (L1)**	
Taxes (L3)	**Taxes (regarded as labor costs)**	**A. Direct wages and salaries**	In-work/social security benefits paid through the government
Payroll taxes	PIT (0%–30%)	• For example, straight-time pay of time-related workers	• Direct immediate benefits → part of net labor income
Social security expenditure (L2)	**Social security contributions (SC)**	B. Renumeration for time not working	**Social assistance benefits (paid through the government)**
Health contributions	Health contributions (fixed amount of US$40 per month for individual insurance and US$60 for family insurance)	• Annual vacation, other paid leave	• Direct immediate benefits (only subsidies at the household level [electricity, gas, water] and not tied to the employment or income status of any of the household members, therefore not included in the mapping)
• Indirect short-term compensation	• Indirect short-term compensation		

continued

TABLE 4B.12 **De jure mapping for independent workers in El Salvador,** *(continued)*

TOTAL LABOR COSTS (L1 + L2 + L3)

NONWAGE COSTS		WAGE COSTS / TOTAL EARNINGS	BENEFITS (PAID THROUGH THE GOVERNMENT)
Pension contributions	Pension contributions (15%)	**C. Bonuses and gratuities**	
• Indirect long-term compensation	• Indirect long-term compensation	• For example, year-end and seasonal bonuses	
Mandatory savings account	Mandatory savings account		
• Indirect contingent compensation	• Indirect contingent compensation	**D. Remuneration in kind**	
Accident insurance contributions	Accident insurance contributions	• For example, food, drink, fuel, and other in-kind payments	
• Indirect contingent compensation	• Indirect contingent compensation		
Unemployment insurance	Unemployment insurance	**E. Cost of workers' housing borne by employers**	
• Indirect contingent compensation	• Indirect contingent compensation	• For example, cost of establishment-owned dwellings	
Severance payment			

Source: Original table for this publication.
Note: Text in blue indicates information specific to El Salvador. Text in light gray indicates categories of general total labor cost that are not present in El Salvador. I3 = in-work benefits and employment-related social security benefits (paid through the government); L1 = gross earnings; L2 = employers' social security expenditure; L3 = other costs (for example, taxes regarded as labor costs); PIT = personal income tax; SC = employee's compulsory social security contributions.

URUGUAY

TABLE 4B.13 **De jure mapping for dependent workers in Uruguay**

TOTAL LABOR COSTS (L1 + L2 + L3)

NONWAGE COSTS		WAGE COSTS / TOTAL EARNINGS	BENEFITS (PAID THROUGH THE GOVERNMENT)
		Net income related to paid employment (L1 + I3 – SC – PIT)	
Firm (L2 + L3)	**Worker (PIT + SC)**	**Gross earnings (L1)**	
Taxes (L3)	**Taxes (regarded as labor costs)**	**A. Direct wages and salaries**	**In-work/social security benefits paid through the government**
Payroll taxes	PIT (0%–36%)	• For example, straight-time pay of time-related workers	• Direct immediate benefits → part of net labor income (AFAM and Hogar constitution)
Training funds (0.1% FRL)	Payroll taxes		
	Training Funds (0.1% FRL)		

continued

TABLE 4B.13 **De jure mapping for dependent workers in Uruguay,** *(continued)*

TOTAL LABOR COSTS (L1 + L2 + L3)

NONWAGE COSTS		WAGE COSTS / TOTAL EARNINGS	BENEFITS (PAID THROUGH THE GOVERNMENT)
Social security expenditure (L2)	Social security contributions (SC)	B. Renumeration for time not working	Social assistance benefits (paid through the government)
Health contributions (5%) (FONASA)	Health contributions (3%– 8%) (FONASA)	• Annual vacation, other paid leave	• Direct immediate benefits (AFAM-PE)
• Indirect short-term compensation	• Indirect short-term compensation		
Pension contributions (7%)	Pension contributions (15%)	**C. Bonuses and gratuities**	
• Indirect long-term compensation	• Indirect long-term compensation	• For example, year-end and seasonal bonuses	
Mandatory savings account	Mandatory savings account		
• Indirect contingent compensation	• Indirect contingent compensation	**D. Remuneration in kind**	
Accident insurance contributions	Accident insurance contributions	• For example, food, drink, fuel, and other in-kind payments	
• Indirect contingent compensation	• Indirect contingent compensation		
Unemployment insurance	Unemployment insurance	**E. Cost of workers' housing borne by employers**	
• Indirect contingent compensation	• Indirect contingent compensation	• For example, cost of establishment-owned dwellings	
Severance payment			

Source: Original table for this publication.

Note: Text in blue indicates information specific to Uruguay. Text in light gray indicates categories of general total labor cost that are not present in Uruguay. AFAM = Asignaciones Familiares; AFAM-PE =Asignaciones Familiares-Plan de Equidad; FONASA =Fondo de Reconversión Laboral Asignaciones Familiares; FRL = Labor Retraining Fund; I3 = in-work benefits and employment-related social security benefits (paid through the government); L1 = gross earnings; L2 = employers' social security expenditure; L3 = other costs (for example, taxes regarded as labor costs); PIT = personal income tax; SC = employee's compulsory social security contributions.

TABLE 4B.14 De jure mapping for independent workers in Uruguay

TOTAL LABOR COSTS (L1 + L2 + L3)			
NONWAGE COSTS		**WAGE COSTS / TOTAL EARNINGS**	**BENEFITS (PAID THROUGH THE GOVERNMENT)**
	Net income related to paid employment (L1 + I3 – SC – PIT)		
Firm (L2 + L3)	Worker (PIT + SC)	Gross earnings (L1)	
Taxes (L3)	**Taxes (regarded as labor costs)**	**A. Direct wages and salaries**	In-work/social security benefits paid through the government
Payroll taxes	PIT (0%) Payroll taxes Training Fund (0.1% of 5 BFC)	• For example, straight-time pay of time-related workers	• Direct immediate benefits → part of net labor income
Social security expenditure (L2)	**Social security contributions (SC)**	**B. Renumeration for time not working**	**Social assistance benefits (paid through the government)**
Health contributions	Health contributions (3%– 8% of 6 for 5 BPC) (FONASA)	• Annual vacation, other paid leave	• Direct immediate benefits (AFAM-PE)
• Indirect short-term compensation	• Indirect short-term compensation		
Pension contributions	Pension contributions (22.5% of 5 BFC)	**C. Bonuses and gratuities**	
• Indirect long-term compensation	• Indirect long-term compensation	• For example, year-end and seasonal bonuses	
Mandatory savings account	Mandatory savings account		
• Indirect contingent compensation	• Indirect contingent compensation	**D. Remuneration in kind**	
Accident insurance contributions	Accident insurance contributions	• For example, food, drink, fuel, and other in-kind payments	
• Indirect contingent compensation	• Indirect contingent compensation		
Unemployment insurance	Unemployment insurance	**E. Cost of workers' housing borne by employers**	
• Indirect contingent compensation	• Indirect contingent compensation	• For example, cost of establishment-owned dwellings	
Severance payment			

Source: Original table for this publication.

Note: Text in blue indicates information specific to Uruguay. Text in light gray indicates categories of general total labor cost that are not present in Uruguay. AFAM-PE = Asignaciones Familiares-Plan de Equidad; BFC = Base ficta de contribución; BPC = Base de Prestaciones y Contribuciones; FONASA = Fondo de Reconversión Laboral Asignaciones Familiares; I3 = in-work benefits and employment-related social security benefits (paid through the government); L1 = gross earnings; L2 = employers' social security expenditure; L3 = other costs (for example, taxes regarded as labor costs); PIT = personal income tax; SC = employee's compulsory social security contributions.

De Jure Analysis Figures

This annex provides figures that allow the analysis of the tax and benefit system along minimum wage brackets, by benefit categories and the distribution of workers along minimum wage categories. Figure 4C.1 shows the total taxes and contributions paid by workers and firms for single-earner households. Figure 4C.2 shows the tax wedge across the minimum wage distribution grouping taxes and contributions by short-term compensation, long-term compensation, contingent compensation, and taxes. Figure 4C.3 provides an overview of all the tax wedges, by country.

FIGURE 4C.1

Total taxes and contributions paid by workers and firms: Single-earner households in select LAC countries

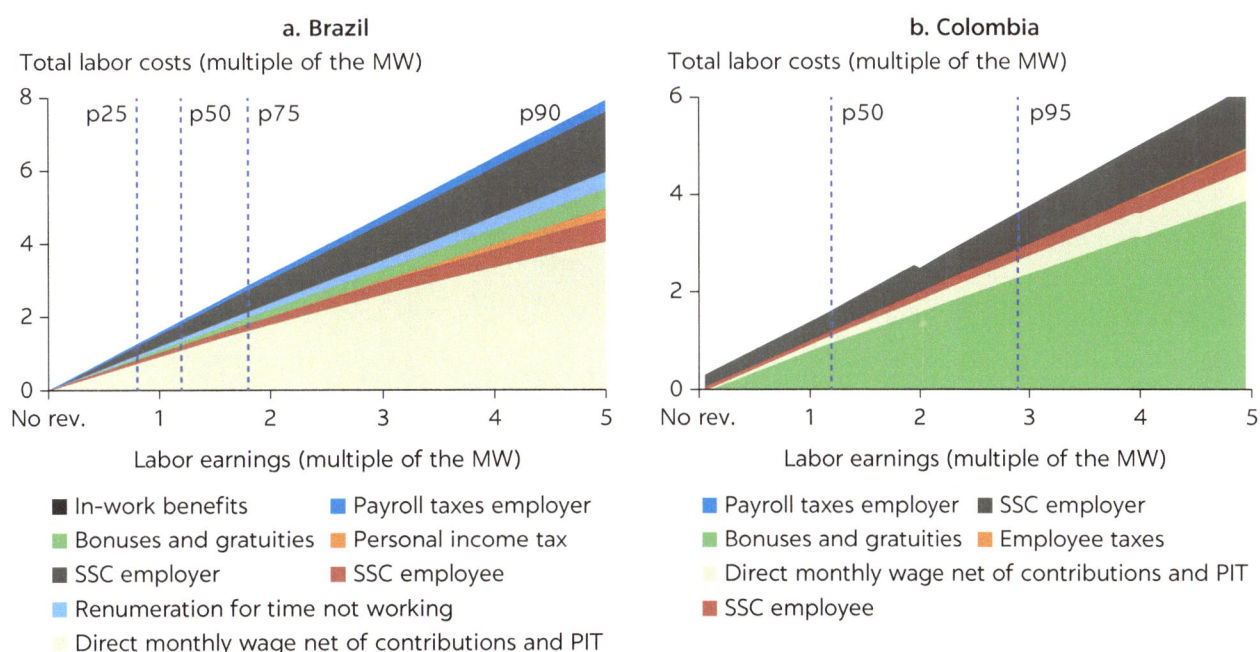

continued

FIGURE 4C.1 **Total taxes and contributions paid by workers and firms: Single-earner households in select LAC countries,** *(continued)*

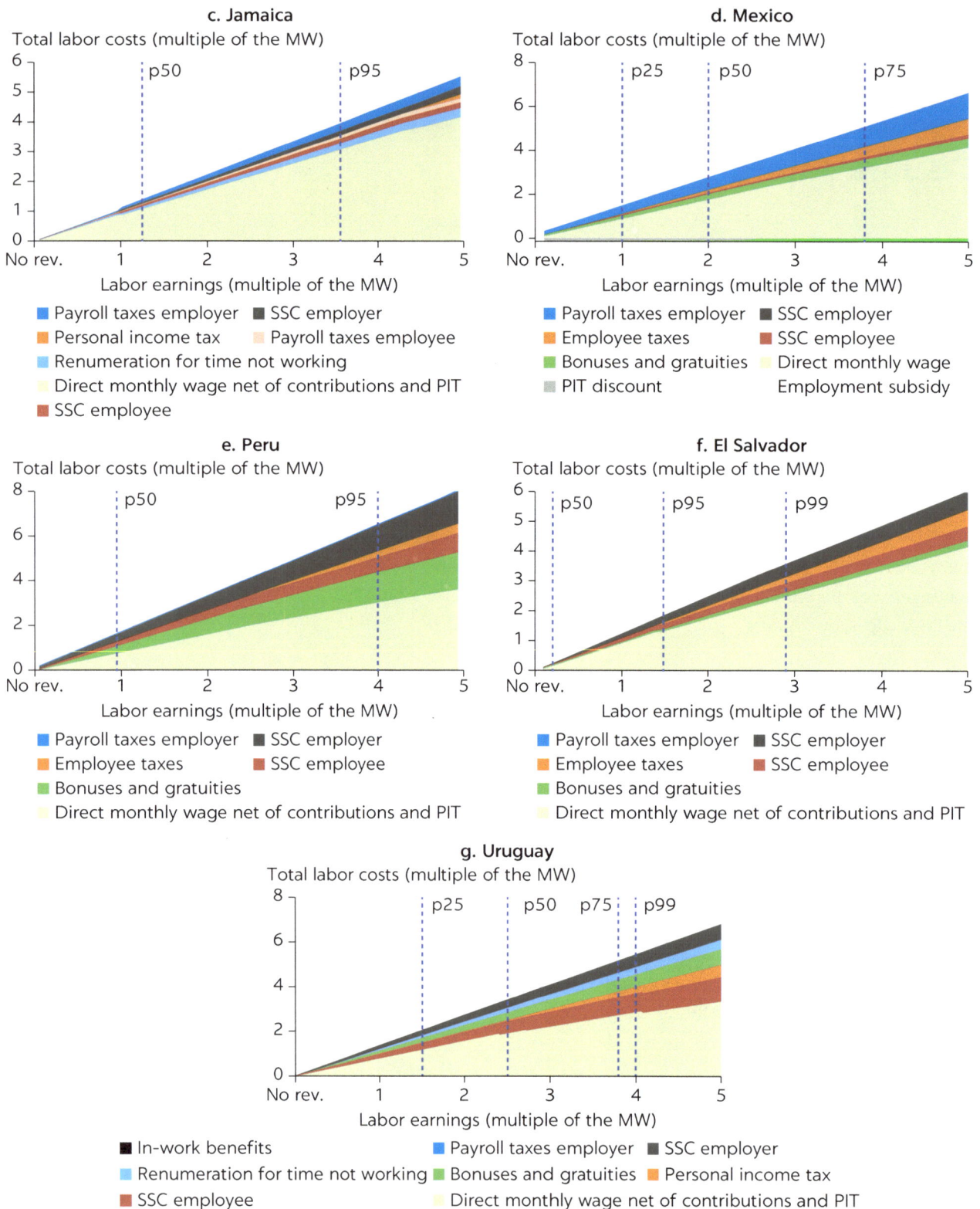

c. Jamaica

Total labor costs (multiple of the MW)

Labor earnings (multiple of the MW)

- Payroll taxes employer
- SSC employer
- Personal income tax
- Payroll taxes employee
- Renumeration for time not working
- Direct monthly wage net of contributions and PIT
- SSC employee

d. Mexico

Total labor costs (multiple of the MW)

Labor earnings (multiple of the MW)

- Payroll taxes employer
- SSC employer
- Employee taxes
- SSC employee
- Bonuses and gratuities
- Direct monthly wage
- PIT discount
- Employment subsidy

e. Peru

Total labor costs (multiple of the MW)

Labor earnings (multiple of the MW)

- Payroll taxes employer
- SSC employer
- Employee taxes
- SSC employee
- Bonuses and gratuities
- Direct monthly wage net of contributions and PIT

f. El Salvador

Total labor costs (multiple of the MW)

Labor earnings (multiple of the MW)

- Payroll taxes employer
- SSC employer
- Employee taxes
- SSC employee
- Bonuses and gratuities
- Direct monthly wage net of contributions and PIT

g. Uruguay

Total labor costs (multiple of the MW)

Labor earnings (multiple of the MW)

- In-work benefits
- Payroll taxes employer
- SSC employer
- Renumeration for time not working
- Bonuses and gratuities
- Personal income tax
- SSC employee
- Direct monthly wage net of contributions and PIT

Source: Original figures for this publication.

Note: LAC = Latin America and the Caribbean; MW = minimum wage; No rev. = no income; p = percentile; SSC = social security contributions.

Panel a, Brazil: in-work benefits = salary bonus and family allowance; SSC employee = employee pension contributions; SSC employer = employer contributions to pensions, individual savings accounts, and accident insurance.

continued

FIGURE 4C.1 **Total taxes and contributions paid by workers and firms: Single-earner households in select LAC countries,** *(continued)*

Panel b, Colombia: SSC employee = pension and health contributions; employee taxes = personal income tax and pension solidarity fund; SSC employer = transport subsidy, health and pension contributions, occupational hazard insurance, severance payment, interest on severance payment, and family compensation fund; payroll taxes employer = Institute of Family Welfare and National Training Service.

Panel c, Jamaica: SSC employee = National Insurance Scheme and National Housing Trust contributions; SSC employer = National Insurance Scheme and National Housing Trust contributions; payroll taxes employer = education tax, Human Employment and Resource Training Trust contributions, and National Health Fund contributions; payroll taxes employee = education tax and National Health Fund contributions.

Panel d, Mexico: SSC employee = health, accident insurance, and pension contributions; SSC employer = occupational hazard, health, accident insurance, pension, child care and social benefits, and housing contributions; net PIT = personal income tax minus employment subsidy for dependent workers; bonuses and gratuities = year-end and seasonal bonuses and profit sharing.

Panel e, Peru: SSC employee = pension contributions; employee taxes = personal income tax; SSC employer = family subsidy, health contributions, accident insurance, and Compensation for Length of Service; payroll taxes employer = National Training Service of Industrial Work.

Panel f, El Salvador: SSC employee = Salvadoran Social Security Institute and Pension Fund Administrator; employee taxes = personal income tax; SSC employer = Salvadoran Social Security Institute and Pension Fund Administrator; payroll taxes employer = Salvadoran Institute for Professional Training.

Panel g, Uruguay: SSC employee = pension, National Health Fund, and Labor Retraining Fund contributions; SSC employer = pension, National Health Fund, Labor Retraining Fund, and Labor Guarantee Fund contributions; PIT = personal income tax.

FIGURE 4C.2

Pure tax wedge paid by workers and firms as a share of total labor cost, one-adult, single-earner households in select LAC countries

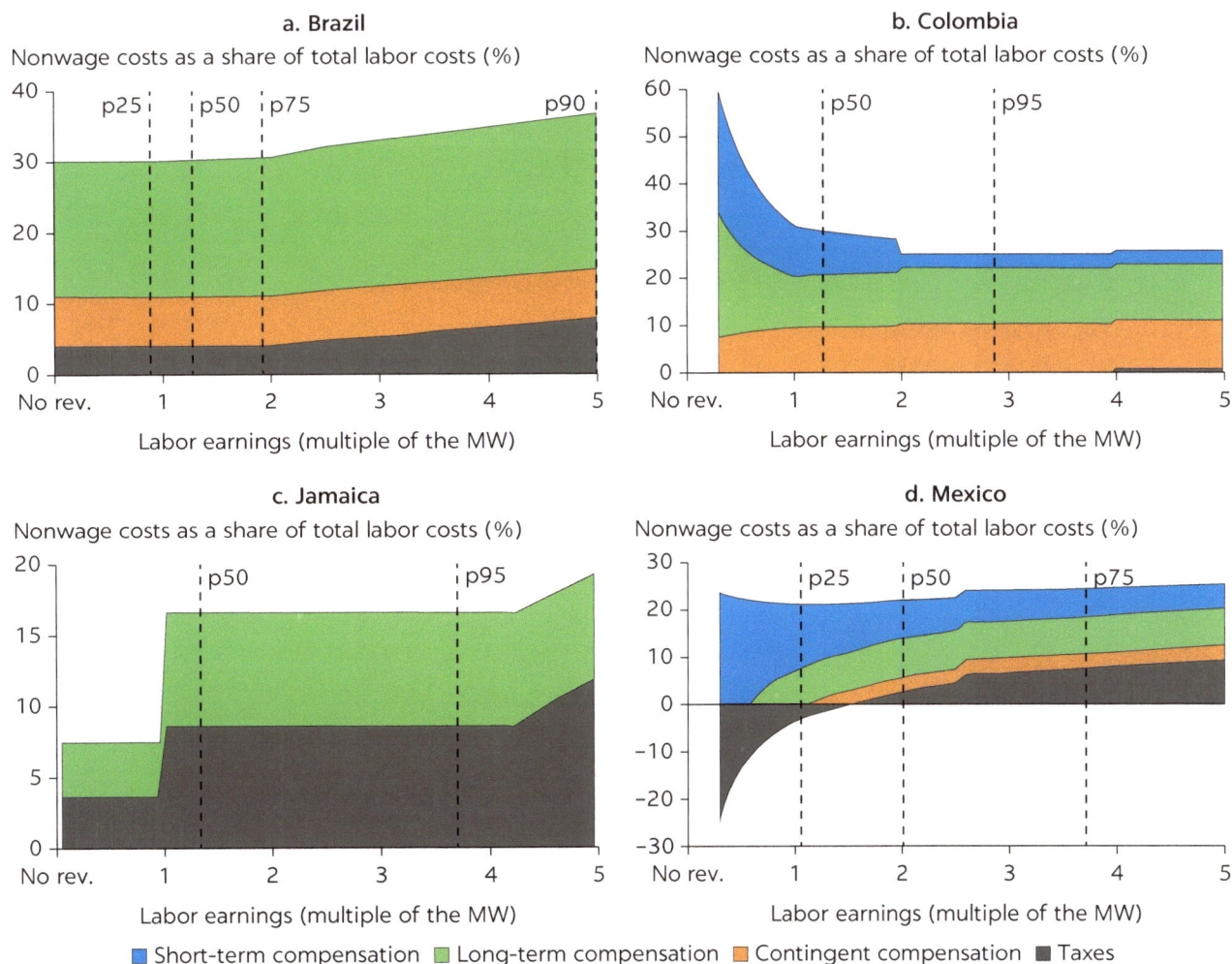

a. Brazil
Nonwage costs as a share of total labor costs (%)

b. Colombia
Nonwage costs as a share of total labor costs (%)

c. Jamaica
Nonwage costs as a share of total labor costs (%)

d. Mexico
Nonwage costs as a share of total labor costs (%)

■ Short-term compensation ■ Long-term compensation ■ Contingent compensation ■ Taxes

continued

FIGURE 4C.2 **Pure tax wedge paid by workers and firms as a share of total labor cost, one-adult, single-earner households in select LAC countries, (continued)**

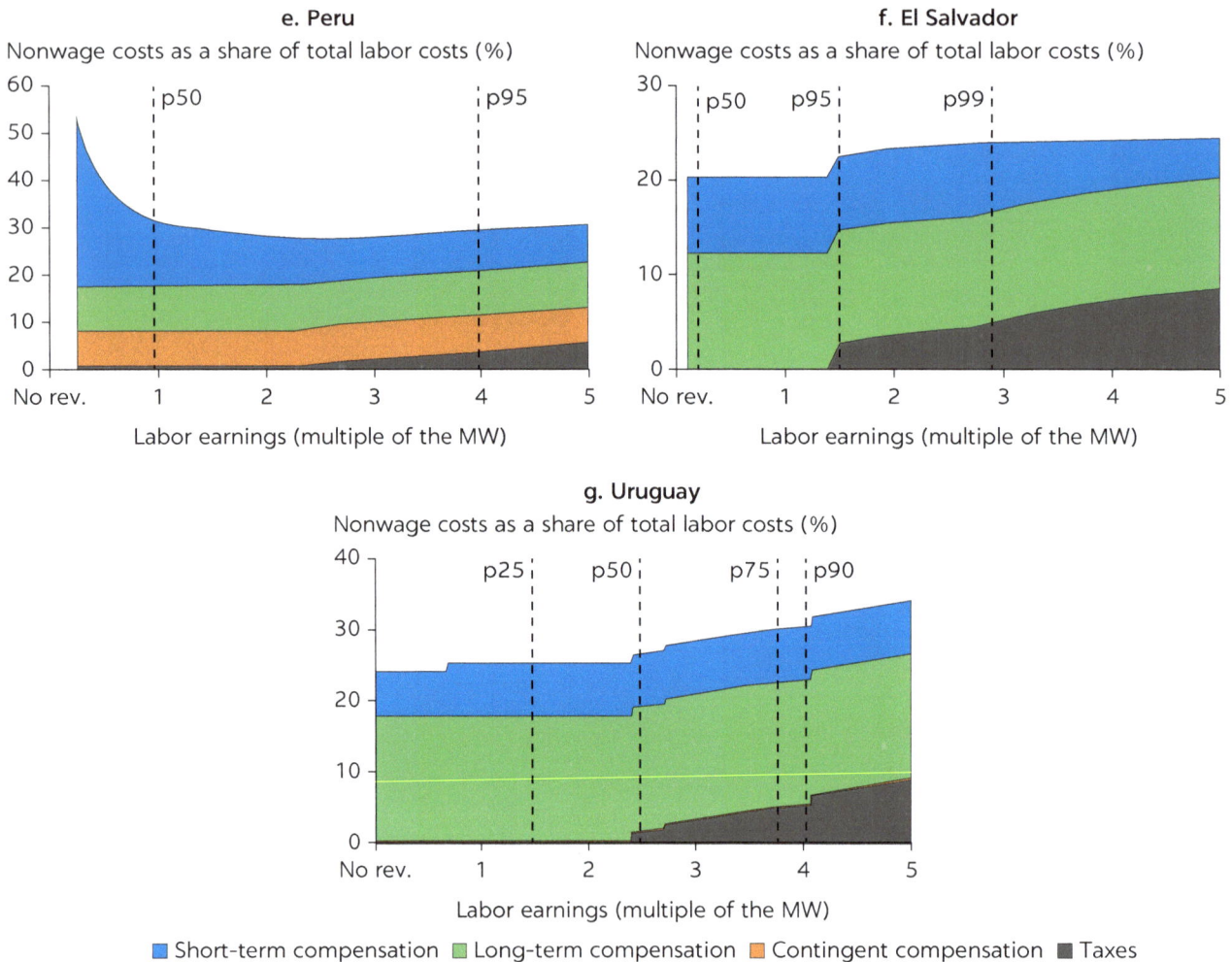

e. Peru

Nonwage costs as a share of total labor costs (%)

Labor earnings (multiple of the MW)

f. El Salvador

Nonwage costs as a share of total labor costs (%)

Labor earnings (multiple of the MW)

g. Uruguay

Nonwage costs as a share of total labor costs (%)

Labor earnings (multiple of the MW)

■ Short-term compensation ■ Long-term compensation ■ Contingent compensation ■ Taxes

Source: Original figures for this publication.

Note: LAC = Latin America and the Caribbean; MW = minimum wage; No rev. = no income; p = percentile.

Panel a, Brazil: contributions toward long-term compensation = pension contributions (National Social Security Institute) and pension contribution (employer's contribution); contributions toward contingent compensation = individual savings account (mandatory employment protection) and accident insurance; taxes = Education Fund (Salario Educacao), National Institute for Colonization and Agrarian Reform (INCRA).

Panel b, Colombia: short-term compensation = health contributions and transport subsidy; long-term compensation = pension contributions; contingent compensation = occupation hazard, severance payment, interest on severance payment, and family compensation fund; taxes = personal income tax, pension solidarity fund, Institute of Family Welfare (ICBF) and National Training Service (SENA).

Panel c, Jamaica: contributions toward long-term compensation = National Insurance Scheme (NIS) and National Housing Trust (NHT); taxes = personal income tax, National Health Fund (NHF), education tax, and Human Employment and Resource Training (HEART).

Panel d, Mexico: contributions toward short-term compensation = health insurance contributions, child care and worker well-being, 13th month of wage, holiday bonuses, and profit sharing; contributions toward long-term compensation = pension contributions, housing contributions (*vivenda*); contributions toward contingent compensations = accident insurance; taxes = personal income tax.

Panel e, Peru: contributions toward short-term compensation = health contributions and family subsidy; contributions toward long-term compensation = pension contributions; contributions toward contingent compensation = accident insurance and Compensation for Length of Service (CTS); taxes = personal income tax and National Training Service of Industrial Work (SENATI).

Panel f, El Salvador: contributions toward short-term compensation = health contributions; contributions toward long-term compensation = pension contributions; contributions toward contingent compensation = payroll tax; taxes = personal income tax.

Panel g, Uruguay: contributions toward short-term compensation = health contributions; contributions toward long-term compensation = pension contributions; contributions toward contingent compensation = Labor Retraining Fund (FRL) and Labor Credit Guarantee Fund (FGCL); taxes = personal income tax.

FIGURE 4C.3

De jure tax wedge for different types of contracts or work in select LAC countries

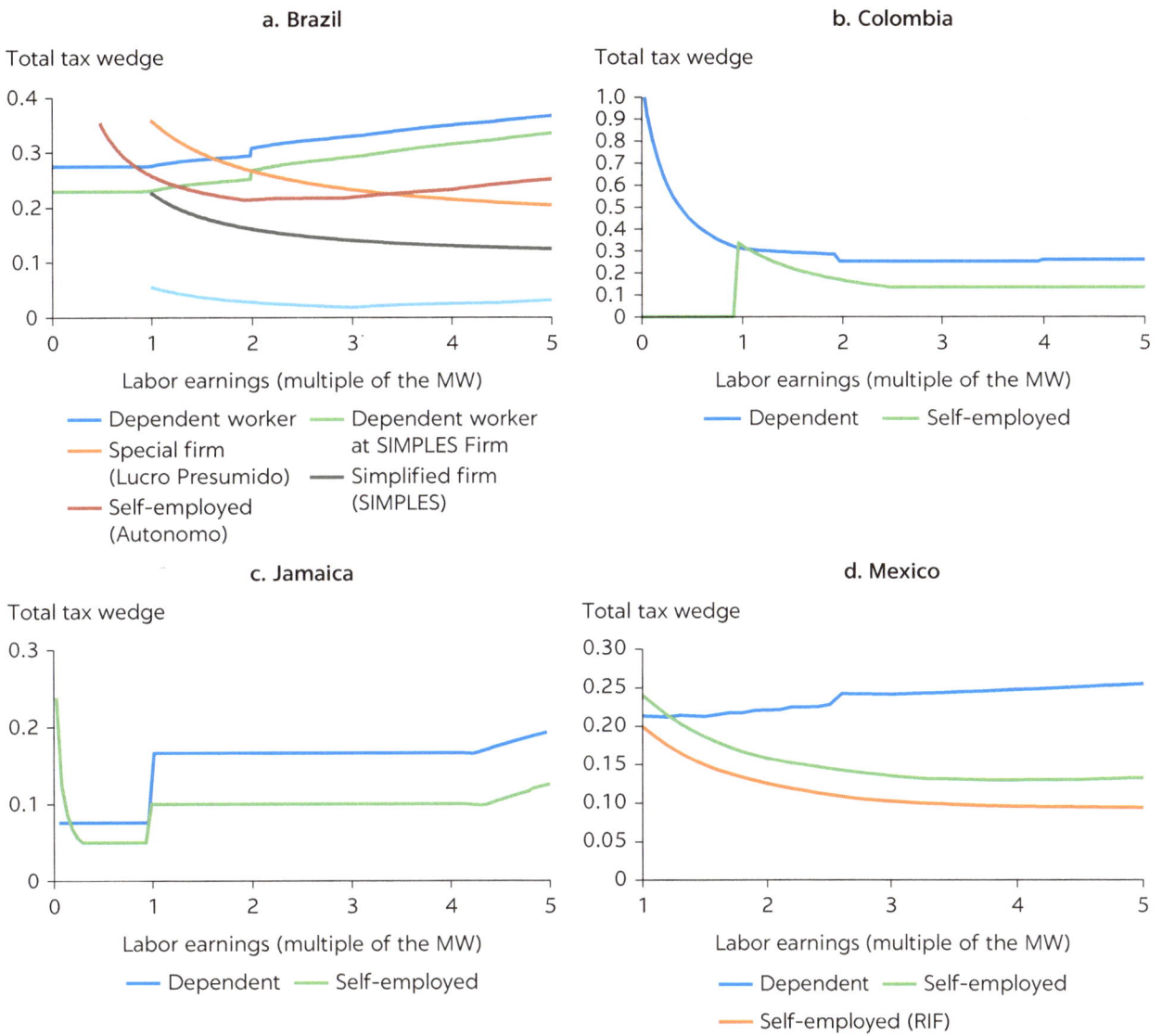

a. Brazil

Total tax wedge

Labor earnings (multiple of the MW)

— Dependent worker — Dependent worker
at SIMPLES Firm
— Special firm
(Lucro Presumido) — Simplified firm
(SIMPLES)
— Self-employed
(Autonomo)

b. Colombia

Total tax wedge

Labor earnings (multiple of the MW)

— Dependent — Self-employed

c. Jamaica

Total tax wedge

Labor earnings (multiple of the MW)

— Dependent — Self-employed

d. Mexico

Total tax wedge

Labor earnings (multiple of the MW)

— Dependent — Self-employed
— Self-employed (RIF)

continued

FIGURE 4C.3 De jure tax wedge for different types of contracts or work in select LAC countries, *(continued)*

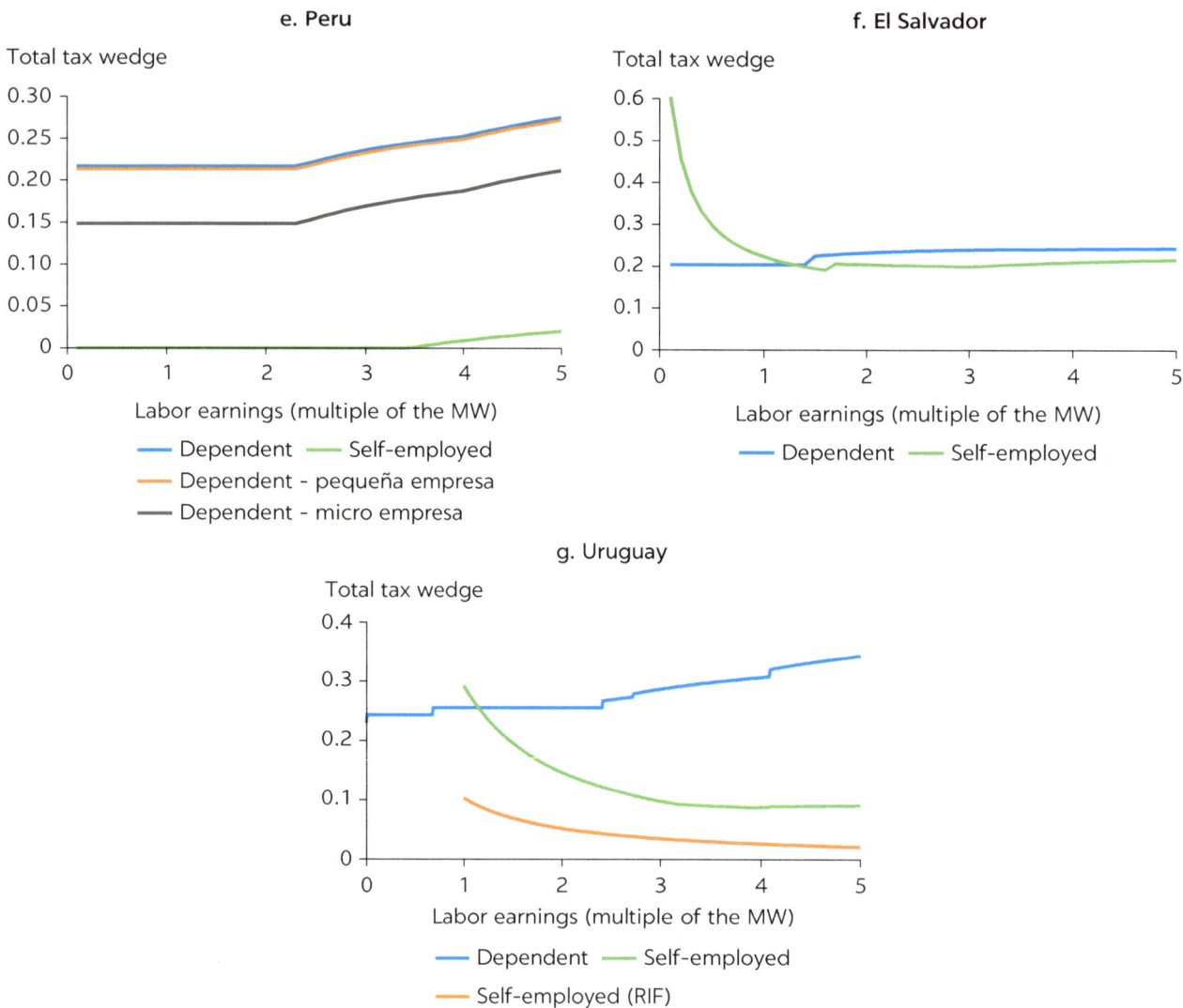

e. Peru

f. El Salvador

g. Uruguay

Source: Original figures for this publication.

Note: LAC = Latin America and the Caribbean; MW = minimum wage; RIF = Régimen de Incorporación Fiscal (simplified tax system); SIMPLES = Regime Especial Unificado de Arrecadação de Tributos e Contribuições devidos pelas Microempresas e Empresas de Pequeno Porte.

Distribution of workers in select LAC countries, by type of employment

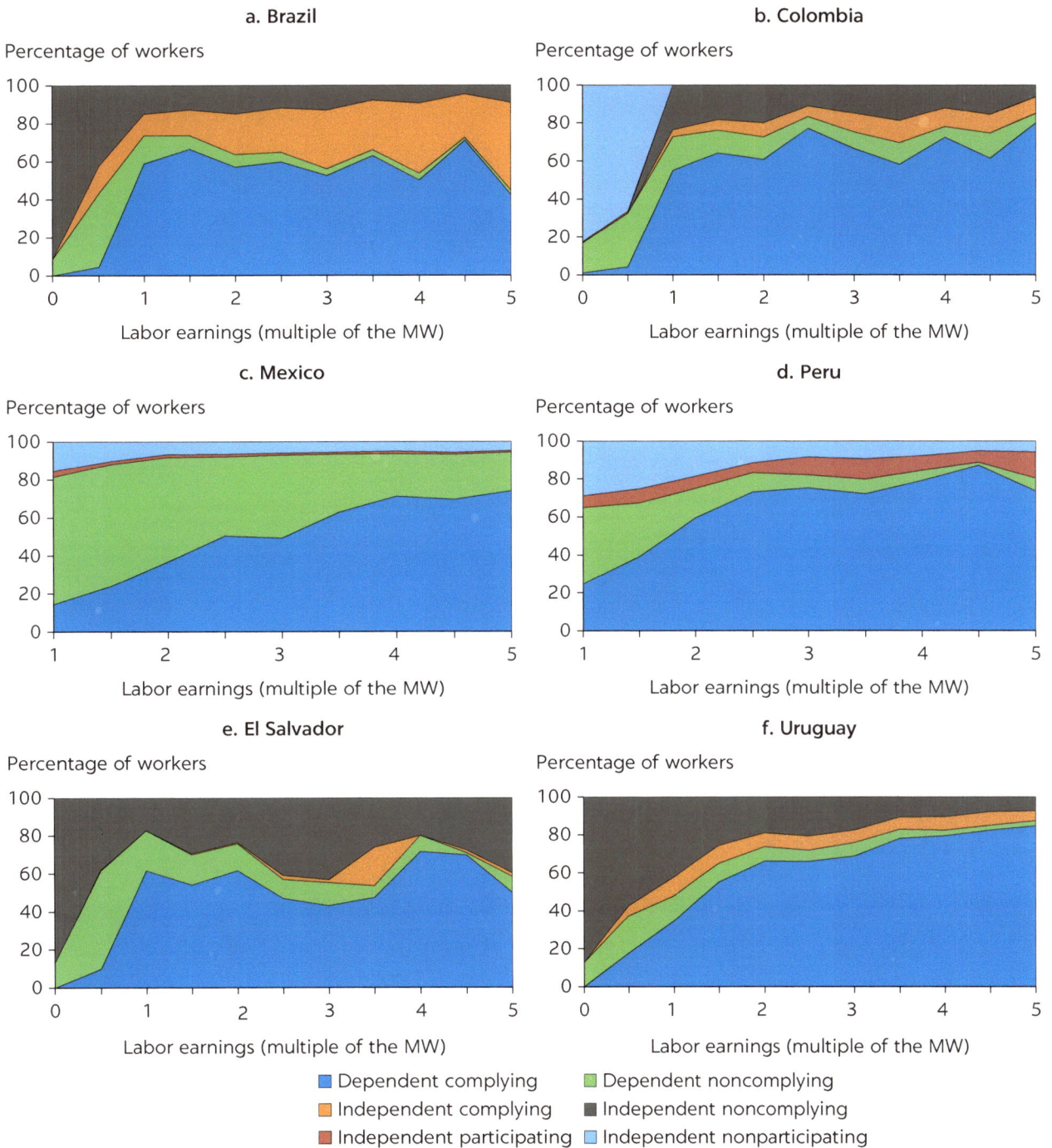

a. Brazil

b. Colombia

c. Mexico

d. Peru

e. El Salvador

f. Uruguay

■ Dependent complying ■ Dependent noncomplying
■ Independent complying ■ Independent noncomplying
■ Independent participating ■ Independent nonparticipating

Source: Original figures for this publication.
Note: The available household data for Jamaica do not allow a trustworthy estimation of the distribution of workers by employment type. Thus, Jamaica's country case study does not include this distribution. LAC = Latin America and the Caribbean; MW = minimum wage.

Steps to Calculate the Formalization Tax Rate

The following procedure describes the calculation of the formalization tax rate (FTR) for workers in a micro dataset containing information on the household and employment characteristics that determine tax and benefit levels, such as an employment survey. This annex describes the computation of the FTR for worker i in household h.

STEP 1: DETERMINE TAXES AND BENEFITS UNDER THE OBSERVED FORMALITY STATUS

Compute the taxes and social security contributions paid, and the transfers received by all members of household h given their existing registration status, earnings level, and other characteristics.

STEP 2: COUNTERFACTUALLY SWITCH THE REGISTRATION STATUS OF WORKER i

Change the employment status of worker i from registered to unregistered or from unregistered to registered while keeping the registration status of all other members of household h as in the data.

The switching logic is as follows:

- Dependent unregistered workers switch to dependent registered workers and vice versa.

- Unregistered self-employed workers switch to registered self-employed workers and vice versa.

The specific registered self-employed regime to which unregistered self-employed workers switch may vary by country, based on local regulations and assumptions.

STEP 3: DETERMINE TAXES AND BENEFITS UNDER THE COUNTERFACTUAL REGISTRATION STATUS

Compute taxes, social security contributions, and transfers for all members of the household, considering the new registration status of worker i.

STEP 4: CALCULATE THE FTR FOR WORKER i

Calculate the difference in taxes, contributions, and transfers obtained in steps 1 and 3. Then apply the following formula:

$$FTR = \frac{\Delta Taxes + \Delta Contributions \times (1 - Valuation) + \Delta Transfers}{Informal\ household\ income}, \quad (5A.1)$$

This formula captures the size of the wedge of nonvalued contributions and taxes normalized by the worker's household income under the assumption that the specific worker is unregistered.

Results of the Simulation Exercises

This annex presents the results of policy reform simulations in Figures 6A.1 and 6A.2. The reforms were chosen to reflect "best-bet" measures to improve incentives for workers and employers to formalize work. The reform measures that are analyzed were chosen to reflect government policy priorities and the best judgment and dialogue of the World Bank Social Protection and Labor and the Poverty and Equity front-line teams in six of our seven case study countries.

Because the simulations are "static" and do not consider worker and employer responses, the results can be used only to determine which workers' incentives are most improved and the size of this improvement, using the formalization tax rate (FTR) as our measure of individual incentives to (in)formalize work.

FIGURE 6A.1

Dimension 1: Policies affecting labor market competitiveness: increase in the minimum wage

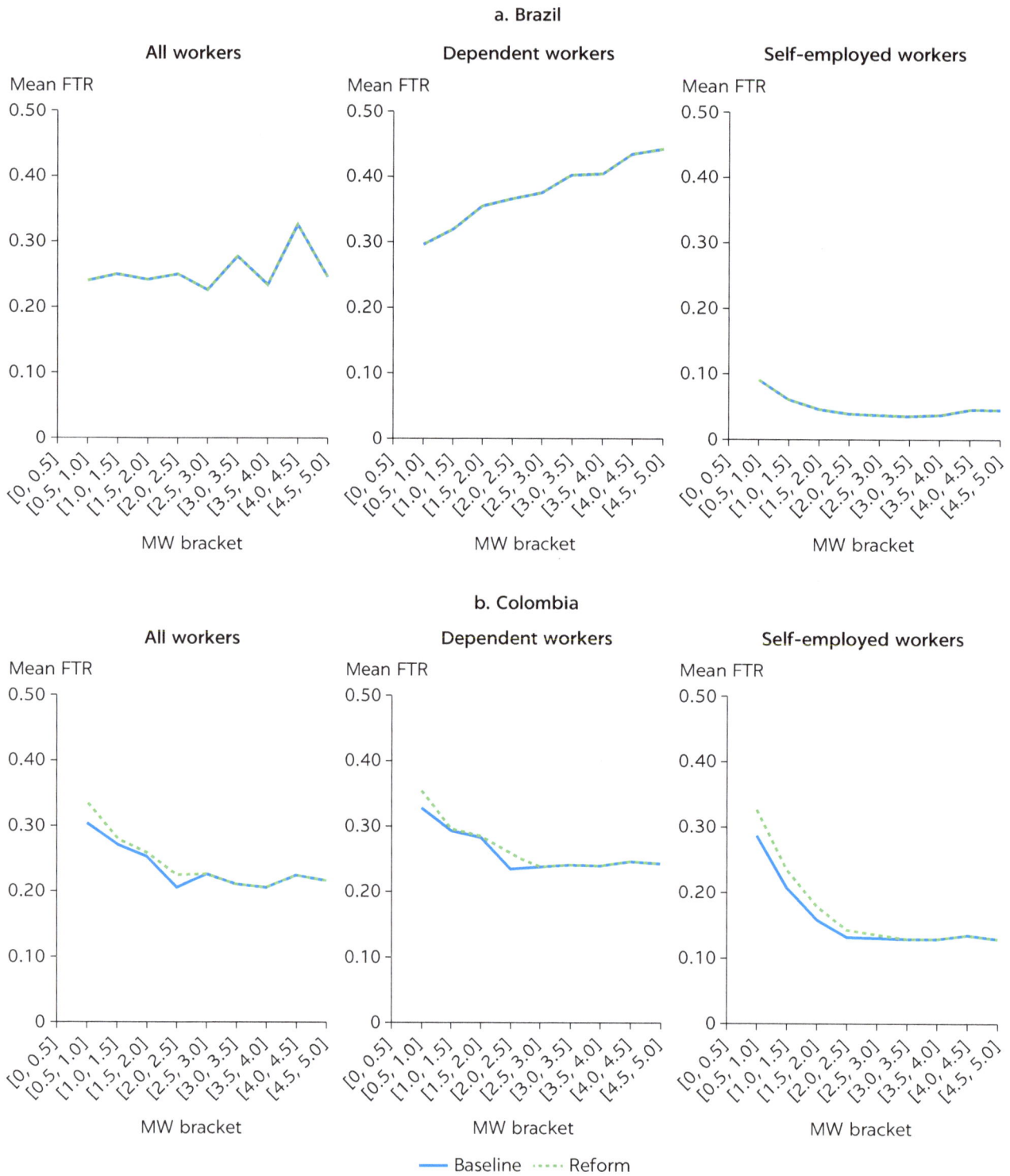

a. Brazil

b. Colombia

— Baseline ····· Reform

continued

FIGURE 6A.1 Dimension 1: Policies affecting labor market competitiveness: Increase in the minimum wage, *(continued)*

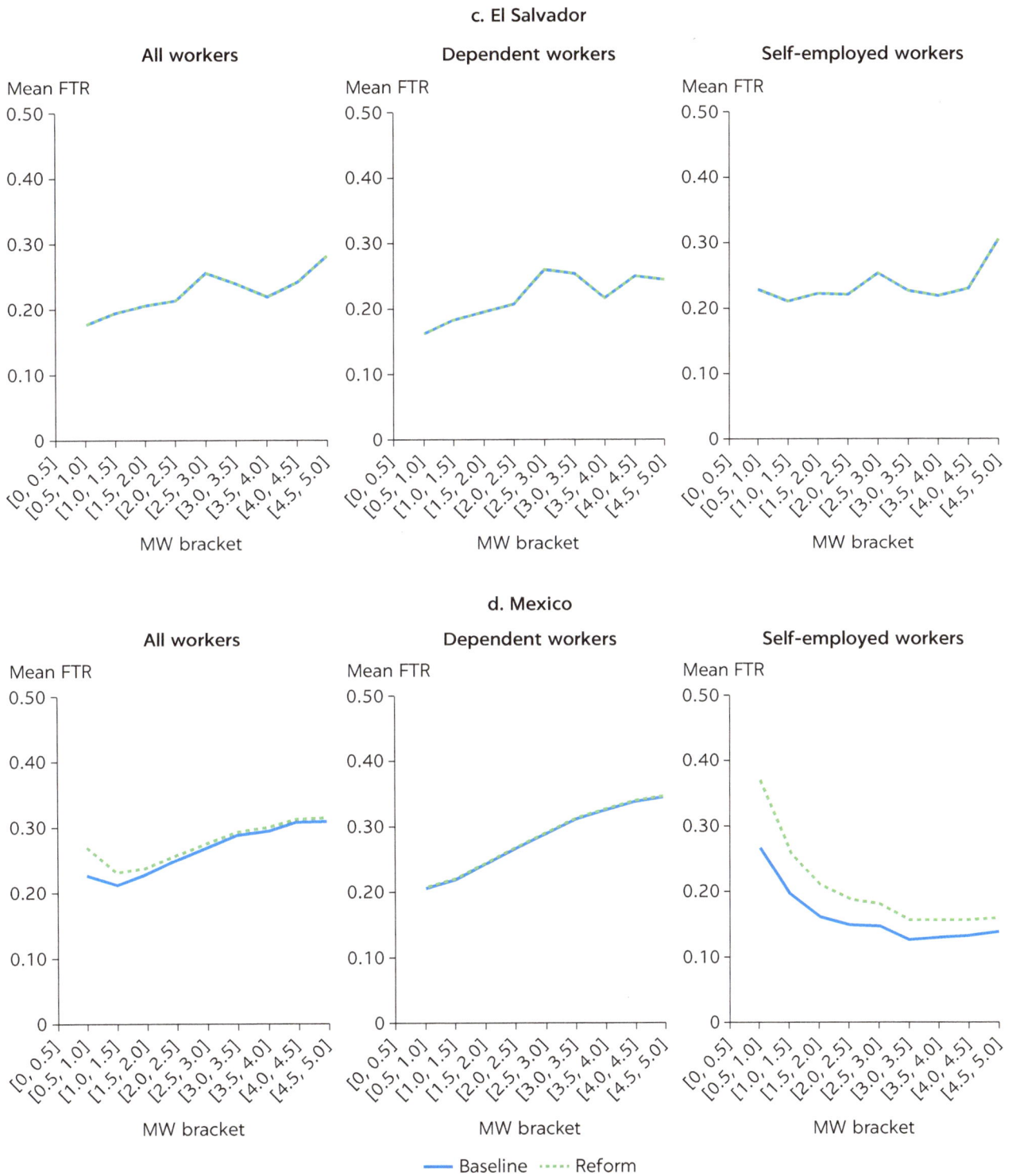

c. El Salvador

All workers · Dependent workers · Self-employed workers

d. Mexico

All workers · Dependent workers · Self-employed workers

Baseline ····· Reform

continued

FIGURE 6A.1 Dimension 1: Policies affecting labor market competitiveness: Increase in the minimum wage, *(continued)*

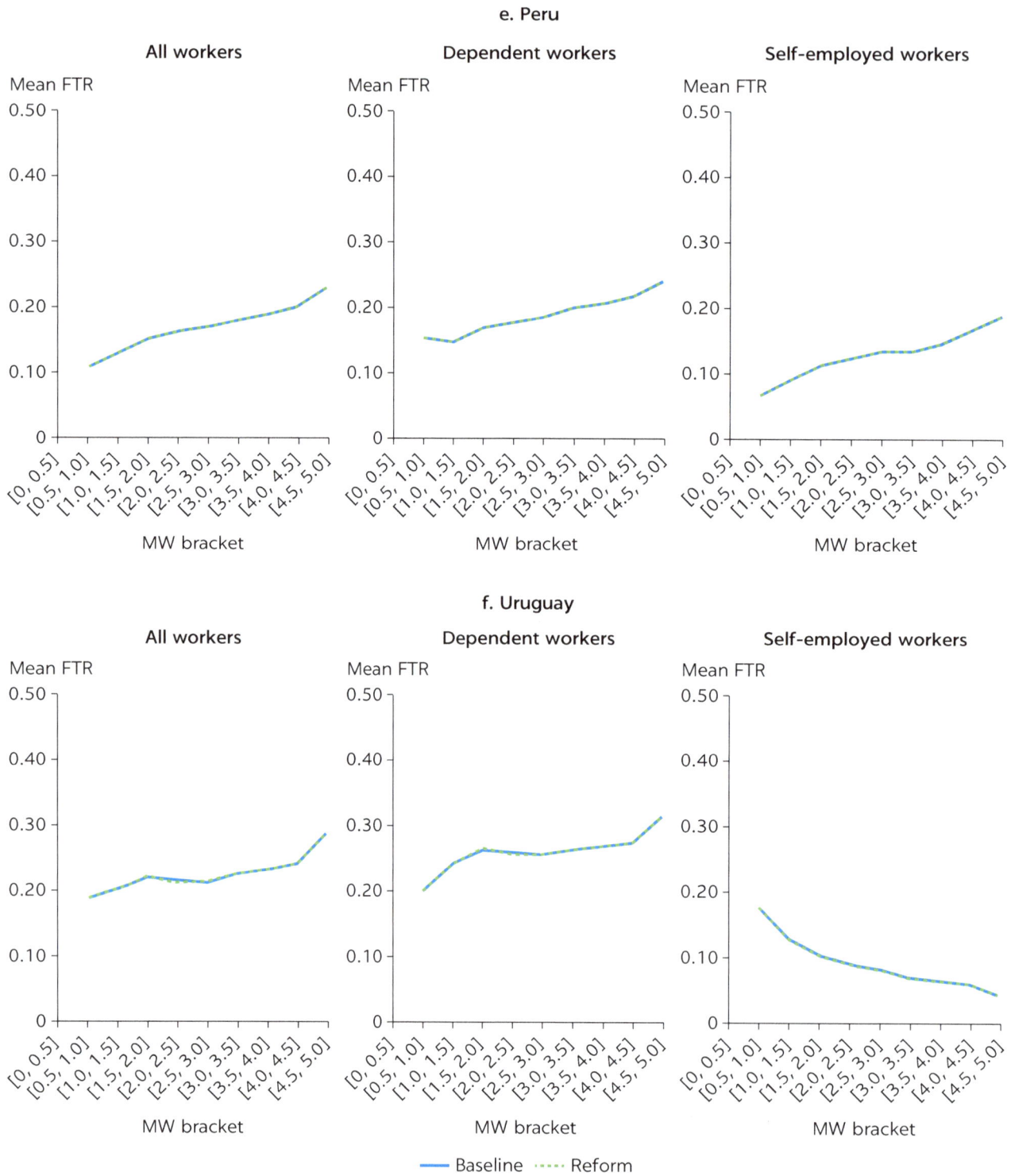

e. Peru

f. Uruguay

Sources: Original figures for this publication using data from the respective Household Surveys: Brazil, 2019; Colombia, 2019; El Salvador, 2021; Mexico, 2018; Peru, 2019; and Uruguay, 2021.

Note: MW brackets are assigned based on formal earnings. FTR = formalization tax rate; MW = minimum wage.

FIGURE 6A.2

Dimension 2: Policies affecting valuation: Reducing direct payroll taxation

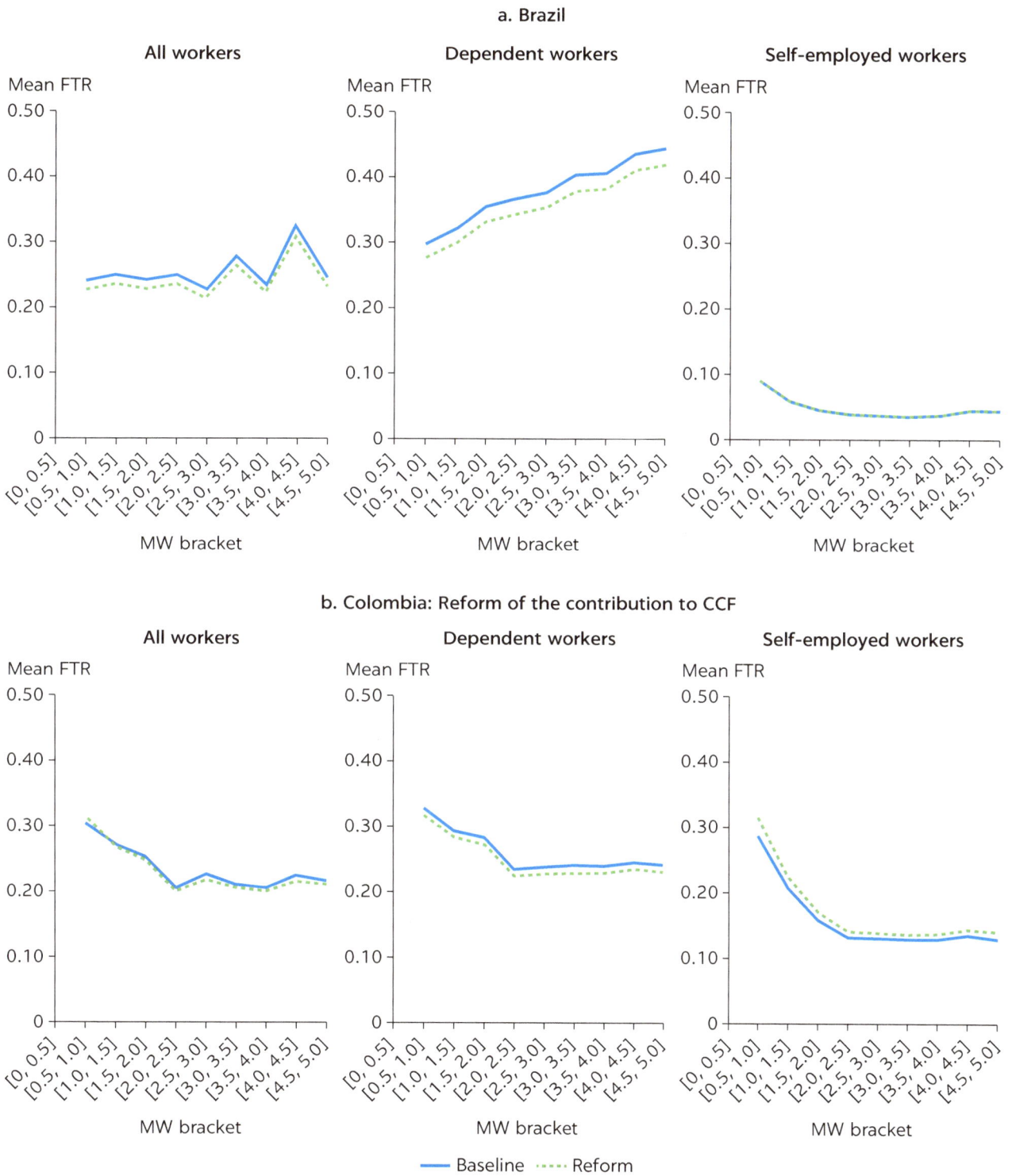

a. Brazil

b. Colombia: Reform of the contribution to CCF

Baseline ····· Reform

continued

FIGURE 6A.2 **Dimension 2: Policies affecting valuation: Reducing direct payroll taxation,** *(continued)*

c. Colombia: Reform of the minimum contribution base

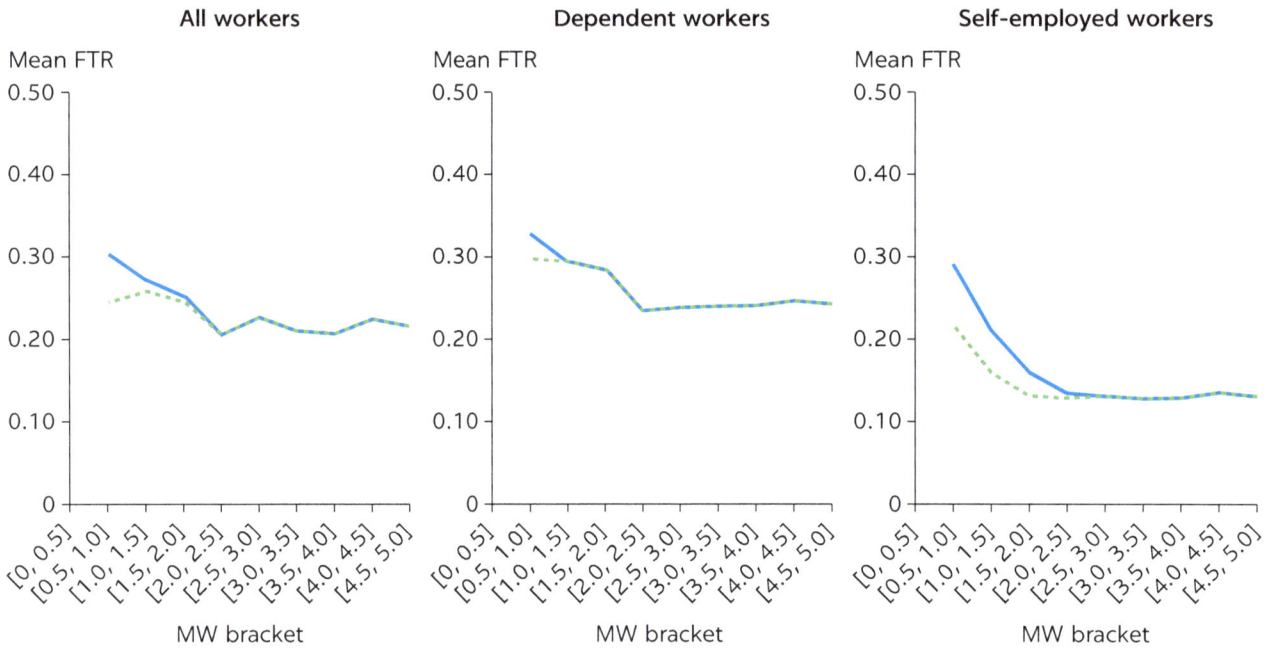

d. El Salvador

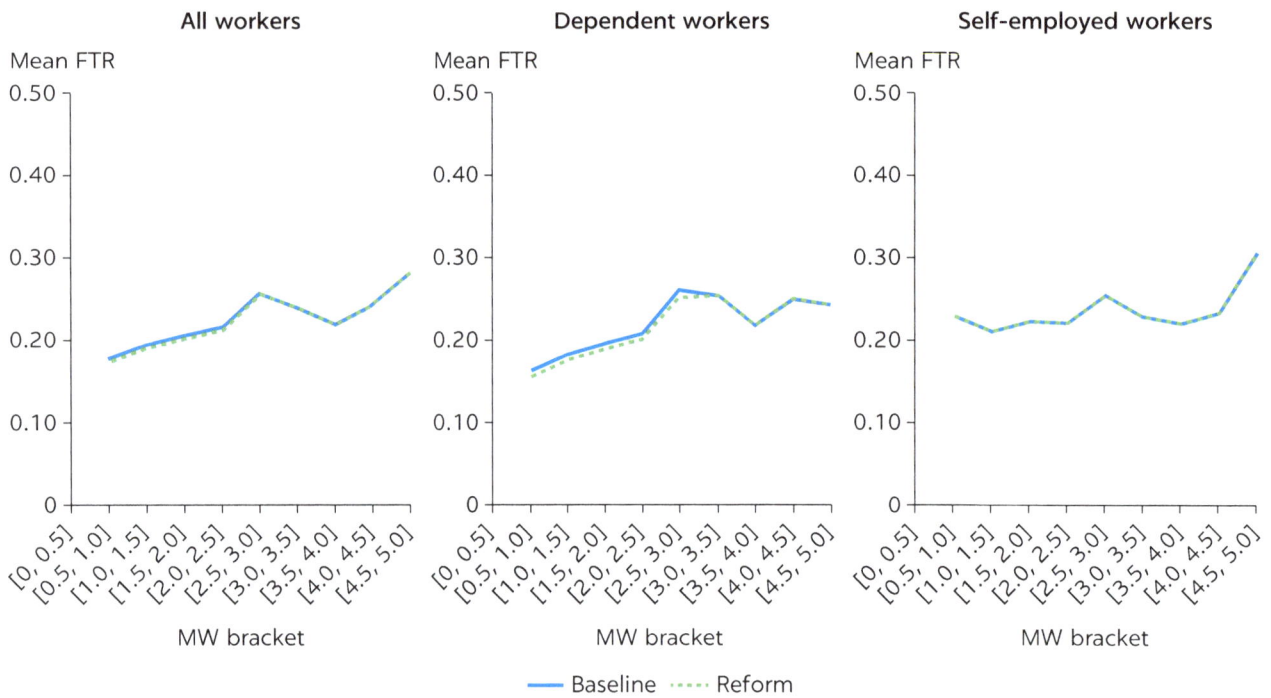

continued

FIGURE 6A.2 **Dimension 2: Policies affecting valuation: Reducing direct payroll taxation,** *(continued)*

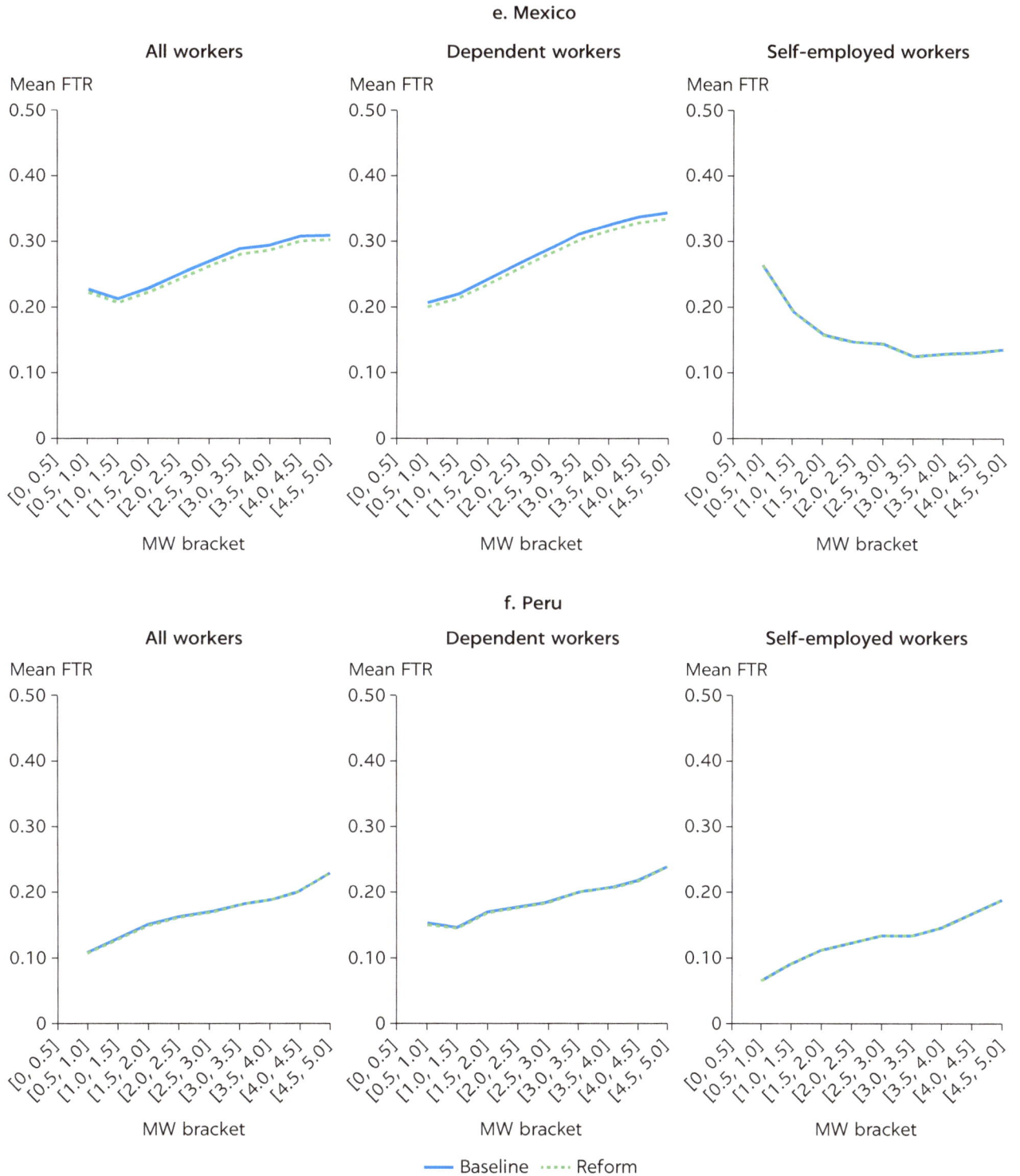

e. Mexico

f. Peru

— Baseline ····· Reform

Sources: Original figures for this publication using data from the respective Household Surveys: Brazil, 2019; Colombia, 2019; El Salvador, 2021; Mexico, 2018; and Peru, 2019.

Note: MW brackets are assigned based on formal earnings. CCF = Cajas de Compensación Familiar (Family Compensation Funds); FTR = formalization tax rate; MW = minimum wage.

FIGURE 6A.3

Dimension 3: Policies affecting valuation: Noncontributory benefits

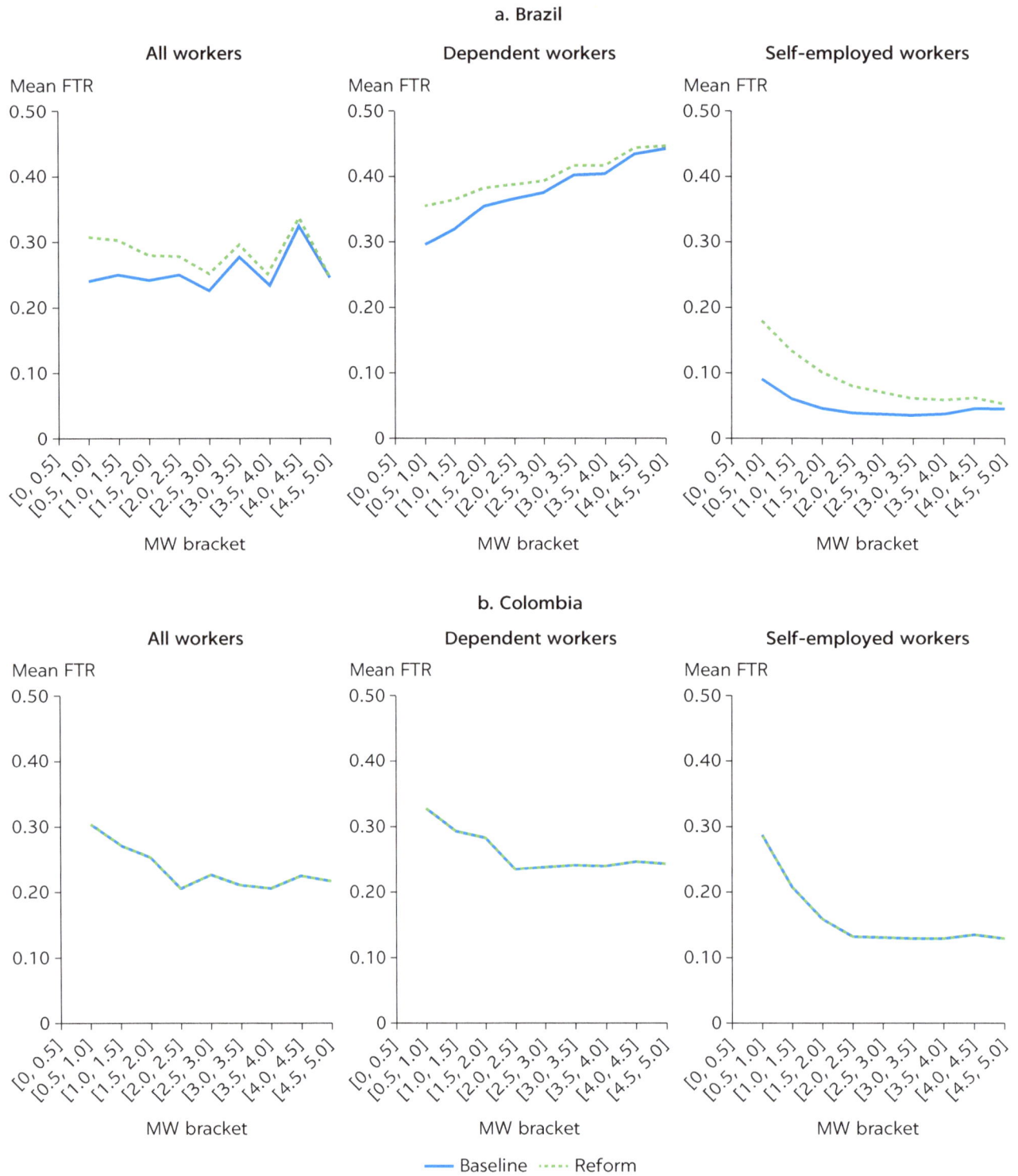

a. Brazil

b. Colombia

— Baseline   ····· Reform

continued

FIGURE 6A.3 Dimension 3: Policies affecting valuation: Noncontributory benefits, *(continued)*

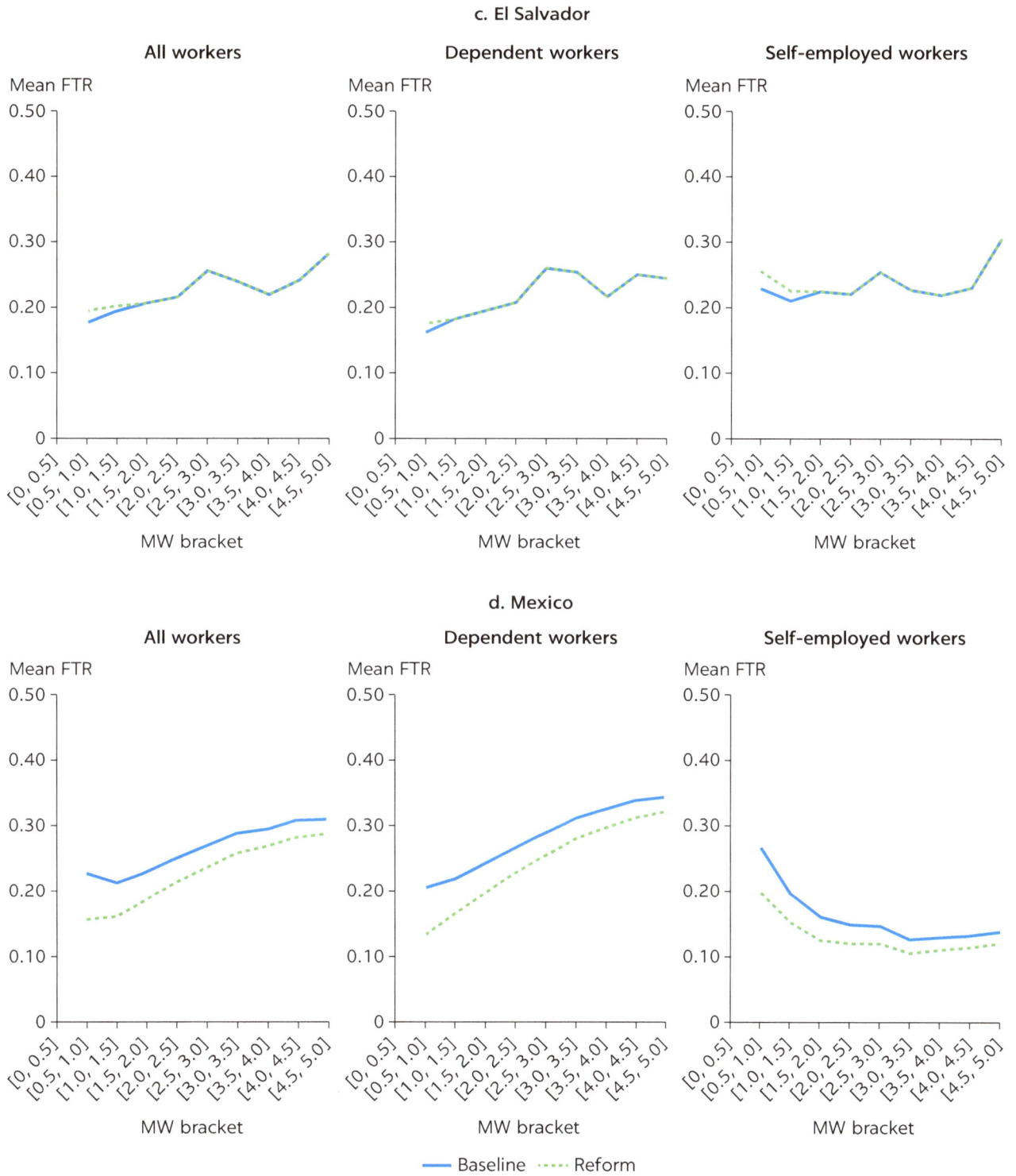

c. El Salvador

continued

continued

FIGURE 6A.3 Dimension 3: Policies affecting valuation: Noncontributory benefits, *(continued)*

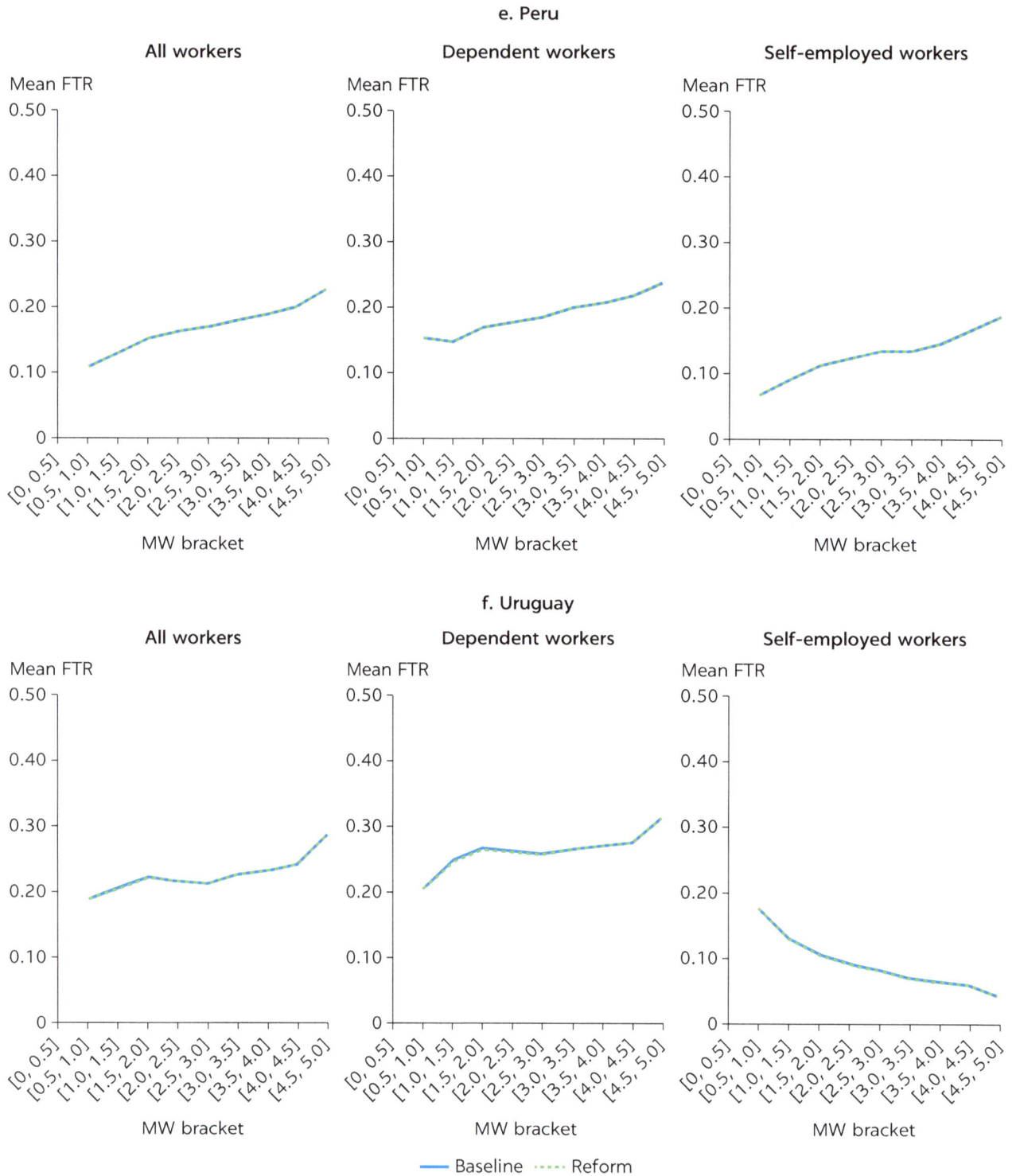

e. Peru

f. Uruguay

Sources: Original figures for this publication using data from the respective Household Surveys: Brazil, 2019; Colombia, 2019; El Salvador, 2021; Mexico, 2018; Peru, 2019; and Uruguay, 2021.
Note: MW brackets are assigned based on formal earnings. FTR = formalization tax rate; MW = minimum wage.

www.ingramcontent.com/pod-product-compliance
Lightning Source LLC
Chambersburg PA
CBHW050906210326
41597CB00002B/36